Bertuna's Children
The history of education in a Suffolk village

Sue Spiller is a retired head teacher. During her 34-year teaching career, she worked in Suffolk in secondary, middle and primary schools and as an advisory teacher, and was the head teacher of Great Barton (CEVC) Primary School for 14 years. During her varied career, she taught a wide range of subjects at all levels and developed a broad knowledge and understanding of the British education system. Since her retirement, she has developed a keen interest in family and local history. She currently lives with her husband in a nineteenth century farmhouse in south-west France and has two children and three grandchildren.

Bertuna's Children
The history of education in a Suffolk village

Sue Spiller

Arena Books

First published in 2017 by Arena Books
Arena Books
6 Southgate Green
Bury St. Edmunds
IP33 2BL

www.arenabooks.co.uk
Distributed in America by Ingram International, One Ingram Blvd., PO Box
3006, La Vergne, TN 37086-1985, USA.

Sue Spiller
Bertuna's Children *The history of education in a Suffolk village*

British Library cataloguing in Publication Data. A catalogue record for this
Book is available from the British Library.

ISBN-13   978-1-909421-92-9

BIC classifications:- HBTB, JNB, JNF, JNA, JNK, JNKH, JNL.

Printed and bound by Lightning Source UK

Cover design
by Jason Anscomb

Typeset in
Times New Roman

CONTENTS

APPENDICES

MAPS, PLANS, FAMILY TREE AND PHOTOGRAPHS

Map 1. Location of Great Barton, Suffolk [© d-maps.com 2015]

Map 2. Parishes in Thedwastre Hundred
[based on map produced by David Addy -
http://www.stedmundsburychronicle.co.uk/domesday/hundreds]

Map 3. Significant buildings in Great Barton, 1871 [based on Map data ©2016 Google]

Map 4. Great Barton in 1904 [reproduced from 1904 Ordnance Survey map, Second edition (6 inches to 1 mile)]

Map 5. Part of Barton Estate, 1915 [www.onesuffolk.co.uk]

Map 6. Old and new school buildings in Great Barton [based on Map data ©2016 Google]

Plan 1. Great Barton Lower School, School Lane [based on drawing (not to scale) by Valerie Mayhew]

Plan 2. Great Barton Senior School, School Road [based on drawing (not to scale) by Valerie Mayhew]

Plan 3. Great Barton CEVC Primary School, School Road, 1967
[© Historic England. From 'England's Schools 1962-88: A Thematic Study'. p.321. Franklin, Harwood, Taylor & Whitfield]

Family tree showing the descendants of the Revd William Bunbury, 5th Baronet of Bunbury and Stanney (Sue Spiller and Ian Bradley)

Sir Henry Bunbury (source unknown)

Barton Hall, Great Barton (http://greatbartonvh.onesuffolk.net)

Holy Innocents' Church, Great Barton (John Dixon)

Commemoration plaque (Lynn Stringer)

Boys from Great Barton School, 1913 (Great Barton History Society)

Certificate of Merit (original certificate donated by Lynn Roberts)

Girls' Schoolhouse, School Lane (Sue Spiller)

Boys' Schoolhouse, School Road (Barton Estate Sale Plan, 1915)

Great Barton Lower School, School Lane, c1960 (Peter Ceurstemont)

Design of the badges for the school cap and blazer, 1964 (Sue Spiller)

Great Barton Senior School, School Road, c1960 (Peter Ceurstemont)

Staff photograph, 1973 (school photographer)

Thurston pyramid of schools

New school badge 1991 (Sue Spiller)

Staff photograph, mid-1990s (Van Cols)

Great Barton CEVC Primary School, 2000 (author)

Thedwastre Education Trust – logos of primary schools at Great Barton, Rattlesden, Thurston and Woolpit

Edward Ernest Reed (Bury Free Press)

Ron Ceurstemont (teaching in United States of America)(Bury Free Press)

TABLES

ACKNOWLEDGEMENTS

Bertuna's Children has been an enjoyable and fascinating book to write. I am extremely grateful to everyone who has given me support and encouragement, especially my long-suffering husband, Roger, who has provided me with hundreds of cups of tea and coffee, read the manuscript, helped to create the index and made many helpful suggestions.

I am very appreciative of all the help I have received from a huge number of people who have contributed information about the school and village.

Firstly, I would like to acknowledge the help and information from people with a connection to the school including Sarah Rees, Lynda Mulley and Peter Woods (current members of staff at Great Barton Church of England Primary Academy); Ron Ceurstemont, Pat Barratt, Wenda Pennells, Reinhild Raistrick, Susan Smith, Doris Mayhew, Sylvia Arbon and Lynn Stringer (ex-members of staff); Peter Ceurstemont, Valerie Mayhew and Michael Harper (family members of ex-head teachers); Charles Johnson, Audrey Osborne-Thomas, Derek Mothersole, Jean Boreham, Peter Fisk, Ann Culpin, Elizabeth Stalley, Michael Nash, Ann Last, David Pearce, Keith Mills, Mark Williams, Angela Bryant, Graham and Linda Mothersole, Debbie Williams, Robin Rayner, Jane Slade, Helen Ellis, Penny Slade, Julie Wright, Graham Borley, Paul Downing, J.D. Bullen, Angela Richards, Rachel Patterson, Kori Buttress, Jade Rutterford, Daisy Henwood, Jess Smith and Roisin Evans (ex-pupils); Lynn Roberts (family member of an ex-pupil) and Tom Scherb (former deputy Education Officer of West Suffolk LEA).

Secondly, I would like to thank various people and members of organisations from the village of Great Barton including Chris Brabrook (Great Barton Pre-school), Richard Leveritt and Andrew Buttress (Great Barton Free Church), the Revd Alan Gates (ex-minister of Holy Innocents' Church, Great Barton), Kate Trevitt (Great Barton Parish Council) and Dr Roger Curtis (the archivist of Great Barton History Society). Also Frank Holmes, the local Family History Research historian who combed the pages of the *Bury Free Press* from the 1850s to the 1930s in search of references to Great Barton and gave me access to his notes and always answered my questions so patiently, and members of Great Barton Women's Institute, who transcribed the burial registers of Holy Innocents' Church, Great Barton, from 1563 to 1992 and cross-referenced the names to gravestones.

Thirdly, I would like to thank the staff at Suffolk Record Office, Bury St Edmunds, for their interest and help in locating relevant documents, and John Dixon, Stephen Adamson, Simon Last and David Dymond, who are all authors in their own right, for useful advice based on their experience of writing and publishing

Fourthly, I would like to acknowledge three very useful websites - www.ancestry.co.uk, for access to census material, records of births, marriages, deaths, probate and military, the British Newspaper Archive for access to articles from the *Bury and Norwich Post* and *the Bury Free Press* and Gillard D (2011) *Education in England: a brief history* www.educationengland.org.uk/history. I can highly recommend them all.

I would like to give very special thanks to some wonderful friends, who have no connection with the school or the village of Great Barton. Denise and Ian Bradley and Jacqui Gregory have patiently read various versions of the manuscript, suggested improvements, edited my maps and plans and encouraged me to keep going. I cannot thank them enough.

Finally, I would like to thank James Farrell and the team of Arena Books for publishing my book and for being so supportive throughout the publishing process.

I would like to acknowledge the following for permission to reprint previously published material:
Historic England for their plan of Great Barton School in 1967;
Bloomsbury Publishing Plc. for use of the first five verses of *An ABC for Baby Patriots* by Mrs Ernest Ames; Daniel Dalet for the use of his base map to show the location of Great Barton; and David Addy for his map of Thedwastre hundred in the nineteenth century.

DISCLAIMER

I have made every effort to check content for accuracy and, to the best of my knowledge, all details are accurate at the time of publication. However, new information is regularly coming to light, some of which could add to, or even contradict, previous knowledge, and I apologise if anything I have written, based on the best evidence available at the time, proves to be inaccurate in the future.

Every endeavour has been made to trace the owners of copyright and I apologise if I have inadvertently overlooked anyone or acknowledged any items incorrectly.

I apologise for the quality of some of the photographs. It has been extremely difficult to find any photographs of the old schools and those that are included are the best ones available.

Map 1. Location of Great Barton, Suffolk

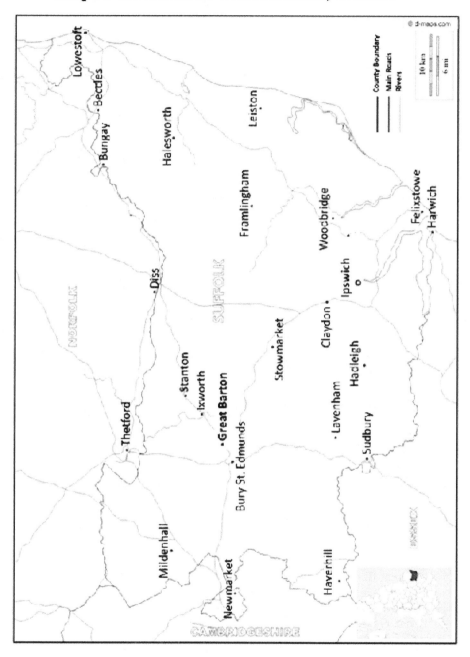

PREFACE

I was the head teacher of the primary school in Great Barton, Suffolk, for nearly 14 years and was always interested in the history of the school. After I retired, I carried out extensive research and discovered its fascinating story.

Bertuna's Children traces the journey of this school from its Victorian beginnings to its present status as an academy, and describes its evolution in response to political, economic, social and local circumstances.

The narrative interweaves the challenges faced by consecutive head teachers and school managers, against a backdrop of social and educational reforms since the early nineteenth century.

Bertuna, the Saxon name for Great Barton, relates to the production of barley. The name is incorporated into the village sign, the first of which was erected in 1978 to celebrate the Silver Jubilee of Queen Elizabeth II. The design, which was inspired by the painting of *The Gleaners* (1857) by Jean-Francois Millet (1814-1875), a French landscape artist, depicts a peasant woman picking up, or gleaning, the ears of corn, left over after the harvest. In 1991, Great Barton Primary School adopted this design as its school logo. The sign was vandalised during the 1990s and was replaced in March 2015 by a new one, which was made of oak and hand-carved by Robert Lewis, a local artisan.

Great Barton is a commuter village, situated alongside the A143, three miles north-east of the market town of Bury St Edmunds known for brewing, malting, and sugar processing. In 1086, the Domesday Book recorded that Great Barton had a population of 103 households, consisting of 22 villagers, 7 smallholders, 4 slaves and 70 free men. During the Middle Ages, the village stored and supplied barley, fish and ice to the Abbey of Bury St Edmunds, which owned the manorial rights of the village.

From Anglo-Saxon times until 1894, England and Wales was divided into 'hundreds', a term which originated when a village, containing about ten households, combined with nine other villages for military, judicial and administrative purposes. Each hundred had a meeting place, known as a moot, one of which was located at Cattishall in Great Barton and became a court of the King's Justices after the Norman invasion. In 1841, the parish of Great Barton comprised the communities of East Barton, Cattishall and Conyers Green and was the third largest parish in Thedwastre Hundred, an area of 40,362 acres, which included 24 parishes in West Suffolk. The Local Government Act 1894 set up Thedwastre Rural District Council, which existed until 1974.

Map 2. Parishes in Thedwastre Hundred

Ampton
Great Livermere
F. G.
Timworth
Pakenham
Fornham St. Martin
Great Barton
Thurston
Rougham
Tostock
Beyton
Rushbrooke
Woolpit
Hessett
Drinkstone
L. W.
Bradfield St. George
Great Whelnetham
Bradfield St. Clare
Gedding
Rattlesden
Bradfield Combuet
Stanningfield
Felsham

L.W.   LITTLE WHELNETHAM
F.G.   FORNHAM ST GENEVIEVE

0   2.5   5   7.5   10 km

Until the nineteenth century, Suffolk had a thriving agricultural economy and was one of the wealthiest areas of Britain. Families who profited from the local production of wool and grain built impressive churches and large manor houses.

However, during the nineteenth century, the economy of East Anglia gradually declined and, as most of its population was dependent upon agriculture, many families suffered from poverty. The Poor Law Amendment Act 1834 grouped parishes in England and Wales into poor law unions for the administration of poor relief.

Thingoe Poor Law Union, which came into being in 1836, consisted of 18 parishes in Thingoe Hundred, 10 in Blackbourn Hundred, 3 in Risbridge Hundred and 15 in Thedwastre Hundred, including Great Barton.

The Bunbury family were the patrons and 'impropriators' (laymen in possession of church property) of Holy Innocents' Church, Great Barton, one of only five churches in Britain dedicated to the 'innocents', the Jewish boys under the age of two, who were massacred by King Herod (*Holy Bible,* Matthew 2:16-18). The benefice of Great Barton was a 'discharged vicarage' in the deanery of Thedwastre until it was transferred to the deanery of Thingoe in 1884. It was in the Archdeaconry of Sudbury within the Diocese of Ely from 1837, and the Diocese of St Edmundsbury and Ipswich from 1914.

Every school is unique, but Great Barton School is unusual in that it was founded by an individual and not an organisation. The first school building was built on the private estate of Sir Henry Edward Bunbury, a wealthy philanthropist, who owned most of the land in Great Barton at the time. At about the time of his death in 1860, a second school building was erected in his memory a quarter of a mile away from the first one. During the nineteenth century, the two schools were known as the Charles Bunbury Schools and were supported by the Bunbury family. Each school was managed as a separate unit, with a headmistress at the Girls' School in School Lane and a headmaster at the Boys' School in School Road.

In 1902, Suffolk Local Education Authority took over responsibility for the schools, which were known officially as Great Barton Church of England Voluntary School, and locally as Great Barton Girls' School and Great Barton Boys' School. They retained their separate identities until 1918, when they united under a single head teacher and became Great Barton Voluntary Mixed School. The younger children were taught in the School Lane building and the older ones in the School Road premises. The majority of pupils remained at the school until the minimum statutory school leaving age of 14, although an increasing number transferred to a local secondary school from the age of 11.

In 1948, the school became Great Barton Church of England Voluntary Controlled (CEVC) Primary School. From September 1953, it was part of a two-tier system, within which all pupils transferred to a secondary school at the age of 11. In 1967, the school abandoned the original premises, which reverted to the ownership of the Bunbury Estate, and moved into new premises. From 1975, the school was part of a three-tier system, within which pupils transferred to a middle school at the age of nine and an upper school after four years. In September 2013, it became part of a two-tier system again and its pupils transferred to Thurston Community College or another secondary school at the age of 11.

On 31 December 2015, Great Barton CEVC Primary School closed. On 1 January 2016, it reopened as Great Barton Church of England Primary Academy, when it joined with three neighbouring primary schools, which were also situated in the original Thedwastre Hundred, to form Thedwastre Education Trust.

No school logbooks for Great Barton School have survived from before 1925, so some of the information about the school during the nineteenth century is derived from newspaper reports. In 1782, Peter Gedge founded the *Bury and Norwich Post* (*BNP*), which tended to support the Liberal cause and in 1855, Thomas Lucia, who worked for the *Bury and Norwich Post*, founded the *Bury Free Press* (*BFP*), *West Suffolk Observer and General Advertiser*. In 1869, J. Merrell founded the *Bury and Suffolk Standard*. Five years later the *East Anglian Daily Times* (*EADT*) started publication, incorporating the *Ipswich Express*, which had been published since 13 August 1839. In January 1932, the *Bury Free Press* bought the *Bury and Norwich Post*, which, by then, had a smaller circulation.

The school logbooks have survived from 1925 to 2000, but they only tell a small part of the story, as illustrated in 'A day in the life of a primary school head teacher' (Appendix II).

In *Bertuna's Children*, a number in square brackets after the name of an individual e.g. Susan Kerry [364] indicates the registration number of their record in the burial register of Holy Innocents' Church, Great Barton.

Further information about the history of Great Barton School and some of the pupils who attended the school during the nineteenth century, can be found on http://www.bertunaschildren.wordpress.com. The author is happy to assist anyone whose ancestors lived in Great Barton with family history research.

Bertuna's Children is a celebration of the history of Great Barton School. Although its details are specific to this school, they provide a historical record the various social and educational changes that have affected British primary schools since the early nineteenth century, and describe the issues that have faced British politicians, teachers and school managers in the past and continue to challenge them today.

SECTION 1   FOUNDATION OF THE SCHOOLS

1
THE BUNBURY FAMILY

Great Barton School was founded by Sir Henry Edward Bunbury, 7th Baronet of Bunbury and Stanney, (1778-1860).

The Bunbury family were descended from St Pierre of Caen who accompanied William the Conqueror to England in 1066 and was granted land in Cheshire. The family acquired the Manor of Bunbury at the beginning of the fifteenth century and adopted the surname of Bunbury, a name derived from Brna, a Saxon name, and burh, a fortress. Through marriage, the seventh descendant of St Pierre acquired the lordship of Stanney, near Chester (*BFP*, 17 Jan 1914).

On 29 June 1681, King Charles II created the baronetcy of Bunbury, Oxon, and Stanney Hall, Cheshire, for Thomas Bunbury (d.1682), who was the Sheriff of Cheshire from 1673 to 1674. As a baronet, he was addressed as 'Sir' and his wife as 'Lady' and he could pass on the title to his oldest male heir.

The family crest, illustrated on the sign outside the Bunbury Arms public house in Great Barton, includes three chess-rooks mounted diagonally through a shield, topped by an emblem composed of two crossed swords through the face of a leopard, a heraldic reference to the family's connection with France. The family motto is *Esse quam videri*, which means 'to be rather than to seem', but the motto on the village pub sign reads *Firmum in vita nihil*, which means 'nothing in life is certain'.

From 1746, the Bunbury family owned the manorial rights of Great Barton, which were held by the Abbey of Bury St Edmunds until the dissolution of the monasteries. These rights were acquired in 1539 by Sir Thomas Kytson (1485-1540), a wealthy merchant and Sheriff of London, in 1553 by the Audley family and in 1704 by Thomas Folkes, a lawyer from Bury St Edmunds. After his death in 1722, they passed to his son-in-law, Sir Thomas Hanmer (1677-1746), the speaker of the House of Commons from 1714 to 1715, who died childless 24 years later and bequeathed the manors of Mildenhall and Great Barton to his nephew, the Revd William Bunbury (1709-1764), Vicar of Mildenhall, who became the 5th Baronet of Bunbury and Stanney.

The Revd William Bunbury had two sons, Charles Thomas and Henry William, both of whom were educated at King Edward VI Grammar School in Bury St Edmunds, Westminster School, and St Catherine's College, Cambridge.

The eldest son, Sir Thomas Charles Bunbury (1740-1821), known as Sir Charles, became a Member of Parliament (MP). His grandfather and uncle, the 3rd and 4th Baronets of Bunbury and Stanney, had represented the constituency of Chester for the Tory Party from 1701 to 1727, and again from 1733 until 1742. Sir Charles was elected as a Tory MP for Suffolk in 1761 when he was one month under the voting age. He subsequently served in nine British parliaments between 1761 and 1784, and 1790 and 1812, and was particularly interested in prison reform and the transport system. Although he was elected to represent the interests of the Tory Party, he often voted with the opposition Whig party and was a friend of Charles James Fox (1749-1806), a radical politician, who was a prominent Whig MP and political rival of William Pitt the Younger, the Tory Prime Minister from 1804 to 1806.

In 1762, Sir Charles married Lady Sarah Lennox (1745-1826), a great-granddaughter of King Charles II and the fourth daughter of the 2nd Duke of Richmond and Lennox. The marriage was not a successful one, and a private parliamentary bill was passed in 1776, which dissolved their marriage and enabled both parties to remarry.

In 1781, Lady Sarah married George Napier (1751-1804), with whom she had five sons and three daughters. Their eldest daughter, Emily, became the second wife of Sir Charles Bunbury's nephew, Sir Henry Edward Bunbury, and one of their granddaughters, Cecilia, married one of the sons of Sir Henry Edward Bunbury by his first wife. After the death of her husband in 1804, Lady Sarah received an annual settlement of £1,000 from King George III, whom she had known from her childhood.

In 1764, Sir Charles became the 6th Baronet of Bunbury and Stanney and moved to Barton Hall, Great Barton, where he established a stud for racehorses and became Senior Steward of the Jockey Club. Legend states that, in 1780, he tossed a coin with Lord Derby to decide whose name should be used for a new race. Lord Derby won the toss, but Sir Thomas ←Charles Bunbury's horse, Diomed, won the first Derby Race in 1780. Sir Charles' stud also produced Eleanor, the winner of the Derby and the Oaks in 1801, and Smotensko, the winner of the Derby in 1813. He also owned property in Grenada in the Caribbean.

In 1806, Sir Charles married Margaret Cocksedge (1745-1822) by special licence in the Parsonage at Great Whelnetham. In 1809, at the village celebrations of the fiftieth year of the reign of King George III, Sir Charles arranged for the distribution of £40-worth of meat and beer to 387 poor villagers in Great Barton. Each individual received 3 lbs of meat, each man a quart of beer, and each woman and child a pint of beer (*BNP*, 1 Nov. 1809). The Prince Regent, who became King George IV in 1820, occasionally stayed at Barton Hall after visiting Newmarket Racecourse.

Sir Charles was a friend of Samuel Johnson, an essayist and literary historian, and belonged to Samuel Johnson's Literary Club. From 1812, he was one of the vice-presidents of the Suffolk branch of the National Society and he built a school for the poor on his estate at Mildenhall in 1817.

Sir Charles' younger brother, Sir Henry William Bunbury (1750-1811), failed to graduate but became a well-known illustrator and satirical cartoonist and amateur actor. He married Catherine Horneck, who was named as 'Little Comedy' in a poem, entitled 'In Reply to an Invitation to Dinner at Dr Baker's' by Oliver Goldsmith (1728-1774) and they had two sons, Charles John and Henry Edward, and a daughter, Annabella. Sir Henry was Lieutenant Colonel of the West Suffolk Militia.

Sir Charles Thomas Bunbury financed the education of his nephew, Charles John Bunbury (1772-1798), who was expected to inherit the baronetcy. Charles John did not excel academically and was expelled from the Royal College of St. Peter in Westminster, better known as Westminster School, for participating in a riot, and was sent down from Cambridge University for brawling and idleness. He served in the British Army, but died in South Africa, at the Cape of Good Hope, at the age of 26.

Henry William's younger son, Henry Edward Bunbury, who founded Great Barton School, was educated for the army, but after the death of his brother in 1821 became the oldest surviving heir and inherited the baronetcy.

Sir Henry Edward Bunbury (1778-1860) - childhood and early career

Sir Henry spent his early years at Mildenhall, where he lived with his mother's sister and her husband, Colonel Francis Gwyn, equerry to King George III. He attended Mr Priest's Academy in Bury St Edmunds, about which he wrote in his *Recollections*:

'The first things which I can recollect were being sent to school at Bury before I was five years old; being disgusted with Gray's Elegy [Elegy Written in a Country Churchyard, by Thomas Gray], by being obliged to learn it by heart without understanding its meaning, and flogged for a lie which I did not tell.'

He subsequently attended a school run by the Curate of Mildenhall for the sons of craftsmen, a school near Windsor, Berkshire, from which he ran away, and, eventually Westminster School, London.

When he was almost 17-years-old, Henry joined the Coldstream Guards as an ensign and served as aide-de-camp to his uncle, Colonel Francis Gwyn, and then to Prince Frederick, Duke of York, the commander–in-chief and second son of King George III.

Descendants of the Revd William Bunbury
(5th Baronet of Bunbury and Stanney)

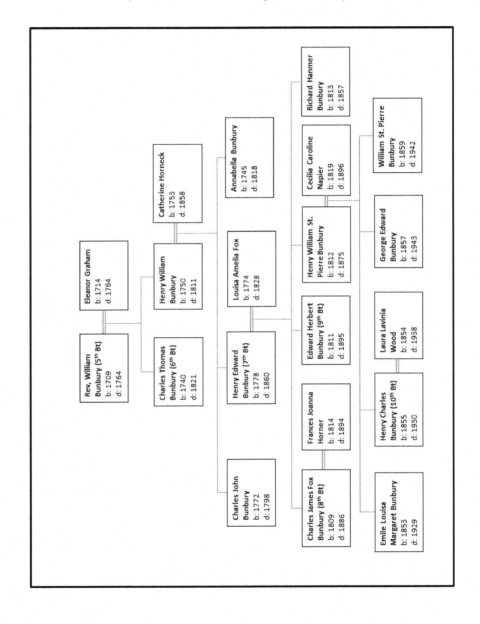

He later received training at the military college at High Wycombe and followed a distinguished military career in the British Army. In 1809, he became Under-Secretary of State for War and the Colonies and worked under the Duke of York at the British Army headquarters, at Horse Guards in Whitehall, London. He was one of a group of reformers who introduced logistical changes to the way the army was run and supplied, and was largely responsible for

Sir Henry Edward Bunbury, 7th Baronet of Bunbury and Stanney, (1778-1860)

LIEUT.-GENERAL SIR HENRY EDWARD BUNBURY, BART., K.C.B.
FROM A PAINTING BY HENRY WILLIAMS, TAKEN IN ROME, 1818

the smooth supply of materials to Spain and Portugal during the Peninsular War (1807-1814), fought between Napoleon's imperial army and those of the allied powers of Spain, Britain and Portugal. He also co-ordinated the distribution of intelligence, collected through espionage, to the relevant officials in the British government, Royal Navy and British Army.

Sir Henry was promoted to under-secretary of state for the war department in 1813, after which he moved back to Mildenhall and lived in the Manor House. A year later, he was promoted to major general and appointed as the War Department's Special Commissioner. On 31 July 1815, following the defeat of the French at the Battle of Waterloo, he accompanied Admiral Lord Keith to H.M.S. Bellerophon to inform the ex-Emperor Napoleon Bonaparte (1769-1821) of the terms of his impending exile to Saint Helena in the South Atlantic Ocean. Henry Bunbury was more fluent in French than Lord Keith, so it was he who translated the letter containing the exile order from Lord Melville, First Lord of the Admiralty. Henry Bunbury was awarded the Order of the Bath (KCB), and rose to the rank of lieutenant general.

In 1816, his post was abolished and he was made redundant from the British Army. Although he never resumed his military career, he wrote books about military campaigns, which included *A Narrative of the Campaign in North Holland* (1849) and *A Narrative of Certain Passages in the Late War with France* (1852).

In 1807, he married Louisa Amelia Fox (1774-1828), the daughter of General Henry Edward Fox (1755-1811) and Marianne Clayton (c1725-1808), niece of Charles James Fox, MP, and a descendant of King Charles II. They had six children, but both of their daughters died before they were two years old.

Mary Marianne Joanne died in 1810 and Emily Georgina in 1819. In 1875, their brother Charles and his wife arranged for stained glass windows, dedicated to their memory, to be fitted at Holy Innocents' Church, Great Barton (*BNP*, 23 Feb. 1875).

Barton Hall, Great Barton

In 1821, Sir Henry Edward Bunbury inherited the baronetcy, together with various properties and estates, which included Barton Hall, on which £2,000 was payable each year in mortgages and annuities. In 1824, he moved into Barton Hall after it had been modernised and was appointed as High Sheriff of Suffolk in 1825.

His wife died in Genoa, Italy, in 1828 and two years later, at Pau in South West France, Sir Henry married Emily Louisa Augusta Napier (1783-1863), the daughter of Colonel George Napier (1751-1804) and Lady Sarah Lennox.

In 1832, Sir Henry bought an estate in north Wales, at Abergwynant, near Dolgelly, and in 1858, sold his Cheshire estates.

Sir Henry Bunbury was a philanthropist, who used some of his wealth to improve the lives of others. He supported a wide range of political and other causes, but of particular relevance to the foundation of the village school is his career as a politician, his support for educational causes, and his concern for the welfare of the labouring classes.

Sir Henry Edward Bunbury – politician

Sir Henry described himself as 'a wise, liberal-minded and reasonable Whig'. In 1830, he stood for parliament as a Whig candidate for the constituency of Suffolk. He was elected, together with Charles Tyrell, defeating the long-standing Tory MP, Thomas Gooch, who had been unopposed for many years.

Sir Henry actively supported the Representation of the People Act 1832 (First Reform Act), which enfranchised 40-shilling freeholders, £10 copyholders, £50 tenants, £10 long-lease holders and £50 medium-lease holders. In Suffolk, this increased the electorate from 6,200 in 1830, to 10,394 in 1832, which included 12 men in Great Barton. Whilst serving as an MP, Sir Henry supported the abolition of slavery, a reduction of the tariff on American wheat imports, and Catholic emancipation in Ireland. He turned down the offer of the post of Secretary of State for War.

However, the Representation of the People Act 1832 abolished the constituency of Suffolk, and Sir Henry, who suffered from rheumatic gout at the time, decided to retire from Parliament at the end of that year. He endorsed the candidacy of Sir William Hyde Parker (1785-1856) of Melford Hall, together with Charles Tyrell, for the constituency of West Suffolk, and spent the next few years travelling with his wife around Europe and sailing to South America.

In 1837, Henry and his son, Charles, both stood for Parliament as Whig candidates - Sir Henry for West Suffolk and Charles for Bury St Edmunds - but neither was successful. An extract from a speech by Charles reflects his views on the importance of education:

'he wished to see political power extended to all those who were qualified to make a good use of it, and to see the blessings of sound and useful education diffused, in order that greater number might be fitted to make use of that power' (*BNP*, 7 Dec. 1836).

Sir Henry Edward Bunbury – supporter of educational causes

Locally, Sir Henry supported the Suffolk branch of the National Society for Promoting the Education of the Poor in the Principles of the Established Church (the National Society) and gave financial assistance to the school at Mildenhall, set up by his uncle in 1817. He built a second school in Church Lane, Mildenhall in 1844 and the two schools were jointly known as the Lady Bunbury Schools. At about the same time, he founded a village school for children of the labouring classes in Great Barton.

Elsewhere, he favoured the establishment of self-supporting agricultural schools, and supported a school for paupers in Bridgnorth, Shropshire.

Further afield, he responded to an appeal from General Sir George Thomas Napier, KCB, (1784-1855), his brother-in-law by his second marriage, who was Governor of the Cape of Good Hope and Commander-in-Chief of the Armed Services in South Africa from 1839 to 1843. After the 1833 war between England and the Kaffirs, General Napier took members of the Fingoe tribe into his protection. He found two missionaries to supervise their religious and moral instruction and to 'bring them into the habits of civilised and industrious life', but needed funds for a chapel and school, and residence for the missionaries. A fund-raising meeting in Bury St Edmunds raised £189. 5s., which included £60 from Sir Henry and Lady Bunbury and £5 from their son Charles (*BNP*, 19 Jun. 1839).

Sir Henry Edward Bunbury – philanthropist

The Bunbury family owned most of the land and farms in the village of Great Barton, where wheat, barley, oats, rye and vegetables were cultivated and cows, sheep and pigs reared. The village was located on the London to Norwich turnpike road, whose route originally passed close to Barton Hall when the section between Bury St Edmunds and Scole, Norfolk, was built in 1769. Sir Henry Bunbury privately funded several Acts of Parliament to alter its direction, which resulted in its final route, which divided the village into two parts, with Barton Hall in the north and Great Barton Church and Vicarage in the south.

Sir Henry was a benevolent and improving landlord. He let land and cottages to labourers at reasonable rates, paid fair wages and did not lay off workers during periods of bad weather. Consequently, Great Barton was unaffected by the widespread riots and protests that affected Suffolk and other rural areas during the early nineteenth century. These protests included sending threatening letters to farmers and landowners, destroying threshing and other machines, and committing various acts of nocturnal 'incendiarism', which included setting light to 160 farms, barns and hayricks in Suffolk.

Sir Henry Bunbury believed that incendiary crimes were symptoms of a smouldering and dangerous discontent, which had many causes. Traditionally, villagers used the common land to graze their animals and gather firewood, hay, berries, nuts and pig fodder. However, between 1770 and 1830, millions of acres of common land in England and Wales were converted to private property, enclosed and fenced by the landlords for their own use. This made life difficult for agricultural labourers, who were paid by the day and reliant on produce from the common land to supplement their income.

Furthermore, at the end of the Napoleonic Wars (1803-1815), the first Corn Law banned the import of foreign corn into Britain until domestic corn reached a price of 80s. per quarter. This led to higher bread prices and widespread unemployment in towns. Workers were forced to spend the majority of their wages on food and had very little money to buy home produced manufactured goods. At the same time, a series of bad harvests and the rise in the use of horse and steam-powered threshing machines led to an increase in rural unemployment. By the 1830s, about a third of Suffolk's working population was unemployed, and there were an increasing number of vagrants moving around the area.

Between 1801 and 1841, the population of Great Barton grew from 523 to 774, during which time the Bunbury family built many cottages for their workforce on the Barton Estate. Some of the cottages were adorned with the face of a leopard, a heraldic symbol of the Bunbury family. Henry Bunbury also built the Bunbury Arms, a public house for the labourers of Barton Estate, in response to a petition from the estate workers. However, its site was selected so that 'his men might choose to imbibe alcohol' but 'he was not obliged to see them doing so'.

In a report of 1850, the Revd Augustus Jessop, Canon of Norwich Cathedral and headmaster of Norwich School, wrote of the 'well-built, airy and commodious cottages on the Bunbury Estate at Great Barton, which contrasted with the miserable hovels in Bury St Edmunds. He described Great Barton as the paradise of the agricultural worker.'

An example of Sir Henry Bunbury's care for his staff was evident in his treatment of Thomas Scott (1827-1900). Thomas's father, William, served with Sir Henry during the Peninsular War and after William's death in 1831, Sir Henry provided his widow and children with accommodation at the Manor House, Mildenhall. At the age of 14, Thomas moved into Barton Hall, and Sir Henry supervised his reading, trained him in property management, and appointed him as general manager and land agent of the Barton Estate.

Sir Henry pioneered the allotment movement and let small parcels of land to cottagers for an affordable rent. From 1816 onwards, he allocated land on his estates at Mildenhall and Great Barton as allotments, for which he charged 15s. p.a. for a half acre, on which he believed it were possible to make an annual net profit of between £3. 10s. and £5. Any tenant who cultivated his land badly paid the full rent but if he cultivated it tolerably or well his rent was reduced to 12s. 6d or 10s. (*BNP*, 24 July 1844). If a tenant were found guilty of any crime, he forfeited his allotment. In 1844, the Royal Agricultural Society invited Sir Henry to write a paper on the subject of cottage allotments.

In September 1844, Sir Henry, together with his son, Charles, and other local landlords, set up the 'West Suffolk Society for the Improvement of the Condition of the Labourers'. Their aims were to ensure that 'the state of the working classes in West Suffolk is generally that of decent comfort; their moral feelings are sound; and the public peace and property are secure.'

In proposing the society, Sir Henry advocated that, in order to reduce the number of vagrants, landlords should provide more extensive and regular employment and should extend the practice of cottage allotments to compensate for the loss of enclosed land. He welcomed the establishment of savings, loan and coal clubs (*BNP*, 30 Aug. 1844). In 1847, he wrote a letter to the allotment holders in Great Barton, advising them not to grow a single crop, such as potatoes. He suggested that they should plant alternate rows with beetroot, parsnips, yellow beetroot, white carrots, peas or Jerusalem artichokes, and informed them of where they could buy the seed (*Essex Standard,* 5 Mar. 1847).

On two successive Sundays in April 1860, Sir Henry gave money to the deserving poor of the parish of Mildenhall at the end of the morning service at St Mary's Church, Mildenhall. On the first occasion, 20 old men received a sovereign each and on the second occasion, 60 men received half a sovereign each. He gave a similar gift of money to the poor of Great Barton (*BNP*, 10 Apr. 1860).

The death of Sir Henry Edward Bunbury

In April 1860, Sir Henry died at the age of 82. On the day of his funeral, shops and businesses in Mildenhall closed for several hours in the middle of the day, many private houses had their blinds drawn, and the church bells were muffled and rung at intervals during the day.

He was buried in a vault in the churchyard of Holy Innocents' Church, Great Barton, and was later remembered in a monument on the wall of the chancel. His coffin was carried by his oldest labourers, for whom he provided a new dark suit. At his funeral, he was mourned as a 'relative, a friend, a landlord and a benefactor'. One mourner said that 'he let people have his land so that they could employ the poor, which was the best way of doing them good' and another said 'he was a wonderful good gentleman to the poor' (*BNP*, 24 Apr.1860).

His obituary described his military career at some length and highly praised his role as a landowner. It mentioned his concern 'to see the people well employed and fairly remunerated', and his provision of the means for the poor to help themselves, rather than for them to be dependent on charity (*BNP*, 17 Apr. 1860). Curiously, there is no mention of the fact that Sir Henry Edward Bunbury founded the school in Great Barton.

His widow, Dame Emily built a second school in Great Barton in memory of her husband, but spent the rest of her life in north Wales, on the family estate at Abergwynant, near Dolgelly. After she died in 1863, her body was returned to Great Barton for burial alongside her husband.

The sons of Sir Henry Bunbury

Sir Henry and Louisa Emilia Bunbury [2] had four sons; Charles, Edward, Henry and Richard, all of whom received a good all-round education, some details of which are recorded in *Life, Letters, and Journals of Sir Charles J.F. Bunbury, Bart.,* edited by his wife, Frances Joanna Bunbury (1814-1894), and published privately by Mrs Lyell, his sister-in-law, in 1894.

Charles James Fox Bunbury (1809-1886) [251], who was born in Messina, Italy, and was the oldest son, inherited the baronetcy. In 1844, he wrote a letter to his father to thank him for 'the excellent education which I have received from you and my dear mother'. His journals record that his father taught him French, arithmetic, geology, mineralogy and Latin, whilst his mother taught him drawing and botany. Of his mother, he wrote:

'she has considerable knowledge of botany and she took great delight in communicating her knowledge to me ....it was not only by regular lessons that she taught us, but by watching, encouraging and guiding our intellectual tendencies and fostering every indication of taste or talent.'

He learnt to appreciate English literature from both his parents and was encouraged to borrow books from his father's extensive library. At meal times, he and his brothers were expected to take part in discussions, including those about astronomy and literature, and, at the age of eight, his father lent him a copy of *The Scientific Dialogues*, which explained the first principles of natural and experimental philosophy, and then asked him for his opinion. Joshua Reynolds (1723-1792) was a family friend and godfather of Sir Henry Edward Bunbury, and the extensive family art collection contained some of his finest paintings, including a portrait of Charles John Bunbury entitled *Master Bunbury*.

In 1822 Frederick Hoskyn Matthews, educated at Shrewsbury School and Trinity College, Cambridge, was employed as a tutor for Charles and Edward. He taught them Latin, Greek and mathematics, in which he was apparently well read, and English literature and French, in which he was less knowledgeable. Charles was given time and encouragement to follow his passions, which included entomology and mineralogy. When he told his father he wanted to draw birds, his father went out and shot some for him to draw. In 1824, at the age of 16, he was taken by his parents to London to visit the British Museum, learn to dance and have riding lessons.

In 1827, Charles studied mathematics and classics at Trinity College, Cambridge, but did not graduate. In 1833, he travelled to Brazil, via Madeira, to work with his uncle, who was minister in Rio de Janeiro, and he spent the next two years collecting plants and making notes on natural history, which were published in *Botanical Fragments*.

On his return, he joined the Holland House circle and became a Fellow of the Royal Society, the Geological Society, the Linneus Society and the Zoological Society. Through them, he met Charles Lyell (1797-1875), an eminent geologist, and Charles Darwin (1809-1882), the author of *On the Origin of Species*, both of whom he invited to speak at the Athenaeum in Bury St Edmunds. He was also a friend of Sir Joseph Dalton Hooker (1814-1879), who became Director of the Royal Botanic Gardens at Kew, and Matthew Arnold (1822-1888), a school inspector. The Revd Charles Kingsley (1819-1875) a historian, naturalist and novelist, stayed at Barton Hall with his family in 1861, just two years before the publication of *The Water-Babies.*

In 1838, he accompanied his uncle, Sir George Napier, to the Cape of Good Hope, South Africa, where, amongst other things, he collected plants. Ten years later, Charles published a *Journal of a Residence at the Cape of Good Hope.* In 1842, he toured France and Italy with his family and visited museums, art galleries and the Royal Courts in Rome and Naples.

In 1844, he married Frances (Fanny) Joanna Horner (1814-1894) [361], the daughter of Leonard Horner (1785-1864), a geologist and social reformer, who served as a member of the 1833 Royal Commission, which investigated the employment of children in the factories of Great Britain. After his marriage, Charles returned to Mildenhall to run the estate, but continued to study fossil botany, keep up his knowledge of Greek, revive his knowledge of algebra and calculus, and learn German.

He and his wife had no children, but took an active interest in the Lady Bunbury Schools at Mildenhall. In 1845, Charles Bunbury wrote in a letter to his stepmother, Lady Emily Bunbury, that 'Fanny has prepared a formidable artillery of school-books and maps to batter the brains of the children at Mildenhall.'

He helped to set up the Albert Middle Class Memorial College at Framlingham, Suffolk, which was founded in 1864 by public subscription as the Suffolk County Memorial to Queen Victoria's husband, Albert, Prince Consort. Sir Charles Bunbury was one of its 26 governors, and the Revd Albert Daymond, headmaster of St. Mark's College Schools, Chelsea, was its first headmaster.

After1860, when Charles became the 8th Baronet of Bunbury and Stanney, he and Fanny moved into Barton Hall. He served as a county magistrate, a deputy lieutenant for Suffolk, and as High Sheriff of Suffolk in 1868. He edited a memoir of his father's life, entitled *Memoir and Literary Remains of Lt. General Sir Henry Bunbury, Bart.*, which was published in1868.

The two schools at Great Barton were jointly known as the Sir Charles Bunbury Schools, and Lady Frances Bunbury took a particular interest in the Girls' School. She was also keen for a secondary school for the working class to be built at Bury St Edmunds, where some of the Cambridge professors could give lectures on two or three days in the week. To this end, she approached the Science and Art Department, which was responsible for the provision of secondary education (*BFP*, 27 June 1876).

Charles continued to try to be a good landlord. At a meeting of Barton Friendly Society in 1872, he told the members that:

'I have always tried to deal fairly with you, and I hope you will always do so with me. If you have any complaint, come openly to me and not mutter secret leagues against me. Barton and Mildenhall Estates have always dealt fairly with good cottages and a good piece of land, which has resulted in Barton being one of the happiest parishes in the County. Great Barton is indeed a model parish and, if all landlords had been equally considerate, we would not have heard of the present agricultural strikes' (*BFP*, 1 June 1872).

In fact, by the time of his death, the Barton Estate was cited as a model village, 'where the labourers have better cottages and larger gardens and allotments at a low rent ...... and the cottages stand, in most cases, in their own gardens and allotments' (*BNP*, 16 July 1889).

He died in 1886 and although he supported the Whig Party as a young man, his obituary stated that, in his later years, he allied himself with the Conservative Party (*BNP*, 29 June 1886). After his death, his widow moved back to the Manor House, Mildenhall, and edited *Botanical notes at Barton & Mildenhall, Suffolk*, written by her husband, which was published in 1889.

Edward Herbert Bunbury (1811-1895) [368] became the 9th Baronet of Bunbury and Stanney in 1886, when his childless brother died.

Edward was educated at home with his brother Charles and, when he was six-years-old, his mother boasted that he could do the longest sum in division without a mistake or difficulty. He attended Trinity College, Cambridge, graduated in 1833 and was a Senior Classic and Chancellor's Medallist. In 1835, he became a Fellow of Trinity College, Cambridge, and was awarded an MA the following year.

He became a barrister and represented the constituency of Bury St Edmunds as a Liberal Party MP from 1847 to 1852. He was an authority on the poets Lord Alfred Tennyson and Robert Browning, well known as a geographer and an archaeologist, and author of *A History of Ancient Geography among the Greeks and Romans*, 1879.

He moved into Barton Hall in 1886 but died at Apsley House in Brighton, aged 84, leaving a gross personal wealth of £32,410.

He bequeathed a portrait of Catherine of Braganza, the wife of King Charles II who had created the Bunbury baronetcy in 1681, to the National Portrait Gallery, London, and a Roman bronze, Quadrissis, to the British Museum.

Most of his estate went to his nephew, Henry Charles John Bunbury (1855-1930) [731], who was educated at Magdalen College, Cambridge, and joined the Royal Navy.

Henry William St Pierre Bunbury (1812-1875) was a soldier and an explorer. He joined the British Army and served in Australia between 1834 and 1837 (see chapter 8). He became a captain in 1838 and served as aide-de-camp to General Sir George Thomas Napier, the governor of the Cape of Good Hope, South Africa, and brother of his stepmother. In November 1852, he married Cecilia Caroline Napier (1819-1896), the daughter of General Napier, at Holy Innocents' Church, Great Barton. He served on the North-West Frontier of India and was promoted to the rank of colonel during the Crimean War (1853-1856), during which he fought at the Battle of Inkerman in 1854 and led the unsuccessful attack on the Redan at Sebastopol in 1855. In March 1855, he returned to Barton Hall to raise a fresh battalion for his regiment (*The Suffolk Chronicle*, 10 Mar. 1855). He retired in 1862 and lived at Barton Place, the family estate at Dolgelly, and Wokingham, Berkshire.

Richard Hanmer Bunbury (1813-1857), the youngest son of Sir Henry Edward Bunbury, joined the Royal Navy at the age of 13 and, whilst serving as a midshipman on the *Asia*, lost his right hand during the Battle of Navarino, which was fought against the Turks in the Greek War of Independence (1821–1832). He served in the navy for 11 years, during which time he reached the rank of captain and received several commendations. In 1838, he married Sarah Susanna Sconce (1816-1897), the daughter of Robert C. Sconce, Chief Commissary of the Navy at Malta, and immigrated to Australia in 1841, where he named one of his homes as Barton Hall. Richard died in Melbourne in 1857 and Sarah returned to England and lived for another 40 years in Brompton, Middlesex, and Eccleston Square, Westminster, London.

They had two daughters and four sons, the eldest of whom, Henry Fox Bunbury (1839-1870), attended King Edward VI Grammar School, Bury St Edmunds, enrolled in the army, and became a captain in the service of the 35th Regiment of the Bengal Native Infantry in India, where he died at Lahore.

Cecil became a colonel in the army, Robert a barrister-in-law, and Herbert a major general in the Royal Artillery.

The legacy of the Bunbury family

The Bunbury family exerted a powerful influence on the village of Great Barton for more than 150 years. Although Barton Hall burnt down in 1914 and the Barton Estate was broken up and sold, the Bunbury legacy has survived in the village street plan, the Bunbury Arms, many of its Victorian buildings and most importantly in its school.

2

SCHOOLS IN GREAT BARTON AREA BEFORE 1840

In 1841, the Bunbury family owned a large part of the parish of Great Barton, whilst Robert Lankester, Captain Philip Bennet and John South Phillips owned most of the remainder.

The Census of England and Wales 1841 was the first modern census. The data for the previous four censi had been collected by overseers of the poor or other leading members of the parish but, for this census, was collected by 35,000 enumerators who worked in census field teams and were required to be 'temperate, orderly and respectable, and to conduct themselves with strict propriety'. In Great Barton, the data was collected by Richard Sillett (1804-1852), the tollgate keeper of Barton Gate and Side Gate on the London to Norwich turnpike road, which produced £642 in tolls in 1841.

Holy Innocents' Church, Great Barton

The village was divided into two enumeration districts. District 9 was situated on the south side of the turnpike road and comprised Barton Mere, East Barton, Cattishall, Shinham Bridge, Manor Farm, Great Barton Vicarage and Holy Innocents' Church. District 10 was north of the road and included the Barton Estate and Conyers Green.

The Census of England and Wales 1841 showed that the population of Great Barton had increased from 523 in 1801 to 774 in 1841 but no children were recorded as scholars. There were twelve farmers and one land agent but the majority of the heads of households in the parish were employed as farm labourers, shepherds or artisans including four blacksmiths, five shoemakers, two wheelwrights, three brick makers, a thatcher and a carpenter. There were also two shopkeepers, a miller and a dairywoman.

Education of the wealthy

The sons of the wealthiest families in Great Barton had had access to education locally since the sixteenth century. These children were expected to play a leading role in public life when they grew up and were educated accordingly. Some were taught at home by a parent, tutor or governess, whilst others attended a preparatory school, before transferring to a grammar or a public school, where they were prepared for university entrance examinations and taught catechism, English, Latin and Greek grammar and the rudiments of Hebrew. The Grammar School Act 1840 added literature and science to the school curriculum. The education of the wealthy often included a Grand Tour of Europe, after which the oldest son returned home to manage the estate and take part in politics, whilst the younger brothers entered the church, armed forces or a profession.

The King Edward VI Free Grammar School at Bury St Edmunds, founded in 1550, was the second King Edward VI School to be built in England. It was founded for the 'sons of all inhabitants', and the 1593 statutes of the school stated that 'they shall, to the best of their power, teach as well the poorest man's child as the richest, without partiality'. However, the fees and the entrance requirements, laid down in the 1665 statutes, included an expectation that a child could already read and write legibly and had a knowledge of *Lilly's Grammar*, a Latin grammar first published in 1540. This effectively restricted the number of 'poor men's children', and no child from a poor family in Great Barton attended the school until the twentieth century.

Pupils who lived outside the town were known as 'foreigners' and within the town as 'royalists'. The Revd John Gay, Vicar of Great Barton in 1639, was educated at King Edward VI Grammar School, as were Sir Henry Edward Bunbury's father and uncle. Other pupils from Great Barton included James Thomas Bennet, born in 1796, who went on to Balliol College, Oxford, and became the Rector of Cheveley, Suffolk, and John South Phillips (1825-1890), who attended the school between 1836 and 1844 and became school captain, before going to Trinity College, Cambridge. Walton Burrell, the father of Frank Burrell, who was to serve as a school manager of Great Barton School from 1915, attended the school in 1815. John Dickenson, the headmaster of the school from 1606 until 1637, died in 1643 and was buried in the churchyard of Holy Innocents' Church, Great Barton.

Wealthy girls were educated at a school for young ladies or by a governess at home. There was no formal training to become a governess, and the quality of teaching was dependent on the standard of the governess's knowledge and level of supervision by the mistress of the house. Girls were taught to embroider, play the piano, recite poetry and perfect other accomplishments, which would enable them to make a 'good' marriage.

Education of the less wealthy

From the eighteenth century, some of the farmers and wealthier artisans in Great Barton sent their children to one of the local fee-paying private academies and schools, some of which were set up by unqualified people in their own homes. In Bury St Edmunds, there were a large number of such schools, some of which offered boarding accommodation.

Education of the labouring classes

Until the end of the eighteenth century, the only full time education available to the children of the labouring classes was in charity schools. There were 40 such schools in Suffolk, including two in parishes near Great Barton. At Ampton, in 1692, James Calthorpe left money in trust to support a charity school for 'the use and residence of a master and six poor boys, of Ampton, Great and Little Livermere, Ingham, and Timworth', with preference being given to children from Ampton. The grant was later extended to eight other parishes, which included Great Barton. In 2015, young students under the age of 25 who lived in any of these 13 parishes were able to apply to the Calthorpe and Edwards Educational Foundation for a contribution of £250 per annum for up to three years, to subsidise the cost of study materials and books required for their further education.

At Rougham, a charity school was set up in 1720, financed by an endowment from Edward Sparke, which accepted four pupils from Thurston in addition to children from Rougham.

There were no charity schools in Great Barton, where benefactors donated money for the welfare of the poor instead. The 'Church and Poor's Estate' was a legacy from the Revd William Howerdly, whose bequest, in 1492, was used to purchase Charity Farm and three cottages, the profits from which were used to defray church expenses and assist the poor. After 1,975 acres of land in the parish were enclosed in 1804, a 50-acre farm in Brand Road, known as Poor's Firing Farm, was allotted to the poor of Great Barton in lieu of their right to cut fuel. The Poor's Firing Farm Charity was managed by a board of trustees, who used the rents from the farm to purchase coal for poor parishioners. In 1828, Lady Louisa Bunbury left money for four almshouses and a small endowment for poor widows of Great Barton.

During the latter part of the eighteenth century, individuals or small groups of people who believed in universal education, set up schools for the poor around the country. In 1784, Mary Wollstonecraft, together with her sister and best friend, set up a school for local children in Newington Green, North London, and used the experience to write a pamphlet, in 1787, entitled, *Thoughts on the Education of Daughters*. Hannah More, the daughter of a schoolmaster, set up 12 schools for local children in Bristol, which taught reading, the *Holy Bible* and the catechism.

However, it was the Sunday school movement in Britain, which prepared the ground for a system of working class education.

It is associated with the work of Robert Raikes (1736-1811), the philanthropic editor of the *Gloucester Journal*, who saw education as a means of preventing children from slum areas from descending into crime. In July 1780, he set up a school in Gloucester that taught boys to read, using the *Holy Bible* as their textbook. Later, girls attended and, within two years, other schools had opened in and around Gloucester. Sunday schools soon spread to other parts of the country, and William Fox and others formed the Sunday School Society in London in 1785. The promoters also opened regular day schools and, by 1787, it was estimated that there were a quarter of a million pupils in Sunday schools.

In 1803, an inter-denominational Sunday School Union was formed, which sold more than 10 million reading and spelling books during the next 50 years.

Some politicians, farmers, clergymen and lawyers opposed the education of the labouring classes, in case it encouraged the poor to challenge the social order of the time. In 1807, during the debate of the Parochial Schools Bill in the House of Commons, Tory MP Davies Giddy warned that:

'However specious in theory, the project might be, of giving education to the labouring classes of the poor, it would, in effect, be found to be prejudicial to their morals and happiness; it would teach them to despise their lot in life, instead of making them good servants in agriculture and other laborious employments to which their rank in society had destined them' (*Hansard*, House of Commons, Vol. 9, Col. 798, 13 June 1807).

Voluntary societies

In 1796, Joseph Lancaster (1778-1838), a Quaker and the son of a shopkeeper, invited children of the poor into his father's house in the London borough of Southwark and taught them to read. In order to teach larger numbers of pupils, he devised the idea of teaching the brighter ones, who could then teach others, and after only two years, the number of pupils had increased from 90 to 1,000. His method of teaching became known as the Lancasterian system.

In 1803, he published *Improvements in Education as it respects the Industrial Classes of the Community*. From his work, the Society for Promoting the Royal British or Lancasterian System for the Education of the Poor was set up in 1808, and renamed in 1814 as the British and Foreign School Society for the Education of the Labouring and Manufacturing Classes of Society of Every Religious Persuasion (the British Society). It built 'British schools', which provided non-denominational religious instruction and was supported by members of

Nonconformist churches. In 1811, a British school was built at Bury St Edmunds for 200 boys, but it closed after the Guildhall schools were opened.

Dr Andrew Bell (1753-1832), a Scottish Episcopalian priest and tutor, worked in India as the Superintendent of the Military Male Orphan Asylum, Egmore, near Madras; an orphanage for the illegitimate and orphaned sons of military officers. In 1796, he observed children teaching the alphabet to other children by drawing in sand, so he adapted the method. He taught the alphabet to a bright 12-year-old boy called John Frisken, who then taught two 'assistants', who each taught a class of about 35 children. His method became known as the Madras system, and later as the monitorial system, as did the Lancasterian method.

In November 1811, Andrew Bell formed the National Society for Promoting the Education of the Poor in the Principles of the Established Church (the National Society). It built schools, known as national schools, in which children were taught basic skills and Christianity as represented by the Church of England. Amongst its supporters were William Wordsworth, Samuel Taylor Coleridge and Robert Southey. Branches were set up throughout the country and, by the time of Andrew Bell's death in 1832, the National Society had built 12,000 schools.

On 25 February 1812, members of the nobility, gentry, clergy and others met in the parish church at Stowmarket and set up the Suffolk Society for the Education of the Poor in the Principles of the Established Church. The Bishop of the Diocese was elected as patron, Marquis Cornwallis as president and Sir Thomas Charles Bunbury (1740-1821) as one of the 14 vice presidents. At this meeting, the members agreed to the building of national schools in Ipswich and Bury St Edmunds, and to support Sunday and other parochial schools in rural areas.

A fundamental rule of the society was that:

'all the children in these schools were to be instructed in the liturgy and catechism of the established church and each child should attend Divine Service in their parish church or other place of public worship 'under the Establishment', on the Lord's Day and that no religious tracts be admitted into any schools, unless they were contained in the catalogue of the Society for Promoting Christian Knowledge.'

During the meeting, £1165. 6s. was raised in donations and a further £239. 2s. promised in annual subscriptions. Sir Thomas Charles Bunbury donated £50 and promised an annual subscription of five guineas, and the Revd Thomas Scotman, the curate of Great Barton, who received an annual stipend of £45 per annum, donated five guineas and promised one guinea a year in subscriptions (*BNP*, 4 Mar. 1812).

The National Society recommended the use of the Madras system and expected children to read the scriptures and learn texts by heart, but at this stage, it excluded the teaching of secular subjects. Their schools accepted children from Anglican and non-Anglican families.

Schools in the Great Barton area in 1818

In 1818, Parliament set up a select committee to investigate the education of the poor in England and Wales. Questionnaires were sent to parish incumbents, and the findings were published in the *Digest of Parochial Returns Made to the Select Committee Appointed to Inquire into the Education of the Poor (1818)*.

Of the 633 parishes in Suffolk, 417 had a day school. Some were dame schools, run by untrained women in their own homes, and others were run by one of the religious societies or a philanthropist.

In 1817, Sir Thomas Charles Bunbury set up a free school for girls at Mildenhall, which was described in 1839 by the Revd Raven, a Diocesan Inspector, as a 'well conducted girls' school, entirely supported by the liberality of Sir Henry and Lady Bunbury' (*BNP*, 2 Oct. 1839).

In 1818, Great Barton had a population of 569, of whom 73 were deemed poor. There was one unendowed Sunday school run on the Madras system and attended by 96 children, and two unendowed day schools attended by 67 children. The Revd Thomas Scotman, the local curate, had contributed to the National Society in 1812, so it is possible that Great Barton Sunday School had operated since 1812.

The *Digest of Parochial Returns (1818)* commented that in Great Barton, 'the poorer classes are not without sufficient means of giving some sort of education to their children; and the Sunday school, conducted on the new system, produces an evident and rapid improvement in the scholars of both sexes.'

Emily Pawsey (1814-1906) [499] was a pupil at Great Barton Sunday School. In 1838, she married John Phillips, a farm labourer, and they had ten children. She lived in Great Barton all her life and when she died at the age of 92, she was still fit enough to walk into Bury St Edmunds. When John [491] died at the age of 91 in June 1906, the *Bury Free Press* stated that they were believed to have been the oldest married couple in England (*BFP*, 30 June 1906). John's obituary mentioned that one of their sons had been in service with Lord Burnham, the founder of the *Daily Telegraph*, and that Emily had 'attended school in church on Sundays, when she was young, and her family had eaten their poor Sunday dinner in the porch or in the churchyard'.

Mary Long (1819-1916) [592] also attended Great Barton Sunday School and was in service to the Bunbury family all of her working life. Her eyesight was still good enough for her to be able to read the *Bury Free Press* in her 90s (*BFP*, 07 Sept. 1912).

When they left Sunday School, both girls may have received a copy of *The Poor Child's Library* (1812) as a leaving present. It cost 4s and was a collection of moral and religious pieces in prose and verse.

Educational provision in 1833

According to the *British Parliamentary Papers, Volume 41,* a survey of educational provision in England and Wales was carried out by parish overseers in 1833. It showed that, between 1818 and 1833, the number of day schools in England and Wales doubled to nearly 39,000, with 1.27 million pupils. The number of Sunday schools tripled to almost 17,000, with 1.54 million pupils. In Suffolk, there were 117 infant schools, 961 day schools and 488 Sunday schools.

The *Abstract of Education Returns (1833)* reported that Great Barton, with a population of 778, had 'one daily school, containing 6 males and 26 females, whose instruction is paid for by their parents, and one Sunday school of 60 males and 71 females supported by subscription.'

The day school was probably taught by Mary Craske in her rented cottage on the Barton Estate. She died in January 1840 at the age of 80 and her obituary in the local newspaper described her as 'the much respected mistress of the school at Barton' (*BNP*, 5 Feb. 1840).

Nationally, there were not enough school places in day schools, especially in towns and cities. It was widely agreed that children whose hours had been limited by the Factory Act 1833 should be offered schooling, if only on a part-time basis. Politicians were divided on the subject of school finance and, whilst some favoured state funding and preferred not to rely on voluntary contributions, others were wary of imposing a compulsory rate or tax, in case some of the philanthropists, who maintained the existing 14,000 non-endowed schools, withdrew their support.

In July 1833, Mr John Arthur Roebuck (1801-1879), the Whig MP for Bath, proposed a motion that Parliament should 'devise a means for the universal and national education of the whole people' for all children in Great Britain and Ireland from the age of six to twelve. This would have been an opportunity to create a universal, state-funded education system, but the motion was withdrawn.

The Education Act 1833 provided state funds for schools and gave a grant of £20,000 'in aid of private subscriptions for the erection of schoolhouses for the education of the children of the poorer classes in Great Britain'. The government hoped that the grant would be matched by voluntary subscriptions or taken up in towns and places, where there were no offers of voluntary subscriptions from wealthy benefactors. The National Society and the British Society administered the grant, and schools that accepted a grant had to agree to inspection by government inspectors, whose objectives were to set guidelines and improve standards.

After the Poor Law Amendment Act 1834, which stressed the importance of education for the labouring classes, the grant was renewed for a further four years. Education was originally free of charge in schools run by the British and National Societies, but some people believed that a greater value was placed on things where a payment was involved, so the 'children's pence' was gradually introduced and many schools made a weekly charge of a few pennies. Wealthy philanthropists continued to set up schools and, in 1836, the Duke of Norfolk built a school in the nearby parish of Fornham St Martin.

Not everyone supported the denominational educational societies and, in 1836, the Central Society of Education was set up, which advocated a national non-denominational system of education with democratic control of schools and government inspection, but this society received only limited support.

Educational provision after 1839

The provision of education became more centralised after 1839, when the Committee of the Privy Council on Education, was set up to administer Treasury money for the provision of elementary schools, which no longer had to be matched by voluntary contributions. James Kay-Shuttleworth, a proponent of state-run education, was appointed as its Assistant Secretary. The Committee created a school inspection system, instigated regulations about teaching methods and school building design, and made provision for teacher training schools, which were eligible for a grant and subject to inspections by Her Majesty's Inspectorate. At first, these schools were known as 'normal' schools because they were expected to establish teaching standards or norms. In 1840, James Kay-Shuttleworth set up Battersea College, the first teacher training college in Britain.

In 1839, 12,524 pupils in Suffolk attended 170 schools, run by the National Society, and a further 11,547 pupils attended schools 'associated with' the National Society, all of which provided secular as well as religious teaching (*BNP*, 2 Oct. 1839).

The school in Great Barton was not funded by a government grant. It was built by Sir Henry Edward Bunbury on the Barton Estate, at his own expense. His decision and timing may have been influenced by the School Sites Act 1841, which encouraged landowners to make land available for education purposes, with the proviso that, if the usage changed, ownership would revert to their descendants. Owners were permitted to sell or donate a maximum of:

'one acre of land, as a site for a school for the education of poor persons, or for the residence of the schoolmaster or schoolmistress, or otherwise for the purposes of the education of such poor persons in religious and useful knowledge.'

The Bunbury family retained the freehold of the school site and premises until the relocation of the school in 1967, after which the land reverted to the Bunbury Estate.

3
THE FIRST SCHOOL

Sir Henry Edward Bunbury, 7th Baronet of Bunbury and Stanney, founded a school in Great Barton for the education of 'children of the labouring, manufacturing, and other poorer class in the parish of Great Barton'.

It was built on the Barton Estate, at the end of School Lane, adjacent to the arboretum. Unlike many other Victorian schools, this one was neither built near the parish church, nor named after it.

The foundation of the school

There is a dearth of evidence about the foundation of Great Barton School. Most schools have a Trust Deed, which provides information about the foundation of the school but there is no evidence of a Trust Deed or any other information about the school's foundation amongst the papers of the Bunbury family, which are held at Suffolk Record Office.

In 1917, the Revd Lipscomb told the Revd F.J. Fulford of Fornham All Saints, the secretary of Sudbury Voluntary School Association, that he was unable to find a Trust Deed for Great Barton School in the records of the National Society, and was 'under the impression that the schools were the private property of Sir Henry Bunbury'.

In 1949, the Revd Duval, the chairman of the school managers, received a letter from the Local Education Authority, which referred to the need to draw up a new Trust Deed and stated that that 'the responsibility for a deed rests with Sir Charles [Bunbury] and the Diocesan Board of Finance, and is no concern of the Local Education Authority'.

The Bunbury family, who claimed the freehold of the school premises, agreed to the school having a 99-year lease, with the Diocesan Board of Finance as the trustee.

In 1962, correspondence about a boundary fence at Great Barton School stated that, 'one must assume that, being kept in private ownership, the school was never subject to such a trust'.

A letter from the National Society to Great Barton School, written in 1966 with reference to the Trust Deed, stated that they did not have any information about the school.

In 1969, correspondence about an indemnity policy for Great Barton School quoted a letter from Mr H.C. Wolton, the solicitor for the Bunbury Estate, to Canon Southwell, written in 1967, in which he stated that 'in his opinion, there was no doubt that the Bunbury family claimed the freehold of these [the school] premises.' The same letter stated that the Registrar of the Diocese of Ely confirmed 'that an exhaustive search was made in the Registry and that no deeds were ever lodged there in connection with Great Barton.'

If Sir Henry Bunbury had applied for a government grant, he would have been obliged to submit plans in accordance with Circular No. 1, November 1839, of the Committee of the Privy Council on Education, but there is no evidence of any such application. Applicants were obliged to include details of the dimensions of every room, the arrangement of the benches, desks, gallery and other apparatus, and a sketch of air-grates and flues.

Date of foundation

The Census of England and Wales 1841 did not list anyone in the parish as a schoolteacher or a scholar. *White's Directory of Suffolk* for 1844 makes no mention of a school in Great Barton.

White's Directory of Suffolk of 1855 states, 'here is a small national school, built in 1854, at the cost of Sir Henry Bunbury and attended by about 50 scholars', but subsequent editions of *White's Directory*, the *Post Office Directory* and *Kelly's Directory* state that a school was built in 1840. In 1886, the *Bury and Norwich Post* reported that the school managers gave Susan Kerry a lamp and teapot, in recognition of her 40 years' service at Great Barton School (*BFP*, 25 Dec.1886).

From this limited evidence, it would seem that the school was established at some time between 1840 and 1846.

Type of school

The Report of Church Schools (1846 to 1847) was based on an inquiry by the National Society and published by Her Majesty's Inspectors (HMI). It gave information about 252 schools in Suffolk, but did not include Great Barton School.

Whilst trades' directories are a useful source of information, they do contain inaccuracies and inconsistencies. *White's Directories of Suffolk* for 1855, 1874 and 1892 described the school at Great Barton as a national school; the *Post Office Directories* of 1869 and 1875 described it as a free school; and *Kelly's Directories* of 1879, 1883, 1888 and 1892 stated that the schools were entirely supported by Sir Charles or Sir Edward Bunbury.

The Annual Report of the Committee of the Privy Council on Education (1879) mentioned that Great Barton School received a government grant and it defined the school as 'being associated with the Church of England', but not run by the National Society. By this time, it was categorised as a 'voluntary' school.

A legal agreement between Sir Henry Charles John Bunbury and the school managers, drawn up in 1918, established the fact that the Bunbury family was the landlord of the school buildings, and stated that the school should be:

'in union with and conducted according to the principles and in furtherance of the ends and designs of the Incorporated National Society for promoting the education of the poor in the principles of the established church throughout England and Wales.'

The above evidence shows that, although the school was the private property of the Bunbury family, it was a voluntary school and was associated with the Church of England.

The teachers

The Census of England and Wales 1851, details of which were collected by John Spooner, the village grocer, recorded that, amongst the 855 inhabitants of the village, there were 2 schoolmistresses and 95 scholars.

One of the schoolmistresses was Mary Last, the 37-year-old daughter of a shoemaker, who lived next door to the Crown Beerhouse in Carpenters Yard, School Lane. Later that year she married Henry Thickson, a glazier, and moved to the London borough of Southwark.

The other schoolmistress was 26-year-old Susan Kerry, who was born in Bury St Edmunds.

There was no national salary scale for schoolteachers. In 1840, the average salary for schoolteachers in Suffolk was less than that of some servants, dressmakers and washerwomen. The HMI Report of Church Schools (1846 to 1847) revealed that teachers' salaries in Suffolk varied from £10 p.a. to £90 p.a., with an average of £33 p.a. In Bury St Edmunds, in 1833, the annual salary of the headmaster of the Central School for Boys was £70 p.a., which was £10 p.a. more than that of the headmistress of the Central School for Girls.

In 1846, the government agreed to grant a pension to those teachers who had taught for 15 years, seven of which had been in a 'school under inspection'. The pension could not exceed two-thirds of their average salary and emolument, and was conditional on a recommendation by the inspector, the trustees and the managers of their school. However, the Revised Code 1862 rescinded this agreement.

Susan Kerry was untrained, although teacher training was theoretically available at the Central School for Girls in Bury St Edmunds, which was classified as a 'normal' school. However, in 1849, the Revd H. B Faulkner, who lived in Long Melford, claimed that no more than two masters and two mistresses had trained at the Central Schools in any year, despite being in receipt of a grant for the training of teachers (*BNP*, 2 May 1849). Subsequently, a committee was appointed in Bury St Edmunds to investigate the training of teachers at the Central Schools.

In 1846, the Committee of the Privy Council on Education introduced the pupil-teacher and teacher training college system. In schools which were judged by an inspector to be suitable, bright 13-year-olds were apprenticed to a teacher for five years, during which time they received training for 90 minutes a day and were required to pass an annual examination, set by HMI. They were trained in class management and routine duties, and girls were expected to supervise sewing lessons for up to two hours each day. Male pupil-teachers received a grant of £10 p.a. at first with increments dependent on their level of success in examinations, rising to £20 p.a. when they were 18-years-old. Female pupil-teachers received about two-thirds of the grant given to males. A head teacher was permitted to have one pupil-teacher for every 25 pupils on the school roll, and the supervising teacher of each pupil-teacher was paid £5 p.a.

At the end of their apprenticeship, pupil-teachers were eligible to compete for the Queen's Scholarship, which would finance a three-year training course at a teacher training college, with a maintenance grant of £20 for women and £25 for men. At the end of the course, pupils received a government certificate and became a certificated teacher. A pupil-teacher who did not choose to take the Queen's Scholarship examination was permitted to teach in a grant-aided elementary school as an uncertificated, or Article 50, teacher.

In 1851, there were 40 teacher training colleges nationally, including 34 run by the National Society and one by the Voluntary School Association, with local colleges at Norwich, Peterborough and Bishops' Stortford. All teacher training colleges run by religious institutions were single-sex until the Second World War.

Educational funding

The Education Census of Great Britain (1851), the only one conducted during the nineteenth century, was organised by George Graham, the Registrar General. Horace Mann, an American education reformer, carried out the survey, which asked each school to complete a detailed questionnaire. The published results included the aggregate of results in registration districts in England and Wales, but not the returns for individual schools. At least 1,206 day schools and 377 Sunday schools refused to supply information, because they were suspicious of government intervention in the voluntary and denominational nature of education. The census defined 'private' day schools as those 'sustained entirely by the payments of the scholars'. These were mainly attended by the children of middle and upper class families.

It defined 'public' day schools as those, which gathered any portion of their income 'from any source besides the scholars' and divided them into four classes of school, which were subdivided into more than 50 subcategories, the majority of them in Class II.

Class I. Schools supported by general or local taxation,
Class II. Schools supported by endowments,
Class III. Schools supported by religious bodies'
Class IV. Other public schools.

Out of 69 schools in the area covered by Thingoe Poor Law Union, 37 were public schools, with 1850 scholars, and 32 were private schools, with 658 pupils. An almost equal number of male and female scholars attended the private schools, but there were 1039 girls and 811 boys on the registers of the public schools. Of the 37 public schools, seven were supported by endowments, 8 by the National Society, 20 by other religious bodies and 2 in (unspecified) other ways. There were no schools run by the British Society. There were 38 Sunday schools; 32 Church of England, 1 independent, 3 Baptist, 1 Wesleyan Methodist and one Congregationalist. The report highlighted an insufficiency of school places, a need for better books and equipment, the inadequacy of many school buildings, the lack of suitable accommodation for teachers, and the need to improve the pay and training of teachers, in order to improve the quality of the instruction.

Schools in receipt of a government grant were inspected by HMI, who examined the qualification of teachers and the school curriculum. Anglican schools could also choose to have a Diocesan Inspection.

Spending on education varied across the country. An education return in 1850 mentioned the insufficiency of books and apparatus in inspected schools and compared 60 of the best schools in various counties. In Suffolk, an average of £3. 1s. was spent annually on books per school, which compared with £10. 2s. 8d. in Surrey.

In 1853, a capitation grant, based on the number of pupils was introduced for rural schools to encourage attendance, and was later extended to all schools. The Parliamentary Return, which reported on the amount of grant to each school, showed that in the year 1859-1860, those schools that received grants contained 917,255 of the 1,675,158 children, who attended public weekday schools. However, the grants were not distributed equally throughout the country and only 46 village schools and

32 town schools in the 575 parishes in Suffolk received a grant (*BNP*, 29 Apr. 1862).

In 1856, to assist the Committee of the Privy Council on Education, the government set up an Education Department, which incorporated the Science and Art Department of the Board of Trade.

The pupils

At Great Barton, boys and girls were taught in a single schoolroom and were divided into standards, according to their age and ability. Pupils sat on long rows of parallel benches, with a marker on a pole at the end of each row to indicate the standard of that row, with Standard I for the seven-year-olds and Standard II for the eight-year-olds etc. The infants sat on a gallery, a stepped or raised seating area.

School days started at 9.00 a.m. and ended at 5.00 p.m., with a two-hour break for lunch. Pupils walked to and from school and, for those living in Cattishall or near the church, it was over a mile; far enough in good weather; less attractive in wet or cold weather, especially as most children were expected to do jobs in the home, before and after school.

A typical school day would begin with registration, followed by an hour of scripture, taught by the Revd William Robert Blake (1800-1868), the Vicar of Holy Innocents' Church, Great Barton. The next hour would be devoted to writing and arithmetic, which might include English grammar, and the third hour to reading (*BFP*, 3 Aug. 1872). For the girls, most afternoons would be devoted to the study of needlework, whilst the boys would study more literacy or numeracy. Some schools also taught geography.

In 1852, the *Bury and Norwich Post* carried advertisements for a series of books, which may have been in use at Great Barton School. *Clarkes Improved Copy Books* (published by T Messrs. Wiggins Teape, and Loder, London) included a sentence at the top of each page for pupils to copy. The Religious Series consisted of seven books, which related to biblical studies, and a further book, which contained biographical sketches of Lord Ashburton, Lord Brougham, Richard Cobden, Benjamin Disraeli and Sir Robert Peel (*BNP*, 14 July 1852).

The highlights of the year for the pupils were the village fêtes. On 25 June 1852, a Grand Musical Horticultural Fête, the second exhibition of the Bury Horticultural Society, was held in the grounds of Barton Hall, and an entrance fee of 1s. for adults and 6d. for children under 12 was charged. Eastern Union Railway Company ran extra trains to and from Bury, Norwich, Diss, and Ipswich, and made an unscheduled stop at Barton Road level crossing, near the grounds of Barton Hall (*BNP*, 16 Jun. 1852).

To enable the children to attend in 1859, Sir Henry Bunbury waived the schoolchildren's entrance fee to the West Suffolk Horticultural Society Show held in the grounds of Barton Hall (*BNP*, 5 July 1859).

Poverty and non-attendance at school

The *Education Census of Great Britain (1851)* reported that in the 46 parishes of the Thingoe Union, 1,510 of the 1,850 registered pupils in the public elementary schools attended school on the day of the census.

In Great Barton, of the 140 working class children in the village, 35 boys and 60 girls were recorded as scholars in the population census of England and Wales 1851. These included 84 children aged five to eleven and nine girls and two boys aged 12 to 15. A further 54 working class children aged five to eleven were not recorded as scholars, and many of those who were registered at school had an irregular attendance record.

Many children did not attend school because their families needed them to help in the home or to earn money. Some rural families were unconvinced as to the value of education for children, especially for their sons, who were destined to work on the land, where observation, shrewdness and practical sagacity were seen as being more essential than the ability to read or write.

The rural population engaged in farming was at its peak in 1851, when, nationally, 1.46 million people worked as agricultural labourers, farm servants or shepherds, and about half of the population were dependent on rural occupations for their livelihood. In 1851, agricultural workers in Suffolk were the worst paid in the whole country, earning an average weekly wage of 7s. 0d. a week, compared with 11s. 6d. in the northern counties, where farmers competed against industrial employers. Wages even compared unfavourably with other parts of East Anglia where the average weekly wage was 7s. 6d. a week in Cambridgeshire, 8s. 6d. a week in Norfolk and 9s. 0d. a week in Essex, so there was little incentive for young men to stay in Suffolk. Although wages rose, they did not keep up with the price of food.

In Great Barton, boys as young as seven worked as farm labourers, and children in Suffolk earned, on average, 8d. per day. Some earned up to 2s. to 3s. a week scaring birds, or 4d. to 8d. a day 'dropping' seeds, such as wheat, peas and beans into holes, previously made with a dibble. Both boys and girls undertook casual farm work, which also included gathering stones, thinning turnips, picking weeds, making hay, and gleaning the leftover grain in August after the reapers had finished. Some boys supplemented the family income by trapping birds, stealing a sleeping pheasant or catching rabbits with a snare or ferret.

Many families were only able to balance their family budget if their children went out to work. This account of the finances a family from a village near Great Barton shows that their income covered the bare necessities, but was not enough for meat, boots or other clothing.

Table 1. Weekly family budget of an agricultural labourer in Lavenham, Suffolk, 1843

Weekly income			Weekly expenditure	
Name	Age	Income	Item	Cost
Robert Crick	42	9s. 0d.	bread	9s. 0d.
wife	40	0s. 9d.	potatoes	1s. 0d.
boy	12	2s. 0d.	rent	1s. 2d.
boy	11	1s. 0d.	tea	0s. 2d.
boy	8	1s. 0d.	sugar	0s. 3½d.
girl	6		soap	0s. 3d.
boy	4		blue	0s. ½d.
			thread etc.	0s. 2d.
			candles	0s. 3d.
			salt	0s. ½d.
			coal and wood	0s. 9d.
			butter	0s. 4½d.
			cheese	0s. 3d
Total		*13s. 9d.*	*Total*	*13s. 9d.*

Source: Report of Special Assistant Poor Law Commissioners on the employment of Women and Children in Agriculture in 1843 (p.233)

A series of bad harvests and the arrival of imports from the American prairies resulted in a serious agricultural depression in Britain, which lasted for about 30 years from the 1850s. Thomas Scott, the general manager and land agent of the Barton Estate, kept a diary of the weather and the state of the farms in Great Barton. The weather in 1860 was particularly wet and cold. On 13 August 1860, he wrote that there was heavy rain, with the Girls' School surrounded by 1 inch of water, and 6.24 inches of rain fell during the month. During 1860, 18.83 inches of rain fell, compared with 11.43 inches in 1862, and 8.12 inches in 1863. On 11 October 1860, Thomas Scott wrote, 'cottage rents received – tenants paid up well – but long and bitter complaints of potato crop being totally destroyed. Allotments of half an acre not having a peck of good ones'. On 25 December 1860, there was 33°F of hoar frost and 4 inches of snow. By the end of the year, the weather was adversely affecting people's health and some animals froze to death.

Thomas Scott was also the secretary of Barton Friendly Society, which provided financial and social services to individuals in the parish.

The wealthy sometimes gave gifts to the poor at special times of the year. According to the Revd Harry Jones in *Dead Leaves and Living Seeds,* his account of village life, published in 1895, Mrs Paine of Elms Farm gave every child a half pint of beer on Valentine's Day.

Severe poverty for some Great Barton children

Some children were unable to attend school because they had no footwear and occasionally parents were tempted to steal shoes, as in the case of the Olley family. Abraham Olley [226], a farm labourer, was born in Guernsey, but moved to Great Barton and, in 1826, married Fanny Foulger. In 1844, Fanny was accused of larceny, when she was caught stealing a pair of clogs from a haberdasher's in the Butter Market, Bury St Edmunds. She was committed for trial but because she had seven children, was pregnant, had had sickness in her house for some time and her husband was of good character, she was released on bail, subject to raising the bail money (*BNP*, 28 Aug. 1844). In October 1844, she was found guilty and sent to the House of Correction in Bury St Edmunds for six months, where she gave birth to Frederick on 9 January. Her ninth child was born in 1847, just two months before her death at the age of 38. Three years after her death, Abraham married Elizabeth Nichols (285) and had six more children.

This family narrowly avoided being taken into Thingoe Union Workhouse, Bury St Edmunds, which was completed in 1836, at a cost of about £5,000, and could accommodate up to 300 paupers. Great Barton was expected to pay for the upkeep of any workhouse inmates born in its parish, even if they had moved away. Sir Henry Bunbury represented the parish of Great Barton on the Board of Guardians, which managed the affairs of the poor law union and the workhouse.

Jane Long was born in 1842. She and her three sisters were born in Great Barton, but moved to Vinefields, in Bury St Edmunds. After their parents died in 1848 and 1849, they were taken to Thingoe Union Workhouse because they had no other means of support. They were stripped of their personal belongings, publicly bathed, and issued with a uniform, which typically consisted of a 'grogram' gown (coarse fabric of mohair and wool, stiffened with gum), a calico shift, a Gingham dress, a day cap, worsted stockings and woven slippers or wooden clogs. They were allocated a bed in a ward with other girls aged 2 to 14 and expected to work for several hours each day in order to earn their keep. They were fed a monotonous although theoretically nutritious diet of bread and gruel for breakfast, a cooked lunch, and bread, cheese and broth for supper.

From 1846, government funding was available for workhouse schools, where children were taught to read and write and the principles of Christianity. The quality of instruction was often poor and the teachers were more concerned with saving children's souls or training them for servitude than providing a general education.

From the age of 14, Jane was expected to live outside the workhouse in spite of the fact that she had no means of support or employment and no alternative accommodation. Having spent most of her childhood in the workhouse, it was the only home she had ever known. After her release, she frequently presented herself at the workhouse gate to demand a bed for the night, in return for which she was expected to contribute two hours of work. This often included picking oakum out of rope using a large metal nail, known as a spike, so that the cleaned hemp from the rope could be used for caulking planks, to make ships watertight. Between the ages of 16 and 20, Jane served 20 prison sentences in the House of Correction in Bury St Edmunds after being found guilty of vagrancy, theft or criminal damage. In July 1862, she was found in the company of prostitutes in a churchyard in Bury St Edmunds (*BNP*, 8 July 1862) after which her destiny is unknown and there are no more newspaper reports of her appearing in Thingoe Magistrates' Court.

By 1858, there were three more children from Great Barton in Thingoe Union Workhouse. John Bray had five children, but after his wife died was caught poaching and fined £5 (*BNP*, 30 Mar. 1858). He was unable to keep a job so he took his three youngest children, aged seven, eight and nine, to Thingoe Workhouse in May 1858. In November 1858, he was found guilty of deserting his family and imprisoned for a month in the House of Correction (*BNP*, 9 Nov. 1858).

These children were later reunited with their father and, by 1861, were living in a house in Eastgate Street, which they shared with an unmarried housekeeper and her two young children.

The class of 1851

Although many of the 35 boys who attended the school in 1851 worked as agricultural labourers in Great Barton when they left school, only a quarter of them remained in the village all their lives. Others moved to nearby villages, towns or the London area, where there were greater opportunities for better paid and more secure employment.

This rural exodus was facilitated by the rail connections to and from Bury St Edmunds, where a station was opened in 1847. By the following year, there were four return trains to London each day via Ipswich, and a return train to Colchester. The train journey from Cambridge to London took three hours, compared with seven hours by mail coach.

Amos Olley (1849-1937) [792], one of the sons of Abraham Olley, was known as 'Tray' to his friends and was an irregular attendee at Great Barton School. He became a farm labourer and earned 3d. a day when he started full-time work in 1861, at the age of 11. He was a superb ploughman and, in 1895, competed against 40 men in a ploughing match at Timworth, where he was judged as the champion ploughman for the best ploughing of a quarter of an acre. During his lifetime, he won 21 copper kettles, a pair of four-tine forks, one two-tine fork, a silver watch, a whip and two half-sovereigns as prizes in ploughing matches. He was a bell ringer at Holy Innocents' Church for over 50 years. He died in 1937, not long after his sixty-fifth wedding anniversary, leaving 7 daughters, 1 son, 25 grandchildren and 14 great-grandchildren, many of whom had attended the village school.

Most of the young men who moved away from the village worked in a farming-related occupation or as a gardener or servant. The exceptions were George Grimwood, who became a timekeeper in an ironworks in Rotherham, Yorkshire, and Edward Parish, who became an inventor.

Edward Parish may have been inspired by the Great Exhibition of 1851, held at Crystal Palace in Hyde Park, London, which attracted 6 million visitors. The displays included new industrial and agricultural machines, medical artefacts, labour-saving devices, transport and new art forms. John Pace, a clock and watchmaker from Bury St Edmunds exhibited a skeleton timepiece in the shape of a pyramid, a skeleton clock, which only needed winding once every three years, and a brass barometer.

Edward Parish was the son of a 'dealer'. He was born in Bury St Edmunds, but moved to Great Barton in 1850 when his grandfather, Edward Cox, took over the Crown Beerhouse in Carpenter's Lane. In 1867, he married Jane Jackaman from Diss and their children were born in Stowmarket, Bury St Edmunds, Sudbury, Cambridge and Leicester, which suggested that they moved home frequently. In Leicester, Edward worked as a general agent for a furnisher, invented a steam cooker, and worked as a 'traveller and manager of patents'. In 1911, at the age of 65, Edward lived in a six-roomed house and was the manager of Parish's Steam Jacketted Cooker Co. In 1917, the Parish's Cooker was advertised in a programme of Crufts Dog Show. His sons worked as clerks, his oldest daughter as a schoolteacher, and his other daughters as typists for companies that manufactured pianos and hosiery.

The choices for the 60 girls who attended the school in 1851 were very limited. Most became a servant, or remained at home to look after younger siblings or a widowed parent, and, where they did find alternative paid work, it was typically as a dressmaker, upholsterer or laundress.

In 1851 and 1861, only four of the 25 female servants of the 13 employers in Great Barton were born in the village. It was common practice not to employ servants from the local area. Employers believed that, not only would it be more difficult for the girls to return home if they were homesick or unhappy, but also there would be less likelihood of trouble from the girls' suitors, or of the private affairs of their employers being discussed in the locality.

Many of these female school leavers left the village, some of whom moved to London. The wealthy had always employed servants but as the population of London and other cities and towns grew, so did the demand for servants from the less wealthy. Victorian newspapers were full of adverts for live-in servants, who received free accommodation, regular meals, a uniform and a small wage, from which they were expected to contribute to their parents. Country girls were popular because they were considered to be more honest, hard-working and biddable, as well as cheaper, than girls from urban areas.

The majority of these Great Barton girls married, but all were over the age of 19 at the time of their marriage. The Marriage Act 1753 (Lord Hardwicke's Marriage Act) fixed the lower legal age of marriage in England and Wales at 14 for men and 12 for women, with parental consent required if the couple were under the age of 21.

The Ages of Marriage Act 1929 raised the minimum age limit to 16 for men and women, with parental consent for those under 21.

The general election and the Royal Commission

In Great Barton, 18 men were eligible to vote in the 1859 election, and it was from amongst them that the school managers were selected. The electors included the landowners, farmers and the Vicar of Great Barton, in addition to two shoemakers, two victuallers (of the Bunbury Arms and the Crown Beerhouse) and Robert Firman (an agricultural labourer).

Voting was made secret in 1872 but until then the votes of the poll of the registered electors in Great Barton were published. Captain Philip Bennett (1795-1866), who lived at Rougham Hall, had been one of the two Conservative MPs for West Suffolk from 1845 to 1859 together with Frederick William Hervey (1769-1859). Philip Bennett received the highest number of votes from the electors in Great Barton, but the seat was won by Major Windsor Parker and Frederick William Hervey, Earl Jermyn of Ickworth Park (1800-1864). Nationally, the Whig Party, led by Lord Palmerston (1784-1865), won the election. At a bi-election in 1864, Lord Augustus Henry Charles Hervey (1837-1875) succeeded his brother as MP for Suffolk and held the seat until 1874.

In 1858, a Royal Commission on the State of Popular Education in England was set up, chaired by the Duke of Newcastle 'to inquire into the state of public education in England to consider and report what measures, if any, were required for the extension of sound and cheap elementary instruction to all classes of the people'.

The Whig government was keen to act on the Newcastle Report (1861) to ensure that the education system was reformed and there were sufficient school places for every child in England and Wales.

By the end of the 1850s, the schoolroom in School Lane, which measured 20 feet by 39 feet, could not accommodate all of the eligible school age children in Great Barton, so it was necessary to extend this school building or erect a new one.

4
THE WIDOW'S GIFT

A second schoolroom was erected in School Road, Great Barton, a quarter of a mile from the first building. Trades directories, written between 1857 and 1912, state that it was built in 1857, whilst those written after 1916 state that it was built in 1860.

Lady Emily Louisa Augusta Bunbury (1783-1863) dedicated this building to the memory of her husband, and a commemoration plaque,

The Commemoration Plaque

built into the wall above the school entrance, stated, 'The widow's gift. Sacred to the memory of Henry Edward Bunbury MDCCCLX.'

The rectangular schoolroom measured 40 feet long, 20 feet wide and 20 feet high and its walls were constructed of brick and flint.

From this time, boys were taught in the second building, which became known as Sir Charles Bunbury's Boys' School, and girls and infants were taught in the original one, known as Sir Charles Bunbury's Girls' School.

A Boys' Schoolhouse was built opposite the Boys' School, on the corner of School Road and Mill Road, to provide living accommodation for the schoolmaster and his family. It was constructed of brick and flint and had three bedrooms, a living room, a kitchen, a pantry and some outbuildings.

A Girls' Schoolhouse was erected on the south side of School Lane, near the Girls' School. It was built of knapped flint and stone from the abbey at Bury St Edmunds, and set in half an acre of garden, behind a brick and flint wall. It was double-fronted with two bedrooms, two sitting rooms, a kitchen and some outbuildings. An upstairs fireplace was added later, together with two ornate chimneys. The internal walls were of wattle (a woven lattice of wood strips), plastered with daub, and made from lime and horsehair. The areas over the front door and both chimneys were decorated with the faces of the Bunbury heraldic leopards.

The Census of England and Wales 1861 revealed that, during the previous decade, the population of Great Barton had declined slightly from 855 to 848, but the number of households had increased from 178 to 208, most of whom were employed in farming, or associated occupations.

The teachers and pupils

William Plummer was the headmaster and Susan Kerry the headmistress of the schools in Great Barton. The Newcastle Report (1861) stated that a schoolteacher needed to have a 'quiet even temper, patience, sympathy, fondness for children, and habitual cheerfulness.'

In Great Barton, 94 of the 134 working class children, aged five to eleven, were recorded as scholars.

Table 2. Number of working class children in Great Barton, recorded as scholars in the Census of England and Wales 1861

	Aged 3 to 7	Aged 8 to 11	Aged 12 and over	Total
Boys	19	20	2	41
Girls	20	22	11	53
Total	39	42	13	94

Source: *Census of England and Wales 1861*

Louisa Strutton was 18-years-old and may have been a pupil monitor. Of the 38 children aged five to eleven who were not recorded as scholars, 15 of the 25 boys were employed on farms. However, according to the 1861 census, 53 'boys' were employed on farms in the village, but this figure included boys over the age of 11.

The ten children of landowners, farmers, and the estate agent were educated privately by a governess or at a private school. The Schools Inquiry Commission 1868 stated that, 'All who devote themselves to agriculture as a class are deficient in their education. The sons of farmers are generally sent to miserably managed, private schools, and farmers are very anxious to give their sons a better education than they themselves had and would be willing to pay for a good education.'

Richard Maillard Scott (1855-1946), the son of Thomas Scott, Sir Henry Edward Bunbury's land agent, was one of the first pupils of the Albert Middle Class Memorial College, Framlingham, which catered for 300 boys and charged 26s. p.a. for board and education.

The Revised Code 1862 (Lowe's Code)

The Newcastle Report (1861) stated that the majority of public elementary schools in Suffolk were associated with the Church of England, many elementary subjects were badly taught, attendance in rural schools was irregular, most boys left school by the age of 11, and there were insufficient school places.

In 1862, Robert Lowe, 1st Viscount Sherbrooke (1811-1892), Liberal Member of Parliament (MP) for Kidderminster and Vice-President of the Committee of the Privy Council on Education in Lord Palmerston's Government, introduced the Revised Code 1862, which set out national standards in education. It laid down the levels of achievement for each standard in reading, writing and arithmetic (the three Rs). Standards I to VI included pupils aged from seven to eleven. Each pupil needed to pass the end of year examination in order to progress to the next standard. By the time pupils left school at the end of Standard VI, they were expected to be able to:-

• read well enough to continue reading in adulthood;
• write and spell sufficiently to compose a letter to their own family or employer;
• know enough arithmetic to be able to keep common accounts, such as items of expenditure, quantities of goods, receipts, or wages.

Annual school grants were linked to school performance in a system known as 'payment by results'. Existing grants to schools were abolished, and government funding of schools and teachers' salaries were contingent on pupil attendance, the condition of the school, and an annual examination in the three Rs of pupils, over the age of seven. Schools could claim 4s. p.a. for each pupil whose attendance record was satisfactory and an additional 8s. p.a., for each pupil who passed the examinations in the three Rs.

Some schools also taught the outlines of geography and history but there is evidence that, as a consequence of the Revised Code 1862, the three Rs were often taught to the exclusion of other subjects. Most teaching involved learning by rote and other sterile, mechanical methods, as teachers concentrated exclusively on preparing the children for the annual visit of Her Majesty's Inspector. In some schools, children read from only one book all year round, so that by the time the inspector arrived they could read it word-perfectly. In spite of this travesty, between 1841 and 1871, according to figures produced by the Registrar-General, literacy rates rose from 67 per cent to 80 per cent of males, and from 51 per cent to 73 per cent of females, but there was no precise definition of literacy. The Revised Code 1862 stipulated that head teachers of all schools in receipt of a grant must keep a school logbook to record events in the school. These were intended to be a permanent record of the history of the school, completed each day by the head teacher, who included matters of significance in the life of the school, the receipt of any report on the school, and the reasons for any temporary closure. Unfortunately, no logbooks for Great Barton School have survived from before 1925.

There was huge opposition to Lowe's proposals from many organisations, including the National and British Societies, who sent a deputation to meet the Prime Minister, Lord Palmerston. School managers, directors and teachers, including the Revd J. Scott from Bury St Edmunds, met Robert Lowe in February 1862 to try to persuade him to withdraw the Revised Code 1862. Their criticisms included the raising of the status of secular teaching above that of religious and moral teaching, failing to include infant teaching, determining the level of a grant by the examination results of a single day, and making judgements without considering local circumstances. They also argued that teachers' certificates had been devalued so that there was no longer an incentive for teachers to train, a fact that was borne out during the next decade, when there was a decline in the number of pupil-teachers and applications to teacher training colleges.

The Revised Code 1862 was modified in 1867, so that geography and history were eligible for a grant, but its main clauses survived for 30 years, in spite of continual criticism.

To encourage the study of Anglicanism, the National Society in the Ely Diocese organised a Prize Scheme Examination and awarded certificates and Bibles each year to pupils and teachers who performed well in an annual examination, which was taken by entrants at a single location away from school. It included questions about the *Holy Bible,* the *Anglican Book of Common Prayer* and the catechism. However, there is no evidence that any candidates were entered from Great Barton during the 1860s.

Village life for the children

When he was resident in the village, and not at the Manor House at Mildenhall or his London home at 48 Eaton Square, Sir Charles Bunbury played an active role in Great Barton. In 1863, he organised subscriptions for a fund to celebrate the wedding of Prince Albert Edward of Wales and Princess Alexandra of Denmark. A total of £38 was collected, which was allocated for the provision of meat and beer to the value of 1s. 6d. to every poor person aged 14 and upwards, and a pound of meat and a pint of beer to those under the age of 14. Farm labourers in the village were given a half-day holiday, and the church bells were rung throughout the day. Sir Charles Bunbury and William Norman King (1824-1914), of Barton Place, provided bundles of wood for a large bonfire, which was set up on the playing fields at Bury St Edmunds.

In 1863, Suffolk County Flower Show was held in Barton Park. It attracted 2,500 people from Bury St Edmunds and the surrounding villages and pupils from The Lady Bunbury Schools at Mildenhall were transported in farm carts to attend the show (*BNP*, 30 Jun 1863).

Children were expected to attend church on Sundays and respect the Sabbath, but not all did so. In Great Barton, three boys were charged with wilfully damaging two statues on either side of the church porch door, and two others were charged and cautioned when they were seen playing 'pitch halfpenny' on a Sunday. In 1863, thieves made a large hole in one of the windows of Holy Innocents' Church and stole an old linen cloth and napkin, used at the sacrament. When the Vicarage was rebuilt in 1869, William Long of Great Barton was caught stealing lead, valued at 1s. 6d., from Mr Jones, the site contractor. He admitted that he had sold the lead to Mr Lock, a marine store dealer in the Buttermarket in Bury St Edmunds for 13d, but, although Mr Jones vouched for William Long's normal good behaviour, the magistrates imposed a custodial sentence of 14 days, which resulted in William Long losing his army pension of 5s.10d. a week, to which he would otherwise have been entitled for a further 18 months (*BNP*, 19 Jan. 1869).

A summer party was held each year at Barton Hall or Barton Vicarage and, in July 1869, the *Bury Free Press* reported that '136 scholars from the school mustered and had a plentiful supply of bread and butter and cakes. Afterwards they enjoyed all sorts of games including cricket, racing, jumping and kiss in the ring, with lots of prizes of books, toys and money'. This was followed by a 'good supper at nine o'clock' (*BFP*, 31 July 1869).

Concerts were often held in the schoolrooms. In November 1869, the church choir, some of the wealthier ladies and their friends from Bury St Edmunds gave a concert to a packed room (*BNP*, 16 Nov.1869), and a similar concert was held at the Vicarage a few days later, during which the vicar's daughter played the piano (*BNP*, 23 Nov. 1869).

The general election, 1868

Great Barton formed part of the constituency of West Suffolk, which returned two Members of Parliament. The Representation of the People Act 1867 (Second Reform Act) extended the vote to all adult male householders in the boroughs, and to male lodgers who paid rent of £10 a year or more for unfurnished accommodation. It made little difference in rural areas, and there was no increase in the number of electors in Great Barton, which remained at 18, although the Revd William Blake died earlier that year, so only 17 votes were actually cast. The remaining electors included Henry and Sir Charles Bunbury, William Norman King, Jacob Lofts, Frederick Paine (1817-1872), John South Phillips, Jonathan Reed Cooper, Edward James Denton, Frederick Sutton, James Manning and Robert Bishop, who were all landowners or farmers. In addition, Thomas Scott (the Barton Estate land agent), William Last and Robert Pollintine (shoemakers), Martin Marriott (the village blacksmith), Robert Firman (an agricultural labourer), and Henry James (a victualler) were eligible to vote.

Charles Lamport, the Liberal Party candidate, received 11 of the Great Barton votes, including one from Sir Charles Bunbury who gave his second vote to Lord Augustus Henry Charles Hervey, the Conservative

Party candidate, who was elected with Major Windsor Parker, also a Conservative.

In 1869 and 1871, Ladies' Petitions were sent to Parliament from Bury St Edmunds, demanding suffrage for women. Although these were signed by many people in East Anglia, there were no signatures of anyone from Great Barton or the 3,000 electorate in Bury St Edmunds.

Nationally, a Liberal Party government, led by William Ewart Gladstone (1809-1898), was elected. Most politicians agreed that it was important to have a better educated workforce and well-informed electorate, and the government was keen to ensure that there was a school place in a public elementary school for every child of school age in England and Wales.

Map 3. Significant buildings in Great Barton, 1871

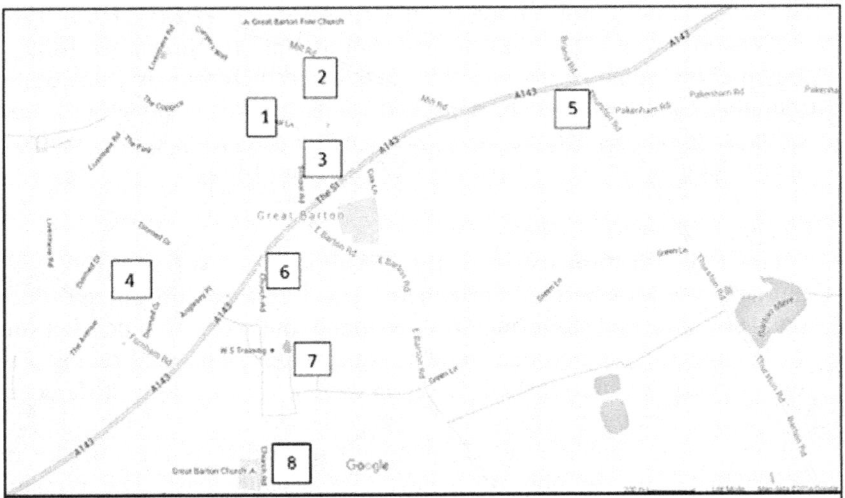

1 Great Barton Girls' School	5 Bunbury Arms Public House
2 Great Barton Boys' School	6 Barton Vicarage
3 Paine's Farm	7 Manor House
(eventual site of new school in Great Barton)	8 Holy Innocents' Church
4 Barton Hall	

5
A SCHOOL IN EVERY PARISH

In 1871, the population of Great Barton was 878, of whom 617 were 'of the class whose children may be expected to attend elementary schools', according to the government inspector, who carried out a local survey.

He concluded that there was insufficient school accommodation for all of the eligible village children in the existing schools at Great Barton. A similar problem was apparent throughout England and Wales, where there were 3,374,100 working class children aged 5 to 13 but only enough school places for 1,824,306 children.

However, the political parties and churches disagreed about which sort of education should be provided. Whilst the National Education Union, supported by members of the Conservative Party and the Church of England (C of E), wanted education to be Anglican in nature, the National Education League, supported by members of the Liberal Party and Nonconformists, believed that it should be non-sectarian and free from Anglican doctrine.

Forster's Elementary Education Act 1870

The Elementary Education Act 1870, drafted by William Forster (1818-1886), a Liberal MP, stated that every child aged 5 to 13 in England and Wales should have the opportunity to receive elementary education in a building of reasonable quality and be taught by a qualified head teacher.

The Act divided England and Wales into approximately 2,500 school districts and, where there was insufficient accommodation in a suitable school, state funding was made available to set up a school board, elected triennially by ratepayers, to oversee the provision of a non-denominational elementary school. School boards were permitted to raise funds from the rates to build and run non-denominational schools, subsidise church schools and, where appropriate, pay the fees of the poorest children.

The Municipal Franchise Act 1869 gave single female ratepayers the right to vote in local elections, serve as Poor Law Guardians and sit on school boards. These rights were extended to some married women in 1894. Dr Elizabeth Garrett Anderson (1836-1917) from Aldeburgh, Suffolk, was elected as a member of the London School Board in 1870, and was the first woman to become a magistrate and to qualify as a physician and surgeon in Britain. One of her sisters, Millicent Garrett

Fawcett (1847-1929), was the co-founder of Newnham College, Cambridge, in 1871.

There was an ongoing debate about whether education should be funded from local rates and provided free to pupils without any obligation to accept religious instruction. In recognition of the fact that, where there was only one school in a parish, parents had no choice between a board or voluntary school, the Elementary Education Act 1870 stated that any public elementary school that wished to receive a government grant was obliged to comply with a 'conscience clause'. This was introduced by William Cowper-Temple (1811-1888), MP for Hampshire South, and stated that, 'No religious catechism or religious formulary which is distinctive of any religious denomination shall be taught in the school'. A public elementary school could not refuse to accept a pupil on religious grounds. If religious instruction were given, it had to be timetabled at the beginning or end of the day. The times of these lessons had to be displayed in the schoolroom so that parents who wished to withdraw their child from religious instruction could do so. Where religion was taught, teachers were permitted to teach the content of the catechism and liturgy, but not insist that pupils learnt the actual words by heart.

School accommodation in Great Barton

In 1873, the government inspectors calculated that Great Barton required a total of 150 school places to accommodate all of the eligible village schoolchildren. They measured the existing schoolrooms and, based on eight cubic feet of space per pupil, judged that 67 boys could be accommodated at the Boys' School and 67 girls and infants at the Girls' School. They suggested that the shortfall of places could be met by making the Girls' School more efficient, by 'supplying a sufficient number of parallel desks, relocating the gallery (a raised area) in the Infants' Department, and appointing a certificated teacher'.

In 1873, Susan Kerry applied for a teaching certificate, which she hoped to obtain without an examination. In 1875, Sir Charles Bunbury's steward wrote to HMI that Lady Frances Bunbury did not desire the Girls' School to receive an annual grant and was indifferent on the subject of a certificate for Susan Kerry. Nevertheless, an HMI, who visited the school in 1875, reported very favourably on the Girls' School and awarded it a pass. He also said that Susan Kerry certainly deserved a certificate under Article 59 and that, if she could fulfil the conditions of the article and complete the relevant paperwork, she could be certificated. However, there is no evidence of whether a certificate was ever granted.

Sandon's Elementary Education Act 1876 increased government grants to voluntary schools. The *Report of the Committee of the Privy Council on Education (1879)* stated that Great Barton Boys' School, which had been receiving a government grant for at least seven years, received £34.16s. p.a. in 1879 (*BNP*, 7 Sept. 1880).

New school building during the 1870s

During this decade, 3,000 to 4,000 schools were built or taken over by school boards in England and Wales, but two and a half times as many pupils were registered in voluntary schools (which included all those set up by religious organisations) than board schools.

In 1870, the 400 schools in the 74 parishes of Suffolk could accommodate only 60 per cent of eligible pupils. Voluntary bodies were given six months to set up new schools in areas where there was a shortfall of places, and the National Society donated nearly £1,200 towards the building or extension of schools. As the result of this additional funding, 80 board schools and 130 voluntary schools were built, extended or rebuilt in Suffolk during the 1870s.

In 1870, within the Thedwastre Hundred, there were existing national schools in the parishes of Bradfield Combust, Drinkstone, Felsham, Hessett, Great Livermere, Pakenham, Rattlesden, Woolpit, Great and Little Whelnetham, and schools, run on similar principles, at Great Barton, Ampton, Fornham and Rougham. During the next decade, the National Society built or extended schools at Thurston (1870), Stanningfield (1871), Rattlesden (1872), Fornham St Martin (1873), Rougham (1874) and Bradfield St Clare (1875). A 'parochial' school was opened at Tostock in 1874 and a board schools was built at Beyton in 1875 and at Woolpit in 1879, where it replaced the national school, built in 1836. Children from the parishes of Little Livermere, Fornham St Genevieve, Gedding, Rushbrooke, Timworth, Bradfield St Clare and Bradfield St George, where there was no school, attended one in an adjacent parish.

In Bury St Edmunds, in 1874, it was estimated that 600 more school places were needed in the town. At a meeting of local ratepayers, representatives of the church spoke in favour of expanding existing church schools and finding money from voluntary subscriptions, rather than raising rates to build new ones. The *Report of the Committee of the Privy Council of Education (1879)* stated that schools in Bury St Edmunds received £500 in parliamentary grants for building work and about £800 in annual grants (*BNP*, 7 Sept. 1880).

By 1880, there was enough accommodation in schools in Bury St Edmunds and the Thedwastre Hundred for all children aged 5 to 13, most of which was provided by voluntary schools. In 2015, within the area covered by the Thedwastre Hundred, the primary schools at Great Barton, Rattlesden, Rougham, Thurston and Great Whelnetham were all C of E voluntary controlled schools and only Woolpit was a community school.

The Census of England and Wales 1871

Joseph Edwards the village wheelwright, and John Farrants, who ran Great Barton Post Office and village store, collected the census data in 1871. Joseph Edwards, together with Martin Marriott, the village blacksmith and postman, invented the Barton Tricycle, which was hand-propelled, steered with the feet, and had a trailer on the back to carry the mail. It is now on display at Moyse's Hall Museum, Bury St Edmunds, which houses a collection of local and social history memorabilia. This collection includes the death mask of William Carter, who, in 1827, was found guilty of the murder of Maria Marten, his lover, in the Red Barn Murder trial.

The population of Great Barton was 878, an increase of 30 since the previous census. The Bunbury family continued to own the schools and most of the land in Great Barton, which had 40 ratepayers and a total rateable value of £5,148. 15s. The largest area of employment was in agriculture and the village had two wheelwrights, a blacksmith, a brickmaker, a bricklayer, a thatcher, a carpenter and a shoemaker.

In 1836, a Borough Police Force was established in Bury St Edmunds and in 1845, the West Suffolk Rural Constabulary was set up under the County Police Acts of 1839 and 1840. These two forces were amalgamated under the County and Borough Police Act 1856. By 1871, Great Barton had its own resident police officer, PC William Offord, who lived on Conyers Green with his wife and baby. He was replaced, in 1874, by PC William Peake, who joined the Suffolk Constabulary in 1871 at the age of 20 and later worked in Ipswich and Beccles. He lived and worked in Great Barton for nearly 13 years, and his son, Charles, attended the village school. There was no organised fire service, but the Barton Estate owned a fire engine, which was stationed at Barton Hall.

In 1800, a Baptist Chapel was established in Bury St Edmunds on Lower Baxter Street and replaced in 1834 by a new chapel in Garland Street. In 1840, Cornelius Elven (1797-1873), the pastor of Garland Street Baptist Chapel, preached in Great Barton for the first time but encountered opposition from the landlord and customers of the Crown Beerhouse, who tried to drown out his words by banging pots and pans. When Sir Henry Bunbury heard about their unruly behaviour, he threatened to evict the tenants of the Crown, should it continue. From then on, each Sunday, Pastor Elven walked the three miles, to and from Bury St Edmunds, to preach at open air meetings and in people's homes in Great Barton. During the 50 years that he was the pastor at Garland Street Chapel, his congregation in Great Barton and the rest of his circuit increased from 40, to over 600 members.

After the death of Pastor Elven in 1873, Richard Maillard Scott, a miller and a biscuit maker, who was the son of Thomas Scott, preached in the village. Between 1875 and 1894, evening meetings were held at Barton Cottage Meeting Place, on Conyers Green.

The teachers

Susan Kerry was the headmistress of the Girls' and Infants' School and was probably assisted by an infant teacher.

The Revised New Code 1871 created an infant stage below Standard 1 for five to seven-year-olds. The infant teacher at the school may have been Jane Prike, the 14-year-old daughter of a Great Barton farm bailiff who was described in the census as an assistant teacher, or Miss Frost who was recorded as an infant schoolmistress but lived at the Rectory in Little Livermere, where there was no school.

William Plummer retired from the Boys' School in 1870 or 1871, but continued to live in the Boys' Schoolhouse.

He was replaced by 20-year-old James Handley from Holborn, London, who lived in a cottage near the blacksmith's shop. He also ran evening classes and was a member of the local cricket team (*BNP*, 27 June 1871).

He was assisted by William Stockley, a pupil-teacher, who was born in Oxfordshire and was the son of a groom-cum-gardener. He attended school at Mildenhall and worked at Great Barton School until 1874 or 1875, when he became a pupil-teacher at the Lady Bunbury Schools, Mildenhall, where he obtained a first-class Queen's Scholarship and a place at the Borough Road Training College in 1876 (*BNP*, 1 Feb. 1876). In 1881, he married a girl from Mildenhall and, in 1888, was a schoolmaster and organist at Abbots Bromley, near Uttoxeter, where he and his family lived in the Boys' Schoolhouse and he earned enough money to employ a servant. In the mid-1890s, he moved to a seven-roomed house in Mildenhall, where he was in charge of a C of E elementary school, and one of his daughters trained as a teacher.

In 1874, James Handley was replaced by John Dorling, who had been teaching since 1860 and was the head master of the school at Bardwell, a nearby village. A recent school inspection judged Bardwell School to be 'in a most satisfactory condition in every way' and praised John Dorling's management (*BNP*, 14 July 1874).

The pupils

Two of the older boys attended school on a part-time basis and worked as gardeners during the remainder of the week.

Twelve village children, aged 5 to 11, were not recorded as scholars and 16 others were educated privately.

Table 3. Number of working class children in Great Barton, recorded as scholars in the Census of England and Wales 1871

	Aged 3 to 7	*Aged 8 to 11*	*Aged 12 and over*	*Total*
Boys	25	21	4	50
Girls	30	31	15	76
Total	*55*	*52*	*19*	*126*

Source: *Census of England and Wales 1871*

In 1875, three schoolchildren from Great Barton, Henry, Harriet (Hetty) and Alice Langham, were sent to Thingoe Union Workhouse. William [35], their father, died in 1870, James [45], their grandfather who was an unemployed shepherd, committed suicide in 1871 (*BNP*, 15 Aug. 1871), and their mother, Catherine, and brother, Arthur, died in 1875 leaving no one to look after them.

The Bunbury family tried to make the lives of the workhouse inmates more pleasant. At Christmas 1877, Lady Frances Bunbury took gifts of tea, sugar and tobacco for the adults, and toys and books for the children in the workhouse (*BFP*, 12 Dec. 1877). In July 1877, 1878 and 1879, she arranged for the workhouse children to be brought to Barton Hall to play games and have a meal (*BFP*, 21 July 1877; *BFP*, 10 Aug. 1878; *BFP*, 1 Aug. 1879).

Unlike Jane Long and her sisters, the Langham children found employment when they left the workhouse. Harriet went to work in Staines in Middlesex as a domestic cook for a 67-year-old lady. Alice became a servant for the family of Henry Bown, a photographer who lived in Camberwell, and then married Henry Winslade, a licensed waterman, from Chiswick in 1899. Her sister was a witness at the wedding. Henry returned to Great Barton to live with Amos Olley, his uncle, and worked as an agricultural labourer, but later moved to Islington, where he worked as a 'railway car man' and lodged with the family of William Taylor, a railway porter.

In November 1871, 15-year-old Walter Foulger(1856-?), an ex-pupil, who was a butcher's apprentice, appeared at Thingoe Petty Session, charged with wilfully breaking a pane of glass at the Boys' School during a class at the village night school, taught by James Handley. On one of the evenings when he had attended the night school, he took a bottle containing powder and, before he entered the building, he lit some touch-paper inside the bottle and placed it outside one of the school windows. Ten minutes later, the bottle exploded loudly, breaking a pane of glass, some of which fell on to the desk of a boy in the class. Walter Foulger was fined 2s. 6d. and ordered to pay 6d. damages and costs of 11s. 6d. (*BFP*, 25 Nov. 1871). In 1878, Walter married Annie Marlton, from Great Livermere, and moved to Bradford, Yorkshire, where he worked as a master butcher. He died at the age of 31, leaving four children, the youngest of whom was born after his death.

Village events for the schoolchildren

Great Barton schoolchildren were treated to a party at the Vicarage at Christmas and in the summer each year. In 1871, the summer party included a short church service, a meal, races in the meadow and a prize-giving, at the end of which each pupil took home a piece of cake, a book and articles of clothing (*BNP*, 25 July 1871).

James Handley took part in winter concerts at the Boys' School. In 1873, he sang the 'Cork Leg' and 'John Littlejohn' and read 'Caudle made a Mason' (*BNP*, 4 Feb. 1873) and, later in the year, he sang 'It is better to laugh than cry' and 'Music has charms' (*BNP*, 2 Dec. 1873).

At Christmas 1875, a musical entertainment included a mix of serious and comic songs, performed by villagers and the staff and pupils of the school. John Dorling sang 'Heart of Oak' as a solo, 'The Wreath' in a trio with Miss and Mr Frost, and 'Winds Gently Whisper', in a trio with the vicar and Miss Frost (*BFP*, 15 Jan. 1876).

At this time, the temperance movement, which urged personal moderation in the consumption of alcohol, was gathering strength. James Handley took part in 'penny readings', which were intended to discourage people from frequenting public houses by introducing them to another form of entertainment at an alternative venue. An admission fee of 1d. was charged for an evening of entertainment, during which the audience could listen to readings of poems or prose, hear musical presentations and sing hymns.

In 1874, the Girls' School hosted a meeting of the Band of Hope, a temperance organisation for working-class children, founded in Leeds in 1847 by the Revd Jabez Tunnicliff. At this meeting, the Revd Hammond, from Liverpool, spoke about 'How to get on in the World' (*BNP*, 7 Nov. 1874).

In 1874 and 1877, the fifth and eighth annual fêtes of the United Temperance Societies of Bury St Edmunds were held at the Barton Estate, where one of the main attractions was the arboretum, with its unique collection of trees and plants from all over the world. The 1874 fête was attended by 4,000 to 5,000 people and the entrance fee for children under the age of 12 was 3d. On the morning of the fête, the Templars met at the Friends Meeting House, and then marched through Bury St Edmunds behind the West Suffolk Militia, the Victoria Fife Pipe and Drum Band and the Mildenhall Temperance Band. After the procession, they travelled to Barton Hall, where the afternoon's entertainment included a flower show, a cricket match between Norfolk and Suffolk teetotallers, a football match, and rural sports, which included a shot-put event. Sadly, the hot air balloon trip had to be cancelled, because one had recently caused a fire. A concert by the juvenile Templars was followed by a huge picnic (*BNP*, 28 July 1874).

The 1877 fête included most of the same events, but the music was provided by the band of the 13th Suffolk Rifle Volunteers. The rural sports included long and high jump, a 100-yard race, a quarter mile race, a sack race, a bell-in-the-ring competition, a consolation race, a one-mile race, and a bicycle race round the park (*BNP*, 7 Aug. 1877). The report in the paper does not mention whether the bicycles were velocipedes, invented in 1863 by French blacksmith, Ernest Michaux, or penny-farthings, invented in 1871 by British engineer, James Starley.

Church Teachers' Association (CTA) in the Archdeaconry of Sudbury

In November 1871, the CTA was set up to discuss issues of concern to teachers and school managers. The Bishop of Ely was the president, and membership was open to all clergymen, school managers, teachers in day and Sunday schools, and other persons known to be interested in schoolwork, provided they were members of the Church of England. Clergy and managers paid a subscription of 5s. p.a., schoolmasters and schoolmistresses 2s.6d. p.a., and Sunday school teachers 1s. In June each year, an Annual General Meeting was held in Bury St Edmunds, which began with a church service and finished with a meal (*BNP*, 21 Nov. 1871). Additional meetings were held at other times of the year at other venues, including Great Barton School.

John Dorling attended the first and subsequent meetings, served on the committee in 1873 and 1874, and often contributed to discussions. CTA meetings were also attended by James Handley, George Stockley and the Revd Henry Percy Smith, M.A., the Vicar of Great Barton between 1868 and 1882. They may have been accompanied by Susan Kerry but, whilst the newspaper reports mention the men by name, most refer to the presence of 'several lady teachers' without publishing their names.

The association, which had about 100 members, was affiliated to the General Association of Church Managers and Teachers and the local branch of the Church School Teachers' Benevolent Institution, and was a supporter of the Royal Society for the Prevention of Cruelty to Animals (RSPCA), founded, in 1824, by William Wilberforce (1759-1833).

In 1872, Henry Bourne addressed a meeting of the CTA, during which he claimed that the average weekly salary of a teacher, which included day and evening teaching and the salary of any family members, was £1. 14s. 7d., which was below that of an intelligent mechanic (*BFP*, 8 June 1872).

The National Union of Elementary Teachers (NUET) was set up in 1870 to unite elementary teachers of all creeds and beliefs. In 1876, some teachers proposed that the CTA should affiliate to the NUET in order that their combined strength would have a greater influence on the Education Department and school boards. However, many of the clergymen in the CTA opposed the idea of supporting non-Anglicans and affiliation was rejected (*BNP*, 30 May 1876).

In addition to its role as a debating forum, the CTA organised summer outings for its members. On 4 July 1874, John Dorling, together with 27 other members and seven children, went to Harwich for the day. They caught a train to Ipswich, and then a boat to Harwich, where they were welcomed at the national school. They walked along the beach and ate lunch before they visited Rogers' famous '*Camera Obscura*', where they were able to see how a photograph might appear, even though it was not actually printed. They then went on a short trip in an open boat, had a dip in the sea, and drank tea at the school, before they caught a boat back to Ipswich and the train home (*BNP*, 28 July 1874).

Most summer trips were to Harwich or Felixstowe, and the 1878 trip to Felixstowe was able to take advantage of Great Eastern Railway's offer of reduced fares.

Amongst the many educational issues discussed at meetings of the CTA were the school curriculum, religious education, school inspections, pupil attendance and school discipline.

The school curriculum

The curriculum, determined by the Education Code 1875, prevailed until the 1890s and consisted of:

- elementary subjects (compulsory) - Reading, wRiting and aRithmetic (the three Rs) for all pupils, and needlework for girls;
- class subjects (optional) - up to two subjects for the whole school above Standard I - grammar, geography, history and plain needlework;
- specific subjects (optional) - for individual scholars in Standards IV to VI, which included grammar, geography, history, plain needlework, foreign languages, branches of pure and applied science (including mechanics, botany and animal physiology), mathematics (including algebra, Euclid and mensuration) and domestic economy.

The Education Code 1876 added English literature to the curriculum.

Class subjects were judged on examination results from the whole class, not on the results of individuals. For each class subject, a grant of 4s per child (calculated on average attendance) was given if the proficiency of the class as a whole reached the required standard. Many teachers continued to concentrate on teaching the elementary subjects, to the exclusion of the other subjects because these attracted the highest grant and, where class subjects were taught, geography was more likely to be chosen instead of history. The teaching of history and geography was often limited to learning lists of dates and names of places by heart, although some educationalists urged teachers to undertake local studies of their parish church and other interesting buildings (*BNP*, 19 June 1877).

In response to the Elementary Education Act 1870, more books were written for use in schools. In their 1875 catalogue, William Collins, Sons and Co Ltd, who specialised in publishing educational and religious books, listed more than 1,000 books. To enable teachers to extend and update their knowledge, various organisations, including the CTA, ran a circulating lending library of educational books.

Mixed age classes presented a difficult teaching challenge. In *Devon Village Schools in the Nineteenth Century*, Roger Sellman described an arithmetic lesson taught by Albert Coles, Master of Puddington School, who taught pupils from five different standards during a single lesson.

'In arithmetic, he had to dictate a sum to Standards I and II, while at the same time writing problems on the board for Standard III and IV, and, in the interval between these operations, give a lesson on compound practice to Standard V and explain the relation between decimal and vulgar fractions to Standard VI, taking care to move among Standards I and II for the purpose of seeing that the sums are correctly taken down and the figures well shaped.'

The Metric Weights and Measures Act 1864 permitted the use of metric measures in trade, and all schools were expected to teach the metric system as part of the government's preparations for the planned conversion of imperial to metric units. However, when metrication was discussed at a CTA meeting, attended by James Handley and John Dorling in 1873, the newspaper report suggested that the metric system was beyond the comprehension of some of the schoolteachers, let alone their pupils (*BNP*, 14 Oct. 1873).

Whether boys should be taught needlework was a controversial subject, and many parents and teachers opposed the idea (*BNP*, 6 Nov. 1877). The Education Code 1877 included a needlework schedule, which John Dorling and other teachers believed was detrimental to the rest of the curriculum and difficult to deliver without the appointment of extra teaching staff. Unless a master was competent to teach it himself, or had a wife who could assist, he had to employ a sewing mistress and pay her from his own salary. The requirement for needlework to be compulsory for boys was amended in the Education Code 1882.

From the 1850s, some teaching took the form of an object lesson, which was inspired by the ideas of Heinrich Pestalozzi (1746–1827). He believed that children learned through their senses and should be led by the teacher from the known to the unknown and from the concrete to the abstract. In order to obtain a teaching certificate, every teacher was required to give two object lessons: one on a subject of his own choice and one selected by the inspector. However, the quality of the lesson relied on the availability of relevant objects, such as a barometer, Davy lamp, telescope, animal tooth or piece of chalk, as well as the knowledge and teaching skills of the teacher.

At Great Barton School, children were taught to respect animals. John Dorling told a CTA meeting that, 'as a practical result of such teaching, there were, at that moment, six or seven nests of young birds in his school grounds' (*BNP*, 2 June 1874).

Meetings of the CTA discussed difficult relations with school managers, but the Revd Henry (Harry) Smith, a manager at Great Barton School, assured teachers that, 'as Christians, the work they were doing was really exceedingly good', which suggests that the teaching at Great Barton School met with his approval (*BNP*, 23 June 1874).

Religious instruction (RI)

The RI curriculum at Great Barton School included the teaching of the Catechism, the Apostles' Creed, the Ten Commandments, the Lord's Prayer, and the sacraments. In October 1873, the National Society re-launched the Prize Scheme Examinations for pupils and teachers, and Bardwell School, where John Dorling was the head teacher, was judged to be well ahead of other schools in this examination. Entrants no longer had to travel to a single location to sit the examination, as they had under the old scheme, but were able to take it at their own school, as long as it was supervised by two independent people and the papers were sent away to be marked centrally (*BNP*, 14 Oct. 1873). A league table of the results was published in the local newspaper each year. In 1876, John Dorling passed the examination and received a certificate of honour from the Bishop of Ely (*BNP*, 28 Nov. 1876). No pupils from Great Barton School were awarded a prize, but the results from the other schools indicate that girls out-performed boys and won more awards.

In 1879, members observed a 'model lesson', when Mr Fleet, of the Church Sunday School Institute, delivered a scripture lesson to pupils at St. James's Girls' School in Risbygate Street, Bury St Edmunds (*BNP*, 29 July 1879).

School inspections

Schools in receipt of an annual government grant were subject to inspection by Her Majesty's Inspectors (HMI), who would observe the day-to-day routine in the schoolroom and playground, scrutinise the timetables and schemes of work and listen to the instruction given by the class teachers. They often set ad hoc exercises to help them to assess pupils' abilities. Members of the CTA unanimously opposed the publication of reports by inspectors, unless the circumstances of each school were included. They also expressed the view that, in the past, the inspector was welcomed as a friend who was keen to find out what the pupils knew, and was a helpful guide or colleague in the educational process, but was now feared by teachers and pupils alike and was seen as an adversary (*BNP*, 24 July 1877).

At a CTA meeting in 1874, John Dorling claimed that the proportion of the children at Great Barton School who failed to pass the standards in which they were presented for examination was only four per cent (*BNP*, 15 Dec. 1874).

Government inspectors were not required to inspect religious instruction in school or examine pupils in this subject. However, church schools were permitted to apply for an inspection by the diocese and 90 schools in the Ely Diocese chose to do so in 1873. Nevertheless, there was an ongoing debate about the future of these inspections and about who should contribute to the Diocesan Inspector's annual stipend of £400.

Pupil attendance

School attendance was not made compulsory by law until 1876.

Truancy and irregular attendance was a perpetual problem, which members of the CTA attributed to parental apathy, difficulty in the payment of school fees, and a lack of suitable clothing or boots. John Dorling also blamed farmers who encouraged boys to leave school as early as possible, in order to employ them.

The 1871 census return for Great Barton recorded that up to 27 'boys' were employed on the farms, which included two 10-year-olds and three 11-year-olds.

The government passed the Agricultural Children's Act 1873, which came into force on 1 January 1875 and stated that no child under the age of eight could be employed, children aged 8 to 10 could only be employed if they had attended school for 250 days that year, and children aged 10 to 12 were required to have a minimum of 150 days' schooling in any single year (*BNP*, 2 June 1874). Some exceptions were permitted during harvest time, when even the younger children might be expected to help with gleaning after the main harvest. In order to leave school before the age of 12, children had to pass Standard IV in the three Rs in the annual examination and obtain a Labour Certificate.

The Agricultural Children's Act 1873 stated that no child under the age of 10 could be employed under the terms of the Agricultural Gangs Act 1867, which regulated the employment of women and children in agricultural gangs and the licensing of gang-masters.

Teachers were concerned about how to deal with short-timers, who were legally able to attend school for three days a week, or in blocks of a few weeks, as long as they attended their allotted number of school days during the year.

The legislation resulted in additional costs for the school and an increase in paperwork for teachers, who were required to keep individual admission books and registers, and produce and award a Certificate of Regular Attendance, and Certificates of Honour for pupils who passed Standard IV before the age of 11 (*BNP*, 6 Nov.1877).

An employer could be fined up to £5 for employing a boy without a Certificate of Regular Attendance; a parent could be fined £1 for allowing their child to be employed; and a teacher could be fined £1 if he or she failed to issue the required certificate. In 1873, a brickmaker in Cavendish was summoned by the sub-inspector of factories and charged with employing a boy, under the age of 13, for more than six and half hours a day, and for neglecting to obtain his attendance certificate. He was fined £2, with 27s. costs (*BNP*, 19 Aug. 1873). During a parliamentary discussion, Clare S. Read, a tenant farmer, stated that he believed that the better educated the children of labourers became, the more useful they would be.

It was suggested at a CTA meeting that truancy could be reduced by offering a prize of a small book or picture for good attendance (*BNP*, 23 June 1874).

The Elementary Education Act 1876 increased government grants to voluntary schools, on condition that they agreed to government inspection. It placed a duty on parents to ensure that their child attended school and established school attendance committees in areas where there were no school boards. Parents were made responsible for ensuring that their children received basic instruction, and the poor law guardians were permitted to contribute towards the payment of school fees for a limited time, if parents were too poor to pay them.

From January 1878, the Education Department required every school to submit a list of the name, residence, and age of every pupil over the age of five who had attended the school during the previous 12 months, with the number of attendances for that year. This list was to be countersigned by the governors, sent to the Local School Authority, and kept for at least 10 years, as were the school registers.

Teachers complained that there were so many returns, registers and certificates that their completion interfered with the proper work of the teacher (*BNP*, 6 Nov. 1877).

In 1879, George Lofts, a farm labourer, was charged with not sending his daughter, Elizabeth, to Great Barton School. In court, his wife, Hannah, claimed that she could not persuade her to go to school. She was almost

13-years-old and did not like to mix with small girls, as she was a 'great girl for her age'. She was subject to fits and was not as bright as the others [so one can assume that she was in a lower standard than the rest of her peer group]. Although The Revd Harry Smith said that she would be allowed to stand with the other tall girls, Elizabeth told the bench that she still refused to attend school. Her father was fined 6s., plus costs of 4s. 6d., and given a fortnight to pay (*BFP*, 17 May 1879). In 1881, Elizabeth was unemployed and living at home, but, ten years later, was employed as a tailor's apprentice to George Sanders and living at Church Gate Street, Bury St Edmunds. She later moved with the Sanders family to a four-roomed house at Well Street, Bury St Edmunds, where she worked as a general domestic servant and, after the death of Mrs Saunders, remained as the housekeeper.

Occasionally, pupils were absent from school due to illness. Some childhood diseases could be fatal. In January 1877, Harry Morris, a pupil at Great Barton School, died from tuberculosis at the age of 11. At his inquest, it was said that 'there were signs of water on the brain with no bruising, but enlarged veins, and brain cavities were full of fluid with signs of tubercular lesions' (*BNP*, 9 Jan. 1877).

On the other hand, some villagers lived to a good age and during a 10-week period in 1874 five villagers died; their combined ages being 417 (*BFP*, 24 Oct. 1874).

The Bank Holiday Act 1871 established bank holidays in England and Wales on Good Friday, Easter Monday, Whit Monday, the first Monday in August, Christmas Day and Boxing Day, most of which fell within the existing school holidays.

School discipline

Teachers were expected to record details of misdemeanours and punishments in a punishment book. Corporal punishment could only be administered by schoolmasters and schoolmistresses, not by pupil-teachers. Alternative punishments included various forms of public humiliation, such as standing on a stool at the back of the class, wearing an armband with DUNCE written on it, or wearing a tall, cone-shaped hat decorated with a large "D".

In May 1872, Great Barton School hosted a meeting, at which the topic of 'Rewards and Punishments' was discussed. The chairman, the Revd Purkiss, stated that he wanted to hear the views of mistresses as well as of masters and his comment that 'he felt that mistresses would not want to be reported as being in favour of corporal punishment' was greeted with howls of laughter (*BFP*, 18 May 1872).

Meetings of the CTA discussed troublesome boys, whose parents were unable to control them at home, and confrontational mothers who interrupted lessons to complain about the way that their child had been disciplined at school (*BNP*, 23 June 1874).

In May 1873, a paper was presented to the CTA on 'The Social Position of a Schoolmaster'. It suggested that teachers were isolated socially, since they were 'intellectually superior to the poor, not accepted by the middle classes, and looked down upon by the upper classes'. Some members believed that teachers who visited the homes of pupils could risk their authority and be treated with contempt, but this was challenged by James Handley, who stated that 'he often visited the homes of pupils, but did not find that the children disobeyed him any the more' (*BNP*, 6 May 1873).

In 1880, the head teacher at Clare Board School in West Suffolk was accused by a parent of assaulting his son, when he thrashed him so severely that he broke his stick. The teacher claimed that he gave his back three or four strokes of the stick, but only after he had been forced to caution the boy several times because of his bad conduct, The magistrate dismissed the case and warned the teacher to be more careful in future (*BNP*, 28 Dec. 1880).

Recurring issues

By 1880, the problem of sufficient and suitable school accommodation in every parish in England and Wales had largely been settled, but many of the issues about the school curriculum, the place of religion in schools, school inspections, irregular pupil attendance and how to manage pupils' behaviour were still unresolved.

6
TEACHERS UNITE

During the 1870s, the number of pupils in the United Kingdom doubled to nearly 4 million, but there was sufficient school accommodation for all children aged 5 to 13 to receive elementary education in a building of reasonable quality. During this decade, thousands of new teachers were employed and the number of certificated teachers rose from 12,467 to 31,422, of pupil-teachers from 14,612 to 32,128, and of uncertificated teachers from 1,262 to 7,652.

Although teaching offered an attractive alternative to employment in service, on a farm or in a factory, it was not an easy option. This decade saw the growth of existing 'associations' of teachers, such as the National Union of Elementary Teachers (NUET) set up in 1870, and the Church Teachers' Association (CTA) set up in 1871 for teachers, clergymen and managers in Anglican schools. New organisations were also set up, such as Sudbury Voluntary School Association in 1884.

The Census of England and Wales 1881

In 1881, John Dorling and Joseph Edwards collected the census data for Great Barton. The population of the village had fallen to 819 as young people had joined the nationwide exodus from the countryside to towns and cities in search of better opportunities.

Two-thirds of the heads of households in the village were engaged in agriculture, and the number of employees on the farms was approximately the same as ten years earlier, with 92 men and 25 'boys' employed on the six largest farms.

Of the 70 women in employment, 54 worked as servants. The 17 female heads of households in the parish were employed as dairywomen, charwomen, laundresses, shopkeepers or dressmakers.

The teachers

Susan Kerry was still the headmistress of the Girls' School. In 1886, the local paper reported that 'the girls of Barton School presented the mistress, Miss Kerry, with a handsome lamp and teapot, a token of respect for her kindness to them, having filled her situation for 40 years' (*BFP*, 25 Dec.1886).

She was assisted by her 23-year-old niece, Kate Kerry, who lived with her in the Girls' Schoolhouse.

Susan and Kate Kerry also taught at Great Barton (Holy Innocents') Sunday School and attended a meeting to set up a Diocesan Sunday School Society in 1883. Concerns were raised at this meeting about the poor standard of teaching in Sunday schools and a lack of teachers, especially male ones.

At a meeting of the CTA, a local clergyman suggested that, 'if day school teachers gave up their Sundays to teach in Sunday schools, they would gain relief by being able to do voluntary work for God and would be more loved by their pupils' (*BNP*, 10 July 1883).

In 1888, the local paper reported that Susan Kerry 'helped with tea and games at the Vicarage' (*BFP*, 28 July 1888).

John Dorling, the headmaster of the Boys' School, was assisted by 12-year-old Frank Last, a pupil-teacher. Frank did not pursue a career in teaching but moved to London and worked as a groom and later as a horse-keeper.

In 1886, John Dorling was replaced by James Daine. He took an active role in village life, participated in fund-raising concerts in the Boys' School and acted as secretary of Great Barton Quoits Club, founded in 1901 by the Revd Hervey.

He played cricket for the village and, in 1889, played in a team of Barton Hall servants in a match against Stowlangtoft Hall servants (*BNP*, 20 Aug. 1889).

The pupils

The Census of England and Wales 1881 recorded 94 girls and 53 boys as scholars. According to *Kelly's Directory* for Suffolk 1883, the average school attendance was 65 girls and 50 boys, but *Kelly's Directory* for Suffolk 1888 indicated a slight rise in the average attendance for girls and infants to 72 but a fall in the average attendance for boys to 44. At this time, there was adequate school accommodation for every eligible schoolchild in the parish within the suggested ratio of 8 cubic feet per pupil.

Table 4. Number of working class children in Great Barton, recorded as scholars in the Census of England and Wales 1881

	Aged 3 to 7	Aged 8 to 11	Aged 12 and over	Total
Boys	22	26	5	53
Girls	23	44	27	94
Total	*45*	*70*	*32*	*147*

Source: *Census of England and Wales 1881*

In the 1881 census, 18 children aged five to ten were not recorded as scholars. Mundella's Elementary Education Act 1880 tightened up the Elementary Education Act 1876. It obliged local authorities to pass byelaws making school attendance compulsory for five to ten-year-olds and available for children up to the age of 13. Any child under the age of 13 was required to have a certificate to show they had attained the required educational standard, and employers of children who were not able to produce a Labour Certificate were penalised. The Education Code 1882 added Standard VII for the older scholars, but some teachers found the challenge of teaching the higher standards too great and believed that it caused undue pressure to both teachers and children (*BNP*, 29 Nov. 1884).

There was a high level of pupil absenteeism and truancy in West Suffolk, although John Dorling told a meeting of the CTA that attendance at his school had increased during the past few years and children attended regularly (*BNP*, 10 July 1883). School attendance officers could impose a fine on parents whose children did not attend school, but in 1885, John Dorling challenged the effectiveness of the law and told a meeting of the CTA that no attendance officers had visited Great Barton School for over six months (*BNP*, 20 Jan. 1885). In 1886, further legislation made it illegal to employ a person under 18 for more than 75 hours per week.

In 1890, Mr Loverock, the school attendance officer for Thingoe District, accused Samuel Phillips of being 14s. 6d. behind with school fees and failing to send two of his children to Great Barton School. This included 11-year-old Agnes, who was still in Standard I with the seven-year-olds and had not attended school for over six months. Since her father and oldest brother were, according to the magistrate, earning good wages, Samuel Phillips was fined 5s. with costs and threatened with a distress warrant if it were not paid within two weeks (*BNP*, 14 Jan. 1890). Agnes and her 11-year-old brother, George, returned to school and were both recorded as scholars in the Census of England and Wales 1891. In 1897, Agnes married Amos Simper, a farm labourer, who was 14 years older than she was, but in 1911, Agnes was living in Bury St Edmunds Union Workhouse (formerly Thingoe Union Workhouse) and her son was fostered out to a grocer's family in the nearby village of Barrow, Suffolk. At this time, it was not unusual for the workhouse guardians to take a child away from its mother if she were in prison, of low moral standing or deemed unfit to take care of her child.

In 1890, one of the school pupils, William Lofts [291], died in Thingoe Workhouse. In 1882, his father Charles [288], who was a woodman, suffered a very severe compound fracture of his right leg, whilst working (*BNP,* 31 Jan. 1882). William's mother, Ellen, died in 1887 and his father, who was then working as a shoemaker, remarried just over a year later. Ten days after the marriage, William's sister found their father in a swill tub house, where he had shot himself. At the inquest, the jury were so sympathetic that they donated their expenses towards the cost of his funeral, and the church allowed Charles Lofts to be buried in the village churchyard (*BNP*, 19 Nov. 1889). William and three of his siblings were sent to Thingoe Workhouse, where nine-year-old William died from tuberculosis in February 1890. His brothers and sisters were sent out to work as soon as they were old enough - Ernest as a farm labourer, Jesse as a coach painter of railway carriages, and John as a grocer's assistant.

Four years earlier, another pupil at the school died in a tragic accident. The nearest doctor to Great Barton was located in Bury St Edmunds, but there was a Doctor's Club in Great Barton, to which members paid a weekly contribution of 2d. or 3d. per family. The Bunbury family paid the salary of a doctor and a nurse, who were available to visit the sick in the village and permitted to order soup and other things from Barton Hall for their patients. This may have explained why the mother of Kate Bishop [245] went to the Hall one Saturday morning to fetch some broth for her children. She left seven-year-old Kate and 11-year-old Alfred at home at Conyers Green with a fire burning in the fireplace, protected by a fireguard. However, whilst her mother was out, Kate reached over the fireguard to wind the clock on the mantelpiece and her apron caught fire. She ran next door, where the neighbour doused the flames with water but by then, Kate's thighs and the lower part of her body were so badly burnt that she died the next day in great pain. At her inquest, a verdict of accidental death was delivered (*BNP*, 12 Jan. 1886).

The class of 1881

Although most of the male school leavers from the class of 1881 worked as agricultural labourers or gardeners as soon as they left school, three-quarters left the village before the age of 30, and 16 of them moved to the London area.

Table 5. Careers of the 1851 and 1881 scholars of Great Barton School

Pupils at Great Barton School	1851	1851	1881	1881
Residence in 1881 or 1911	in 1881 Male	in 1881 Female	in 1911 Male	in 1911 Female
Limited or no information	10	23	3	7
Died before age of 30	4	3	5	10
Emigrated	1	1	0	2
Great Barton	7	7	9	13
Another rural area in East Anglia (Suffolk, Norfolk, Cambridgeshire, North Essex)	3	11	8	13
A town in East Anglia (Bury St Edmunds, Ipswich, Newmarket, Haverhill, Peterborough, Thetford, Lowestoft, Beccles, Braintree)	4	7	6	15
London or south east (south Essex, Kent, Surrey, Sussex, Hampshire, Dorset)	3	6	16	26
South West England	0	0	0	1
Midlands or northern England	3	2	5	8
Total	**35**	**60**	**52**	**95**

Source: derived from Census returns of England and Wales 1851, 1881, 1911

Some were employed as carpenters, joiners, blacksmiths, farriers, cobblers. Others worked as bakers, butchers, shop assistants, carters, coachmen, chauffeurs, gardeners, waiters, servants or warehouseman. Several worked for the police service or a railway company, but only three worked in industry.

Arthur Phillips moved to Burntwood, Staffordshire, married Sarah Ann Hollyhurst, who came from a coal-mining family, and worked as a hewer in a coal mine. Thomas Calthorpe was employed as a maltster in a brewery in Burton on Trent, Staffordshire, and Frederick Nunn as a labourer at the brewery in Bury St Edmunds.

Farming was not without hazards and in 1895, 23-year-old Robert Newman, who was a shepherd, was struck and killed by lightning at Littleport, Cambridgeshire (*BFP*, 31 Aug. 1895).

Some of the young women stayed at home after they left school, but by 1901, at least 50 were employed as domestic, living-in servants, at a time when over 30 per cent of all adult working women were employed as domestic servants.

Widows often needed to work and find a job that they could combine with childcare. Maria Fisher, the daughter of a hawker was widowed in 1900 after the death of her husband, Alma Smith, who was in the Royal Engineers based at Aldershot. She and her children moved to Bury St Edmunds, where she ran a convenience store from her five-roomed home at 46 Eastgate Street.

Some married women also found paid employment. Sarah Holmes, the wife of a wheelwright, was a 'monthly' nurse, who looked after mothers for the first few weeks after the birth of their baby. Ellen Nunn, who was married to a house painter, became a housekeeper in a ten-roomed house in Warwick Road, Kensington, London, which was owned by a teacher and her brother and took in teachers as boarders.

Some girls helped their husbands to run a business. Harriet Hazelwood worked in the bakery at St Andrews Street South, Bury St Edmunds; Ada Jane Bentley in the bakery in Out Westgate Street, Bury St Edmunds; Annie Firman helped to run the family's stationery business; Lucy Trudgett was the landlady of the Angel Inn, Stanton, Suffolk; Margaret Foulger was the landlady of Ye Olde Cock Inn, Sevenoaks, Kent.

Sometimes family members moved out of the village at different times, but to the same location. Five of the Newman family moved from Great Barton to Leytonstone, Essex. Mary, who worked as an under housemaid for William Norman King at East Farm, Great Barton, married William Miller, a coachman, in 1892, and they moved to Lambeth, south London, and then to Leytonstone. Nine years later, her sister, Susan, married John Mingay, a labourer on the Great Eastern Railway, and they moved to Leytonstone with her mother and sister, Charlotte, who was a dressmaker. Charlotte married William Pye, a carpenter, and they moved in next door. After Susan died, in 1909, her sister, Ann [122], who worked as a housemaid at Wanstead, north-east London, moved in with John Mingay and looked after Susan's nine-year-old daughter, Edith.

Middle class pupils from Great Barton

Alexander Robert South Phillips (1857-?), the son of a Great Barton landowner, worked as an assistant teacher at Framlingham College and then became a clergyman.

Francis Samuel Farrants, the only son of Hannah and John Farrants, who ran Great Barton Post Office, village shop and bakery, was privately educated for at least nine years and became a pharmacist. In 1899, he married Dora Saxton, originally from Mildenhall, who lived in Tottenham Court Road, London, in a building with 37 other young, single women, most of whom, including Dora, worked as drapery assistants. After their marriage, Francis and Dora moved to Orpington, Kent, where Francis worked as a 'druggist and chemist at home'. Before the founding of the Pharmaceutical Society in 1841, anyone could work as a pharmacist, but the Pharmacy Act 1852 introduced the first statutory register and, after the Pharmacy Act 1868, all pharmacists had to register with the Pharmaceutical Society and pass one of the society's exams to become a chemist, druggist or pharmaceutical chemist. By 1911, Francis was a qualified pharmacist and, together with Dora, ran a successful chemist shop on The Parade, in Orpington High Street, where they lived above the premises in six rooms, with their only child, Frances Dora. When Francis died in Bromley in 1921, he left £5,489. 4s. 2d. to his wife.

Some middle class girls were educated by governesses, most of whom were untrained and unqualified. Governess training for girls over the age of 12 years was available at the Governesses' Benevolent Institution, in Queen's College, London, but the number of places was limited. In 1887, Charlotte Maria Shaw Mason (1842-1923) formed the Parents' National Education Union and opened the House of Education at Ambleside, Lake District, in 1892 as a training institution for governesses. In 1871, the National Union for Improving the Education of Women was set up and within 30 years, middle class girls were able to attend one of the 30 fee-paying boarding schools for women.

Better educated girls, like the daughters of Hannah and John Farrants, had a much greater opportunity of obtaining higher-paid employment and leading an independent life.

Fannie Farrant, their oldest daughter, was educated at a boarding school for young ladies at Northbury House, Northgate Street, Bury St Edmunds. She married Walter Firman, a hosiery agent, and moved to Urmston, Lancashire. After John Farrants died in 1882, his widow, Hannah, became the village sub-post mistress and ran the general store with the help of her daughters, Josephine and Hannah Jnr, until she retired during the late 1890s. She sold the business to William Copsey and moved to Urmston with her daughters to live with Fannie and Walter. Neither Hannah Jnr, nor Josephine, married. Josephine Farrant became a post office telegraphist, and Hannah Farrant, an artist and a textile designer. Josephine died in Norwich in 1939, leaving nearly £500 to her sister, Hannah, who lived for another 23 years.

Education and the political agenda

The Representation of the People Act 1884 (Third Reform Act) extended the franchise to men who paid an annual rent of £10 or more, or held land valued at £10. This enfranchised 60 per cent of male householders over the age of 21 and included some farm labourers. However, it would not have enfranchised the head masters of Great Barton School, because they paid less than £10 p.a. in rent.

The Redistribution of Seats Act 1885 reduced the number of Members of Parliament (MPs) for Bury St Edmunds from two to one. Great Barton became part of the newly created constituency of Stowmarket, which existed until 1918, during which time it swung back and forth between Liberal and Conservative Party MPs.

In 1885, education was high on the election agenda, especially as 50,686 of the 5.5 million men with the right to vote were illiterate. Liberal and Conservative candidates held different views about whether parents should pay for their child's education. At a meeting in a tent in the grounds of Barton Vicarage, Felix Thornley Cobbold (1841-1909), the Liberal candidate for Stowmarket, said:

> 'The education laws had been made by people who lived in towns, who did not know a plough from a turnip, and who forgot that the greater part of the education an agricultural labourer needed was learnt on the fields rather than between the walls of a schoolroom. Either he should like to see compulsory education abolished or to have it made free' (*BNP*, 27 Oct. 1885).

At his adoption meeting, held at the Athenaeum in Bury St Edmunds, Lord Frances Hervey (1846-1931), the Conservative candidate for Bury St Edmunds, stated that:

> 'Parents did not seem to value the education of their children unless they had to pay for it. He thought that parents felt that, in contributing a small sum towards the education of their children, they had some interest in that education, and he believed all were willing to do that. What was required was that working men should be able to earn more money, so that they could afford to pay for their child's schooling' (*BNP*, 17 Nov. 1885).

In 1885, Henry Charles Bunbury, Sir Edward Bunbury's nephew and heir to the baronetcy, presided over a Conservative Party meeting, in support of Sir Thomas Thornhill. However, Felix Cobbold was elected as MP for Stowmarket and Lord Francis Hervey for Bury St Edmunds, which had been represented by members of his family, almost continually, since 1826. Nationally, the Liberal Party, led by William Ewart Gladstone, won the highest number of seats in the House of Commons, but not an overall majority, so another general election was called in 1886.

Sir Edward Greene (1815-1891), who lived at Nether Hall, Pakenham, and whose family owned Greene's brewery in Bury St Edmunds, had been one of two Conservative Party MPs of Bury St Edmunds since 1865. In 1886, he was elected as MP for Stowmarket and Lord Francis Hervey as MP for Bury St Edmunds, which now had only one MP. Nationally, the Conservative Party won this election, and Robert Cecil (1830-1903) became Prime Minister. His government set up the Cross Commission to inquire into elementary education in England and Wales.

The Local Government Act 1888 established county councils and county borough councils in England and Wales, which became the basis of Local Education Authorities. In Suffolk, there were two separate administrative counties of East Suffolk and West Suffolk, and Ipswich became a county borough. Although women were still not eligible to vote in general elections, this act gave over half a million female ratepayers in Britain the right to vote in county and borough council elections, but not stand for election as a councillor. In January 1889, Henry Charles Bunbury was elected unopposed to represent Mildenhall on Suffolk County Council (*BFP*, 26 Jan. 1889).

The need for educational reforms

At this time teachers, especially those who taught in small voluntary or denominational schools, had many concerns about the education system. The teachers at Great Barton School joined the CTA and the NUET, which changed its name to the National Union of Teachers (NUT) in 1888.

The NUET, which was open to teachers in both board and voluntary schools, campaigned for better pay and conditions, pension rights for teachers, and reforms to extend and improve the system of state education. It aimed to raise the social and professional status of teachers and ensure that their views were represented in Parliament. By 1887, local membership of the CTA was falling, whilst that of the NUET was growing.

Teachers were particularly concerned about school inspections, especially as their salary was dependent on the results. In 1882, members of the CTA were informed about a letter, written by the Archbishop of Canterbury, which recommended the use of preliminary examinations in advance of a government inspection. The evidence showed that whereas 83.1 per cent of pupils in board schools and 80.4 per cent of pupils in voluntary schools passed the examination, 92.8 per cent of pupils passed in schools that had undergone a preliminary examination. Consequently, the average grant per head of pupils was 16s. 7½ d. in board schools, 15s. 5d in voluntary schools and 17s 5¾ d. in those schools which held a preliminary examination. John Dorling was in favour of the use of a preliminary examination and told the meeting that many schools, including his own, 'adopted the practice of submitting their school to examination by neighbouring teachers' in advance of the inspection (*BNP*, 21 Mar. 1882).

During the 1880s, teachers and others expressed their concerns about educational pressure. Dr Elizabeth Garrett Anderson, a member of the London School Board, delivered a paper to the Social Science Association in London on this subject, in which she advocated a reduction in the school curriculum and in the number of hours in a school day (*BFP*, 15 May 1880).

In 1884, the CTA branch, of which Great Barton was a member, sent out questionnaires to 24 schools, seeking the opinion of teachers about the causes of the excess pressure and possible solutions. Nineteen replies were received, including one from John Dorling, which confirmed that teachers and pupil-teachers were suffering from 'over-pressure'. The main causes cited were the excessive demands of the educational codes, the irregularity of pupil attendance, the insufficiency of staff and the salaries being too dependent on the grant. Teachers suggested that the pressure could be eased by allowing more flexibility to modify class and specific subjects, enforcing better attendance, making salaries independent of the school grant, abolishing payment by results, reducing the number of school sessions to a maximum of two per day with none on Saturdays, and setting up higher schools for Standard V and upwards (*BNP*, 20 Jan. 1885).

This excess pressure was certainly experienced by John Dorling, who was so overwhelmed by the job and his fears about the outcome of the forthcoming school inspection that, in April 1886, he 'committed suicide, whilst in a state of insanity, by cutting his throat with a razor' (*BNP*, 4 May 1886) (appendix I iii).

During the following term, the *Bury Free Press* reported that Miss James, the head mistress of the parochial school at Thurston (a neighbouring village to Great Barton) had 'been compelled to resign through ill-health, brought [about] by mental anxiety' (*BFP*, 13 Nov. 1886).

At Great Barton Boys' School, James Daine was appointed as the new headmaster and at the next school inspection in May 1888, the school performed well and the inspector recommended the highest available grant.

James and Emma Daine both attended meetings of the CTA and the NUT. Although the two organisations agreed on many subjects, and even organised joint social events, the CTA believed that the teacher in a Church of England school was the servant of God, and schools were nurseries of the Church.

This view was summed up by the Revd F. R Chapman, Archdeacon of Sudbury and Cannon of Ely Cathedral, who stated at a CTA meeting that:-

'Schoolmasters and schoolmistresses could never do any real good to their children unless they had some higher aspiration - some desire to bring about a marked good in the character of the children under their care. The schoolmaster was somewhat in the nature of a missionary; for there was the same ignorance to meet, the same planting of new ideas required. He must look for his reward in something higher than what he received from the Royal Mint' (*BNP*, 28 June 1887).

All teachers welcomed the Report of the Cross Commission on Elementary Education (1888), which included a recommendation for public funding for the secular curriculum in voluntary schools and the end of the system of payment by results.

However, the NUT wanted even more reforms and, in August 1888, the National Executive Committee of the NUT sought to address some of the concerns of teachers and submitted a petition to parliament, asking that:

- payment by results be completely abolished;
- a consultative council be set up, which would include teachers, to work with the Education Department to reform the education system;
- teachers be allowed full liberty to classify the scholars according to their attainments and abilities, and use the most intelligent methods of teaching;
- the inspection of schools be conducted by persons who possess a knowledge of the theory and practice of education and have had adequate practical experience of the work of teaching in elementary school;
- the work of the local authorities, charged with the duty of enforcing attendance at school, be made effective;
- the duty of granting certificates to teachers be vested in a council, consisting of representatives of the education department, the Universities, and the teaching profession, and that in future the annual endorsements on teachers' certificates be abolished;
- a scheme of superannuation for teachers be provided to enable managers to keep up the efficiency of the school staff by the retirement of aged and incapacitated teachers;
- additional pecuniary help be given to schools which are necessarily small, to enable them to provide an efficient staff and suitable school appliances (*BNP*, 21 Aug. 1888).

The Revd Harry Jones – priest, philanthropist and author

In 1882, the Revd Harry Percy Smith was replaced by the Revd Harry Jones (1823-1900), who described himself as a 'bigoted old liberal' (*BNP*, 6 June 1882). In 1895, he published *Dead Leaves and Living Seeds* in which he described Great Barton as having 'a notable admixture of gentry, farmers and peasants' and claimed that 'the labourers attended church well'.

The Revd Jones was educated at St John's College in Cambridge and served as a curate in Suffolk and Cambridge, before he moved to London and became Prebendary of St. Paul's Cathedral, Chaplain-in-Ordinary to the Queen, Vicar of St Luke's Berwick Street and then Rector of St George-in-the-East, Stepney. Whilst in London, he supported the creation of board schools and accepted that religious education in them should be non-denominational. He improved the area's water supply, organised the provision of school dinners in his parish and allowed children to leave the church service before the sermon, because he knew that they could become bored. In 1882, his wife Emily had a serious accident, so they left London and moved to the family home at Barton Mere, Pakenham, where Harry Jones' father was the parish vicar between 1845 and 1861, and his brother, Charles, between 1861 and 1904. Harry and his brother, Charles, inherited Barton Mere from their mother, Mary, the only daughter of Thomas Quayle of Barton Mere.

In 1883, the Revd Jones set up Great Barton Village Club and Reading Room for working and middle class men over the age of 16, under the patronage of Sir Charles Bunbury. Club membership cost 9d. a quarter or 2s. 6d. a year and members could be expelled from the room, or even the club, if they used bad language or gambled (*BNP*, 15 May 1883). The Revd Jones enjoyed playing quoits and chess and was impressed by the enthusiasm for chess shown by the villagers.

In 1883, he provided a summer treat for about 300 schoolchildren from Pakenham and Barton in the grounds of Barton Mere. After a communal meal, there was a tug of war between the two parishes using an extra-long rope, which was won by the team from Great Barton. The day ended with a firework display by the mere (*BFP*, 15 Sept. 1883).

In 1884, a party was organised for Great Barton Sunday School pupils in a large barn, lit and decorated by Jonathan Reed Cooper (1831-1902). The curate, the Revd Tanqueray, and the teachers arranged the room so that the children could watch a Punch and Judy Show, brought from London by the Revd Jones. The hand bell ringers gave a 'polished performance,' which included a rendition of their new peel (*BFP*, 12 Jan. 1884).

During the 1885 and 1886 general elections, the Revd Harry Jones spoke at Liberal Party meetings in Great Barton. He was considered by the villagers to be an able, untiring and enthusiastic worker, and when he resigned in 1886, he was presented with a silver fuse-box and an electroplated tray, wrapped in a blue pocket-handkerchief, as a leaving present. He moved back to Piccadilly, London, where, amongst other things, he wrote children's books. *Field and Street, or Boys with a difference* (SPCK 1893) was about a city lad, whose life went astray until he went to live in the country. *Prince Boohoo and Little Smuts* was described as:

'really good nonsense..... and inspired by a quite delightful insouciance.' (*The Spectator*, 5 Dec. 1896, p.9).

The Revd Jones eventually returned to Barton Mere, where he died in 1900 and left effects valued at £18,434. In 1912, he was described by Mary Steer, who ran the non-denominational Bridge of Hope Rescue Mission in Betts Street, in St George-in-the-East, as 'a broad-minded, generous man, big and strong, and of imposing appearance, and he was also a man of peace'.

In 1886, the Revd Jones was replaced by the Revd Henry Stewart Gladstone, who worked in Great Barton for eleven years until he moved to the parish of East Tuddenham, Norfolk in 1897.

Barton Hall

In 1886, Sir Charles Bunbury died and, as he had no children, his brother, Edward, a barrister-at-law, inherited the baronetcy. Edward moved into Barton Hall, which continued to be used for fêtes and other village events.

At the Annual Temperance Fête in 1886, held three months after the death of John Dorling, his widow, Charlotte, came equal-first in the knitting, netting and crochet competition (*BNP*, 3 Aug. 1886). In 1887, the village celebrated the jubilee of Queen Victoria and Great Barton Annual Show of Vegetables and Industrial Work, the first show of its kind in the village, was held in the coach houses at Barton Hall. It included contributions from 100 cottagers (*BNP*, 13 Sept. 1887).

In January 1888, Sir Edward Bunbury invited 60 men who were employed on the Barton Estate, together with their wives to a New Year's Supper at Barton Hall (*BFP*, 14 Jan. 1888).

Hopes for the future

The 1880s was a difficult time for Great Barton School, especially after the death of John Dorling. Teachers hoped that the government would respond positively to the demands of the NUT and introduce educational reforms, which would not only make the education system more efficient, but also improve the working conditions of teachers.

7

EDUCATIONAL REFORMS

Between 1880 and the 1890s, the number of certificated teachers rose from about 31,000 in 1880, to 47,000 in 1892 and 53,000 by 1895. There was an even greater increase in the number of unqualified teachers. The Census of England and Wales 1901 recorded that there were nearly a quarter of a million qualified and unqualified teachers, of whom nearly three-quarters were female.

By the 1890s, there was a pressing need to reform the education system. The Education Department, renamed the Board of Education in 1899, introduced many reforms to address some of the issues highlighted in the parliamentary petition of the National Union of Teachers (NUT) and the Report of the Cross Commission on Elementary Education (1888). However, some of the educational reforms stretched the resources of small rural schools, and Great Barton School was obliged to build an additional classroom, at its own expense, in order to comply with the new regulations.

In 1893, in order to promote the interests of small rural schools to the National Executive Committee of the NUT, the Bury St Edmunds branch of the NUT set up a branch of the Confederation of Rural Teachers (*BNP*, 6 June 1894). Membership of the NUT nationally reached 38,683 by 1898, which represented a majority of schoolmasters, but not schoolmistresses (*BNP*, 29 Nov. 1892).

The teachers

In 1891, Susan Kerry retired as headmistress of the Girls' School after 47 years, having worked alongside four different headmasters of the Boys' School. She was replaced by Emma Daine, the wife of James Daine, the current headmaster of the Boys' School. Since Emma and James were already living in the Boys' Schoolhouse, Susan Kerry was able to continue living in the Girls' Schoolhouse with her niece, Kate.

Kate Kerry taught the infants class until her marriage, in September 1894, to Godfrey Holmes, an ex-pupil of Great Barton School and the son of the village thatcher. He lived at home and worked as an agricultural labourer when he left school, and later joined the Suffolk Regiment, based at Colchester, Essex.

After their marriage in Holy Innocents' Church, Great Barton, Kate and Godfrey moved to Taplow, Buckinghamshire, where Godfrey worked as an assistant gamekeeper, and then to Ware, Hertfordshire, where he worked as a game keeper.

Kate Kerry was replaced by Frances Margaret Firman, who was born in Great Barton, but brought up at East Donyland, Essex, by her older sister, Ann, who was married to a schoolmaster and took in teachers as boarders.

She taught the infants for eight years and received a china tea service as a leaving present in July 1901. Frances married George Alfred James Nobbs, another elementary schoolteacher, on 14 August 1901, and they moved to Watford, Hertfordshire, but Frances died in 1905, at the age of 32, from 'vascular disease of the heart and tachycardia exhaustion'.

Annie Corley and Agnes Mary Trudgett, who were both 15-years-old, were pupil-teachers at the Girls' School.

In 1893, James Daine took early retirement from teaching, on grounds of ill health. He was replaced by James Killick, a qualified teacher, who worked at the school for three and a half years, assisted by Walter Foulger. In 1897, Robert Evans was appointed as the new headmaster.

Robert Evans, and James and Emma Daine were members of Bury and Stowmarket Teachers' Association, the local branch of the NUT, which charged 8s. p.a. membership for head teachers and 7s. p.a. for assistant teachers, with an option to donate 2s. p.a. to a legal defence fund.

The Education Act 1899 made provision for the establishment of a register of teachers. However, voluntary teacher registration did not actually begin until 1914, although it did include retrospective records of some teachers who started their careers during the 1870s.

The Census of England and Wales 1891

This was the first census to employ female enumerators and the first to record employment status. In Great Barton, the data was collected by James Daine and Joseph Grimwood Edwards, who was a wheelwright and the son of a previous enumerator. It revealed that there had been a further decline in the population of Great Barton from 819 to 766, and that only half the heads of households were born in Great Barton. It included the Bunbury family, the farmers of Conyers Green Farm, Elms Farm, Hall Farm, Cattishall Farm, Manning Farm and East Barton Farm, a pork butcher, a thatcher, a miller/baker, a blacksmith, a wheelwright, a postmistress, a laundress, and a thatcher/grocer as employers. It also listed eleven self-employed people including five men, who worked as a hawker, farm worker, tailor, brickmaker and butcher, and six women, three of whom worked as bakers, and the others as a dressmaker, laundress and servant.

The Revd Henry Stewart Gladstone was replaced as vicar of Great Barton by the Revd James Arthur Hervey (1855-1948). He was the grandson of Frederick William Hervey, Marquis of Bristol, also known as Lord Jermyn, and the son of Lord Arthur Charles Hervey (1808-1894), Bishop of Bath and Wells. The Revd James Hervey attended Eton College and Trinity College, Cambridge and was Vicar of Alfreton in Derbyshire, before he moved to Great Barton, in 1897, with his wife, Margaret Augusta, and their 11-year-old son, Thomas Percy Arthur.

In 1887, PC William Peake was promoted to sergeant and left the village to work in the nearby village of Woolpit (*BNP*, 3 May 1887). From there, he moved to Newmarket, where he was promoted to superintendent, and then to the Boxford Division of West Suffolk on 1 April 1900. His replacement was PC Robert Rix, from Cromer, Norfolk, who stayed in Great Barton for 13 years until he moved to Stanton, Suffolk, in 1900.

The school managers

The Revd Hervey, William Norman King, Robert Fyson and Richard Scott were the school managers, with Richard Scott as a representative of the Nonconformists.

Pupil attendance

The minimum school leaving age was raised from 10 to 11 by the Elementary Education (School Attendance) Act 1893 and to the age of 12 by the Elementary Education (School Attendance) Act 1899.

Table 6. Number of working class children in Great Barton, recorded as scholars in the Census of England and Wales 1891

	Aged 3 to 7	*Aged 8 to 11*	*Aged 12 and over*	*Total*
Boys	19	34	8	61
Girls	20	30	8	58
Total	*39*	*64*	*16*	*119*

Source: *Census of England and Wales 1891*

Four boys and five girls, from working class families in Great Barton, were not recorded as scholars in the 1891 census, but this could have been explained by the fact that four of the girls were five-years-old and may have started the following term, and one of the eight-years-old had special educational needs.

Table 7. Average attendance at Great Barton School, 1892 to 1901

	Girls and infants	*Boys*	*Total*
1892	70	46	116
1896	46	40	86
1901	63	32	95

Source: *Kelly's Directory of Norfolk and Suffolk, 1892 and 1896; The Return of Voluntary Schools, (County of West Suffolk, 1902)*

For those scholars who were registered at the school, many attended irregularly. The situation was not helped by the fact that parents of pupils in many schools were expected to make a weekly contribution. In 1891, a table was published in the *Bury and Norwich Post*, which showed the annual fees per pupil of a sample of 25 schools in West Suffolk, but did not include Great Barton School. The table showed that fees, locally, ranged from 3s. 6d. p.a. at Bardwell Church School, to 12s. 3d. p.a. at St James Boys' School, Bury St Edmunds, with the average rate per head of 5s. 10¼d. Some elementary schools charged extra for books (*BNP*, 1 Sept. 1891).

The Elementary Education Act 1891 effectively abolished school fees from 1 September 1891, after which schools could choose instead to receive an annual government grant of 10s. for each child aged 3 to 15, based on average attendance. Fees could either be reduced by the amount of the grant or abolished entirely, and most schools abolished the fees. During a parliamentary debate in December 1893, it was stated that the percentage of children under the age of ten on school registers in England and Wales increased from just 77.7 per cent to 79.98 per cent between 1891 and 1893 (*BNP*, 28 Aug. 1894).

School attendance was not always good in West Suffolk. Some teachers blamed this on the ineffectiveness of school attendance committees, the willingness of parents to allow their children to work for farmers, market gardeners and others, and the fact that some of these employers sat on the attendance committees (*BNP*, 29 Nov. 1892). A meeting of the NUT in 1894 added indifference to education as a further cause of the irregularity of attendance (*BNP*, 02 Jan. 1894).

However, some absence was the result of illness. Infectious illnesses, including measles, scarlet fever, whooping cough, typhoid, diphtheria, influenza, pneumonia and tuberculosis, could all be fatal. In October 1891, 13-year-old Agnes Jane Trudgett, who suffered from caries of the vertebrae and curvature of the spine, died from tuberculosis. In 1892, the schools in Great Barton were closed as the result of an outbreak of whooping cough and then of scarlet fever.

In February 1892, all of the children in one family caught diphtheria. On investigation, it was discovered that the privy was near the back door of their house and that a drain ran within a few feet of a shallow well, from which the family's water supply was obtained. The house was thoroughly disinfected by the Inspector of Nuisances, but the woman who nursed the children passed it on to other children, one of whom died at the Borough Infectious Hospital a few hours after admission (*BNP*, 28 Feb. 1893).

In 1898, the harvest holiday at Great Barton School was extended to nine weeks because of an outbreak of measles (*BNP*, 13 Sept. 1898).

In 1900, there was at least one case of diphtheria in the village, but this time it was not fatal.

In 1893, four pupils had a lucky escape when the newly thatched roof of their home at Clay Cottages, owned by Sir Edward Bunbury, was set alight by a spark from a traction engine, which had stopped in front of their cottage to allow a horse and vehicle to pass. Neighbours helped the families to remove their furniture and belongings, and, although the roof was destroyed, no-one was hurt (*BNP*, 4 Apr.1893).

Some of the villagers were unemployed and others were poorly paid so during the winter of 1890 to 1891 a soup kitchen was opened at the Girl's School using a new boiler, which was installed in the school kitchen at one end of the schoolrooms. The soup kitchen was organised by Herbert Bourke, a retired Royal Navy lieutenant, who worked as the political agent for the Conservative Party and lived in Barton Cottage during the election campaign. Henry and Laura Bunbury, Mrs Gladstone, Mrs Bourke and two or three other village ladies helped to serve about 150 pints of soup a week, at a charge of a halfpenny a pint. The following summer, at the Fox Inn at Pakenham, William Foulger publicly accused Herbert Bourke of pocketing some of the takings. Sir Edward Bunbury organised a public meeting at the Boys' School, where Herbert Bourke presented the accounts and successfully defended himself.   William Foulger apologised and withdrew the accusation but because of the controversy, Sir Edward Bunbury refused to allow the soup kitchen to continue (*BNP*, 18 Aug. 1891).

Special educational needs

Four of the nine children of Samuel and Harriet Howe, who moved to the village around 1880, had special needs. According to the 1891, 1901 and 1911 census information, Lavinia was 'blind from birth', Elizabeth was an 'idiot from childhood', Ellen was an 'imbecile' and 'feeble-minded' and Alfred James was 'sad and deserving'. The Elementary Education (Blind and Deaf Children) Act 1893 made grants available for specialist education for blind and deaf children and required school authorities to establish specialist schools. Alternative education was provided by asylums, in which adults were taught a trade and the children taught the three Rs and technical and domestic skills. Each inmate was supported by a voluntary subscription and was sponsored and elected by those with voting qualifications.

In 1898, the local paper appealed for people to sponsor 17-year-old Alfred James Howe for a place in the Eastern Counties' Asylum for Idiots at Colchester, Essex (*BNP*, 5 Apr. 1898). Alfred was awarded a place, but died soon afterwards from tuberculosis. In October, there was another appeal to the same sponsors to transfer their votes to his 23-year-old sister,

Elizabeth. Her case was strongly recommended by leading residents of Great Barton, including Sir Henry Charles Bunbury, William Norman King, Frank Baldwin, the Revd Harry Jones and the Revd James Hervey. She received the fifth highest number of votes and received sponsorship for five years (*BNP*, 4 Oct. 1898).

Child protection

Two families of the pupils were accused of child neglect. In 1894, Ethel May Sargent [358], the ten-month-old sister of Percy and Annie, died in tragic circumstances. Their mother put Ethel May to bed at noon and tied her loosely to the bed with a pinafore sash so that she would not roll down to the bottom of the bed and get her head caught between the bars. Her mother found her three hours later, suspended from the bed by the loop, with her chest on the edge of the chair, which was beside the bed. The tightness of the loop, with the weight of the body on the chair, prevented breathing and caused death from asphyxia. The jury returned a verdict of 'death from misadventure' and added a rider to the effect that they considered the mother should be censured for her negligence in tying up a young child and leaving her alone for so long (*BNP*, 19 June 1894).

Thomas Bishop (1851-1923) [655], a farm labourer, and his wife, Alice (1855-1935) [776], lived at Conyers Green and had nine children, one of whom, Kate, had died in 1886 as the result of a tragic accident (chapter 6). In 1893, the local clergy brought the family to the attention of the National Society for the Prevention of Cruelty to Children. In 1895, Alice and Thomas Bishop were taken to court at Thingoe and Thedwastre Petty Sessions, accused of child neglect, having already received several warnings. It was stated that the family took home 25s. or 26s. a week, which included the wages of 18-year-old Alfred and 19-year-old James, but no money was spent on soap, and the children were always in a verminous and filthy condition. The two oldest brothers had recently suffered from sore throats, and the five younger children were sent to school with sore throats and were allowed to run around the village. Five of the ten children caught scarlet fever and their skin peeled off their hands like a glove. At one point, Emma Daine told the children to stay at home for three weeks until they were 'purified and fit to attend'; and made an entry in the school logbook to that effect. However, the children returned the next day with shaved heads. Their mother, Alice, who appeared in court with a baby in her arms, was given a prison sentence for 21 days, and the magistrate said that her husband must have the house and children thoroughly cleaned in her absence (*BFP*, 30 Nov. 1895; *BNP*, 3 Dec. 1895). Alice had two more children after her release; Thomas in 1896 and Agnes [441] in 1901.

Educational reforms

The vice-presidency of the Committee of the Privy Council on Education was held by Sir William Hart Dyke (1837-1931) between 1887 and 1892, Sir Arthur Herbert Dyke Acland (1847-1926) between 1892 and 1895, and Sir John Eldon Gorst (1835-1916) between 1895 and 1902. All three were determined to bring about reforms.

Sir John Eldon Gorst was a colourful figure, who cycled through London to the Department of Education on his bright red bicycle. He was a Conservative MP, but his political views became increasingly independent, and he stood unsuccessfully as an Independent Free Trader in 1906.

The fragmentation of the education system

By the 1890s, six different government departments oversaw the provision of education. The Education Department was responsible for board bchools, voluntary schools, higher elementary schools, teacher training colleges, and evening continuation schools. The Local Government Board was in charge of poor law schools; the Home Office in charge of industrial schools and reformatories; the Science and Art Department was responsible for secondary and technical schools and the provision of training in drawing for elementary school teachers; and the Board of Agriculture was in charge of colleges for advanced education in agriculture. Endowed schools and public schools came under the auspices of the Charitable Commission and the Charitable Trusts Acts.

In 1892, Mr C.T. Addiscott, a member of the Executive of the NUT, spoke of the need to consolidate the educational system. He quoted Matthew Arnold (1822-1888), who admired the regularity of the continental educational system compared with the chaos of the British one (*BNP*, 29 Nov. 1892).

This division of the education system resulted in an inefficient use of public funds. It also created barriers for poor pupils who wished to continue their education beyond the minimum school leaving age, but had not been appropriately prepared by their elementary school for further education.

In 1896, John Gorst put forward an Education Bill, by which he hoped to address the issues of the fragmentation of the educational system, the inequality of school funding between voluntary and board schools, and the religious issue. It proposed the creation of a single department for the administration of education, with local supervision provided by municipal and county councils.

However, the bill was opposed by Arthur Balfour, a Conservative MP, and was heavily amended and eventually rejected, although many of its ideas were included in the Education Act 1902.

School funding

Great Barton School was a member of the Confederation of Rural Teachers and of the Voluntary School Association, both of which were concerned about the unfair financial advantages enjoyed by board schools.

Until 1891, voluntary schools were funded by a government grant, voluntary contributions and school fees, whilst board schools were funded by a government grant, local rates and school fees. After the abolition of school fees in 1891, board schools were able to receive additional funding from local rates, but voluntary schools had to raise money from voluntary subscriptions, which many found difficult.

The system of payment by results was gradually phased out after 1892 and replaced by fixed grants, the exact level of which was determined by Her Majesty's Inspectors (HMI), who took school equipment and the age of the teacher into consideration, when making their judgements.

Many voluntary schools were inefficient, unable to afford to update or repair their premises, and poorly resourced. They were only able to offer lower salaries and were more likely to employ pupil-teachers and Article 68 teachers, instead of qualified ones. In rural schools, pupils were more likely to be malnourished and part-time attendees, and less likely to attend evening continuation classes than in urban schools. Furthermore, inspectors often found that the teaching in voluntary, denominational schools was inferior to that of board schools.

Inferior education was suggested as one of the reasons for the difference between the crime rates in different cities. In Liverpool, where schools were predominantly denominational, the crime rate was three times higher than in Birmingham, where most education was provided in board schools. However, the government could not afford to replace all of the voluntary schools, so sought to make the existing ones more efficient.

The Church of England was concerned about the viability of small church schools, which were unable to afford to maintain and update their buildings in order to comply with government regulations. In 1890, it proposed the establishment of confederations of Church Schools with an Organising Master, who could give advice to schools and raise funds from across each diocese in order to support those schools in greatest need (*BNP*, 18 Nov 1890).

A questionnaire was sent to every parish and, in 1893, in the Thedwastre Hundred, nine parishes approved of the confederation scheme, two were doubtful, two were opposed, two had no school, two had board schools and one did not reply (*BNP*, 2 May 1893).

From 1895, the government provided grants for schools in small villages where the population did not exceed 500 within a two-mile radius of the school, so that they could appoint extra staff, offer higher salaries, employ certificated teachers and improve working conditions, including security of tenure. However, Great Barton School did not benefit, because more than 500 people lived within two miles of the school.

The Education Bill 1896 included a proposal that voluntary schools could be federated into associations, each of which would be eligible to receive a lump sum from a Special Aid Grant Fund. The associated schools could share managers and teachers, although there were logistical problems for teachers who worked in more than one school and had to cycle or walk between schools.

Some members of the local CTA favoured such an arrangement, but others feared that the Anglican church could lose some of its influence if a school of one denomination federated with a school of a different one (*BFP*, 27 June 1896).

Funding for voluntary schools was increased by the Voluntary Schools Act 1897, which provided grants for voluntary schools on condition that they agreed to jointly administered inspections.

From 1900, schools received a block annual grant of 17s. per infant, and 21s. or 22s. for each older pupil, the precise level of which was determined by an HMI, based on the attendance record, the 'suitability of the instruction to the circumstances of the children and the neighbourhood, the thoroughness and intelligence with which the instruction was given, the sufficiency and suitability of the staff', the discipline and the organisation (*BNP*, 10 Apr. 1900).

The religious question

The question of the teaching of denominational religious instruction remained contentious.

The Anglican Church claimed that it had a right to preserve the link between itself and the schools that it funded. However, in villages or areas where the only school was a voluntary one, Nonconformists objected to their child receiving Anglican teaching. Other people were concerned that the teaching of religion was at the expense of other subjects.

The Elementary Education Act 1870 did not make religious education a compulsory subject in board schools but where it was provided, the Cowper-Temple clause allowed pupils whose parental conscience was offended by religious teaching to arrive after, or leave before, the lesson. However, the Report of the Cross Commission on Elementary Education (1888) stated that few parents exercised their rights under this 'conscience clause'.

In 1893, the Revd Harry Jones, the ex-Vicar of Great Barton, wrote an article in the *Education Review*, entitled 'Religious Education: Ways and Means', in which he suggested three alternative solutions. A teacher who had a conscientious objection to teaching religion could be replaced for an hour a day by a curate or lay preacher, scholars could receive daily instruction from the minister of their own church, or there could be no religious instruction in school.

Many of the Great Barton schoolchildren came from Nonconformist families, whose numbers were steadily increasing in the village. Richard Scott (1855-1946), who was a school manager and parish councillor, was the lay preacher between 1873 and 1899. He ran the village mill, which manufactured wheat meal biscuits, which were so popular that he moved to Ipswich in 1899 to live nearer his customers (*BFP*, 01 April 1899).

Baptist meetings were held at Barton Cottage Meeting Place on Conyers Green until 1894, when it was proposed that a Mission Hall, which could hold between 150 and 200 people, be built in Great Barton in association with the Garland Street Baptist Church, Bury St. Edmunds. Some of the villagers, including members of the Church of England, signed a petition to ask Henry Charles Bunbury to donate a piece of land for a Baptist Mission Hall. He agreed to give the Baptists a plot of land near the junction of Livermere Road and Vicarage Farm for a nominal rent, on condition that the hall would not be used for political meetings (*BFP*, 28 April 1894).

The Baptists commenced fund-raising straight away and John Watson, one of the deacons, who was a builder, offered to start building the hall as soon as half of the money was raised. In 1895, work began on the building, and an additional £8 was raised for the purchase of a new organ.

In 1895, a grand opening was planned for Whit Sunday, in a tent large enough to hold 600 people. However, on the morning of the event, Sir Henry withdrew his permission to erect the tent so Richard Scott arranged for the tent to be set up in one of his meadows on the edge of Barton Park. People travelled from up to 14 miles away to attend the opening service, which was addressed by George Nokes, known as the 'Bishop of Whitechapel'. Afterwards 350 people sat down to eat tea in the tent and, in the evening, 700 people came to hear speeches by George Nokes and others.

Most travelled by horse and trap, carrier pony, bicycle or on foot, but any who travelled on a mechanically propelled vehicle were subject to the Locomotive Act 1865 (Red Flag Act) which set a speed limit of two miles per hour in towns and four miles per hour in the countryside. On 28 January 1896, Walter Arnold of East Peckham, Kent, was fined 1s. for travelling at 8mph. He was the first person to be fined for exceeding the speed limit and was caught by a police officer, who had given chase on a bicycle. The act was amended in 1896, when the speed limit was raised to 14mph.

Baptist gatherings were held regularly in the Mission Hall, which was often decorated by some of the children with fruit and flowers supplied by Richard Scott and others. In June 1898, the fourth Baptist Annual Meeting was addressed by George Nokes. In September 1898, a thanksgiving meeting was addressed by the Revd G. F. Wall of Bardwell on behalf of Garland Street Baptist Chapel, Bury St Edmunds (*BNP*, 20 Sept.1898).

The school curriculum

In 1893, the Education Department issued a special circular to Inspectors on the *Training and Teaching of Infants* (Circular No. 322, 6 February 1893), which declared that the Department wanted to see kindergarten methods used more widely. These included the recognition of the child's spontaneous activity, the stimulation of this activity in certain well-defined directions by the teachers, and the harmonious and complete development of the whole of the child's faculties.

Learning to draw was considered a good method of improving powers of observation, but the provision of drawing lessons often presented problems for teachers in small rural mixed schools, who had to teach drawing to boys and needlework to girls at the same time. This was less of a problem at Great Barton School, where the boys and girls were taught separately, and Edith Evans, who had taught sewing at her previous school, was available to teach the older girls from 1893 onwards. To enable teachers to obtain a drawing certificate, classes in freehand, geometry, model, and perspective were held in Bury St Edmunds, from October 1891 (*BNP*, 10 May 1892).

Schools in rural areas were permitted to teach agriculture, but it was not taught in any of the elementary schools in the Bury area before 1892, so a series of lectures, entitled 'Agricultural Geology', were arranged for teachers in elementary schools by the Technical Instruction Committee in Bury St Edmunds, held in the anteroom of the Athenaeum. The Education Code 1894 added domestic economy as an optional subject for girls.

Physical exercise was not compulsory in British schools, as it was in Germany, France, Sweden and Switzerland. However, the Education Code 1894 stipulated that the higher grant would not be paid to any school, unless drill and suitable physical exercise were taught. It also made provisions for elementary schools to provide lessons on temperance and the importance of abstaining from alcoholic drink. The Education Code 1895 extended provision for physical education and stated that expenditure on footballs, skipping-ropes and other items for teaching games was a legitimate use of public money. Drill was seen as useful training for military service.

Recitation was effectively a compulsory subject because schools were unable to attract the higher grant unless scholars achieved a satisfactory level. Scholars were expected to be able to recite an increasing number of lines of poetry or other text by the end of each standard, from 20 lines of poetry at the end of Standard I, to 150 lines at the end of Standard VI.

Robert Evans was a keen gardener and, in 1899, was highly commended for his presentation of a graceful flower arrangement by *The Gardener* at a local show (*BNP*, 16 May 1899). In 1900, an inspector from HMI sanctioned a scheme of instruction for the Boys' School which included a two-hour period of gardening each week. Daniel Pawsey (1848-1926) [682], the gardener and coachman at Barton Vicarage and an enthusiastic and talented horticulturist was appointed as an instructor (*BFP*, 4 Aug. 1900).

The Education Code 1900 abolished the grant for class subjects and offered schools the opportunity to adopt a curriculum tailored to the circumstances and capabilities of their scholars. In infant classes, the code stipulated that there should be 'suitable instruction in the elementary things' and 'simple lessons on common things'. For pupils aged 7-years-old and upwards, the school curriculum consisted of:

- elementary subjects (compulsory) - the three Rs, drawing for boys and needlework for girls, which were all compulsory, in addition to lessons in drill and physical exercise;
- class subjects (optional) - singing, recitation, drawing, English, geography, science, history and domestic economy;
- specific subjects (optional) - mechanics, chemistry, physics, animal physiology, agriculture, navigation, languages, shorthand, cookery, laundry and dairy work.

In an effort to improve the standard of handwriting, a national competition was held each year with prizes of money, books and certificates. In 1899, Winifred and Dorothy Evans, aged eight and nine, the daughters of the head teacher were each awarded a prize (*BFP*, 24 June 1899).

By 1900, the Board of Education had abandoned the standards system, in which pupils remained at one standard until they passed the test, which allowed them to move up to the next one.

School inspections

During the 1890s, annual examinations were replaced by an unscheduled visit from an HMI, who was now also required to include a judgement on discipline and moral training. However, these visits from an inspector were criticised by teachers, who felt that it was unfair to judge the performance of a school on a single day. Inspection reports were published, but schools had the right to appeal against the report.

Some members of the Ely Diocese were in favour of Diocesan Inspectors being empowered to inspect secular matters as well as religious ones in voluntary schools, but this idea was not pursued at national level.

In 1892, Mr H. T. Knowles, the Diocesan Inspector, reported that there were 126 schools in the Archdeaconry of Sudbury, of which three had received a preliminary warning from the Education Department, and that the average grant was 16s 9½d. per head, compared with 17s. 8d. per head in all church schools in England and Wales. He was concerned that schools in this area were losing financially, through inefficiency, and hoped that, instead of looking upon the visit of the Diocesan Inspector as an inquisition, teachers would regard it as a friendly aid to help them to secure and maintain the efficiency of their school (*BNP*, 10 May 1892). However, although the Education Department also expressed the desire that its officers should aim at being helpful and sympathetic, teachers were not convinced that this would happen in practice.

Great Barton School was certified by the Secretary of the Education Department as 'efficient' in 1891. Eight years later, the Diocesan Inspection for Great Barton Schools reported:

> Girls' and Infants' School: The results of the examinations are creditable to the teachers with painstaking and thorough religious teaching. The infants repeated their memory work accurately but could improve their answering. Singing – very good.
> Boys' School: Very satisfactory. The boys are interested and show much intelligence. Although examined at the end of a long morning, they were keen and eager. Memory work and written work neat and good. Singing – very good (*BFP*, 1 July 1899).

The Education Code 1894 relaxed inspection rules for infant schools, so that the formal annual visit of the inspectors could be omitted or relaxed if there had been two previous formal visits without notice.

In 1900, the Revd G. H. D. Jones, the Diocesan Inspector, carried out the annual scripture tests and reported that he was satisfied with the results in both schools, but added that 'the boys should be checked. During the same year, the school was inspected by HMI, who awarded the school the maximum grant based on his report, which stated that:

> at the Boys' School, The boys attend well, and the general progress is highly creditable to the master;
> at the Girls' School, the pupils continue to be extremely well taught and disciplined;
> in the infants' class, the pupils continue to make fairly good progress.

The school premises

The Education Code 1890 recommended that new school buildings should allow ten cubic feet per pupil, and, in 1893, the government issued Circular 321, which required inspectors to investigate and report on the condition of buildings and apparatus of each public elementary school. In 1896, new legislation restricted class sizes.

An HMI inspection of the school premises concluded that more accommodation was required at the Girls' and Infants' School, where no more than 52 pupils could be accommodated. In 1891, P. Scott wrote a letter to the Education Department on behalf of the school, in which he suggested that the area marked 'kitchen' on the plan could be utilised as a separate infants' room.

George Betts, one of the school managers, drew up a plan, with a new classroom to accommodate 47 infants, but his original plans were rejected by the Education Department because they did not provide enough light. He amended and resubmitted them, with an accompanying letter, which stated that, 'I have ventured to place one large window in the west side, instead of two smaller ones, for the reasons that an ample left hand light is thereby afforded to all the desks, now placed at right angles to the west wall; and also that the outside effect is better'.

There were further discussions about whether the infant boys and girls should be taught separately and whether it was necessary to erect a fence, but the plans were finally approved on 17 May 1899. Sir Edward Bunbury immediately arranged for the alterations to be made at his own expense. The infant classroom, which measured about 345 square feet, was built at right angles to the existing classroom and was officially completed on 2 August 1900.

In 1900, Margaret Hervey, the wife of the Revd James Hervey, organised a rummage sale at the Girls' School, which raised ten guineas, to defray the heavy expenses which the schools had 'been compelled to incur' (*BFP*, 17 Feb. 1900).

School discipline

The Education Code 1890 insisted on the keeping of records of school punishments. Schools were urged to avoid corporal punishment, and some teachers were summoned to court. However, the views of magistrates varied, so that there was no conformity in the sentencing and some MPs suggested that there should be national guidelines on the management of pupil behaviour.

During the 1890s, the law courts in Suffolk backed teachers in their use of the cane. In 1895 Mr Savage, a teacher at Kedington, was accused of using undue severity against a boy, causing wheals on his skin, but the case was dismissed by the court as being vexatious. The chair of the bench stated that the boy got what he thoroughly deserved and fined the father 1s. with 4s. costs (*BNP*, 25 June 1895).

Fines were imposed in 1894 to discourage boys from making slides on footpaths in bad weather (*BFP*, Dec. 1894).

Teachers' pensions

In 1888, an NUT petition asked the government to set up a superannuation scheme for teachers, to encourage aged and incapacitated teachers to retire. The situation was still unresolved by 1892 and the Executive Committee of the NUT argued that every certificated teacher in a public elementary school or training college should receive a retirement pension when they reached the age of 60, if male, and 55, if female. In addition, they argued that teachers should receive a pension at a younger age if they had achieved a certain length of service, or became incapacitated by 'infirmity of mind or body'. They pressed for pensions to be one-sixtieth of the retiring salary for every year of service. In 1892, the Bury and Stowmarket Teachers' Association appointed a committee, which included James Daine, to organise a deputation to lobby MPs on the issue of pensions and demand that teachers should be recognised in the same way as civil servants, soldiers, sailors, and police officers, who all received pensions (*BNP*, 5 Apr. 1892).

Under the Education Code 1892, a global sum of £5,580 was made available for pensions of £20, £25, and £30 p.a. to 'decayed teachers' who had entered their teaching career on the understanding that they would receive state assistance at the end of their careers. The total amount for distribution in 1893 was raised to £10,580 p.a. In 1893, the local branch of the NUT passed a motion stating that, 'We thank the government for the additional sum granted for teachers' pensions, but venture to hope that the time will speedily come when every teacher will be entitled to a state pension' (*BNP*, 28 Mar. 1893).

The Elementary School Teachers' (Superannuation) Act 1898 met some of their demands and contributed to teachers' pensions in several ways.

- An annuity fund was set up, into which men paid in £3 p.a. and women £2 p.a., and each teacher received whatever annuity their payments would buy at the age of retirement.
- In the event of someone retiring from the profession before the age of 65, he or she would still, on attaining that age, be entitled to an annuity in proportion to the amount paid.
- In addition to superannuation, a teacher would receive 10s. p.a. for every year of service after 1898, and an additional 3d. for every year of service before 1898.
- A 'break-down fund' was available for anyone who had a mental or physical break down, as long as they had worked for over ten years, with a man eligible to receive £20 p.a., plus £1 for every year over ten years served beyond that time, and a woman £15 p.a. plus 13s. 4d. for every year over ten years served beyond that time.

Extra-curricular duties

During the 1890s, the Confederation of Rural Teachers discussed the question of compulsory extra-curricular duties, and the NUT continued to put the case for the right of teachers to refuse to carry out extra-curricular duties without jeopardising their career.

In Great Barton, both head teachers played a significant role in the life of the village, where they were expected to accompany pupils to village events and participate in social events at the school outside school hours.

Emma Daine and Edith Evans organised Great Barton Sunday School. Emma Daine was also the treasurer of several village organisations, including the Doctor's Club, the Clothing Club and the Children's Boot Club. Robert Evans ran evening continuation classes, was a part-time journalist, played the church organ, ran the church choir and performed in village concerts. He was clerk of the Parochial Church Council for several years, clerk of the trustees of the Poor's Firing Farm Charity from 1908 until 1925, a rate collector from 1912, a parish councillor, a lay reader from 1917 and secretary of the Church Institute.

Evening continuation classes

The Revised Code 1862 stated that, 'schools may meet three times daily; viz., in the morning, afternoon, and evening'. A night school for adults operated in Great Barton in 1871 when classes were taught by James Handley, but evening classes had been discontinued by the 1890s.

Nationally, attendance at evening continuation classes fell from just over 73,000 in 1870 to under 30,000 in 1886. This was due to a number of factors including the requirement under the Revised Code 1862 to study at least one of the elementary subjects as well as class subjects, so that most classes only offered reading and writing, which effectively repeated the work covered in elementary day schools. Moreover, the grant for evening classes depended on examination results, which further discouraged many students.

This attendance compared unfavourably with Germany, where 50 per cent of children aged between 12 and 17 attended evening classes (*BFP*, 14 Oct. 1893).

During the early 1890s, many new evening classes for adults were established in the UK, especially after the range of subjects on offer was increased.

The Evening Continuation School Code 1893 stated that classes were open to anyone over the age of 14 and could be taught by any lay or clerical person over the age of 18 who was approved by the inspector. Each evening school was to open on at least 30 evenings during the school year and the registers were to record the number of hours attended by each student in each subject. The annual examination was to be replaced by unannounced inspections by HMI, and the level of grant would be determined by the HMI report and the number of attendances by the students.

The subjects that could be taught included:
*   elementary subjects – reading, writing and composition, reading and writing, arithmetic;
*   English subjects– English, geography, history, the life and duties of the citizen;
*   languages - French, German, Latin, and Welsh for Wales;
*   mathematics — Euclid, algebra, mensuration;
*   science subjects - agriculture, horticulture, botany, bookkeeping, vocal music, domestic economy, needlework.

Later codes included industrial, commercial, domestic and rural subjects and allowed teachers to select branches of instruction suited to the students in their district. Nationally, the number of students rose, including a growing number of female students, who studied needlework and domestic subjects.

From September 1897, evening classes were held at Great Barton Boys' School, set up by the school managers in conjunction with West Suffolk County Council, and organised by Robert Evans. Classes were held on Monday evenings, from seven o'clock onwards, and students were charged 1s. for a period of six months (*BFP*, 25 Sept. 1897).

The Evening Continuation School Code 1898 provided state grants, which were based on attendance rather than examination results.

In 1898, the managers at Great Barton School decided to open the evening class one hour earlier and offer some form of entertainment before the lesson (*BNP*, 27 Sept. 1898).

From October 1898, this included a monthly magic lantern picture show, which was an early form of image projector, invented in the seventeenth century, and was originally illuminated by a candle and later by acetylene gas. One week, Robert Evans used the lantern to give an illustrated lecture on a journey from John O'Groats to Land's End (*BNP*, 14 Nov.1899).

In March 1899, Lady Laura Bunbury sponsored six lectures on home nursing, given by Miss Morgan, a lecturer employed by Suffolk County Council, and the average attendance was 50 (*BFP*, 25 Mar. 1899).

HMI made unannounced visits during classes in order to observe the manner in which the classes were conducted and question students on the work. In 1899, HMI inspected Great Barton Evening Continuation School and reported that, 'the master works hard to make the evening school a success', and awarded the school the higher grant (*BFP*, 29 May 1899).

In 1900, ten youths enrolled at a joinery class (*BFP*, 9 Oct. 1900) and, at the end of the autumn term, the boys of the evening continuation school presented Robert Evans with a silver mounted walking stick (*BFP*, 1 Dec. 1900).

Great Barton Sunday School and church choir

Robert Evans played the organ for church services and ran the church choir. Emma Daine and Edith Evans were both involved with Great Barton Sunday School activities.

In July 1891, members of Holy Innocents' church choir and Sunday school enjoyed a day trip to Felixstowe (*BNP*, 28 July 1891). In July 1893, the church choir travelled to Ipswich by train from Thurston Railway Station, the nearest station to Great Barton, and then by boat on the River Orwell to Harwich (*BNP* 18 July 1893).

In July 1898, the children of the Sunday school took floral offerings to the church for a Flower Service, after which the flowers were taken to the Dr Barnardo's Hospital (*BNP*, 5 July 1898). In 1900, the flowers from the service were given to West Suffolk General Hospital and the Infirmary.

In August 1898, the church congregation paid for the choir's trip to Felixstowe. The choir members caught the six o'clock train from Thurston to Ipswich, where they ate breakfast, and then went by river on the *Essex* to Felixstowe, where they ate lunch, rode on donkeys and enjoyed other beach amusements. At the end of the day, they sailed back to Ipswich on the *Suffolk* and caught a train to Thurston (*BNP*, 2 Aug. 1898).

In December 1898, Robert Evans accompanied the church choir and bell ringers to a party at Barton Hall, where 40 guests were entertained by Miss Evans, Tom Hervey and the Bunbury children, who all performed in costume. After the meal, he accompanied the choir on the piano (*BNP*, 10 Jan. 1899).

The Christmas parties for the children of Great Barton Sunday School, organised by Emma Daine and Edith Evans, were held in a classroom at the Girls' School. In December 1898, Lady Laura Bunbury presented books as prizes to 60 pupils, including Lucy Clutterham, Rose and Lily King, Mary and Alfred Cage, Victor Sturgeon, Walter Aldous and George Wright, who all achieved full marks. The prize-giving was followed by a magic lantern show, which illustrated the story of *Bluebeard* (*BNP*, 3 Jan. 1899).

Amongst these books, given as prizes, would have been the 'classics', which provided the main diet of children's reading. *Gulliver's Travels* (Jonathan Swift) and *Robinson Crusoe* (Daniel Defoe) were both written in the eighteenth century. Nineteenth century classics for children included all of the books by Charles Dickens, *Alice's Adventures in Wonderland* and *Through the Looking Glass* (Lewis Carroll), *What Katy Did* (Susan

Coolidge), *Lorna Doone* (R. D. Blackmore), *Treasure Island* and *Kidnapped* (R. L. Stevenson), *Coral Island* (R. M. Ballantyne), *Little Women* (Louisa M. Alcott), *Swiss Family Robinson* (J. R. Wyss), *Heidi* (Johann Spyri), *Robin Hood* (Howard Pyle), *Ivanhoe* (Walter Scott), *Children of the New Forest* (Frederick Marryat), *Tom Sawyer and Huckleberry Finn* (Mark Twain), *Black Beauty* (Anna Sewell), *Tom Brown's Schooldays* (Thomas Hughes), *Agnes Grey* (Ann Bronte), *Jane Eyre* (Charlotte Bronte), *Wuthering Heights* (Emily Bronte), *The Mill on the Floss* (George Eliot), *Jungle Book* (Rudyard Kipling), *Vanity Fair* (William Makepeace Thackeray), *The Treasure Seekers* (Enid Nesbit) and *The Water Babies*, written by Charles Kingsley.

In December 1899, three of Lord Bunbury's children attended Great Barton Sunday School's Christmas party, during which, tea was provided at the Girls' School, which was followed by a prize-giving at the Boys' School, where 67 prizes of Bibles, prayer books and hymn books were awarded. Victor Sturgeon, who achieved full marks for the second year running, was presented with a certificate and money, in addition to a book.

Afterwards, Margaret Hervey, the wife of the vicar, entertained the children with a magic lantern show, which illustrated the story of *Puss in Boots* (*BNP*, 6 Jan. 1900).

Attendance at village events

Sir Henry Charles Bunbury regularly invited the schoolchildren and their teachers to Barton Hall. The Bunbury daughters, Laura and Cissie, who were taught by a governess at home, were often available to help with parties for the children, but both of their brothers attended boarding schools during term time.

Charles Henry Napier Bunbury (1886-1963) attended Eton College, and Henry William Bunbury (1889-1956) attended Rottingdean in Sussex, Eton College and Trinity Hall, Cambridge University.

At the Christmas party in 1894, the children ate a special tea, pulled Christmas crackers, and sat around the Christmas tree to receive presents from the Bunbury family. At the end of the party, they were given buns and sweets to take home.

At a summer party for the children, the children ate tea at long tables on the lawn, played games, competed in races and took cake and an orange home at the end of the party (*BNP*, 6 Aug. 1895).

On 20 June 1897, Queen Victoria celebrated her Diamond Jubilee Accession Day at Windsor Castle. Celebrations were held throughout the country, including at Great Barton, where a party was organised by the Revd Henry Gladstone, who had officially left the village. It was held in the grounds of the Vicarage and included tea and supper, an adult cricket match and games until twilight. Later, pupils were given a medal as a memento of the jubilee.

Barton Cricket Club, which included ex-pupils, played in the grounds of Barton Hall and competed against teams from nearby villages, the Bury Early Closing Team and Bury Tradesmen. In 1898, Sir Henry and Lady Laura Bunbury presented a cap to each member of the club with specially made ribbons in the Bunbury colours and neckties to match (*BNP*, 5 July 1898). At the end of the season, the club presented Sir Henry with a ball, mounted on a solid silver stand, and a silver shield with an inscription that commemorated the seven wickets taken by him for 25 runs at Ampton on 30 July 1898. Lady Laura was given a framed photograph of the team, to thank her for providing the teas, and her daughter, Cissie, was presented with a pencil case, engraved with her initials, to thank her for her contribution as score-keeper (*BNP*, 13 Sept.1898).

On the last Saturday of September 1898, Laura and Cissie Bunbury organised a party for the schoolchildren and the teachers. Before tea, the older boys played football, whilst the other children played lawn games. After tea, the girls watched a tug of war between the boys all of the children competed in races. At the end of the party, the girls and younger boys were each given a toy to take home, and the older boys were given footballs (*BNP*, 27 Sept. 1898: *BFP*, 01 Oct. 1898).

In 1898, William Norman King, a school manager who had been a county councillor since 1888, invited villagers to his home at Barton Place for a harvest lunch of roast beef and plum pudding, after which there was a tug-of-war and other games. At the end of the afternoon, all the guests sat down to tea, before they played more games and joined in a sing-song (*BNP*, 27 Sept. 1898). In 1899, he invited the 60 members of Great Barton Women's Help Society to his home (*BNP*, 08 Aug. 1899). The object of this organisation, which had about 150 groups, with 12,000 members, was to 'establish and maintain homes or clubs for the poorest classes of women and girls in all parishes where the clergyman so desires' (*The Spectator*, 14 Mar. 1903, p17). The society had 107 members in Great Barton by 1901.

Great Barton Bicycle Club was set up in 1888 (*BNP*, 17 Apr. 1888). In 1899, a bicycle gymkhana, in aid of the Eastern Counties Asylum for Idiots at Colchester and West Suffolk General Hospital, was held at Barton Hall and presided over by Frank Riley Smith (1866-1912) who lived at Saxham Hall. Miss Betts, daughter of the estate manager, won first prize for best-decorated bicycle, and 13-year-old Laura Bunbury, who was dressed as a jester, won second prize. Cissie Bunbury won both the egg and spoon and the tortoise race for the under 15-year-olds. Other attractions included a labyrinth race, a three lap's race, a hoop race, a bandbox race, a Victoria Cross race, a churchwarden's race and competitions which involved tilting at the ring, threading needles, making Turk's heads and slicing lemons (*BNP*, 12 Sept. 1899).

The summer party for 120 schoolchildren was held at the Vicarage in 1900. The children participated in or watched a game of cricket, during which Cissie Bunbury, who was captain of one team, scored 12 runs. After tea, the Revd Hervey, Sir Henry and Lady Bunbury arranged activities with prizes, and gave toys to the younger children, 'carts' to the older ones, and 'thoughtful gifts' to the teachers (*BFP*, 18 Aug. 1900).

In the same month, Emma Daine was in charge of one of the stalls at a garden fête, held at the Vicarage in aid of the Church of England Homes for Waifs and Strays. It was attended by 300 parishioners and raised £6.7s. 6d. (*BFP*, 4 Aug. 1900).

Attendance at the school outside school hours

By an agreement, dated 13 December 1890, Sir Edward Bunbury 'reserved, to himself, the exclusive use and control of the school rooms, playgrounds and offices at all times during the tenancy, except during school hours, from nine o'clock to five o'clock.' A wide variety of local organisations held meetings at the schools, which were also the venue for many social events and fundraising concerts.

In 1891, a concert and magic lantern show raised money for the family of 30-year-old John Ambrose, who died whilst sawing branches from a tree for William Norman King. The concert raised £6. 5s. for his widow, and 10s. to cover the use of a room for the inquest at Mrs Clarke's house, and the attendance expenses of the jury (*BNP*, 27 Jan. 1891).

A series of winter concerts raised money for a variety of good causes, including the National Society for the Prevention of Cruelty to Children (NSPCC) in 1893 and 1898 (*BFP*, 14 Jan. 1893; *BFP*, 1 Oct. 1898).

In 1895, adults and schoolchildren performed a concert to raise funds to buy coal for the widows of the parish (*BFP*, 5 Jan.1895). A variety show was held, which included waxworks, vocal and instrumental music, and a humorous dialogue entitled 'Silence under Difficulties' (*BNP*, 29 Jan 1895).

In 1898, the Boys' School was decorated with flags for a concert in aid of the church. A baby grand piano was borrowed from Mr J Last from Bury St Edmunds, and the concert included songs, music and readings. Cissie Bunbury sang and accompanied herself on the guitar, and Miss Tollemache, dressed in Japanese costume, sang Japanese songs (*BFP*, 10 Dec. 1898).

In 1899, the Revd Hervey organised a Christmas concert, which included songs and piano pieces from Dorothy and Winifred Evans, and a choir from the Girls' School, conducted by Emma Daine. Amongst the other contributions were 'The Yellow Coon', sung by Laura Bunbury, and

'The Picanninies', sung by Gwendoline Oliver (*BFP*, 23 Dec. 1899), both of which would be unacceptable in the twenty-first century. In 1894, the CTA held one of a series of Shakespearean evenings at the school.

On Shrove Tuesday 1898, the Revd Hervey arranged a social event, with an admission fee of 1d. Tables and chairs were set out for draughts and other games, and the son of the vicar served food and drink. The entertainment included songs from Robert Evans, who sang 'The Powder Monkey' and 'Golden Slippers', piano pieces by Robert's daughters, Dorothy and Winifred, and musical drill by six of the schoolboys (*BNP*, 1 Mar. 1898).

In 1899, Lady Laura Bunbury, Margaret Hervey, Edith Evans and others prepared a tea for a musical evening, interspersed with games. Since the admission charge was only 1d, the profit of £2. 4s. 6d. suggested that it was well-attended (*BFP*, 5 Apr. 1899).

Use of the schoolrooms for political meetings
During the 1890s, meetings of North West Suffolk Workmen's Liberal Association and the local Conservative Party were held at the school. In 1891, there was a by-election in Stowmarket after the death of the Conservative MP, Sir Edward Greene. His son, Walter, stood as the new Conservative candidate, but was defeated by Sydney James de Stern (1845-1912) the Liberal Party candidate, who was created a peer in 1895 and became the First Baron Wandsworth.

In May 1894, Sir Edward Bunbury, who had served as the Liberal MP for Bury St Edmunds from 1847 until 1852, gave permission for a Conservative Party meeting and smoking concert to be held in a marquee in the grounds of the Bunbury Arms, in support of Sir Ian Zachary Malcolm (1868-1944), the Conservative candidate (*BNP*, 8 May 1894).

In November 1894, Henry Charles Bunbury, heir to the baronetcy, chaired a packed meeting in the schoolroom addressed by Sir Ian, who described Barton as a 'stronghold of conservatism', and accused Sydney Stern, of being more concerned with the Home Rule for Ireland and increasing death duties than with raising wages (*BNP*, 13 Nov. 1894).

At the 1895 general election, Sir Ian Malcolm was elected as MP for Stowmarket, which he subsequently represented for 11 years, during which time he married the daughter of the infamous Lillie Langtry, a mistress of Edward, Prince of Wales. Robert Cecil, Marquis of Salisbury, became Prime Minister and appointed several members of his family to his cabinet; giving rise to the phrase, 'Bob's your uncle'.

The departure of the Bunbury family from Barton Hall
Sir Edward Bunbury died, childless, in 1895 and the baronetcy was inherited by his nephew, Henry Charles Bunbury, who became the 10th

Baronet. Henry's sister, Emilie Louisa Margaret Bunbury (1853-1929), who was two years older, was unable to inherit the baronetcy by reason of her gender. This situation was still true in 2016, following the failure of the Equality (Titles) Bill in 2014, which would have made provision for the succession of female heirs to hereditary titles.

The Bunbury family were no longer as wealthy as they once had been. At his death in 1895, the personal wealth of Sir Edward Bunbury amounted to £32,411. 1s. 6d. (net value £23,493. 18s. 11d) and his heir had to pay death duties, a progressive tax, calculated on the estate of the deceased.

During the 1890s, the family sold their coin collection and raised £3,000 at a five-day sale of the Bunbury Library, which included a first edition of *The Deserted Village* by Oliver Goldsmith (*BFP*, 18 July 1896). In 1901, they sold the family's porcelain collection for £2,421. 13s. 6d. (*BFP*, 06 July 1901).

Sir Henry Charles Bunbury vacated Barton Hall in December 1900 and moved to the Manor House, Mildenhall, to live on his smaller estate.

He leased Barton Hall to Frank Riley Smith who was living at Saxham Hall, a 38-roomed stately home near Bury St Edmunds. Frank continued to live at Saxham Hall whilst extensive alterations, including the installation of electric lighting and the renovation of the stables, were carried out at Barton Hall.

During this time, PC William Baker, the village police officer, lived at East Lodge and worked as a gatekeeper for Barton Hall.

The end of an era

The educational reforms of the 1890s brought about some improvements to the education system. By 1900, there was more school accommodation, a broader school curriculum, a pension for teachers, a more flexible inspection regime, free schooling, an end of the system of payment by results, and an increase in school finance.

The issues of having a multiplicity of educational providers, a fragmented education system and inadequate funding for voluntary schools were partly addressed during the following decade, which saw the establishment of a national system of public education.

The year 1901 marked not only the end of an era for Great Barton, during which the Bunbury family had dominated the village, but also the end of an era for Great Britain, following the death of Queen Victoria.

During her 64-year reign, many pupils and others from Great Barton had left the village, some of whom had gone overseas. Some had emigrated from Suffolk to the New World and British Colonies, whilst others had joined the armed services, worked abroad for a short time or enjoyed foreign travel.

8
FAR AND WIDE

During the Victorian era, a number of individuals from Great Barton travelled overseas for work or pleasure, and several families emigrated.

Organisations, such as the Religious Tract Society run by Nonconformists, encouraged working class people to emigrate. Newspapers published reports of meetings and letters, which glowingly described the new lives of émigrés in the United States of America or one of the British colonies. Some young men saw the armed services as a means of escaping the poverty of their village life, serving their Queen and country and seeing the world. One or two young people from wealthier families in Great Barton sought their fortune overseas or travelled abroad for pleasure, whilst one young man joined an important expedition of discovery.

United States of America

Between 1836 and 1914, more than 30 million people emigrated from Europe to the United States of America (USA). In 1850, the *Bury and Norwich Post* published many articles about life in the USA. One article reported that Mr Mann of New Lisbon, Ohio, had discovered gold on his farmland, from which he collected 300 dollars-worth of gold in a few days (*BNP*, 02 Jan. 1850). Another stated that the wheat crops in the west of the country were 'never more satisfactory' (*BNP*, 14 Aug. 1850), and yet another that 'the electric Ohio, Indiana, and Illinois Telegraph Company had built 1,000 miles of line through a country covered with dense and almost impervious forests' (*BNP*, 02 Oct. 1850).

Sometimes a parish contributed to the Assisted Passages Scheme in order to reduce the number of families who were dependent on them for assistance. In 1851, the *Bury and Norwich Post* published a letter, written by a family from Playford, Suffolk, who emigrated in 1849 with the assistance of their parish. It claimed that the state of Ohio had rich, fertile, prairie soils, which enabled wheat to be grown for up to six years in succession without a break, and for Indian corn to grow up to 14 foot high. It also stated that cucumbers, various kinds of melons, pumpkins and squash gourds grew without needing extra heat, and grapes, cherries, gooseberries, cranberries and walnuts grew spontaneously. It even dispelled the problems of the dangers of wild animals and Indians, and claimed that both had been forced to move west when Europeans settled on the land (*BNP*, 30 Apr. 1851).

The *Nunn family* was attracted by the promise of these fertile lands. In April 1851, Charles and Miriam Nunn and their seven children lived in Turnpike Road, Great Barton. Charles worked as a baker and six-year-old Frederick attended the village school. Charles and his family sailed on the *Margaret Evans* from London and arrived in New York on 16 June 1851. From there, they travelled to Medina, Ohio, a thriving settlement, which had grown from 163 people in 1818, to 2011 people in 1850. It had six churches, 15 stores, one newspaper office, one woollen factory, one axe factory, one flourmill, and one iron furnace. Charles Nunn farmed the virgin land of the prairie and constructed a wooden cabin for the family to occupy. He and his wife had four more children, and Frederick helped his father on the farm.

The American Civil War began in 1861, and an estimated 1,500 men from Medina County enlisted in the Union Army, two-thirds as volunteers. Amongst them was 18-year-old Frederick Nunn, who, in July 1863, joined the 85th Infantry Regiment at Camp Chase, Columbus, Ohio, under Colonel Barnabas Burns, a lawyer, businessman and politician. His regiment participated in the chase of General John Hunt Morgan, a Confederate general and cavalry officer, and joined the successful expedition to capture Cumberland Gap, Tennessee. Frederick's regiment remained on guard duty from September 1863 until February 1864, during which time 37 enlisted men died from disease, but Frederick survived.

After the war, Frederick and his family moved to Greenfield Township in Huron, Ohio, where his father continued to farm until his death, at the age of 80. In 1870, nine children lived at home; Frederick and his brother, Josiah, worked as farm labourers, and his sister, Eliza, as a schoolteacher. Ten years later, Frederick was still living at home and was working as a sawyer. Eventually, he moved to Michigan, Ohio, and then to Illinois to live in Tuscola, with one of his sisters, and later his nephew. He never married and died on 17 October 1921, at the age of 77.

Walter and Martha Pawsey lived in one of the cottages by the Crown Beerhouse, and Walter worked as a farm labourer and later as a coachman. From 1888, their family emigrated to New England on the east coast of the USA, where 2,138 people from Norfolk, Suffolk, Lincolnshire, Essex and Cambridgeshire had settled during the puritan-led Great Migration of 1630.

The first family member to emigrate was their eldest daughter, Maude Sophia Pawsey (1866-1927), who worked as an under housemaid at Brent Eleigh Hall in Suffolk, the home of Walter Thomas Brown, a magistrate and High Sheriff of Suffolk. In 1887, she married Joseph Biggs (1865-1964) who was a groom at Thornham Rectory, Suffolk, and the following year, they sailed with their baby daughter from Liverpool to New York, USA. From there, they travelled northeast to Glastonbury, Hartford County, Connecticut, where they lived for the remainder of their lives, and Joseph worked as a cutter in a woollen mill. They had five children, the eldest of whom trained as a nurse.

During the next four years, Maude was joined by the rest of her family. Her sister, Ethel (1872-1940) who worked as nurse and housemaid at Onehouse Rectory, near Stowmarket, Suffolk, sailed to New York, in 1891, on the *SS Alaska,* an American passenger ship. She married Richard Smith, a farm labourer, who was born in Connecticut, and they lived in Glastonbury, where they had three children. Richard died in 1912, but Ethel lived there for nearly another 30 years. Their children worked as an insurance underwriter, a stenographer on the railways, and a bookkeeper in a bank.

After Walter's father died in 1892, Walter and Martha emigrated with 16-year-old Agnes (1876-1953) and 14-year-old Bertie (1878-1954). They travelled to New York on the *Arizona*, the ship in which Oscar Wilde had sailed to America in 1881.

In 1898, Agnes married George Archebald McLean, who came from Connecticut and worked at a local woollen mill. They moved to Williams Street, named after James B. Williams, the owner of the first commercial soap manufacturers in the world, based in Glastonbury, and George worked in the soap factory as a labourer and later as an electrician. They had at least five children, one of whom worked as a stenographer.

Walter and Bertie worked in the woollen factory at Glastonbury, and Bertie married a local girl. All of the Pawsey family lived in rented homes in Hartford and were buried in St James' Cemetery, Glastonbury. Many of their descendants still live in Connecticut.

Eliza (Lizzie) Scott (1857-1938*)* was the daughter of Thomas Scott (1827-1900), the general manager of the Barton Estate. Following the death of her mother in 1868, 11-year-old Lizzie was brought up by her father and stepmother and educated at home. During the 1860s, she met Edwin Merritt Fulcher (1840-1924), the son of a 'gentleman' from Mildenhall, who was born in Poplar and worked as a warehouseman in Bow when he was 21-years-old. He emigrated to the USA, but became engaged to Lizzie on one of his return visits to the UK. Although Lady Bunbury tried to persuade Lizzie to marry him in Great Barton rather than the USA, Lizzie chose to sail to New York in 1879 and marry him in Chicago. Edwin worked as a bookkeeper and accountant, and Lizzie and Edwin enjoyed a comfortable lifestyle at Evanston, near Chicago, where they owned their own house

In 1891, Eliza and Edwin travelled to South Africa, and their youngest daughter, Gwyneth, was born in Kimberley, South Africa. The family travelled back to New York on *SS State of Nevada*, in 1892. Their son, Gordon, studied science at Massachusetts and worked as a university teacher and research physicist and, in 1933, was in charge of the physics section at Chicago's World Fair entitled, 'A Century of Progress'. The older daughter, Eleanor, was a kindergarten teacher before her marriage, and Gwyneth, who never married, became a private secretary.

South Africa

Eliza's sister, *Eleanor (Nellie) Maria Scott*, married Peter Berry Owen in 1883, and they emigrated to Kimberley, South Africa. She died, three years later, at the age of 32, leaving a two-year-old son, Cecil, who returned with his father to the UK. He was brought up by his grandfather, Thomas Scott, and was educated at a boarding school at Aldenham, Hertfordshire.

Both Eleanor and Peter are recorded as being buried in the churchyard at Holy Innocents' Church, together with Thomas Scott, Anna Maria Scott and William John Scott, who died at the age of ten months (gravestone 329).

In September 1888, *Thomas Lancelot Reed Cooper* (1863-1944) from Manor Farm, who was educated at King Edward VI Grammar School, Bury St Edmunds, went to South Africa for a long holiday and, on his return in 1890, gave a lecture at the Boys' School about his experiences.

He sailed from Southampton and travelled via Lisbon, Madeira and the Canary Islands. He arrived 21 days later at Cape Town, where he admired the scenery, but found the town dirty and disappointing, although the suburbs were pretty. Three days later, he arrived at Port Elizabeth, where he visited the Botanical Gardens and the ostrich feather market, as well as some farms. He continued his journey to Durban, via East London, near the Buffalo River, where he saw whales, and from there to Pietermaritzburg, 40 miles away, which was adjacent to Fort Napier, the headquarters of the Natal forces. He described Pietermaritzburg as being one of the prettiest cities in Africa, with wide boulevards, impressive buildings, an excellent shopping area, beautiful tree plantations, magnificent gardens, and abundant flowers. He was, however, less flattering about Johannesburg, where he found filthy streets and fleas, which were the 'hardest working portion of the community, for they never rest' (*BFP*, 04 Jan. 1890). On his return, he moved to Glasgow, Scotland, and then Ealing, London, where he worked as an electrical engineer.

Canada

Edward Adams (1824-1856) was born in Great Barton, where his family had lived since the 17th century. In 1844, his father worked as a land agent and the family lived at Hall Farm. Edward Adams qualified as a surgeon in 1847 and worked at the Royal Navy's Haslar Hospital in Gosport, Hampshire, and then the Naval Hospital at Devonport. In 1848, he joined the expedition of James Clark Ross (1800-1862) which was organised by the Admiralty to locate and rescue Rear-Admiral Sir John Franklin (1786-1847), a British Royal Navy officer, and his crew members who disappeared whilst attempting to chart and navigate a section of the Northwest Passage in the Canadian Arctic. Adams sailed on *HMS Investigator*, which spent 18 months searching unsuccessfully for survivors of Franklin's crew.

In 1850, Edward Adams returned to Canada as assistant surgeon on *HMS Enterprise*, an Arctic discovery ship, to continue the search. He landed on the Yukon delta and spent several months searching inland, before re-joining his ship, which proceeded to sail further inland than any previous ship had done. *Arctic Hell-Ship: The Voyage of HMS Enterprise 1850-1855* by William Barr, which describes the progress of this expedition, is illustrated with some vivid paintings by Edward Adams. In 1855, Adams returned to England and became a fully qualified naval surgeon. The following year, he travelled to West Africa, where he died of typhus and was buried in Sierra Leone. The White-billed Diver (*Gavia adamsii*), which breeds in the Arctic in Russia, Alaska and Canada, was named after him by his friend George Robert Gray (1808-1872).

Henry Heigham (1836-1890), the son of John Heigham of Hunston Hall and brother-in-law of John South Phillips of Great Barton, moved to Canada, where he became the Chief of Police. In 1888, he married Winifred Rose Sophia Griffin from Ontario, but died two years later, without an heir.

Australia

Great Barton had associations with the Australian colonies through the two youngest sons of Sir Henry Edward Bunbury.

Henry William St Pierre Bunbury (1812-1875), the third son, was a lieutenant in the 21st Royal North British Fusiliers. He was promoted to the rank of lieutenant in 1833 and transferred to the 21st Regiment, a Scottish regiment, which was on duty in Tasmania (Van Diemen's Land). In 1834, he sailed to Sydney on the *Susan*, a convict ship, with 300 convicts and their guards, to join his regiment in Tasmania, Australia. During such voyages, which lasted about 100 days, it was common for one of the convicts to be appointed as an Inspector of Schools, and for all of the convicts to be taught Bible stories and to read and write.

When the ship landed in Sydney, Henry Bunbury was appointed as an Aide de Camp to Governor Richard Bourke at Sydney. Whilst there, he kept a journal which included caricatures of Governor Bourke and some of the convicts. When the governor was shown the journal by his valet, he took offence at some of the caricatures. Henry Bunbury was demoted and he rejoined his regiment at Eagle Hawk Neck on the Tasman Peninsula. Whilst there, he gardened, read and sketched, but was bored, so he volunteered to go to Western Australia.

On 6 March 1836, Henry travelled on the *Maria* as an officer in charge of 150 troops, who were detailed to protect the settlers from attacks by Aborigines, the indigenous people of Australia. He arrived at the Swan River Colony, an uncharted area of Western Australia, and was sent by Sir James Stirling, the first Governor and Commander-in-Chief of Western Australia, to Pinjarra, to form a military post. He established a land route between Pinjarra, the Vasse River settlements, and the Port Leschenault area, 109 miles south of Perth, where the governor intended to form a military post in the Busselton district. In his journal, Henry Bunbury mentioned 'the metallic sands along the beaches near Bunbury and Busselton', the value of which was unappreciated at the time. Today, those heavy mineral sands are used to produce titanium dioxide pigment for paint. He also wrote, 'A township has been formed, or at least laid down on the maps, comprising the southern promontory and part of the north beach at the entrance of Port Leschenault Inlet, which the Governor renamed 'Bunbury' in compliment to me.' In 2015, this was a thriving town, with a population of about 34,000. In November 1837, Henry sailed back to England on the *Hero*, and later served in South Africa, India and the Crimea.

His youngest son, **William St Pierre Bunbury** (1859-1942), was educated at Beaumaris Grammar School. In 1878, he was given a commission in the Royal Field Artillery and, from 1885 until 1888, he served in Australia, where he established the School of Gunnery at Middle Head, Sydney.

Richard Hanmer Bunbury (1813-1857), the youngest son of Sir Henry Edward Bunbury, lost his right hand during the Battle of Navarino in 1826 and retired from the navy in 1837, with the rank of captain. In 1838, he sailed to Australia on the *Argyle*, accompanied by Sarah (his wife, who was eight months pregnant), Robert Sconce (Sarah's brother), Elizabeth (Lizzie) Catherine Sconce (Robert's pregnant wife), a pet monkey, and 10 to 12 tonnes of luggage. They landed at the colony of Port Phillip, in Victoria, after a journey of 110 days, and moved into Forest Hill Cottage, Brunswick Street, New Town, where they set up home with the furniture from their cabin and some items borrowed from Georgiana Huntly McCrae (artist and diarist), who had travelled on the *Argyle* with them.

Richard was appointed Superintendent of Water Police at Williamstown, on Port Philip Bay, and later as Harbour Master. Within two years, Robert and Lizzie had moved out of Brunswick Street and Robert Sconce had been appointed as Anglican Minister of St. Andrews,

Sydney. Richard invested in land, and he and Sarah moved ten miles away to a seven-roomed farmhouse at Darebin Creek, which Richard named as Stanney, a reference to his ancestors. In 1841, he became a magistrate, but he had financial problems and needed to borrow money from his father. He took over the squatting rights of a 38,000-acre cattle station in the Grampians, 160 miles west of Melbourne, and bought 300 cattle with the intention of setting up a dairy farm. He named the homestead on the site, Barton Hall, a sketch of which, drawn by him in 1844, hangs in the National Gallery of Victoria, Melbourne. During her time in Australia, Sarah Bunbury painted pictures to document and share her family's travel and life experiences with her family in England. They had six children, but Richard's health was poor and he died in 1857 at the age of 44. Sarah returned to the UK, where she lived for another 40 years.

The transportation of convicts from the UK to New South Wales ended in 1850, but continued to Western Australia until 1868. In order to colonise Australia with free settlers, especially farmers, the British Government sold crown land in Australia to ex-soldiers and emancipists (ex-convicts), and used the proceeds to fund the Assisted Passages Scheme for migrants from the UK who could not afford the fare. By 1850, 18,700 free settlers had emigrated from the UK to Australia under this scheme, which was administered by the Colonial Land and Emigration Commission until 1876. Preference was given to farm labourers, shepherds and domestic servants. The ships that took these free settlers to Australia returned to the UK, laden with supplies of cotton, wool and wheat.

Samuel Webb, a Great Barton shepherd, was accepted for the Assisted Passages Scheme. He paid £5 for his wife, Charlotte, his five children and himself to sail on the *Humboldt* from Plymouth to Port Jackson, New South Wales, where they arrived in December 1852. Samuel was able to read and write; the two oldest children, aged 12 and 14, could read, but not write; whilst Charlotte and the three younger children could neither read nor write. The family settled in Grafton, New South Wales, where Samuel worked as a gardener, and Charlotte gave birth to three more children. Charlotte died in New South Wales in 1884 and Samuel in 1904 at the age of 92.

By 1869, 162,000 men and women had been transported to Australian penal colonies on 806 ships, and the population of Australia had reached one million. British colonists lived in New South Wales, South Australia, Western Australia, Victoria, Queensland and Tasmania, each of which had its own system of parliament, which reported to the British Government. South Australia, which was the only Australian state to be settled entirely by free settlers, granted restricted suffrage to women in 1861 and universal suffrage in 1895.

Amelia Rolfe emigrated to Queensland. The daughter of the village carpenter in Great Barton, she worked as a servant and then a cook for a bank manager in London, until her marriage to William John Bines, the son of an Ipswich carpenter, on 3 October 1872. Five days later, they travelled on the *Royal Dane*, a passenger ship, to Brisbane, where they landed on 15 January 1873. They set up home 90 miles from Brisbane, at Gympie, where William found employment as an engine driver. After his death in 1917, Amelia was eligible for a means-tested pension, as she had been an Australian resident for over 20 years. Her youngest daughter was a schoolteacher before her marriage to James Devonport Walker, and one of her grandsons became a schoolteacher in Brisbane.

Thomas Shipp Gissing, a miller in Great Barton from 1855 to 1880, emigrated with his wife and family on an unassisted passage from Plymouth to New South Wales, on the *SS Assaye*. They settled in Sydney and, in 1901, his daughter, Catherine, married William Allen Peairs, the son of a wagon maker, from Ohio, USA. After their first four children were born, they left Australia and sailed to America, where five more children were born. They settled in Des Moines, Polk, Iowa, where William owned the Dyola Dye Company. He frequently travelled for his work, and visited China, as well as Quebec, Canada. William died in 1932, at the age of 70, but Catherine lived for another 45 years, and died in Yorba Linda, Orange County, California.

The rest of Catherine's family remained in New South Wales. Her sister, Priscilla, remained single and lived to the age of 91, whilst Martha married George Henry Abbott, an amateur collector of coins, President of the Royal Australian Historical Society, and fellow of the Sydney University Senate.

John Paine (1858-?), the youngest son of Frederick Paine who owned Elms Farm, joined the Merchant Service, qualified as Master in 1884 and served as a lieutenant on *HMS Aurora* in 1891. Under the command of Captain Edward Henry Bayly, *HMS Aurora* took part in the Boxer Rebellion in 1901, a peasant uprising in China, which attempted to drive all foreigners, including Christian missionaries, from China.

In defence of the British Empire

During the nineteenth century, uncertainty of employment in farming made the armed services an attractive option for boys from a rural background, especially where they were from a large family. Britain was at the heart of a huge empire, and education put great emphasis on the importance of patriotism and loyalty to Queen, country and empire.

The Evening Continuation Class Code 1893 included a detailed scheme of instruction on 'The life and duties of the citizen'. It stated that pupils should be taught to know what was best for their country, to place the interests of the country above that of class or party, and be willing to take trouble for every public community to which they belonged from the parish to nation (*BNP*, 10 Oct. 1893). Mary Francis Ames, born Mary Frances Leslie Miller (1853-1929), wrote and illustrated children's books, under the name of Ernest Ames or Mrs Ernest Ames. One of her most well-known books was *An ABC for Baby Patriots* (1899), which contained a rhyme for each letter of the alphabet and began:-

A is the Army, that dies for the Queen; it's the very best army, that ever was seen.
B is for Battles, by which England's name, has forever been covered with glory and fame.
C is for Colonies. Rightly, we boast, that of all the great nations, Great Britain has most.
D is the Daring, we show on the field, which makes every enemy, vanish or yield.
E is our Empire, where the sun never sets; the larger we make it, he bigger it gets.
F is the Flag, which wherever you see, you know that beneath it, you're happy and free.

© *Mrs Ernest Ames, 'An ABC for Baby Patriots', first published 1899, this edition 2010, Old House Books, used by kind permission of Bloomsbury Publishing Plc.*

Three of the sons of Abraham and Fanny Olley (see chapter 3) joined the British Army. Charles Olley was enrolled in the 1st East Suffolk Regiment and, in 1861, was stationed at Otahuhu, New Zealand. Alfred Olley joined the 54th Foot Regiment in 1858 and became a colour sergeant. After his discharge, he married, and, was a Chelsea Pensioner and Barracks Servant in the 26th Brigade Depot, at Normanton in Derby in 1881. John Olley joined the 12th Regiment as a private and served in Australia. He sailed on the *Empress Eugenie* to Melbourne, where he arrived on 3 November 1854. He was stationed in Tasmania and worked as a servant for Major Edward Hungerford Eagar at Anglesea Barracks, Hobart. On 23 May 1860, he married Emmeline Christina Bourne at St Georges' Church, Battery Point, Hobart, and their son, Jeffery John, was born 19 Dec 1861. However, John and Emmeline separated in July 1861, and John slept in a stable at the barracks. In June 1862, he died at the military hospital, after he inhaled carbon monoxide from a portable stove in his room (*Coroner's report, No. 5322, 17th June 1862*). He was only 27-years-old and was described in the report of the inquest, in the *Hobart Mercury*, as a 'quiet steady man'.

John and William Morris came from a family of 12 children. They both joined the 33rd Regiment of Foot, which had fought in 1815, at the Battle of Waterloo, under the command of the Duke of Wellington. During the 1860s, their regiment was on duty in India, but, in 1867, was sent on a mission to Ethiopia to rescue some British citizens who had been taken hostage by the self-appointed Emperor Tewodros II, and were incarcerated in a mountain fortress at Magdala. The attack, led by General Robert

(Cornelius) Dundas Napier (1810-1890) was successful, but resulted in the deaths of hundreds of Ethiopians, and, subsequently, of Emperor Tweodros II, who committed suicide in 1868.

William Bishop, who was also from a large family, joined the 2nd Battalion of the Coldstream Guards, whose origins date back to 1684. He was based at Chelsea, London, during the 1870s, but was on active service in Egypt in 1882, where the Coldstream Guards were part of the force that defeated the Arabi Pasha at Tel el-Kebir.

Several old boys from Great Barton School fought in the Anglo-Boer Wars, in South Africa. William Pettit joined the Royal Fusiliers in 1860, at the age of 17, and became a sergeant in the 2nd Battalion. He served in India and South Africa during his 21 years of service, and, after the First Anglo-Boer War (1880–1881), was awarded the South Africa Medal and clasp, and the Good Conduct Medal. After his discharge in 1881, he became a coachbuilder in Bury St Edmunds (*BFP*, 19 Apr.1919).

Walter Sturgeon joined the 3rd Grenadier Guards and served under Lord Methuen, at the Modder River in South Africa, during the Second Anglo-Boer War (1899-1902). In 1899, Walter wrote a letter to his mother, Eliza, in which he described how he had fought a big battle against the Boers and had won a medal and a bar. He told her that, during the last two days, he had eaten only one biscuit, had very little to drink, and was very dirty (*BNP*, 26 Dec. 1899). On his return to England, he lodged with a dredging bargeman in Enfield, north London, and worked as a storekeeper. In 1909, he married Daisy Annie Reach, from Bury St Edmunds, and moved to Bromley, Kent, where he worked as an orderly surgeon in a Royal Arms Factory.

William Burrell (1866-1949), of Cattishall Farm, a leading member of Great Barton Cricket Club, was posted to the Cape of Good Hope, South Africa, in November 1899, for six months. He was engaged by the War Office as an assistant engineer and attached to the 45th Company Balloon Section and Steam Transport at Aldershot, Hampshire. William's family were farmers and his father was educated at King Edward VI Grammar School, Bury St Edmunds. However, William and three of his siblings, who were deaf from birth, were educated at a school for the deaf in Willesden, Middlesex. Whilst in South Africa, William Burrell caught enteric fever, also known as typhoid, as did many other soldiers, but he survived and returned in 1900 to Great Barton, where he lived at Cattishall Farm with his brother Frank who was one of the original managers of Great Barton School in 1903.

The 3rd Suffolk Regiment fought its first major battle during the Second Anglo-Boer War on 5 January 1900, when it attacked a hill near Colesberg, between Blomfontein and Pretoria, which was renamed Suffolk Hill by the Boers, in recognition of their courage during the assault. 18-

year-old David Long, who was serving with the 4th Norfolk Regiment, was amongst the 30 men who left for South Africa on 11 February 1900 as part of the 2nd Volunteer Battalion from Bury St Edmunds.

One of the most famous incidents of the Second Anglo-Boer War was the victory of the British Army in May 1900, after a seven-month siege of Mafeking, by 5,000 Boers. The success was widely celebrated in the UK, and schools were granted a half-day holiday by the government. The war ended with the Treaty of Vereeniging, signed in May 1902. In Bury St Edmunds, a memorial was unveiled in the town centre on 11 November 1904, which listed the names of 193 Suffolk soldiers who had died during the conflict.

Both sons of the Revd Henry Percy Smith, Vicar of Holy Innocents' Church, Great Barton, were lieutenants in the militia by the age of 20. Herbert served with the Cambridge Militia, and Rennell with the Royal Artillery, where he rose to the rank of major.

These Great Barton men eventually returned to an Edwardian Britain, where Victorian attitudes, including those of loyalty to the British Empire, prevailed for many more decades.

9
A NEW PAIR OF BOOTS AND A SCARLET CLOAK

In 1902, Great Barton School became a state-run, voluntary school, controlled by West Suffolk County Council and managed by a representative board of managers. The Bunbury family continued to own the school premises, but after they moved out of Barton Hall, they gradually reduced their involvement with the school.

During the Edwardian Era (1901-1910), Great Barton was dominated by the colourful figure of Frank Riley Smith [552], the new tenant of Barton Hall, who was a Yorkshire man and joint owner of the John Smith Brewery in Tadcaster, Yorkshire. As Lord of the Manor and village squire, he expected people to touch their forelock when they met him, but was particularly popular with the schoolchildren in 1905, when he gave a new pair of boots to each boy and a scarlet cloak to each girl. Frank Riley's life in Great Barton, where he was 'master of the hounds', is described in *A Life of Riley*, by Frank Holmes.

School reorganisation and funding

In order to mitigate the inefficiencies of the fragmented education system, improve the overall quality of educational provision and increase funding for voluntary schools, the government passed Balfour's Education Act 1902, which established the framework of educational administration until 1944. It unified the school system by abolishing the 2,568 school boards and 14,238 other bodies of school managers, and handing over their power to 328 local education authorities (LEAs). These were under the control of the county and county borough councils, which elected an education committee, which could levy rates. Suffolk County Council governed schools throughout Suffolk, except in Bury St Edmunds and Lowestoft, where those councils opted to have Borough Education Committees.

From 1902, there were two types of elementary schools. 'Provided' or council schools corresponded to the old board schools; 'non-provided' schools included voluntary, denominational and other schools. In most cases, the local Vicar and other church members served as managers at 'non-provided' schools, thus retaining their influence over the education of the pupils at these schools. Denominational schools were guaranteed as much funding for running costs as non-denominational schools, on condition that the LEA oversaw secular education within denominational schools.

In 1902, Great Barton School became a voluntary school, under the new arrangements. The accounts for the financial year 1901 to 1902 show that the grants from the government were insufficient to cover the salaries of the teaching staff, and the school relied on subscriptions to make up the shortfall. *The Return of Voluntary Schools* recorded that it was the only voluntary school in West Suffolk with a loan debt.

Table 8. Annual account for Great Barton School, year ending May 1902

Annual income		*Annual expenditure*	
Annual Government Grant	£143. 0s. 6d.	Salaries	£182. 8s. 8d.
Voluntary Schools Aid Grant	£30. 0s. 0d.	Building repairs	£16.11s. 6d.
Subscriptions	£77. 8s. 6d.	Other expenses	£47. 18s. 0d.
Endowments	none		
Other receipts	£1. 11s. 6d.		
Total	*£252. 0s.6d*		*£246.18s. 2d.*

Source: *The Return of Voluntary Schools (County of West Suffolk, 1902)*

After 1902, LEAs were entirely responsible for the provision of council schools, but only responsible for the maintenance, not the provision, of voluntary schools. Council schools were responsible for keeping the school fabric in good repair, although ordinary wear and tear was funded from the local rates, and they were expected to allow the LEA to make use of the building for educational purposes, free of charge, up to three times a week. Voluntary schools were expected to finance their own building repairs.

The managers of both council and voluntary schools were permitted to appoint their own teachers, subject to the consent of the LEA, who was responsible for the payment of teachers' salaries. The LEA made decisions about the salary and qualifications of teachers, the school curriculum, teaching methods, timetables, textbooks and equipment.

School funding was based on average pupil attendance. Between 1900 and 1909, the Board of Education paid each school 17s. p.a. for each pupil under eight-years-old, and 22s. p.a. for older pupils. The Code of Regulations for Public Elementary Schools in England 1909 reduced the grant to 13s. 4d. p.a. for pupils under five, and 21s. 4d. p.a. for all others.

Of the 20 schools in the Thedwastre Hundred at that time, only those at Beyton and Woolpit became council schools; the remainder chose to be voluntary ones. From 1906, the terms 'British' and 'national' were discontinued in the title of a school, and, in most cases, 'national' was replaced by 'Church of England'.

Secondary education

In 1901, the Fabian Society published a tract entitled *The Education Muddle and the Way Out,* which condemned the lack of educational opportunities for the working class. The Education Act 1902 attempted to extend the academic opportunities for young people from working class backgrounds by allowing LEAs to provide secondary and technical, as well as elementary, education.

At the age of 11, elementary school pupils could either remain in their elementary school until the minimum statutory leaving age of 12, or transfer to a county secondary school, maintained by the LEA, or an endowed grammar school, which received grant-aid from LEAs. From 1905, Great Barton pupils could transfer to West Suffolk County Secondary School (a co-educational school in Northgate Street, Bury St Edmunds) or King Edward VI Grammar School for Boys, which relaxed its entry requirements for pupils who lived outside the town, but expected them to wear a cap and gown, until the Second World War when national clothing restrictions were imposed.

The Education (Administrative Provisions) Act 1907 introduced a scholarship system for secondary education, so that some pupils could attend a secondary school free of charge.

By 1914, there were over 1,000 secondary schools in England and Wales, including 349 schools for girls. The provision of state-run secondary schools was, in theory, a good route for working class children to progress up the educational ladder, but, in reality, the number of pupils who could take advantage of the new opportunities was limited by their family's ability to afford the direct and indirect costs involved. However, George Daine and Robert Evans Jnr, the sons of the head teachers, were both awarded a place at King Edward VI Grammar School, and George Daine won an exhibition, which contributed towards his fees.

Robert Evans continued to run evening classes at Great Barton, but in 1905, they were attended by only six pupils.

The religious question

The Education Muddle and the Way Out (Fabian Society, 1901) stated that, 'What is special about education in this country is that it is thought necessary to give religious instruction (RI) in elementary schools, as part of the national system'. The Education Act 1902 allowed local rates to be used to fund denominational RI in schools, but stated that no pupil or teacher should be required to conform to a particular religious belief. RI lessons were held at the start or end of the day, so that pupils could withdraw from the lessons, in response to a parental request.

In 1906, the Liberal government put forward an Education Bill, which proposed that teachers should be permitted to teach religious instruction in schools whatever their beliefs, religious education tests for head teachers should be abandoned, and children should be able to receive religious instruction from the provider of their parents' choice, outside school hours. The bill was opposed by members of the Conservative Party and the Church of England, who organised a large protest meeting at the Royal Albert Hall in London in 1906. Anglican Bishops circulated letters to be read out in churches and, in March 1907, the Revd John Elwin Eddis (1859-1928), who succeeded the Revd James Hervey as Vicar of Great Barton in 1902, called a meeting at the school to discuss the proposed changes. He said that, 'although he did not want to become involved in political matters, he invited parents to sign a petition objecting to the changes' (*BFP*, 24 Mar. 1907). The bill was passed by the House of Commons, but amended to such an extent by the House of Lords that it was effectively a different bill and was subsequently rejected by the House of Commons.

At the same time, many Nonconformists and others withheld all or some of their rates as a protest against their money being used to fund the teaching of Anglicanism or Roman Catholicism. The protesters were prosecuted and, in most cases, goods to the value of their underpayment were taken from them and sold. By 1906, over 170 members of the National Passive Resistance movement had been imprisoned for refusing to pay their rates.

Map 4. Great Barton in 1904

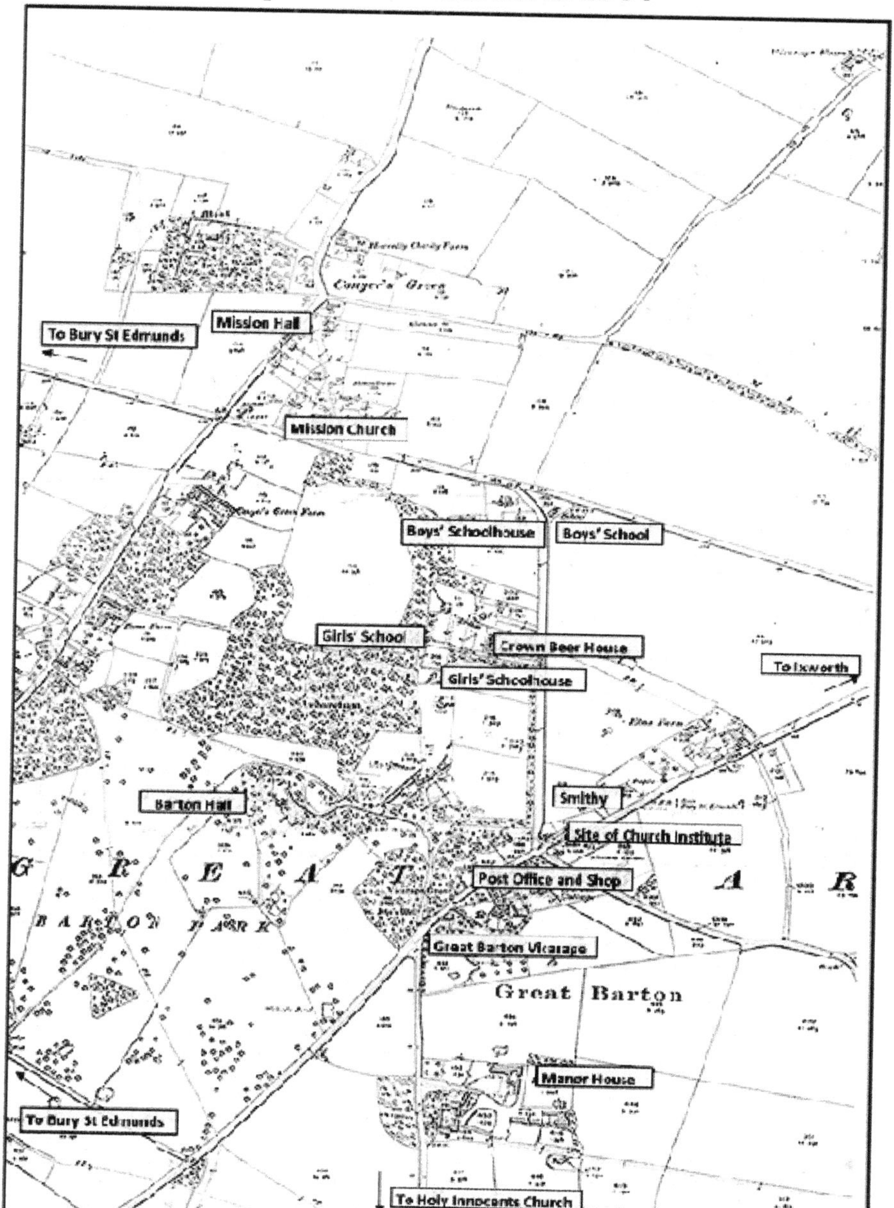

The school managers

On 17 March 1903, Sir Henry Charles Bunbury signed an agreement with William Norman King, Robert Fyson and George Betts which stated that, 'the school should be managed by a Committee consisting of the principal officiating minister for the time being of the parish of Great Barton and three other persons being bona fide members of the Church of England. Vacancies in the number of the said three other persons were to be filled by co-option.'

In 1903, a special meeting of Great Barton parishioners was held to elect the board of school managers of Great Barton Church of England Voluntary School. Frank Baldwin and Frank Riley Smith were appointed in addition to William Norman King, Robert Fyson and George Betts. At the first meeting, held on13 July 1903 at Barton Vicarage, the Revd Eddis was unanimously elected as the correspondent.

In 1907, George Betts was replaced by George Edward Clinton (1840-1908), who was one of the enumerators of the Census of England and Wales 1901, together with James Daine.

George Clinton started his career as the landlord of the Sir Robert Peel Public House in Shoreditch, in the East End of London, joined the army and then worked as an estate agents' clerk, an assistant overseer and a rate collector. He died in 1908, and his widow, Mary Ann, remained in the village and lived at North Lodge with her mother and two youngest daughters, Lilian and Jennie, both of whom became teachers at Great Barton School.

The Qualification of Women (County and Borough Councils) Act 1907 allowed some women to be school managers and, after the death of George Clinton in 1908, Mary Riley Smith replaced him as the county council representative on the Board of Managers. In 1912, she was replaced by Margaret King, a Sunday school teacher and widow of William Norman King, who had previously been a school manager.

The movement for women's suffrage was garnering support in Suffolk as elsewhere. In Bury St Edmunds in 1912, a branch was set up of the National Union of Women's Suffrage Society (NUWSS), known as suffragists, whose national president from 1897 until 1919 was Millicent Fawcett. Her older sister, Dr Elizabeth Garrett Anderson joined the militant Women's Social and Political Union (WSPU), founded in 1903 by Emmeline Pankhurst (1858-1928) and known as suffragettes.

In 1907, there was a by-election in Bury St Edmunds, but the Liberal government refused to make any concessions to the women's suffrage movement. Sylvia Pankhurst (1882-1960), a leading suffragette, campaigned in support of the Conservative candidate, Walter Edward Guinness (1880-1944), a member of the brewing family, who represented Bury St Edmunds as Member of Parliament from 1907 until 1931.

The teachers

In 1901, Robert Evans was the head teacher of the Boys' School, and Emma Daine of the Girls' and Infants' School. Although they were both certificated, Robert Evans received a salary of £80 p.a., plus £5 p.a. allowance, whilst Emma Daine was paid £70 p.a., plus £3. 10s. p.a. allowance. These salaries compared badly with the average salary of a certificated teacher in England and Wales at the time, which was £128 for men and £86 for women.

In 1904, the Equal Pay League was established as a pressure group within the National Union of Teachers (NUT). In 1906, it was renamed as the National Federation of Women Teachers and eventually became the National Union of Women Teachers (NUWT).

In 1902, Jessie Fraser was paid £30 p.a. as an Article 68 teacher. By 1900, there was a restriction on the number of hours that a pupil-teacher could work, so it was sometimes more economical to employ Article 68 teachers, later known as supplementary teachers, whose hours were unlimited. These teachers were required to be over 18-years-old, approved by Her Majesty's Inspectors (HMI) and have passed a medical examination.

In September 1903, James Daine, the previous headmaster, applied for the post of assistant master as a qualified or an Article 68 teacher. The managers resolved that 'provided a certificate is produced to the effect that Mr Daine's presence amongst children be not detrimental to their health, the post of assistant master, at the rate of £40 p.a., is offered to him for a period of three months.'

During this probationary period, they would judge whether James Daine and Robert Evans could work in harmony, and, if so, offer a permanent appointment to James Daine. However, the arrangement was short-lived, so it does not appear to have been a successful arrangement.

In 1903, the Girls' School placed an advertisement in the press for an Article 50 assistant teacher, one who had undertaken training as a pupil-teacher, but was not certificated. However, there were no applicants.

Instead, the school appointed an Article 68 teacher. Elizabeth Edwards, the daughter of James Edwards, the village blacksmith, who was appointed to teach the infant class at a salary of £25 p.a. She was born in the village but, in 1903, lived with her aunt and uncle in Kingston upon Thames, in south-west London, and was employed by her uncle as a picture dealer's assistant. She taught at the school until her marriage in 1904, when she received a silver hot water jug as a leaving present from the teachers and pupils (*BFP*, 13 Aug. 1904). Her husband, William Austin Robinson, was a groom from Kimbolton, Huntingdonshire, and after their marriage, they moved to Windsor, Berkshire.

She was replaced by Lilian Clinton, who was paid an annual salary of £20 until her eighteenth birthday, in March 1905, when it was increased to £25. When Lilian resigned in June 1907, she was replaced by her 17-year-old sister, Jennie, who was paid £30 p.a.

Teacher training improved during this decade. From 1900 onwards, pupil-teachers had to be over 15-years-old, pass a medical examination and be approved by HMI. They were also required to pass a Board of Education examination in reading and recitation, English, history, geography, arithmetic and algebra, in addition to Euclid for boys or needlework for girls. They were not allowed to teach more than five hours a day or 20 hours a week and, at the end of their training, they could sit the Queen's / King's Scholarship Examination for entry into a training college, although fewer than half were accepted in 1900, because there were insufficient places. In 1904, the minimum age was raised to 16 and, from 1905, their contact hours were reduced, and they were given an entitlement of 30 hours approved training in a year, in a Pupil-Teacher Centre where possible.

Herbert Rudling, a 21-year-old pupil-teacher from Norwich, was appointed to the Boys' School in 1903. He was unqualified, but intended to sit for a King's Scholarship Examination, and was offered the post of assistant master at a salary of £40 p.a., on condition that he gained the appropriate qualification and remained at the school for a reasonable period. In 1904, he took the examination twice, but failed both times. The managers agreed that he could continue to teach, subject to the approval of HMI. He eventually passed the exam and remained at the school until he was appointed as a teacher at Mildenhall Elementary School in 1907.

In 1906, the King's Scholarship Examination was replaced by the Preliminary Examinations for the Certificate, which was in two parts. Part I was compulsory and had to be passed before taking Part II, in which English, history and geography were compulsory, with options of three further subjects, chosen from within three groups. Successful candidates were eligible to attend training college. From 1907, the pupil-teacher system was gradually replaced by the bursar system, which gave a grant to aspiring teachers who wished to stay at school until the age of 17 or 18, and then enrol at a teacher training college for two or three years, or become a student teacher at a public elementary school.

Mr A. M. Wright, who replaced Herbert Rudling in June 1907, passed the Preliminary Examination for the Certificate, with a distinction in geography (*BFP*, 19 July 1908). In 1910, he was placed sixth out of 530 candidates in the scripture examination and secured an award of £10 towards his fees and entry to St Peter's Church of England Training College at Saltley, Birmingham, an all-male college with 300 students (*BFP*, 7 May 1910). After the first year, he was placed in the first division with two distinctions (*BFP*, 19 Aug.1911) and, on completion of his training in 1913, was appointed as head teacher of the Diocesan College for Native Teachers in Zululand (*BFP*, 31 May 1913). He was replaced at the Boys' School by Stanley Thompson, and then by Mr W.D. Giles, in 1912.

In 1908, 28-year-old Mary Frost, from Hargrave School, near Bury St Edmunds, was appointed as an uncertificated teacher. She passed the first two parts of the Preliminary Examination for the Certificate, achieved a distinction in history, a first class award in elementary science and theoretical and inorganic chemistry, and a second class award in freehand drawing and model drawing. In December 1909, she was awarded the Board of Education Certificate. She resigned the following year and received a gold bracelet as a leaving gift from staff and pupils of Great Barton School (*BFP*, 2 June 1910). She was appointed to Lavenham Council School and was replaced by Clara Amy Weller, Miss Pinpoint and then Catherine Hogg, who were all unqualified teachers. In April 1912, Winifred Evans, the daughter of the headmaster, was appointed as a teacher.

In 1913, the school logbook recorded that, 'Notice is received from Mrs Daine that her school was now in Grade 3', but revealed no further explanation. The managers reported the fact to the LEA and recommended that Emma Daine should receive an increase in her salary, commensurate with that grade. At the same time, they requested a pay rise for Robert Evans, whose salary was £11 p.a. less than that of other local head teachers.

The number of newly recognised pupil-teachers fell from 11,018 in 1907 to 1,691 in 1914, amongst whom was Archibald Barnett, the son of the schoolmaster at Fornham All Saints School, who was a pupil-teacher at the Boys' School. He passed Part I of the Preliminary Examination for the Certificate in February 1914 and Part II in June (*BFP*, 14 Feb. 1914, 27 June 1914) and was appointed as an assistant teacher at the Boys' School, in July 1914. When war was declared in August 1914, he enlisted in the army.

The pupils

By 1901, three-quarters of the population in the United Kingdom lived in urban areas and rural depopulation was evident in Great Barton, where the population declined steadily from 878 to 645, between 1871 and 1901, although it temporarily increased to 718 in 1911, before decreasing to 666 in 1921. In 1912, the Inspector of Nuisances recorded that there were 43 three-bedroomed houses, no evidence of overcrowding and several empty houses in the village (*BFP*, 19 Oct.1912).

The families of most of the children who attended Great Barton School were mainly employed in agriculture as horse keepers, stockmen, cattlemen, stationary engine drivers or gardeners, or as rural artisans, shop workers or publicans. Many worked directly or indirectly for the Bunbury Estate, which owned nine farms, the smithy and wheelwright's workshop, the laundry, both public houses and the village shop.

Table 9. Working class children in Great Barton recorded as scholars in the Census of England and Wales, 1901

Great Barton Schools -1901	Aged 3 to 7	Aged 8 to 11	Aged 12 and over	TOTAL
Boys	20	24	11	55
Girls	15	22	10	47
Total	35	44	21	102

Source: *Census of England and Wales 1901*

The figures for the Boys' School and Girls' School differ from those returned by the school for the *Return of Voluntary Schools*, which were published the following year.

Table 10. Capacity, pupil roll and attendance of Great Barton School, 1902

Great Barton Schools -1902	Boys' School	Girls' School	Infants' School	TOTAL
School capacity	55	48	36	139
School roll	35	42	37	114
Average attendance 1901-01	32	36	27	95

Source: *The Return of Voluntary Schools (County of West Suffolk, 1902)*

In 1908, the Board of Education reassessed the school capacity, and the Code of Regulations for Public Elementary Schools in England 1909 recommended that the maximum class size should be reduced from 80 to 60 pupils.

Table 11. Capacity, attendance and accommodation of Great Barton School, 1908

Great Barton Schools -1908	Boys' School	Girls' School	Infants' School	TOTAL
School capacity	88	52	47	187
Average attendance 1907-08	48	52	32	132
Revised accommodation	72	47	40	159

Source: *Board of Education. Reassessment of Accommodation (Memo. to Inspectors, E. No. 8)*

Two pupils at Great Barton School died in 1905 and their teacher and classmates were involved in their funeral arrangements. Dorothy Evans played the organ at the funeral of 11-year-old Ethel Fuller [473], where Ethel's friends threw spring flowers on her grave (*BFP*, 1 Apr. 1905). Ernest Chaplin [481] died from bronchitis at the age of four. His coffin was carried by four schoolboys and other children laid flowers and wreaths on his grave *(BFP*, 21 Oct. 1905).

In 1893, a deputation of working men raised the subject of a grant for school meals with Arthur Herbert Dyke Acland, the Minister for Education, from 1892 to 1895, but he saw it as an issue that should be dealt with by a London municipality (*BNP*, 14 Feb. 1893). However, the Liberal government of 1905 to 1915, which was keen to improve the well-being of children, took up the issue and, in recognition that hungry children cannot learn properly, passed the Education (Provision of Meals) Act 1906, which allowed LEAs to provide meals for necessitous children at lunchtime. The LEA would be required to provide land, buildings and apparatus for the Canteen Committee and levy a charge on parents for the meal. To subsidise those parents who were unable to afford to pay for the meals, the LEA was empowered to levy a rate not exceeding a halfpenny in the £1.

Many authorities were slow to respond to this legislation, and Great Barton School did not provide lunches until 1944. Until then, pupils had to walk to and from home at lunchtime. Unfortunately, not all children were provided with a lunch when they arrived home, and one ex-pupil reported that he 'often just ate raw turnips', which he dug from the fields.

In the early 1900s, the Army Medical Corps discovered that about half of the men who applied to the armed forces were not physically fit enough to fight.

The government passed several reforms, which included the Education (Administrative Provisions) Act 1907 which required LEAs to provide medical inspections for all pupils as soon as possible after they started school, and arrangements to be made for children during school holidays. The problem of poor health persisted throughout the next decade, when nearly 40 per cent of volunteers were rejected by the armed services during the First World War on medical grounds.

The school curriculum

In 1905, the Board of Education issued the *Handbook of Suggestions for Teachers in Elementary Schools*, which encouraged 'innovation and experimentation by teachers'.

'The only uniformity of practice which the Board of Education desires to see in public elementary schools is that each teacher shall think for himself, and work out for himself such methods of teaching as may use his powers to the best advantage and be best suited to the particular needs and conditions of the school. Uniformity on details of practice (except in the mere routine of school management) is not desirable, even if it were attainable.'

In 1905, five of the recently appointed women HMIs conducted an inquiry about infant education. Their report, published in 1905, concluded that children aged between three and five did not benefit from school instruction, and that the mechanical teaching in most schools dulled their imagination and weakened their powers of independent observation.

The Code of Regulations for Public Elementary Schools in England 1909 recommended an end to the system of pupil-monitors in public elementary schools, greater responsibility of the head teacher for general control and supervision of instruction, and a new school curriculum, which directed that:

- younger infants should learn games, singing, and breathing exercises, rather than set drill, together with language development;
- older infants should learn to draw, read and write, acquire elementary knowledge of number, practise suitable songs, sing simple musical intervals, and learn sewing and knitting, with care taken to avoid fine work and injury to eyesight;
- scholars, over the age of eight, should learn English language, handwriting, arithmetic, drawing, observation, nature study, history, citizenship, singing, hygiene, physical training including swimming and geography including knowledge of the British Isles and the British Dominions beyond the sea;
- all girls should learn domestic subjects, including the proper performance of ordinary domestic duties, needlework and knitting;
- older girls should learn cookery, laundry work and housewifery.
- all pupils should receive moral instruction, directed to the inculcation of courage, truthfulness, cleanliness of mind, body and speech; the love of fair-play; consideration and respect for others; gentleness to the weaker; kindness to animals; love of one's country and an appreciation of beauty and nature in art.

The government encouraged schools to play organised games to foster team spirit. Poems like *Vitaï Lampada* by Sir Henry Newbolt, written in 1897, urged pupils to 'Play up! Play up! And play the game!'

Both the vicar and Sir Henry Bunbury played cricket for Great Barton Cricket Club, and schoolboys played for the church choir, Barton Juniors,

East Barton Boys and West Barton Boys. The school purchased a football in 1908. Pupils may have been inspired to take up more sport after the 1908 Summer Olympics, which were held in London, instead of Rome, after Mount Vesuvius erupted.

Rewards

At the end of each school year, one of the school managers awarded prizes of books to the pupils for successes in gardening, arithmetic, needlework, nature study, writing and general good work. At the annual Christmas party, teachers presented prizes to the schoolchildren for drawing and other achievements. Each year, pupils won prizes of money in the annual hand writing competition.

In 1912, every child in the country received a special cake to celebrate the hundredth anniversary of Charles Dickens' birth on 7 February 1812.

Suffolk County Council awarded quarterly good attendance certificates, which were presented to pupils by one of the school managers. This Certificate of Merit was set against a background, which included a picture of King Alfred at study, various family shields and significant dates in British history. The selected dates were those of the accession of various monarchs, which reflected the importance of the teaching about kings and queens at the time - 1066

Certificate of Merit awarded for Regular Attendance during school quarter ending 30 November 1904

(William I), 1154 (Henry II), 1413 (Henry V), 1603 (James I), 1689 (William III), 1714 (George I) and 1837 (Queen Victoria).

In 1908, attendance at the school reached over 96 per cent and the Revd Taylor presented medals to those pupils with the best attendance, who included Robert Evans Jnr who lived opposite the school and Arthur Long who lived over two miles away.

At the end of each school year, the vicar spoke to the boys who were leaving school. In 1908, he commented that farm work was a healthy life and advised them that:

'there is a big difference between sport and cruelty and told them they should be 'good sports' when after rabbits and give them a fair chance, rather than cornering them... the worst sport is letting pigeons out of a trap and shooting them, adding that 'shooting wild pigeons is true sport' (*BFP*, 15 Aug. 1908).

In 1909, Robert Evans reported that he was pleased with the end of year results and that, for the first time, boys stayed on at school and developed not only their minds, but also their bodies (*BFP*, 28 Aug. 1909).

School discipline

Schools had been required to keep a record of punishments since the 1870s, but from the early 1900s, the LEA provided punishment books to record details of offences, as well as punishments. Two of these books survived for Great Barton School from 1907, but were lost during the 1990s.

During his time at the school, Robert Evans recorded his use of the cane on 48 occasions, and he caned several boys on more than one occasion. The first entry in the book records that three cuts on the back of a ten-year-old were given for marking his book with ink, and subsequent entries record one or two cuts on pupils' buttocks, back or shoulders. About a quarter of the boys were caned for being late, very late, habitually late or incorrigibly late. Other 'crimes' included throwing stones, bullying, biting a boy's arm, producing an indecent drawing, taking pheasants' eggs and interfering with nests, taking food from dinner bags, getting boots dirty and retaining a found knife. Two boys were caned for breaking the gates by rough usage, wilfully damaging school property during the lunch hour, and interfering with a boy on a whip horse. Respect for girls was expected, and insulting a girl, or 'interfering with a girl after repeated warning', was punished with two cuts on the back. Only one boy was caned for producing careless work.

In February 1915, Robert Evans made this comment about a nine-year-old boy:

'Disobedience. This boy has always been allowed to do as he likes by his parents. If he is reproved, he simply yells for all he is worth. I had a screamer today.'

Alternative punishments were also used. A pupil who left Great Barton School in 1913 revealed that, on one occasion, he had had to stand in the corner of the classroom for an hour with a pile of slates on his head. When they fell on the floor and broke, he was punished again.

In 1909, George Carter, Archibald Lingwood and John Phillips, who were all aged 12, were charged with stealing two rat traps, valued at 1s. 6d. from Edward Coe, a labourer. PC Warner, the village policeman, said that, on information received, he visited the Boys' School to ask these boys whether they had been on Ixworth Heath on 7 January. At first, they denied it, but then admitted they were on their way from Ixworth to

Livermere, and they eventually brought the traps into school from home. Since it was a first offence, they were released, subject to the costs being paid. Archibald's father appeared in court to speak on behalf of the boys and promised the bench that he would 'give his lad some good advice and a sound thrashing' (*BFP*, 30 Jan. 1909). It is pleasing to note that, at the end of the school year, Archibald Lingwood was awarded a geography prize by Suffolk County Council.

In 1913, Frank Baldwin, one of the school managers, reported the theft of 'half a peck of blue peas' valued at 1s. 6d., which had been stolen from a drill, which he had left in his field overnight. Small footprints were seen near the drill, so PC Arthur Manning, the village policeman, spoke to the boys at the school to discover the culprit. Two boys admitted the theft and were placed on probation for six months (*BFP*, 14 June 1913).

School inspections

His Majesty's Inspectors (HMI) observed day to day routines in the schoolroom and the playground, listened to the instruction given by teachers, and inspected the timetable and schemes of work. In 1904, both schools received a favourable HMI report (*BFP*, 4 July 1902).

In 1905, the HMI report commented on a drop in pupil numbers but praised the headmaster for 'working with undiminished energy and success' (*BFP*, 22 Apr. 1905).

In 1906, HMI wrote that, 'the schools deserved their usual excellent report' (*BFP*, 24 Apr. 1906).

A more rigorous inspection system was introduced in 1909, which required inspectors to question pupils and give them exercises to complete, to enable a 'fair judgement of the intelligence, alertness and responsiveness of the pupils, their interest in their studies and power of applying their knowledge and the thoroughness, carefulness and accuracy of their work'.

On 22 and 25 May 1914, the school was inspected by F.W. Thompson, an HMI, who submitted the following observations to the Board of Education on 6 June 1914:

- Boys' Dept. The effect of the teaching has been to make the boys alert and interested. The upper class deal intelligently with problems in arithmetic and are appreciative of their reading about which they talk readily. They have retained a good amount of information about the geography they have learnt. Observation out of doors is especially encouraged. Their physical exercises do not reach as good a standard as most of their other work.
- Girls' Dept. The teaching is thorough. Satisfactory work is being done. The arithmetic of the first class is good; the working of the examples is set down clearly. Lessons are well prepared and the girls keep careful notes. The elder girls need desks better suited to them.

Diocesan Inspectors also visited the school. In 1902, he judged both schools to be 'very satisfactory', but commented that, at the Boys' School, 'the offices [toilets] are too near the school and should be removed at a greater distance' (*BFP*, 4 July 1902). In 1904, HMI made recommendations about the need for small windows near the ceiling and a drainage system in the school playground.

In March 1913, the Revd A. Donald Perrott inspected the Girls' School and wrote the following:

- Written work. Standards VI and VII - Each pupil wrote two abstracts from Old and New Testament. The work was excellent.
  Standard IV - Creed, Lord's Prayer, Commandments were excellent. Did not find any mistakes all.
  Standards I to III – Lord's Prayer and Commandments. Very promising work.
- *Viva Voce*. Infants. Very bright class.
  The elder children answered all their questions splendidly, and the younger ones showed they had made a beginning. The amount of work taken was very large. I would suggest the learning of very simple home prayers.
  Girls. Excellent work in all subjects, and it was intelligently understood. The complete syllabus was not quite covered this year, owing to special circumstances. The tone and reverence the children made the inspection a very gratifying one.

There are no further details of these 'special circumstances' but the following year, the same Diocesan Inspector was so satisfied that he granted the children a half-day holiday (*BFP*, 14 Mar. 1914).

The school premises
The Bunbury family owned all of the school buildings. The Boys' School was located at the end of School Road and consisted of a single room, within which two teachers taught two groups of pupils. A toilet block was located in the playground, away from the school building. The Girls' School, situated a quarter of a mile away at the end of School Lane, was an L-shaped building, within which there were two classrooms, set at right angles to each other with a common entrance hall. There was a small shed attached to the rear of the girls' schoolroom and a toilet block at one end of the playground, away from the school building.

On 17 March 1903, Sir Henry Charles Bunbury leased the school premises to the school managers at a peppercorn annual rent, terminable at 12 months' notice. The schoolhouses were let to West Suffolk Education Committee on a yearly Michaelmas tenancy, determinable on six months' notice, and sublet to the head teachers. In 1905, both head teachers complained to the school managers that £3 had been deducted from their salaries towards the cost of internal repairs to their houses. The managers agreed to refund the money. In 1908, Robert Evans requested that the floor of the scullery be re-laid at his house.

Sir Henry Charles Bunbury and the managers were responsible for carrying out building repairs of the schools and the schoolhouses. In 1904, the managers agreed to set up a Managers' Fund to pay for building repairs and the affiliation fee of two guineas per annum to the Sudbury Voluntary School Association. They sought subscriptions for a building repair fund and received contributions from Frank Riley Smith (£5), Sir Henry Bunbury (£2) and William Norman King (£1) by November 1904. In April 1906, the fund stood at £4. 16s.10d. but was in deficit by November 1906.

The classrooms were heated by stoves, but these were inefficient and the pupils were often cold. In March 1904, Frank Riley Smith paid for a new stove for the infants' classroom out of his own pocket, and arranged for cocoa and soup to be provided for the schoolchildren, on alternate days, during a period of very cold weather (*BFP*, 2 Mar. 1904).

During the night on November 1907, there was a break-in at the Girls' School. The following morning, Ellen Louisa Phillips, the school cleaner and caretaker, found a broken window and damaged clock but although the schoolmistress's desk had been forced open, no money had been stolen from either a box in the desk or the mission box on the shelf. The only missing items were a duster and a reading book, valued at 1s. 4d. Enquiries were made by PC Manning, who interviewed Albert Edward Patrick Barker Soanes [who sounds as if had stolen a few names], at Morley's Lodging House in Bury St Edmunds. He admitted the charge of entering and stealing, and appeared before Thingoe Magistrates at Ixworth, where Emma Daine and Ellen Phillips gave evidence. Albert Soanes said that he had nowhere to sleep and could not afford lodgings, so had broken into the school. Since it was dark, he had taken the clock off the wall to see the time, but it had landed on his head and had broken. He was committed for trial and granted bail of £5 with a surety of £5 (*BFP*, 17 Dec. 1907). The *Bury Free Press* did not report the name of the reading book or the eventual outcome of the trial.

Ellen Phillips left soon afterwards, but continued to live in the village until her death in 1921 (*BFP*, 17 Dec. 1921). She was replaced as cleaner and caretaker by Mrs Sturgeon, who was dismissed in November 1908, after a dispute with the managers and replaced by Mrs Calver from 1 July 1909.

In January 1909, the girls' schoolroom at the Girls' School still contained the infant's gallery (a raised area of the room), in spite of the fact that the infants had been taught in a separate classroom for 10 years. The minutes of the managers' meetings recorded that, 'the Chairman was asked to look into the request for desks to replace the gallery'. The request was repeated in June. In 1914, the LEA purchased new furniture for the schools, which included 12 double desks for the Girls' School.

In 1909, the school managers proposed that part of the playground, measuring 17 yards by 14 yards, should be converted into school garden plots. However, the land did not meet the requirements of the LEA so an alternative piece of land was rented from Sir Henry Charles Bunbury at an annual rent of 5s. Daniel Pawsey, who was already employed under the West Suffolk Education Committee scheme, continued to give practical gardening instruction to the boys.

In 1910, in response to another HMI report on the school, new windows were fitted in the west wall of the girls' classroom. In 1913, the playgrounds, which were poorly drained, were covered with new gravel.

Use of the schoolrooms outside school hours

Until 1905, the schoolrooms were regularly used by Great Barton Sunday School and other church-related activities.

On New Years' Eve, 1900, the Boys' School was used for a Cinematograph Exhibition, organised by the Rev. Hervey, during which the audience watched '*The Cinderella Pantomime*' and '*The Street Procession of Barnham's Great Show*' (*BFP*, 5 Jan. 1901). In January 1901, Frank Burrell arranged a concert at the Boys' School in aid of church funds, which included performances by himself, his family, and Robert Evans, together with other villagers (*BFP*, 12 Jan. 1901).

Emma Daine and Edith Evans both served on the committee of the Missionary Society, formed in 1901, which held meetings and a meal at the Girls' School. In April 1901, members walked to the Boys' School after the meal to listen to various songs performed by Miss Phillips and Robert Evans, and hear a talk about life in Madagascar (*BFP*, 20 April 1901).

No general elections were held between 1910 and 1918, but, in 1913, the North West Suffolk Conservative and Unionist Association held a meeting at the Boys' School, presided over by Sir John Reid Smiley (*BFP*, 13 Dec. 1913).

The Church Institute

In 1903, after a harvest tea in the coach house at Barton Hall, the Revd John Eddis proposed the idea of building a Church Institute in the village. The idea was enthusiastically supported by Frank Riley Smith, who offered to chair a fundraising committee, and the Bunbury family offered a suitable site at the southern end of School Road, next door to the Smithy for a nominal rent. George Betts drew the plans, and Mr W.R. Green prepared the legal documents and a lease.

It was estimated that the hall would cost £200 to build. In 1903, Frank Riley Smith invited local 'county' families to a fund-raising concert in the library at Barton Hall, which included a piano solo, sketches, songs, recitations, card tricks, amusing stories and whistling solos by both Mr and Mrs Charles Capper, who were popular performers of the day. This was followed by a tea and a sale of handmade goods. A similar concert for the villagers was held at the Boys' School in the evening.

By 1904, £140 had been raised, so an opening event was arranged during which Lady Bunbury laid the foundation stone and the band of E and F Companies of the 2nd Volunteer Battalion of the Suffolk Regiment played music. After a short service of dedication, there was a fund-raising fête, which raised £30. Villagers danced on the Vicarage lawn, and the children played sports.

By 1905, the fund had reached £186. 6s. and, in order to raise the remainder, two concerts were arranged, which raised a further £10. In the second one, entitled *The Sleeping Children of Mrs Bountiful*, Mary Riley Smith played Mrs Bountiful, and the children acted the parts of the babes.

On 5 October 1905, the Church Institute was officially opened by the Revd Hodges, Archdeacon of the Sudbury Diocese, and up to 300 villagers and guests sat down to eat tea in the new building. From this time onwards, the focus of village activities moved away from the schools, and the Church Institute was used by Great Barton Sunday School, Bible and catechism classes, the Communicant's Guild, the Mother's Union, Barton Cricket Club, a Working Men's Club and a Bowls Club, and as the venue for village concerts and whist drives.

In 1908, a farewell tea was held in the Church Institute for the Revd John Eddis, who was moving to the Isle of Wight, and the local paper reported that the boys from the school sang 'Ten Little Nigger Boys'.

His replacement was the Revd Taylor, who graduated from Gonville and Cais College Cambridge in 1897, was ordained as a priest and became curate at Lavenham Church and a priest in the parish of St James in Bury St Edmunds. He was editor of the *Diocesan Calendar* and travelled extensively on the continent and in the Middle East. He was a manager of the West Suffolk General Hospital and a farmer at Lavenham, where he was an expert in the culture of wheat, sugar beet and roses. Whilst at Great Barton, he created a bowling green in the garden of the Vicarage, installed a new treble bell, and commissioned a wooden font cover, carved by Alfred Pollintine, an ecclesiastical carver, who was one of the first pupils to attend Great Barton School.

In November 1911, the parish library, located in a large cupboard in the Church Institute, was officially opened by the Revd Taylor. Winifred Evans was appointed as the librarian and books were donated by Frank Riley Smith, the Revd James Hervey, Revd John Eddis and Mr Paget and catalogued by Emma Daine. The library was open to parishioners every Tuesday at 3.30 p.m. for one hour (*BFP*, 18 Nov. 1911).

During the same year, a village concert was held at the Institute, which included some 'waxworks' by pupils, including the children of Robert Evans (*BFP*, 2 Dec. 1911). In 1913, Emma Daine organised a 'long-night' dance for villagers in the Church Institute (*BFP*, 25 Jan. 1913).

Coronations and pageants

Between 1901 and 1914, the village celebrated two coronations and participated in a huge pageant.

The first Empire Day was observed on 24 May 1902, Queen Victoria's birthday, although it was not widely celebrated until the end of the following decade.

On 25 May 1902, Great Barton Parish Council met in the Boys' School to consider how the village should celebrate the coronation of King Edward VII. It was proposed that a committee be formed, with representatives 'from every class of person in the parish'. Frank Riley Smith was elected as chair and George Clinton as secretary, together with a committee, composed of Robert Evans, and eleven other men, including four of the school managers. A subscription list was opened and, by the end of the meeting, £40 had been donated, which included a donation of £25 from Frank Riley Smith.

The coronation, originally scheduled for 26 June, was postponed until 9 August, because King Edward VII needed an emergency appendectomy. In Great Barton, the village celebrations were held on 5 August 1902. They began with a church service at 2.30 p.m., followed by a peal of bells. Then the villagers walked to Barton Hall, where Mr C.H. Taylor, of the Golden Fleece Public House, served tea for 150 ladies and children, and a meat tea and beer to several hundred men and boys, inside a huge marquee on the lawn. Invalids, who were unable to attend the meal, received 2s. After tea, the band of the 2nd Volunteer Battalion of the Suffolk Regiment played the British National Anthem, and children participated in sports. At the end of the party, they were given nuts, sweets and chocolates, and a commemorative medal, donated by Frank Riley Smith. The finale of the evening was a firework display (*BFP*, 31 May 1902).

In 1906, Bury St Edmunds celebrated the 300th anniversary of its Town Charter. The Bury St Edmunds Pageant, written by Louis Napoleon Parker, Master of the Pageant, was held in the Abbey Gardens the following year, during the second week of July. It depicted seven events from the history of Bury St Edmunds, from the time of Queen Boudicca to Queen Elizabeth, including the beheading of St Edmund. Everything in the pageant was made locally, and 1,800 local residents were involved. Mary Riley Smith designed and made some of the costumes, and her husband, Frank, loaned several of his horses and acted the part of Charles Brandon, Duke of Suffolk. The performances were accompanied by a choir of 200 singers, and music was played by the 1st Battalion of the Suffolk Regiment and local musicians, directed by Mr Shann, the organist of St James' Church. The pageant made a profit of about £750.

In January 1911, a committee was set up to organise a village event to celebrate the coronation of King George V (1865-1936) and Queen Mary. Frank Riley Smith was elected as chairman and Robert Paul Fyson, of Manor Farm, as treasurer. The celebrations, held on 27 June, were attended by Sir Henry and Lady Laura Bunbury and one of their daughters, but not the Riley Smiths, who were at Tadcaster at the funeral of Frank's brother, Henry. The celebrations began with two church services, after which 160 children, waving flags and carrying banners, accompanied by their teachers and a band, walked to Manor Farm, where tables on the lawns were decorated with bunting and flags and laid out with food. After tea, everyone walked to Barton Hall, where sports' activities were arranged by Mr Clarke, and prizes presented to the winners by Lady Laura Bunbury. Each child was given a commemorative mug and medal, donated by Frank and Mary Riley Smith, and the day ended with a Punch and Judy show and a grand firework display by Sullings of Ipswich (*BFP*, 1 July 1911).

Great Barton Sunday schools

Emma Daine was the superintendent of Great Barton Sunday School. On Holy Innocents' Day, the children attended a special service at the church and then walked to the Girls' School for a meal, and the Boys' School to receive prizes and be entertained by a magic lantern picture show (*BFP*, 05 Jan. 1901).

In November 1907, nearly 160 children from the Sunday school met at the Church Institute for tea and cake followed by a talk on Rangoon, Burma, by Bishop Knight, a friend of the vicar (*BFP*, 16 Nov. 1907).

In July 1908, 180 children gathered at the Church Institute for a summer party and walked to the Vicarage with Margaret King, the superintendent of the Sunday school, to play games in the field. The winners were allowed to choose their own prizes from 'a collection of useful items' (*BFP*, 18 July 1908). In October 1908, there was a Children's Flower Service at Holy Innocents' Church, after which the flowers were sent to West Suffolk General Hospital (*BFP*, 03 Oct. 1908).

In August 1909, a party for the children from Great Barton Sunday School was held at the Vicarage. The children ate tea, played sports and cricket on the meadows, and received prizes (*BF*P, 28 Aug. 1909).

In 1910, a Christmas party was organised for the children from the Bible and catechism class in the Church Institute. After tea, the children gathered around a Christmas tree and received presents and prizes, and mothers were given cakes to take home to youngsters who had been unable to attend the party (*BFP*, 31 Dec. 1910).

In 1913, the Revd Taylor and his wife organised a Children's Festival for the 130 children of the Sunday school (*BFP*, 04 Jan. 1913).

A summer party was held for the children from the Baptist Sunday School on a meadow on the Rougham Estate, owned by George Agnew (*BFP*, 12 July 1913).

Christmas parties for the schoolchildren

In 1902 and 1903, the schoolchildren met at the schools and walked to Barton Hall with their teachers, where they ate tea in the servant's hall and sang for their hosts. Afterwards, they sat around a huge decorated Christmas tree in the Coach House and the children received presents of work baskets, boxes of carpenters tools, knives, paint boxes, drawing slates, and pretty toys, whilst the teachers were given what the local paper described as 'useful presents' (*BFP*, 27 Dec. 1902).

In 1904, 130 pupils were given buns and milk at school and then taken to the Church Institute, where a huge Christmas tree was loaded with presents, including gifts and clothes for the children, donated by Mary and Frank Riley Smith (*BFP*, 24 Dec. 1904).

In December 1905, Frank Riley Smith presented each boy at the school with a new pair of boots, and each girl with a scarlet hooded cloak (*BFP*, 12 Dec. 1905).

In January 1908, 200 children attended a service at Holy Innocents' Church and then a Christmas party at the Church Institute, organised by the Revd Taylor and the teachers. After the meal, they pulled Christmas crackers and received prizes. Then Father Christmas [Robert Evans] handed out 'suitable gifts', donated by the vicar, which were draped over a brilliantly lit Christmas tree, decorated by Emma Daine (*BFP*, 7 Jan. 1908).

In 1911, the children took home 'especially made boots' after a Christmas service at the parish church (*BFP*, Dec. 1911).

At Christmas 1911, the children took home boots, and the adults took home two rabbits and a prime cut of beef after the church service. Widows received money from the Poor's Firing Farm Charity (*BFP*, 2 Dec. 1911).

In December 1913, each child was given an orange on the last day of term. A Christmas party was held at the Girls' School with a Christmas tree laden with presents, donated by William Norman King, one of the school managers.

Each child was given an apple and orange, a cracker and a bag of sweets, which may have included Jelly Babies, a chocolate bar, peanut brittle or liquorice allsorts that were all popular sweets of the day. Some children were invited to the annual 'horkey' [harvest supper], arranged by William Norman King for the workers on his farm and their families.

Boys' clothes

There was no school uniform. The photograph of pupils from the Boys' School in 1913 shows them wearing a hat, jacket, wide collared shirt, long or short trousers, heavy boots and extra-long socks. Some boys wore a tie and a waistcoat, even when they were working in the school gardens

Great Barton Boys' School 1913

Barton Hall – 1901 to 1914

Frank Riley Smith (1866-1912)

After the death of his brother in 1911, Frank Riley Smith decided to leave Barton Hall and move back to Tadcaster in Yorkshire. However, he was still living at Great Barton when he died from cancer in March 1912.

His impressive funeral at Holy Innocents' Church was attended by hundreds of people, including the village schoolchildren. The cortege was led by a large horse-drawn carriage, which was draped in purple and decorated with floral tributes. The procession walked three quarters of a mile from Barton Hall to Holy Innocents' Church, where the service was conducted by the Revd John Eddis, who returned from the Isle of Wight especially for this occasion.

There were 150 floral tributes, including two from the schoolchildren. The one from the Boys' School read, 'a spontaneous offering from the Great Barton schoolboys and teachers, with love, for their friend'. The other from the Girls' School simply read, 'from the scholars of Great Barton Girls' and Infants' School.'

In December 1912, there was a pilgrimage by villagers to his grave, where ex-employees and schoolchildren laid wreaths. In the church today, there is a marble tablet, dedicated to his memory, on the south wall of the Church and a stained glass window, which was donated by members of the Suffolk Hunt.

After his death, his widow married George Cochrane, and moved to Athelhampton in Dorset, where she died in 1932, at the age of 67.

Sir John Reid Smiley (1876-1930)

In 1912, Barton Hall was leased to Sir John Reid Smiley, who was living at Saxham Hall, near Bury St Edmunds, and was from a wealthy Ulster-Scot family, who owned a stately home in Larne, County Antrim, Ireland.

His mother, Elizabeth Kerr of Gallowhill, Paisley, Scotland, was heiress to a fortune from the manufacture of sewing thread.

His father, Sir Hugh Houston Smiley, an iron manufacturer, was created a baronet in 1903, at which time he was a Justice of the Peace for Renfrewshire, Scotland, and County Antrim, Ireland, as well as a deputy lieutenant and the main owner of the *Northern Whig* newspaper, based at Belfast in Northern Ireland.

Sir John Smiley, the oldest son, had a distinguished military career. He fought in South Africa in the Second Anglo-Boer War as a lieutenant in the Sixth Dragoon Guards (Carabineers) and then as a captain in the North of Ireland Yeomanry.

In 1903, he married Valerie Champion de Crespigny, the youngest daughter of Sir Claude Champion de Crespigny, a baronet, jockey, balloonist, sportsman and adventurer. In 1906, Sir John stood for the parliamentary seat of Belfast West as a candidate for the Liberal Unionist Party, which had held the seat since 1892. However, Joseph Devlin, the Irish Parliamentary Party candidate, beat him by 16 votes. Sir John moved to England, where he remained living, even after he inherited the baronetcy in Ireland.

Changes

During the Edwardian period, the village of Great Barton and its schools had undergone many significant changes, but events during the following decade totally transformed the village and the school.

10

YOUR COUNTRY NEEDS YOU

In August 1914, there were just over 730,000 soldiers in the British Army, half of whom were serving overseas, policing the British Empire. Professional soldiers enlisted for 12 years, seven of which were spent in full-time service with the British Army, followed by five years in the Army Reserve. In addition, there were part-time members of the Special Reserve, introduced in 1908 to train a pool of army reservists, who could enlist for six years and renew for a further four years until the age of 40 if they chose to do so. Training began with full-time preliminary training for six months, during which time a reservist was paid the same as a regular soldier, after which he was expected to undertake three to four weeks of training each year.

About 145 men from Great Barton, including 120 'old boys' of Great Barton School, enlisted in the armed forces during the First World War, many of whom served with the Suffolk Regiment.

Great Barton service men and preparations for war

At the outbreak of the First World War, the Suffolk Regiment had two active battalions in the regular army: one at home and one elsewhere in the British Empire. In addition, the West Suffolk Militia, set up in 1759, had been designated as the 3rd Battalion of the Suffolk Regiment since 1881.

Percy Eastlea was serving with the 1st Battalion of the Suffolk Regiment at the Mustafa Pasha Barracks in Alexandria, Egypt, and was on garrison duty in Khartoum, Sudan, in August 1914. His brother, Harry, was serving with the 2nd Battalion of the 1st Cavalry Brigade of the 19th Hussars, which had spent time in India.

Russell Mortlock was serving with the 1st Battalion of the Lancashire Fusiliers in the British Indian region of Punjab. Robert Frost enlisted in the Royal Regiment of Artillery in 1903 and, by 1914, was a corporal in the 4th Dragoon Guards at the Shrapnel Barracks at Woolwich, Kent, a veterinary hospital and stable for army horses. Charles Prentice was serving in Potchefstroom in the Transvaal, South Africa, with the Household Cavalry, with the 3rd (King's Own) Hussars, which he joined in 1906, with William Frost and Edward Hunt.

In 1902, Robert Bishop joined the Royal Hussars and Royal Field Artillery for 12 years. His brother, Walter Bishop, who was also a soldier, drowned in Malta in 1908, at the age of 19, in a tragic accident. Whilst attending the funeral of another soldier, Walter disembarked from a tug into a smaller boat, which then capsized when it was caught on the tug's propeller.

Stephen Phillips, a farm labourer, signed up for the Special Reserve in 1912, at the age of 17. Two years later, he enrolled in the Royal Army Medical Corps for three years and the Army Reserves for nine years.

There had been some form of home defence in West Suffolk since 1859. In 1864, William Norman King, a leading member of the parish, had permitted the Volunteer Rifle Corps to set up camp and train on the fields opposite his farm in East Barton (*Suffolk Chronicle*, 16 Apr. 1864). In 1900, Mr J. W. Greene, an enthusiastic supporter of home defence, volunteered as a subaltern of the unofficial Rifle Corps for the parishes of Fornham and Great Barton, which was associated with the 1st Suffolk and Harwich Artillery Volunteers. The 59 members of the corps included 16 from Fornham All Saints, 27 from Fornham St. Martin and 14 from Great Barton. However, when they requested more rifles, the government refused to give official sanction to the Rifle Corps, but agreed to recognise a Rifle Club, as long as it affiliated to the National Rifle Association (*BNP*, 15 May 1900).

The Territorial and Reserve Forces Act 1907 created the Territorial Force to provide home defence. The East Anglian Division, which included the Norfolk and Suffolk Brigade, was formed in 1908.

In November 1910, the National Service League held its first meeting in Great Barton Church Institute, and, in response to Mr J. W. Greene's call for volunteers to join the Territorial Army, Great Barton men joined the 6th Battalion (Cyclists), which had been set up in 1908, together with the 4th and 5th Battalion (Cyclists) of the Suffolk Regiment.

The County Associations, which organised the Territorial Force, maintained the National Reserve, a register of trained officers and men, which included the names of 215,000 men in October 1913.

In 1914, the British Expeditionary Force (BEF) consisted of six infantry divisions, five cavalry brigades, and the Special Reserve.

'Old boys' of Great Barton School

Britain declared war on Germany at midnight on 4 August 1914, after she failed to receive assurances from Germany about the neutrality of Belgium. The war was fought between the Entente Powers, known as the Allies, which included the British Empire, French Republic and the Russian Empire, and the Central Powers, which included the German Empire and the Austro-Hungarian Empire at the beginning of the war, and later included the Ottoman Empire and the Kingdom of Bulgaria.

The day after war was declared, the British Parliament passed the Aliens Restriction Act 1914, which categorised every foreigner born in Germany or Austria-Hungary as an 'enemy alien' and required all foreign visitors to register with their local police station. Amongst these were 31-year-old, Henrietta Foulger (née Threin), the German-born wife of Walter George Foulger from Great Barton, who served with the Grenadier Guards from 1902 to 1905. Walter and Henrietta married in 1905 and lived in Poplar, in the East End of London, where Walter worked as a constable in the London docks area. As an alien, Henrietta would have been expected to register at her local police station and be subject to various restrictions, but as the wife of a British citizen, she may have been exempted from registration.

On 11 August 1914, Field-Marshal Lord Horatio Kitchener (1850-1916) Secretary of State for War, issued a call for volunteers to enlist for a new form of short service, under which a man could serve for three years, or the duration of the war whichever was the longer. These recruits became known as Kitchener's New Army. The 7th, 8th, 9th and 10th Battalions of the Suffolk Regiment were created in 1914, the 11th at Cambridge in September 1914 and the 12th and 13th in 1915.

Recruits had to be between 18 and 38 years of age, taller than 5 foot 3 inches and have a chest size greater than 34 inches. They enlisted for seven years full-time service, followed by five years in the Army Reserve and were not sent overseas until the age of 19. Those in the 11th Battalion of the Suffolk Regiment were paid 1s. per day, plus a 3d. 'messing allowance'.

In Great Barton, 15 men had enlisted by 15 August 1914 and a further seven by 7 September 1914. During the following week, 18 more men were recruited at an open air meeting on Conyers Green addressed by the Revd Taylor, Miss Trafford Rawson of Coldham Hall, Hugh Copinger-Hill, Robert Fyson, O.A. Clark and W.T. Fox. By the end of September 1914, 50 men from Great Barton had volunteered, most of whom were sent to Brighton and Shoreham, Sussex, for training.

Recruits had to pass a physical fitness test and several Great Barton men were rejected on medical grounds, including Edward Banham, an ex-secretary of Great Barton Agricultural Labourers' Union, who was told that he would not be accepted unless he had an operation. This was arranged immediately, after which he joined the 7th Suffolk Regiment who were sent to France in May 1915. He took part in the Battle of Loos during which he was killed on 30 November 1915, and he was buried in Vermelles British Cemetery in northern France.

William Fuller joined the Royal Marines as a boy and was discharged just before the outbreak of the war, by which time he had served for 13 years. When he tried to re-enlist, he was advised that he needed to have an operation first, which he did, and then joined the 1st Suffolk Regiment, with whom he fought in Salonika, Greece.

Walton Burrell (1863-1944), who was profoundly deaf, taught himself photography and did voluntary work at the Red Cross Hospital at Ampton, opened in October 1914, which treated 6,568 soldiers during the next four years. Other Great Barton men, rejected as unfit, joined the Blue Cross Army Veterinary Corps, which cared for military horses.

Some men were so keen to volunteer that they falsified their age, which was easy to do, since no proof of age was required until the introduction of conscription in 1916. When Bob Burton, a Barton scholar, joined the Territorial Force on 29 August 1914, he claimed to be 18 years and 6 months old, although he was, at the time, just over 17-years-old.

In 1915, in order to attract more recruits, the 2nd and 3rd Battalions of the Suffolk Regiment passed through Great Barton, stopped in the main street, and displayed their flags (*BFP*, 21 Aug. 1915). Until 1916, volunteers were encouraged to join up with their friends and were allocated to local regiments.

The majority of 'old boys' from Great Barton School who fought in the war served as a private, a soldier of the lowest military rank. A few were promoted to be non-commissioned officers (NCO), which was below a commissioned officer and referred to as 'other ranks'. Sydney Banham, George Sargeant, Benjamin Frost, Robert Bishop and Albert Long became lance corporals, and Harry Eastlea and Walter Doel became corporals. Percy Eastlea and Charles Crack, who both served with the Suffolk Regiment, became sergeants, as was Charles Fuller, who served with the First Sherwood Foresters (Nottinghamshire and Derby Regiment).

George Daine, the son of Emma and James Daine, attended King Edward VI Grammar School, Bury St Edmunds, where a Cadet Corps attached to the 3rd (Reserve) Battalion, the Suffolk Regiment, was formed in 1900. After he left school, George served with the Royal Regiment of Artillery, until his 'dishonourable discharge' on 20 February 1908 [no further explanation given on the discharge form]. He re-enlisted after 1914, served with the 4th Battalion of the Suffolk Regiment and, by 1918, was a sergeant major and instructor at Seaford Army Camp in Sussex.

Commissioned officers from Great Barton

Initially, only the sons of farmers, clergymen, public-school educated boys and the wealthy were appointed as officers, but there were exceptions especially if the soldier was an experienced one. Robert Frost, who was the son of a Great Barton farm worker, served in the regular army from 1903 and became a first lieutenant in the Royal Berkshire Regiment.

Three men from Great Barton became second lieutenants. Thomas Hervey, who was the son of the Vicar of Great Barton from 1897 to 1902, served with the Kings Royal Rifle Corps. Robert Evans Jnr, who attended King Edward VI Grammar School, Bury St Edmunds, served with the 4th

Battalion of the Suffolk Regiment. Austin Baldwin who was the son of a farmer and school manager, served with the 2nd Battalion of the Suffolk Regiment.

Robert and Christopher Fyson, the sons of Robert Fyson, a school manager, who lived at Manor Farm, were educated at a private boarding school in Bishop Stortford, Hertfordshire. Robert, who served as a lieutenant, was wounded twice in Egypt in 1917. After 1 April 1918, he transferred to the Royal Air Force, trained as a pilot and served in Palestine and France. Christopher was granted a commission in the Indian Army in 1918. In December 1916, their sister, Helen, married Second Lieutenant Herbert Charles Nutter, who served in the 5th Battalion of the Suffolk Regiment, but she was widowed six months later, when Herbert was killed on active service in France.

At least three members of the Bunbury family fought in the First World War. Henry William Bunbury (1889-1942) was a captain in the Suffolk Regiment (Special Reserve) and the Royal Air Force. Sir Charles Henry Napier Bunbury (1886-1963) was a lieutenant in the Coldstream Guards (Special Reserve) and the Royal Wiltshire Regiment. William St Pierre Bunbury (1859-1942), their uncle, who had retired from the Royal Field Artillery as a major in 1897, was recalled for service with the Royal Field Artillery in 1914, fought in France and retired in 1918 with the rank of lieutenant-colonel.

Hugh Copinger-Hill, who lived at The Cottage, Great Barton, was educated at Snettisham Grammar School and a teacher at Framlingham College, Suffolk, before the war. He was promoted to the rank of major and then lieutenant colonel.

Sir John Smiley, who leased Barton Hall until 1914, was a captain and honorary major in the Royal Garrison Artillery in France, where he won a medal in 1917, and became a major.

His youngest son, David, who became a colonel, fought in the Second World War in Palestine, Iraq, Persia, Syria, Western Desert and with Special Operations Executive (SOE) in Albania and Thailand. He was awarded an OBE in 1946 and, after his death in 2009, it was suggested that John le Carré, the author of *Tinker, Tailor, Soldier, Spy*, took David Smiley's surname for that of his hero, George Smiley (*Daily Telegraph*, 12 Jan. 2009).

Further recruitment and conscription

By May 1915, recruitment had slowed down, so the upper age limit for entry to the armed services was raised from 38 to 40. The National Registration Act 1915 was passed to stimulate recruitment and ascertain details of the trades and employment of men between the ages of 15 and 65. The National Register revealed that almost 5 million men of military age were not in the armed forces. This included 1.6 million in 'starred' occupations i.e. those deemed vital for the war economy.

In October 1915, Edward Stanley, 17th Earl of Derby (1865–1948) was appointed as Director General of Recruiting. Under the Group Scheme, commonly known as the Derby Scheme, men aged 18 to 40 were informed that until 15 December 1915 they could either enlist voluntarily or attest with an obligation to enlist if called up after January 1916. In Great Barton, the Revd Lipscomb (1874-1948), Vicar of Holy Innocents' Church, served as secretary of the scheme, which was managed by Robert Fyson and Isaac Banham, both of whom had sons fighting in the war (*BFP*, 27 Nov. 1915).

However, the voluntary scheme did not produce enough volunteers, so Parliament passed the Military Service Act 1916, which introduced compulsory conscription for all single men, aged 19 to 41, unless they were ministers of religion, or widowers with children. In May 1916, compulsory conscription was extended to include married men and 18-year-olds, and conscripts no longer had a choice of unit. War casualties were heavy and many conscripts failed to pass the medical tests, so it was necessary to amend the Military Service Act 1916 several times during the course of the war and, by 1918, all men, single or married, aged 18 to 50, were liable for conscription.

Appeal Tribunals were set up to consider applications from conscripts for deferment, or exemption from military service on the grounds of ill health, occupation or 'conscientious objection'. In June 1916, Mr First, a miller and farmer in Great Barton, applied for exemption on behalf of his 33-year-old employee, who was a miller and stone dresser. He stated that he had 40 acres of hay, 8 acres of barley, 10 acres of mustard and 16 acres of grass with clover and sainfoin, which he needed to harvest, and, if he failed to do so, he would be unable to pay his income tax of 5s. in the £1. The chair of the tribunal told him that he was 'damned lucky to be paying tax' (*BFP*, 10 June 1916). In February 1918, a Great Barton butcher appealed against being conscripted, but Thingoe Tribunal granted him exemption for only one month (*BFP*, 16 Feb. 1918).

About 16,000 men refused to fight for religious reasons or because they were pacifists. Approximately half of them agreed to serve in a non-combat service, and many were employed as stretcher-bearers.

From December 1914, the Government War Office recognised a Central Association of Volunteer Training Corps, consisting of those men who had been granted an exemption from military service. Local units had to be financially self-supporting. Members had to provide their own uniforms, which could be any colour except khaki, wear a red armband bearing the letters "GR" (*Georgius Rex*), and use dummy weapons for training. In January 1915, Sir George Agnew called a meeting at Rougham to form a unit, and James Hales was appointed as commandant. Robert Evans was in charge of Great Barton Volunteer Training Corps, and each volunteer was given a cap and a belt (*BFP*, 16 Jan. 1915). At their first meeting in Great Barton in March 1915, they decided to hold training sessions twice a week but only eight men signed up at the first meeting and two more at the second (*BFP,* 13 Mar. 1915; *BFP*, 03 Apr. 1915).

In November 1916, Sir Henry Charles Bunbury, who had served in the Royal Navy during the 1870s for seven years, became a temporary captain in the Suffolk Volunteer Training Corps at the age of 61 (*BFP*, 11 Nov. 1916). He received a special mention by the Under Secretary of State for War, for services rendered, was nominated for special mention by Eastern Command, and was praised for being the best shot of the 5,500 members, for which he was awarded the Regimental Cup.

Great Barton roll of honour

Men from Great Barton served in all theatres of war. In 1915, there was a framed roll of honour in the church porch, which listed the names of 58 serving men, who had either been born in the village or lived there. It also included the names of men who had volunteered, but had been rejected. A second roll of honour, containing the names of local inhabitants and 'old boys' of the school, was maintained at the Boys' School (*BFP*, 24 Apr. 1915).

In 1992, a poster was discovered at the back of a drawer in a map chest at Great Barton Primary School, entitled, '*In Memory of the Men of this Parish of Great Barton, who served in the Great European War 1914– 1919*'. It lists 120 'old boys' of Great Barton School, who fought in the war and includes Walter Bishop who died in 1908.

Two future head teachers of Great Barton School fought in the war. Cecil Frank Channell served with the Hertfordshire Yeomanry, and Ernest Reed with the Warwickshire Horse Artillery.

Men from Great Barton who made 'the supreme sacrifice'

Five members of the Royal Navy and 30 members of the British Army, who were from or associated with the village of Great Barton, were killed during the First World War.

The Royal Navy

In August 1914, the Grand Fleet of the British Navy, which consisted of 20 big gun 'dreadnought and super dreadnought' battleships, and 4 fast battle cruisers, was larger than the German High Sea Fleet, which had 13 German dreadnoughts and 3 battle cruisers.

Some of the Royal Navy was deployed in the North Sea to ensure the safe movement of supplies and troops, and blockade German ports. Within

32 hours of the outbreak of war, Staff Paymaster Joseph Gedge, the grandson of William Norman King, was killed in action (*BFP*, 15 Aug.1914). Joseph served on *HMS Amphion*, a light cruiser, which set sail from Harwich, on 5 August, with destroyers of the 3rd Flotilla. Information was received from a trawler, which had spotted a boat laying mines in the Thames estuary, so the Flotilla gave chase. *HMS Amphion* searched and found the *Königin Luise*, a German auxiliary minelayer, which had previously been a Hamburg-Holland holiday ferry boat. Two destroyers, *Lance* and *Landrail*, were despatched to sink it, and 46 of the 100 crew of the Königin *Luise* were rescued by the Flotilla. On its way back to Harwich, *HMS Amphion* hit a mine and, although some of the crew were saved, a second mine sank the cruiser, with the total loss of about 150 men, including Joseph Gedge and 19 of the rescued German sailors.

William Newport, who joined the navy before the war, served with the Royal Marine Light Infantry, and was a crewmember on *HMS Hawke*, which was engaged in operations in the North Sea. On 15 October 1914, *HMS Hawke* was torpedoed by the German submarine *U-9,* and broke up and sank, with the loss of her captain, 26 officers and 497 men, including William.

Paul Leathley Eddis, the youngest son of the Revd John Elwin Eddis, joined the navy in 1908, at the age of 17, and served as a midshipman on the *Canopus 16*, a 'pre-dreadnought' battleship. During the war, he was a lieutenant on *HM Submarine, E13*, which grounded on the Island of Saltholme, off the Danish coast, after being torpedoed by a German destroyer on 19 August 1915 (*BFP*, 28 Aug. 1915). He was rescued from the wreck and survived. After the war, he served as lieutenant on *HM Submarine L21*, and then as commander of *HM Submarine L24*, which was sunk, after a collision with the battleship *Resolution*, during an exercise off Portland Bill in the English Channel, on 10 January 1924. There were no survivors, and a memorial to the crew was erected at St Ann's Church at His Majesty's Naval Base, Portsmouth.

Arthur Manning, the eldest son of the village baker, was 16-years-old and the youngest 'old boy' to be killed. He joined the Merchant Marine Reserve and was a signal boy on *HMY Aries*, a former 268 ton luxury yacht, built in Barrow, Cumbria, in 1880, used by the Royal Navy to inspect suspicious vessels in the Dover area. On 31 Oct 1915, *HMY Aries* struck a mine from the German submarine *UC-6*, and sank in the English Channel off Leathercote Point, Kent. All 22 of the crew drowned, and their bodies were never recovered.

Thomas Robert Scott (1887-1917), the son of Richard Maillard Scott, and a lay preacher like his father, served as a stoker on *HMS Hannibal*. On 16 April 1917, he was killed in action in the Mediterranean Sea and buried on the island of Ekinosa in Greece. In 1921, his body was reburied at Syra New British Cemetery, on a Greek island in the Adriatic.

Ernest Bean, born in Kent, joined the Royal Navy before the war and married Ruby Gillings from Great Barton. In July 1917, Ernest was serving on *HMS Vanguard*, when it exploded at Scapa Flow, in the Orkney Islands, Scotland. The explosion was probably the result of an accident, when a fire in the boiler room caused the bulkhead to overheat and ignite ammunition stored nearby. *HMS Vanguard* sank almost instantly, with the loss of 804 men. There were two survivors, but Ernest was not one of them. His only daughter, Ernestine, born two months after his death, attended Great Barton School, obtained a free place at West Suffolk County Secondary School in 1928, and became a teacher.

The Western Front

The BEF was mobilised on 5 August 1914 and four infantry (1st, 2nd, 3rd and 5th) and two cavalry divisions (1st and 2nd) crossed the English Channel to northern France. The 5th Division, which included the 2nd Battalion of the Suffolk Regiment, fought at the Battle of Le Cateau on 26 August 1914 and suffered heavy casualties. Private Peter Frost, who was a regular trooper in the Royal Irish Dragoon Guards, took part in the Retreat from Mons in northern France, in August and September 1914. In a letter, written to his family the following June, he mentioned that the soldiers' great coats had often become frozen during the winter (*BFP*, 26 June 1915). He was severely wounded with a shrapnel injury to the head in June 1915 and returned home in October 1915.

Harold Albert Simmonds, whose parents lived at East Barton, was killed in action in northern France in October 1914. Lance Corporal William Meadows [616] was badly wounded during the First Battle of Ypres and was taken to Germany as a prisoner of war. Six months later, he was exchanged for a German prisoner of war and three months later was declared unfit for service. He became landlord of the Greyhound Public House at Wickhambrook, Suffolk and, when he died in November 1919, he was buried in Great Barton churchyard with full military honours (*BFP*, 22 Nov. 1919).

Harry Elliston and Percy Eastlea served with the 1st Battalion of the Suffolk Regiment, which landed at Le Havre in January 1915. They were both killed on 24 April, the third day of the Second Battle of Ypres, after a ferocious battle during which the Germans used poison gas, and 56,000 British soldiers died during a single month. Harry left a wife and five daughters, under the age of six, the youngest of whom was born just after her father was killed.

Several battalions of the Suffolk Regiment took part in the Battle of Loos on 25 September 1915, including at least one of the sons of William and Harriet Frost, who received a letter from the King, in July 1915, congratulating them on having four sons in the army (*BFP*, 10 July 1915). Edward, who was in the 2nd Battalion of the Suffolk Regiment, died on 30 September 1915, but his brothers survived the war. Lance Corporal Robert Frost was in the Coldstream Guards, when his horse rolled on top of him and, whilst being treated in hospital in Oxford, caught pneumonia. Lance Corporal Ben Frost, who was in the Mounted Brigade in Egypt, caught malaria.

Sidney Gillings, who was in the 2nd Battalion of the Suffolk Regiment, was killed in January 1916; Harry Everett, who served with the 9th Battalion, in April 1916; George Steggles, who served with the 10th Battalion, in May 1916. Corporal Fred Werner, who was not an 'old boy', but was associated with the village, was killed on 1 July 1916, whilst serving with the London Regiment, 2nd City of London Battalion (Royal Fusiliers).

Six battalions of the Suffolk Regiment fought at the Battle of the Somme, which lasted from July to November 1916, and was intended to be a decisive breakthrough. It was the scene of indiscriminate slaughter, at the end of which, the Allies had only advanced a few miles, and nearly one million men had been killed or wounded.

Amongst the dead were Frederick Harry Sturgeon, Herbert Bishop, William Banham and Herbert Nichols, who all served in the 9th Battalion, together with Albert Sturgeon and Second Lieutenant Thomas Hervey, who both served with the Kings Royal Rifle Corps.

Five battalions of the Suffolk Regiment fought in the Battle of Arras in 1917, during which Samuel Steward and Ernest Bishop were killed. Ernest, a gunner in the Royal Field Artillery, died in April, when a shell dropped in front of his gun, and shrapnel hit him in the shoulders and neck.

Before the war, Robert Pawsey was an experienced footman and butler at Nonsuch Park, Surrey, and, after he enlisted at Knightsbridge in the London Regiment, in December 1915, was transferred to the Machine Gun Corps, where he was the batman [personal servant] for Second Lieutenant Mutch. He was killed in the trenches at Arras in June, and was buried in front of the chemical works at Arras (*BFP*, 30 June 1917).

Two of the six sons of David Thomson, a dairy farmer died in action. Their family moved to Great Barton in October 1916 and Walter and William Thomson both joined the London Scottish Regiment, whose uniform included a kilt. Walter Thomson was killed in May 1917 (*BFP*, 19 May 1917) and his brother in November that same year.

As the battle for control of the Western Front continued, Robert Mayhew was wounded in November 1916 and died in June 1917, Sergeant Charles Crack and Lance Corporal George Sargeant died in September 1917 and Alfred Howe, in January 1918.

During the spring of 1918, German forces launched a major offensive on the Western Front. In May 1918, the *Bury Free Press* published a letter, written by an unnamed British soldier fighting in northern France, who wrote that this village 'was completely deserted and was a mass of ruined houses and cafes. Not a single dwelling stood in one piece and you could look through the broken walls at crockery, ornaments and curtains, which had been left, but were undamaged. Cats and dogs roamed the streets, but soon made friends with the British Tommies. The church was in ruins, but part of the tower and clock remained, and statues, which had been torn from their bases, lay in ruins on the ground. The crucifix was undamaged, as were some fine paintings, but the village was being shelled every day' (*BFP*, 25 May 1918). Most of northern France was in a similar state, and 3,400 French civilians died during the war, many from malnutrition and disease.

William Simmonds was killed in June 1918, and William Sparham and Charles Prentice in August 1918, when the Allies successfully fought back at Marne and Amiens against the Central Powers. Two of Charles Prentice's brothers survived. Ebor Prentice was wounded three times and sent to a hospital in Yorkshire. William Prentice, together with Alfred Howe, another 'old boy', were each awarded a Military Medal, one side of which was inscribed 'For Bravery in the Field'. These were awarded to 'other ranks' of the British Army and Commonwealth Forces for acts of gallantry and devotion to duty under fire.

The Gallipoli Campaign (25 April 1915 to 9 January 1916)

The 1/5th Battalion was part of a Territorial Force, formed in Bury St Edmunds in August 1914, as part of the Norfolk and Suffolk Brigade, 54th (East Anglian) Division.

In February 1915, the British government mounted a naval expedition to bombard and take control of the Gallipoli Peninsula and Constantinople, in the Ottoman Empire, so that they could link up with the Russians, defeat Turkey, and persuade the Balkan states to join the Allies. The Mediterranean Expeditionary Force, later considered an ill-conceived campaign, was led by General Sir Ian Standish Monteith Hamilton, and the allied forces included troops from the UK, France, Australia, New Zealand, India and Newfoundland. Over 100,000 men were killed at Gallipoli during this campaign.

Major Hugh Copinger-Hill and several 'old boys' from Great Barton School, including Charles Rogers, Cecil Crick, Frederick Lingwood and George Wright, took part in this campaign. Their regiment embarked at Liverpool on 30 July 1915, sailed on the *Aquitania* to Gallipoli, via Mudros, Greece, and landed at Suvla Bay on 10 August. Charles Rogers was killed in battle on 21 August 1915, on the same day that 15 men from Hadleigh, Suffolk, were killed.

On 19 December 1915, the 1/5th Battalion of the Suffolk Regiment was successfully evacuated to Alexandria, Egypt, and spent the rest of the war in Egypt and Palestine. Frederick Lingwood, who had been a journalist before the war, sent a letter to a friend, in which he wrote that, at Christmas 1915, they had enjoyed plum pudding and wine, and that a draw had been organised to win presents from England (*BFP*, 15 Jan. 1916). He also wrote that his unit had camped in the sand and he was able to catch a tram into the nearest town (*BFP*, 22 Jan 1916). In March 1916, whilst troops were training in Egypt, Frederick Lingwood wrote that he had been on a route march past the Pyramids and the Sphinx, and that there was a Young Men's Christian Association (YMCA) hostel with shower facilities (*BFP*, 04 Mar. 1916).

Some troops had their first sighting of tanks, which were employed during the unsuccessful First Battle of Gaza, in March 1917, when the Egyptian Expeditionary Force attempted to invade the south of Palestine. During the Second Battle of Gaza in April 1917, which was also a failure, Cecil Crick was wounded in the ankle and arm. In November 1917, during the Third Battle of Gaza, which was successful, Cecil fought with A Company, whose role was to capture two hills. They took the first one but, as they tried to take the second, the Turks opened fire and a shell burst near Cecil, who died soon afterwards. He was buried in Ramleh War Cemetery, near Jerusalem, in December, the same month that the Allies captured Jerusalem.

The Commander of the 1/5th Battalion, Lt Colonel Frederick Hargreaves Arbuthnot Wollaston, frequently visited Great Barton to talk to the families of the dead or wounded troops, but was killed on his return from one of these trips to France by a one-tonne bomb, dropped on London on 8 March 1918.

The home front

When Britain declared war on Germany on 4 August 1914, Emma Daine and Robert Evans were the head teachers of Great Barton School. They were assisted by Winifred Evans, Jennie Clinton and Archibald Barnett, who had been a pupil-teacher at the Boys' School. Archibald volunteered for the Royal Garrison Artillery as soon as war was declared, became a corporal and was sent to the front in 1915 as a motor despatch rider, but was wounded in May 1916 (*BFP*, 20 May 1916).

Teachers, women and children, as well as those men who were ineligible to enlist, all contributed to the war effort at home.

Robert Evans was in charge of Barton Volunteer Training Corps and, as this involved him in extra work in preparing the Assessment Books, his salary was increased in 1916 (*BFP,* 29 Apr.1916). As clerk to the trustees of the Poor's Firing Farm Charity, he received a gratuity of £1 p.a., which was increased to two guineas in 1921. The farm was let on a seven-year lease to Mr Nunn from 1913 at an annual rent of £60. However, he struggled to pay his rent, so the farm was run by the War Agricultural Committee and West Suffolk County Council from 1917 until December 1920. Coal was purchased from the rents and given to 100 parishioners, each of whom received 5 cwt [quarter of a ton] of coal in 1915 and 1916, with an extra half portion for larger families (BFP, 1 Jan. 1916), and 3.5 cwt in 1917, after the price of coal increased to two guineas per ton. Recipients were means-tested and had to have been resident in the parish for longer than 12 months.

Many village women raised money for the war effort and joined working parties to make gifts for the troops. Some attended weekly meetings of the Red Cross Working Party, where they sewed and knitted 'comforts for the sick and wounded'. Others raised money for Belgian refugees, organised regular collections for the West Suffolk and other hospitals, raised money for the Seaman's Mission and arranged whist drives, one of which raised £4. 5s. towards the Wool Fund (BFP, 27 Nov. 1915). Some joined the Women's Institute, formed in 1915 to revitalise rural communities and encourage women to become more involved in food production.

Women were encouraged to work on the farms to replace the men who were serving in the armed services. In March 1917, a meeting was called to form a branch of the Women's Land Army, which was part of the National Service Scheme. Lilias D'Arcy Hutton, the registrar for Great Barton, kept a register of women agricultural workers who could help local farmers, and recruits were trained at local centres or farms to work in agriculture, the Women's Forage Corps or the Women's Forestry Service.

There was a special children's service at Holy Innocents' Church during the summer holidays in 1915, and the schoolchildren contributed to the war effort by collecting eggs for West Suffolk General Hospital. In 1916, the Girls' School collected 70 eggs and 2s. 6d. in cash during a Children's Special Week (*BFP*, 4 Mar. 1916), and donated a further 340 eggs in 1918 (*BFP*, 27 Apr. 1918). The egg collections continued after the war and the girls donated 1,032 eggs in 1922 (*BFP*, 10 June 1922), 1,000 eggs in 1923 (*BFP*, 2 June 1923) and 880 eggs in 1933(BFP, 6 May 1933).

Schoolchildren also collected blackberries in support of the National Blackberry Scheme, organised by the Board of Education in co-operation with the Food Production Department of the War Office.

In January 1918, the Girls' School raised 13s. for the YMCA. That year, they also donated £8. 19s. for the Blinded Soldiers' Children's Fund, some of which they raised through the sale of flags, postcards, poetry and poster stamps, commissioned by Winox Ltd, of Richmond, Surrey, to raise money for war charities (*BFP*, 19 Jan. 1918; *BFP*, 3 Aug. 1918).

Children's toys and magazines were designed to encourage support for the war effort and, in 1918, a collection of patriotic nursery rhymes entitled *Wartime Nursery Rhymes: A First World War Collection* by Nina MacDonald was published. One of its verses read:

> This little pig flew to Margate, and this little pig went too,
> The first little pig dropped a bomb on the town,
> And the second dropped another, then flew,
> But both little pigs were shot in the air, and fell in the ocean blue.

In February 1916, a National Savings Scheme was introduced. On 21 May, daylight saving (British summertime) was introduced to enable factories and farmers to work longer hours.

Voluntary food rationing was encouraged from May 1917, and the 9d. loaf was introduced six months later. In February 1918, compulsory rationing was imposed in the south of England, with stiff penalties for offenders. Rationing of meat, butter and cheese was extended to the whole country in April and July 1918, and every individual had to register with a butcher. Bacon and ham came off rationing on 28 July 1918, but raw meat was rationed until 15 December 1918. Allotments became very popular and, in 1918, an allotment of just over 1 acre on Conyers' Green was sold for £50 (*BFP*, 21 Sept. 1918).

The Defence of the Realm Act 1915 gave emergency powers to the government to censor the press, requisition property and control workers' jobs, pay and conditions. In spite of the fact that wives and dependents of servicemen were able to claim a separation allowance from their husband's wages and a pension in the event of his death, many families suffered financial hardship.

In January 1915, Frank Burrell, who farmed at Cattishall, gave a brace of rabbits and two cwt of coal to each cottager at Cattishall (*BFP*, 2 Jan. 1915). At Christmas 1915, the employees of Barton Stud each received a joint of beef (*BFP*, 1 Jan. 1916), and those of Red Castle Farm, Cattishall Farm and Manor Farm all received a Christmas bonus (*BFP*, 29 Dec. 1917).

The Prime Minister, David Lloyd George (1863-1945), renounced alcohol and even persuaded King George V to do the same. Bank Holidays, Guy Fawkes' night, the football league, race meetings and the Oxford and Cambridge Boat Race were all cancelled, suspended or postponed.

Throughout the war, everyone lived in fear of bombing raids by German airships, manufactured by the German Zeppelin Company. The Kaiser initially banned the bombing of London, in case a member of the

Royal family, to whom he was related, was killed, but he sanctioned attacks on industrial targets. On 16 December 1914, the first shelling of British civilians by the Imperial German Army took place at Scarborough, Hartlepool and Whitby, Yorkshire. On the night of 19 January 1915, two zeppelins, which were heading for Humberside, were diverted by strong winds and dropped bombs on Yarmouth and Kings Lynn, killing four people. The *Bury Free Press* commissioned a chart of weather conditions to show when zeppelin raids could be expected, and, in May 1915, the Buttermarket in Bury St Edmunds was bombed, although the only casualty was a collie dog (*BFP*, 7 May 1915). Throughout 1915 and 1916, much of East Anglia experienced air raids, and 28 people were killed and 44 wounded in April 1916. In September 1916, 13 zeppelins attacked eastern England and caused a great deal of damage, although one was destroyed over the south of the area and crashed into the sea. On the morning of 17 June 1917, the *L48 Zeppelin*, the last one to fly over East Anglia on a bombing raid, was shot down over Theberton, near the coast about 45 miles away from Great Barton, and 17 of the 19 crewmen were killed.

Peace services and celebrations in Bury St Edmunds and Great Barton

An armistice was declared at Compiègne, France, which came into effect at 11.00 a.m. on 11 November 1918. To celebrate the ceasefire, a Festival of Freedom was organised in Bury St Edmunds with a torchlit procession from the Abbey Gardens and a firework display (*BFP*, 16 Nov. 1918). The town was presented with a collection of guns captured from the Germans by the Suffolk Regiment.

Some of the 185,000 prisoners of war started returning home. Amongst these were John (Jack) Phillips, Cecil Lofts, Harry Eastlea, Charles Everett, Peter Frost, Horace Sturgeon and Arthur Floyd who were all from Great Barton. In January 1919, Bury St Edmunds Borough Council organised a reception for the returned prisoners of war, who marched from Angel Hill to the Corn Exchange behind a band. At the Corn Exchange, 800 men and guests were treated to a meal of chicken, tongue, ham and turkey, donated by well-wishers (*BFP*, 25 Jan. 1919). In February 1919, the 1/5th Territorial Battalion of the Suffolk Regiment held a reunion dinner in the Corn Exchange.

On 15 March 1919, the Suffolk Regiment Cenotaph was dedicated at St Mary's Church, Bury St Edmunds. The Regimental Chapel at St Mary's Church commemorates 360 officers and 6,513 other ranks of the Suffolk Regiment and includes the names of some men from Great Barton.

In June 1919, more than 50 men of the 2nd Battalion of the Suffolk Regiment returned to Bury St Edmunds by train, and marched from the railway station to Angel Hill, where they received a rapturous reception from the public.

On 28 June 1919, Germany and the Allied Powers signed the Treaty of Versailles. In July 1919, a massive Peace Service was held on Angel Hill, Bury St Edmunds, and a Festival of Peace and Victory was organised. The following day, a Peace Procession was held in London.

In Great Barton, flags were displayed throughout the village, and there was an early morning peal of bells and a Communion Service at Holy Innocents' Church. At the Church Institute, which was decorated with flags, flowers and fairy lights, 40 demobilised soldiers were provided with a meal of beef, chicken, turkey, tongue and vegetables, and given an ounce of tobacco, a box of matches and a packet of cigarettes (*BFP*, 26 July 1919).

Amongst the ex-soldiers were the six sons of John Aldhous, the butcher in School Lane, all of whom had fought in the war and survived. In the afternoon, 150 children assembled at the school, walked to the Church Institute for tea, and afterwards to the Vicarage for a village party. Gramophone music was played all afternoon and there were swings on the lawn, and glasses of mineral water or cups of tea for the children, who were able to join in races with medals presented by Catherine Fyson, one of the school managers. The men played bowls, and took part in a tug of war competition for a prize of 3s. for each member of the winning team. Older parishioners were given a gift of meat, the men were given an ounce of tobacco, and the widows of the parish were given a meat tea.

Sir Edward Hulton gave a gift of £1 to each of his employees at Lodge Farm, to commemorate the peace (*BFP*, 2 Aug. 1919).

Great Barton war memorials

In July 1917, a memorial service was held at Holy Innocents' Church, Great Barton, with lessons read by Robert Evans and Frank D'Arcy Hutton, a churchwarden. The vicar asked the congregation to remember the following men who were from, or associated with, Great Barton: - Edward Banham, William Banham, Herbert Bishop, Ernest Bishop, Charles Crack, Harry Everett, Percy Eastlea, Harry Elliston, Edward Frost, Charles Gillings, Alfred Howe, William Manning, Robert Mayhew. Herbert Nichols, Robert Pawsey, George Sergeant, Harold Simmonds, Albert F. Sturgeon, Frederick Harry Sturgeon, Samuel Steward, Walter Hallam Thomson, Charles Frost, Herbert Charles Nutter and Fred Werner.

In January 1919, another memorial service was held at Holy Innocents' Church, where the Revd Yeo, the Rector of Rougham, read out the names of the men who were from, or associated with, the parish of Great Barton and had been killed whilst fighting in the First World War (*BFP*, 1 Jan. 1919).

Numerous meetings were held in Great Barton to discuss how to commemorate those who had died in the war, and three different committees were formed between July 1919 and July 1920. The vicar suggested that there should be a plaque on a wall inside the church, inscribed with the names of the fallen, and the idea was accepted by 46 to three votes. Further ideas included the building of a village hall, a public bath, or a recreation ground. The committee agreed to send a circular to all villagers, to request their views and ask for a promise of a subscription, but this was never done. By the end of November there was £100 in the fund, with a stipulation that there should be a memorial outside the church as well as a plaque inside. At a meeting in December, it was agreed by 29 to six votes that £55 should be spent on a plaque, and £42 on a memorial cross in the churchyard. Robert Evans opposed the decision because he had only contributed to a plaque. Thomas Nice promised to donate a further £50, if nine other people donated the same amount, for a village recreation ground.

Finally, in July 1920, it was agreed that a plaque, measuring 2 foot 9 inches by 1 foot 8 inches, in deep relief brass with an ornamental edge, would be placed on the inside north wall of the church, facing the porch. A 10 foot 6 inch high octagonal memorial cross of Portland stone, designed by Archie Ainsworth Hunt, a school manager, would be erected at the entrance to the churchyard. The committee continued to pursue the idea of buying land for recreational purposes.

In April 1921, over 500 people attended a memorial service at Holy Innocents' Church. Robert Evans Jnr carried a cross and led the choir in a procession as they sang, 'Oh God our Help in Ages Past', accompanied by Gunn Lipscomb on the violin. Major Hugh Copinger-Hill, of the 1/5th Battalion, the Suffolk Regiment, unveiled the stone war memorial in the churchyard, which was 'dedicated' by the Revd Lipscomb. Many wreaths were laid, including one that read, 'In proud memory of the boys from the school on the hill, from the schoolchildren.' Major Hill then read out the names of the 22 men on the memorial, which was inscribed with 'Erected to the men of this parish, who gave their lives in the Great War 1914-1918'. Afterwards the crowd entered the church, sang hymns accompanied by Dorothy Evans on the organ, and listened to a sermon, preached by the Revd Lipscomb. The inscription on the plaque read 'Men of Great Barton, who made the supreme sacrifice in the Great War 1914-1918. To the Glory of God and in memory of '..... and listed the same names as on the war memorial cross, which included 17 'old boys' from Great Barton School and five others (Baldwin, Mayhew, Scott and the Thomson brothers), who did not attend the school, but were associated with the parish of Great Barton. The name of Samuel Steward was added to the memorial cross in 2002.

The Baptist War Memorial at the Garland Street Church, in Bury St Edmunds, includes the names of Herbert Henry Bishop and Arthur William Manning.

The names of Alfred James Howe, Charles Albert Rogers, William and Harold Simmonds, William Sparham and George Steggles were omitted from the memorial, in spite of the fact that they were all 'old boys' and had all been killed during the war.

Similarly, there was no mention of Ernest George Bean, Joseph Theodore Gedge, Sidney Gillings, William James Newport, Herbert Charles Nutter and Fred Werner, all of whom were associated with the village.

Table 12. Men of Great Barton, killed during the First World War

Servicemen (rank)	Regiment	Servicemen (rank)	Regiment
Elliston, H.W. (Private)	1st Suffolk	Sturgeon F.H. (Private)	9th Suffolk
Estlea, P.W. (Sergeant)	1st Suffolk	Pawsey R. (Private)	Machine Gun
Frost E.C. (Private)	2nd Suffolk		Corps
Baldwin A.P. (2nd Lieutenant)	2nd Suffolk	Thomson W.H. (Private)	London Scottish
		Thomson W. (Private)	London Scottish
Crick C.H. (Private)	3rd Suffolk	Bishop E.W. (Gunner)	Royal Garrison
Banham E.A. (Private)	7th Suffolk		Artillery
Banham W.H. (Private)	9th Suffolk	Prentice C.J. (Trooper)	15th King's
Bishop H.H. (Private)	9th Suffolk		Hussars
Crack C. (Sergeant)	9th Suffolk	Sturgeon A.W.	King's Rifle
Everett H. (Private)	9th Suffolk	(Rifleman)	
Mayhew R. (Private)	9th Suffolk	Manning A.W.W. (Able	H.M.S. Aries
Nichols H.J. (Private)	9th Suffolk	Seaman)	
Sargeant G.S. (Lance Corporal)	9th Suffolk	Scott T. (Stoker)	Royal Navy

Source: Great Barton war memorial

After the First World War

Worldwide, 65 million soldiers from 30 countries, including 2.67 million volunteers and 2.77 million conscripts from the United Kingdom, fought in the First World War. During the conflict, 10 million members of the armed services and 7 million civilians were killed. The estimated number of UK servicemen who were killed varied between 826,746 and 1,012,075, which amounted to between 1.79 per cent and 2.2 per cent of the UK population at that time and created 136,000 widows and 300,000 fatherless children. In addition, there were over one and a half million wounded UK servicemen. Some had lost limbs, some had been gassed in the trenches and endured visual and respiratory problems, and others were emotionally wounded and found it difficult to adjust to civilian life.

The men who returned to Great Barton after the war found a very different village from the one they had left behind.

11

THE DENOUEMENT OF THE BARTON ESTATE

During the second decade of the twentieth century, the Barton Estate was broken up and sold, the Bunbury family moved out of the village, and the two Great Barton schools amalgamated and became Great Barton School.

Sale of Barton Estate

In 1914, Barton Hall was leased to Sir John Smiley. At about midnight, on 14 January 1914, a fire broke out on the upper floor, which destroyed or damaged most of the mansion. It took an hour for the horse-drawn fire engine to arrive from Bury St Edmunds, only to discover that the well, which supplied Barton Hall, was too deep for the extraction of water. In spite of great efforts by many villagers, most of the furnishings and many valuable books and paintings were destroyed. The building became one of six country houses in Suffolk that were destroyed by fire in the twentieth century and never rebuilt.

John Smiley moved to Canterbury on 1 February 1914 and Sir Henry Charles Bunbury decided to sell his 2,136-acre estate at Great Barton. This included Barton Hall and 130 acres of wooded parkland, the Bunbury Arms public house, the Crown Beerhouse, the wheelwright's workshop and house, the smithy, the laundry, the post office and grocer's shop, both schoolhouses, three large private residences, 100 cottages and nine mixed farms. The Bunbury family retained ownership of the two school premises.

Under the terms of the Bunbury family Trust Deed, the Barton Estate had to be sold in its entirety, rather than in separate lots, and it was bought by George Grant Stephenson, an oil magnate from Kent. He also acquired the Lordship of Great Barton and all manorial and other rights, which dated back to the year 1281 and produced an annual income of £6. 8s. 9d. in 1915.

On 16 and 17 July 1915, Barton Estate was resold in about a hundred individual lots at a public auction, organised by Messrs. Norbury-Smith and Co., a London firm of auctioneers. Conyers Green Farm was divided into three smaller holdings, and most of the farms were bought by the sitting tenants.

The site of Barton Hall itself was withdrawn when the bidding only reached £875, so the timber was sold in lots, whilst the house, pleasure grounds, arboretum and gardens were sold in smaller lots for individual development. In January 1916, the ruins of Barton Hall were finally demolished and sold privately to T.W. Rodwell of Hacheston, Suffolk. The materials, which included a fine old stone porch with its massive oak door, 10,000 Queen Anne red bricks, ornamental stoneware, slates, poles and boards, were auctioned in 280 lots (*BFP*, 8 July 1916). In March 1916, Southeby, a London auction house, sold 2,000 volumes from Sir Henry Bunbury's library, which raised £232. 5s. 6d. (*BFP*, 4 Mar. 1916).

Map 5. Part of Barton Estate, 1915

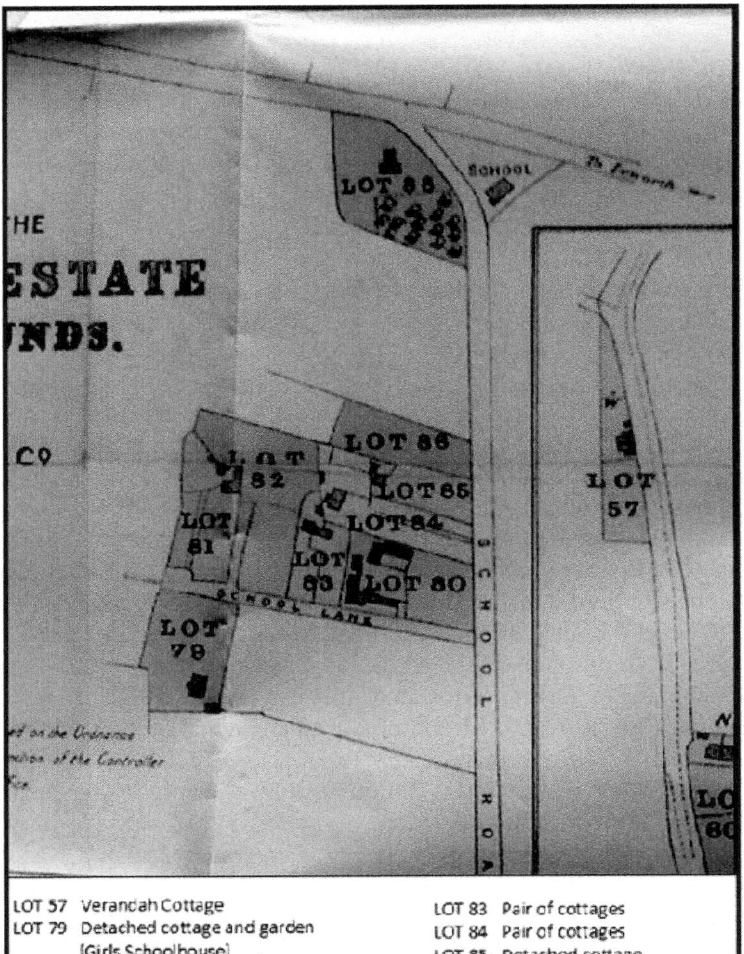

LOT 57	Verandah Cottage	
LOT 79	Detached cottage and garden	
	[Girls Schoolhouse]	
LOT 80	Crown Beerhouse and butcher's shop	
LOT 81	Cottage with garden	
LOT 82	Paddock and allotment	
LOT 83	Pair of cottages	
LOT 84	Pair of cottages	
LOT 85	Detached cottage	
LOT 86	Allotment	
LOT 88	Pair of cottages and gardens	
	[Boys Schoolhouse]	

The post mill, built in 1783, was demolished in 1918. The Church Institute was leased to the vicar and churchwardens for 99 years from 11 October 1903, for a ground rent of 5s. p.a. The Mission Hall was let to the deacons of the Baptist Church (*BFP*, 17 July 1915). The lordship of the manor was withdrawn from sale when the bidding failed to reach more than £250 (*BFP*, 10 Oct. 1915).

Sale of the schoolhouses

The Girls' Schoolhouse (Lot 79), occupied in 1915 by Emma Daine, was described in the Barton Estate sales catalogue as a 'detached double-fronted, freehold cottage' with half an acre of garden, situated on the southern side of School Lane. It was built of brick and flint, and had two bedrooms, two sitting rooms, a kitchen and outbuildings. In 1915, the Girls' Schoolhouse was let for £5p.a. to Suffolk Education Committee who sublet it to Emma Daine for £7. 10s. p.a. The house was withdrawn from sale after the bidding only reached £150, but was sold privately for £150, on 11 October 1915, to Fred Cowley, who named it Lane End.

Girls' Schoolhouse, School Lane

Fred Cowley was born in April 1873, in Whittington, Derbyshire, and was the son of a gamekeeper. In 1881, his family lived at Downton, Wiltshire, but Fred left home before he was 17 and worked as an assistant gamekeeper at Follifoot, near Knaresborough, Yorkshire. In 1897, he married Sarah Elizabeth Parry in Crickhowell, Breconshire, and they moved to Cumnor, Berkshire, with a baby and two of Fred's brothers, one of whom also became a gamekeeper. They later moved to the Round House, Park Lodge; a six-roomed house at Rougham where Fred worked as head gamekeeper and he and Sarah brought up five children. When he enlisted in the army on 9 June 1916, Fred gave his address as Rougham

Hall, not Great Barton, so Emma Daine may have rented it from him until the end of 1916. He served in the Dorset Royal Garrison Artillery for nearly three years, during which time he was based at Weymouth, Portsmouth and Aldershot. He was discharged, on grounds of disability, in February 1919. He died on 26 July 1956 at Mill Lodge, Rougham, and left assets, valued at £3,546. 19s. 8d. to his wife and youngest son, Oswald, who was a police sergeant.

On 10 March 1924, Fred Cowley sold Lane End for £375 to John Sutherland Hall Esq, from Plaistow, London E13, who sold it, on 16 Apr 1930, for £675 to Dorothy Turner George of Chapel Farm, Great Ashfield, Suffolk, who had inherited her father's estate, valued at over £37,000, in 1924. By 1943, Dorothy had moved to Bury St Edmunds and rented out Lane End to Eric Tom Fairweather, a motor mechanic from Sicklesmere.

Lane End was sold to Phyllis Eaton Russell for £1,000 on 20 May 1953, and then to Brian Lord of 3, Laundry Cottages, Great Barton, for £5,700 on 22 March 1968. In 1970, it was bought by Alan Roger Moad, who lived there for 38 years, extended the house and changed its name to Pipers' Piece after new houses were built and it was no longer the last house in the lane. In 2008, Mr and Mrs Garrard bought the house, which they sold on 16 April 2010 for £480,000 to Justyn and Julia Randall, who carried out further renovations and extensions.

Robert Evans lived in the Boys' Schoolhouse (Lot 88), a semi-detached cottage which occupied a corner position nearly opposite the Boys' School. It was described in the Barton Estate sales catalogue as one of 'two capital freehold cottages, with exceptionally good gardens and outbuildings' and was built in brick and flint, with a slate roof. It comprised three bedrooms, one living room, kitchen and a pantry. In 1915, the Boys' Schoolhouse was let to Suffolk Education Committee for £3 p.a. Mrs Sturgeon, who occupied the other half of the cottage, paid £4 p.a. in rent.

LOT 88.

Boys' Schoolhouse, School Road

After the cottages were sold on 16 July 1915, the school managers were concerned about the housing arrangements for Robert Evans. They sent a letter to West Suffolk Education Committee on 12 August 1915, which stated that:

'The Managers at their meeting tonight, decided to apply to the Education Committee for consent to terminate Mr Evans's engagement as head teacher of the Boys' School, so that more satisfactory arrangements may be made with him for the future. 'There is no desire to dispense with Mr Evans' services, but simply to alter existing arrangements with regard to the provision of a house.'

The Managers' Minute Book recorded that, in December 1915, the managers gave Robert Evans notice to quit and recommended that West Suffolk Education Committee should consider re-appointing him as a continuation of his existing appointment. It later stated that the new arrangement was considered by the managers to be satisfactory.

The Boys' Schoolhouse was renamed Ramblers. In July 1933, the house was bought by Joseph Mayes, who moved from the nearby village of Troston. His five-year-old son, Peter, and 11-year-old daughter, Peggy, both attended Great Barton School. The house was subsequently bought by Dorothy Kate Dixon, Francis Thoburn (a school manager), Yvonne Pamela Faiers, and David and Diane Elaine Hardwick.

Land ownership and leading people in Great Barton after 1915

In 1916, Kelly's Directory of 1916 listed six landowners in the village.

Sir Edward Hulton (1869-1925), a newspaper proprietor, purchased Westerfield Farm and Lodge Farm and turned them into a stud farm to breed racehorses. His father had established the *Sporting Chronicle* (1871) and the *Athletic News* (1875), and Edward took over control of both in 1894. He started a halfpenny newspaper called the *Manchester Evening Chronicle* (1897), produced the *Daily Dispatch* (1900) and the *Daily Sketch* (1909), and began publishing the *Sunday Herald* (1915). He was knighted in 1921 and retired in 1923, when he sold all his publishing interests to Allied Newspapers for six million pounds. He died in 1925, at the age of 56, leaving a quarter of a million pounds to his wife, Florence Elizabeth Millicent Warris Lindon, a former actress, whom he married in 1907. His son, Edward, published magazines and set up the Hulton Picture Library in 1945, created by cataloguing photographs from *Picture Post*, a photojournalist magazine.

Sir Edward Walter Greene, DL, JP, (1842-1920) owned Nether Hall, Pakenham, and land in Great Barton and served as the Conservative Member of Parliament for Bury St Edmunds from 1900 until 1906.

Major St John St George Ord, who had been the private secretary and aide-de-camp to the governor of Newfoundland, Canada, during the 1870s and 1880s, owned property in Great Barton and Fornham.

Frank Baldwin owned Elms Farm, a 180-acre farm previously known as Paine's Farm, which he sold, in 1920, to West Suffolk County Council, who used it as a 'County Farm'. A new village school was built on part of the land in 1967.

Robert Paul Fyson owned Manor Farm and allowed the villagers and the schoolchildren to use one of his meadows to play cricket and football. His son, Robert [690], fought with the Royal Air Force and found employment in London at the end of the war, but was killed in a motor car accident in 1926 in Newmarket, at the age of 29, on his way to visit his parents in Great Barton.

Mrs Bennett owned Barton Grange, which she later sold to Frank Burrell, a farmer at Cattishall.

The Revd Henry Taylor, Vicar of Holy Innocents' Church, Great Barton, died in January 1915, aged 43, after a serious attack of influenza. He was buried in his home village of Hawstead, Suffolk. Robert Fyson was appointed as the People's Warden until 17 July 1915, when the Revd William Hatt Lipscomb was appointed as the new vicar. He had previously worked in Canada and London, was ordained as a deacon in 1905 and as a priest in 1906 in Ontario, Canada, where he served as a curate at St Paul's Church in Kingston, Ontario, and then priest-in-charge of Gananogue, Ontario. He returned to London in 1909 to be a curate at Maida Vale in West London until 1912, when he was appointed as a hospital chaplain in Paddington (*BFP*, 19 June 1915).

James Maulkin King, JP, a director of Greene King Brewery in Bury St Edmunds, lived at Barton Lodge, but suffered from advancing paralysis and, in January 1917, was found dead in his bathroom where he had shot himself in the head with a revolver (*BFP*, 20 Jan. 1917).

Walter Morley owned Barton Place. He was a farmer and an elder of the church and, in 1918, was fined for taking his wife to chapel in a car at a time when wartime regulations restricted the use of petrol to 'public duty'. He defended his action on the grounds that he could not afford to buy a horse, but was fined £1 (*BFP*, 1 Mar. 1918).

William Picken, a baker, owned land in Shinham Bridge Road and eight cottages in The Street. He ran the village store and post office, and his daughter, Monica, was a pupil at Barton School and a talented pianist (*BFP*, 26 July 1919).

In addition to the above, Major Hugh Copinger-Hill of Barton Cottage, David James Thompson of Cattishall Farm and Harold and Lilias d'Arcy Hutton who lived at Old House were leading members of the village community.

In 1919, PC Manning, the village police officer, was replaced by PC Briggs a Royal Navy ex-serviceman.

Amalgamation of the Barton schools

In 1915, Robert Evans was the head teacher of Great Barton Boys' School and Emma Daine of Great Barton Girls' School. The Revd Lipscomb, Frank Baldwin, Mrs Copinger-Hill, William Picken, and Robert and Catherine Fyson were the school managers. The Revd Lipscomb, Frank Baldwin and Robert Fyson were also trustees of the Poor's Firing Farm Charity, together with John Aldhous.

In 1915, West Suffolk Education Committee decided to amalgamate the two schools and create a mixed school, which would be more educationally efficient and financially viable.

West Suffolk Education Committee offered Emma Daine alternative employment as head teacher of Tuddenham Elementary Mixed School. She was happy to accept since she had 'not felt comfortable, since the arrival of the new Vicar of Great Barton and welcomed the opportunity to move to a new school' (internal note, written by member of Board of Education).

In December 1916, the *Bury Free Press* reported that 'the village very much regretted the resulting departure of the girls' and infants' school headmistress for over 20 years, Mrs Daine. She had enjoyed the complete confidence of the Education Committee and school managers throughout, and had seen some 700 to 800 pupils pass through the school. Her ex-pupils were spread far and wide (*BFP*, 23 Dec. 1916).'

At her leaving assembly, Emma Daine was presented with gifts from many people including Lady Laura Bunbury and Mary Riley Smith. Betty Stiff, the youngest girl in the school, presented her with a silver-handled, silk umbrella on behalf of all the pupils and staff (*BFP*, 6 Jan. 1917).

Florence Pickworth was appointed by Suffolk County Council as a temporary, head teacher of the Girls' School until the amalgamation was finally agreed. She made only one entry in the girls' punishment book, which stated that, in November 1917, one stroke of the cane was administered to a girl for inking her arithmetic book.

There are no entries in the Managers' Minute Book for 1916, but the amalgamation of the schools did not have the unanimous support of the managers. A majority wanted the post of head teacher to be advertised in order to seek external applications, whilst a minority wanted the post of head teacher to be offered to Robert Evans. This latter group included the Revd Lipscomb who was afraid that if the post were opened up to external applicants, Robert Evans would leave the village, which would then need to appoint a new church organist and choirmaster as well as a teacher.

A long-running dispute ensued, and the Revd Lipscomb and Frank Baldwin, chair of Great Barton Parish Council, resigned as school managers on 19 February 1917 and were replaced the following week by Mr R. G. Saint and John Aldous, with Robert Paul Fyson as chairman and correspondent. On 5 March 1917, the new board of managers passed a motion stating that, 'owing to the complex conditions which have arisen, the managers have decided not to amalgamate the Great Barton schools'.

Following this decision, Sir Henry Charles Bunbury wrote to the school managers giving them notice to 'deliver up the schools on the sixth day of April 1918', the next date on which the annual lease was due to be renewed. This risked the closure of the school, in the event of which Great Barton children would have to travel to Thurston, Pakenham, Rougham or Bury St Edmunds to attend a school.

On 17 August 1917, the Local Education Authority (LEA) wrote to the Board of Education to explain the situation. The letter stated that Robert Evans was in his sixtieth year and was, 'by no means a bad fellow, but that evidently there was much feeling for and against him in the parish'.

On 21 August 1917, the National Union of Teachers suggested to the Board of Education that the school should be taken over either as a council school or as a non-provided school under a new body of managers.

On 25 August, R.F. Fulford the secretary of the Sudbury Voluntary School Association asked the Board of Education for permission to build a new school if the existing one were closed. The same letter asked whether the Ministry of Munitions had the power under the Courts (Emergency Powers) Acts, in relation to the arbitrary eviction of tenants, to suspend the enforcement of the eviction notice until the end of the war.

The situation was still unresolved on 3 November 1917 when the board of managers resigned *en bloc* and handed over all the relevant paperwork to West Suffolk Education Committee.

At this point, further negotiations were held, following which Sir Henry Charles Bunbury agreed to withdraw the eviction notice on condition that the Revd Lipscomb and Frank Baldwin were reappointed as managers.

On 4 January 1918, a new board of managers was appointed consisting of Frank Burrell, David Thompson, Frank Baldwin (County Council representative) and Percy Haddon (Parish Council representative) with Archie Ainsworth Hunt as vice-chair and school correspondent and the Revd Lipscomb as chairman. They unanimously agreed to the amalgamation of the two schools and the appointment of Robert Evans as head teacher of Great Barton Voluntary Mixed School.

On 16 January, the Board of Education were asked for a formal date for the reappointment of Robert Evans as head teacher.

Tenancy agreement

In January 1918, the following agreement was signed by Sir Henry Charles Bunbury and the new school managers:

'Memorandum of Agreement made this 7th January One thousand nine hundred and eighteen BETWEEN Sir Henry Charles John Bunbury of Manor House Mildenhall in the County of Suffolk (hereinafter called "the Landlord") of the one part and William Hatt Lipscomb, Archie Ainsworth Hunt, Frank Burrell and David Thompson (hereinafter called "the Tenants") of the other part, WHEREBY the Landlord agrees to let, and the Tenants agree to take those buildings situated in the parish of Great Barton aforesaid called or known as the Great Barton Boys' School and the Great Barton Girls' School respectively together with the playground and appurtenances thereto with the Landlord's fixtures and fittings therein, more particularly described in the Schedule hereunder written. To hold for the term of one year, to commence from the sixteenth day of April 1918 and then from year to year until either party shall give to the other notice to determine the tenancy hereby created, in manner as hereinafter provided, at the clear yearly rental of one peppercorn, or one shilling, if demanded. And the tenants agree to pay the rent reserved and to keep, use, and occupy the said premises as and for the purpose of a School for the education of children and adults or children only, of the labouring, manufacturing, and other poorer class in the Parish of Great Barton and as a residence for the teacher or teachers of the said school, which said school shall always be in union with and conducted according to the principles and in furtherance of the ends and designs of the Incorporated National Society for Promoting the Education of the Poor in the Principles of the Established Church throughout England and Wales, and shall be managed and controlled by a Committee consisting of the principal officiating Minister for the time being of the said Parish, who shall be ex-officio Chairman of the Committee, and three other persons being bona fide members of the Church of England, of whom the following shall be the first appointed – that is to say, Archie Ainsworth Hunt, Frank Burrell and David Thompson and vacancies in the number of the said three other persons shall be filled up by the nomination on the part of the continuing or surviving members of the said Committee of another person or persons being bona fide members of the Church of England. And it is further agreed that at the expiration of the said term of one year either of the said parties shall be at liberty to determine the said tenancy by giving to the

other twelve months' notice or warning in writing, expiring on either of the usual quarterly days, except Christmas Day. And also that in the event of any breach of the agreements on the part of the Tenants hereinbefore contained the Landlord may determine the tenancy by giving to the Tenants one calendar months' notice in writing to that effect, and may after the expiration of such notice resume possession of the premises and remove therefrom all property belonging to the Tenants without any process of Law or further authority on that behalf.'

It was signed by Sir Henry Charles John Bunbury, William Hatt Lipscomb DCL, Archie Ainsworth Hunt LRIBA, Frank Burrell and David Thompson.

In essence, control of the schools was handed over to the school managers, although the Bunbury family retained the freehold of the land.

Alteration of the school premises

In 1918, Archie Ainsworth Hunt, who was an architect as well as a school manager, drew up plans for converting the school to a mixed one. These plans, which included the creation of separate entrances, cloakrooms and playgrounds for boys and girls, were sent to Sir Henry Bunbury for his approval.

The managers wrote to the principal ratepayers of the parish to request subscriptions towards the estimated cost of £110 for the alterations. A total of £92 had been raised by July 1918.

On 5 April, the school submitted detailed plans to the Board of Education for changes to the 'offices' and the cloakrooms. The plans were approved 'except for the piped disposal of the liquids from the urinals'. The school was advised that 'if a filter or irrigation area is impracticable, the waste from the urinals should be taken to a water-tight cesspool as described in the building regulations'.

William Moyse, a local builder, was asked to proceed with the work. However, on 22 April 1918, the Board of Education informed the LEA that they proposed that the building work should be postponed until the end of the war in view of the shortage of labour and materials. They also stated that 'even when it becomes possible to proceed with the alterations, the distance separating the premises will necessitate the appointment of a head teacher for each of the Departments (senior and junior) and that the question of amalgamating the Departments under a single head teacher will have to be postponed until the provision of the infant's classroom, indicated on the plan, enables all the children to be accommodated in the same premises'.

By June 1918, the cost of the building work had risen to £180, but the Board of Education rejected an application for a loan and suggested that the alterations be postponed until the end of the war. West Suffolk

Education Committee challenged the Board of Education's decision about postponement on the grounds that the work would be carried out, 'with local supplies of labour, which are unavailable for agricultural or munitions work, and of materials, which are not likely to be drawn upon for munition purposes.'

On 3 July 1918, the school was given permission to go ahead with the alterations and asked William Moyse to carry out the work. On 30 October 1918, an Architects' Certificate was issued by the Board of Education for Great Barton School to become a mixed and infants' school with up to 158 pupils.

From 8 November 1918, the school became Great Barton Voluntary Mixed School. The younger children were taught in the School Lane building and the older ones in the School Road building.

The teachers

In 1918, there were four members of staff and about 80 pupils. The teaching staff consisted of Robert Evans and Winifred Evans who taught the older pupils (Standards III to VII), Emily Reed (née Brunning) who taught the lower juniors (Standards I and II), and Jennie Clinton, who was in charge of the infant class.

Emily, who was appointed as Emily Brunning in July 1917, married Ernest Reed in October 1917, who was to become a future head teacher of Great Barton School.

In 1920, Jennie Clinton, who had worked at the school since 1907, married David Thomson, and the school gave her a valuable tea service as a present. The minutes of the managers' meeting state that:

'She had been loyal to the Vicar and the Master. She was beloved by the children and her valuable work in the day schools, as superintendent of the Sunday school, and her work generally in the parish would not be quickly forgotten.'

The schoolchildren were given a half-day holiday. After the service, the vicar thanked Jennie for her 'loyalty to the vicar and the schoolmaster' (*BFP*, 06 Nov. 1920). This comment provoked a short article in the local paper, which challenged the idea of a teacher being expected to owe a loyalty to a parish vicar (*BFP*, 13 Nov. 1920).

After her marriage, Jennie resigned her posts as teacher and as the superintendent of Great Barton Sunday School.

A third of all LEAs operated a marriage bar before 1914 but, in London and some rural areas, it was generally accepted that women could continue to teach after marriage. In most places, the bar was lifted during the First World War. However, in 1921, only 19 per cent of women teachers in elementary schools were married. From this time, most LEAs operated a marriage bar for teachers to solve the problem of male teacher unemployment and thousands of married women teachers were dismissed.

Jennie Clinton was replaced by Miss Addison, a 'supplementary teacher', who taught the lower junior class (Standards I and II).

West Suffolk Education Committee arranged a course of cookery and domestic classes for the older girls at the Church Institute. In 1919, the class was run by Miss Faulkner, a part-time teacher, and attended by 18 girls, six of whom walked three miles each way from Fornham (*BFP*, 7 June 1919). Miss Faulkner also ran an evening class at the Church Institute.

In 1921, Doris Robinson and Cicely Clara Bloomfield were appointed as pupil-teachers, and Cicely Bloomfield passed the pupil-teacher examination in December 1922. Robert Evans advised the managers that she was, 'the first to have done so in the history of the school'.

The school curriculum

The Education Act 1921 reaffirmed the right of a parent to withdraw their child from religious observance or instruction. However, the school admissions register at Great Barton School indicated that very few children opted out of religious instruction lessons in spite of the fact that some pupils were Roman Catholics and others attended Great Barton Baptist Chapel, where Edward Johnston was superintendent until 1942.

The Education Act 1921 consolidated previous legislation relating to the education and employment of children and young persons and removed exemptions that enabled pupils to leave school before the age of 14. It required LEAs to ensure that elementary schools provided 'practical instruction suitable to the ages, abilities, and requirements of the children'.

Mr Creek, a horticultural and gardening instructor, worked with the older boys in the school gardens. He taught them how to grow fruit, flowers and vegetables, gave demonstrations of digging, ridging, trenching, budding, grafting and pruning, and gave talks entitled 'soils and manures', 'espalier apple trees', 'seeds and their germination', 'pests and how to destroy them' and 'how to grow roses'. He took seeds to the school, checked the condition of the tools and, in 1929, helped some of the boys to creosote the inside of the shed. The produce was sold to raise money for the school and to purchase more seeds.

One year, Frank Burrell, a school manager, presented a gardening prize of 10s. In August 1920, a summer tea party with games and sports was held for the schoolchildren at the Church Institute, and Archie Ainsworth Hunt presented prizes, which included two for the best school garden (*BFP*, 14 Aug. 1920).

Post-war events for the schoolchildren

During the war years, no parties or visits were arranged for the pupils from Great Barton School, but children from the Sunday school and the bell-ringers were invited to a Christmas party each year at the Vicarage.

On 7 November 1919, newspapers published '*The King's Letter to his People*', which asked that, 'at the eleventh hour, on the eleventh day of the eleventh month of every year, people throughout the British Empire would observe a two minutes silence and suspend all duties, in order to remember '*the glorious dead*'.' At Great Barton School on 11 November 1919, the letter was read to the pupils and the children and staff observed a two-minute silence.

From 1919, Empire Day (later known as Commonwealth Day) was celebrated, often with fireworks and community bonfires, and parties and annual outings resumed. The Church Choir travelled to Felixstowe by train, boat and charabanc, and enjoyed time on the beach, and dinner and tea in the Grand Hotel (*BFP*, 09 Aug.1919). The Baptist Chapel organised an outing and a garden tea party for 120 people for their annual Whitsun gathering (*BFP*, 14 June 1919). The Primitive Methodists held a rally at the Oakeries, the home of William Frost (*BFP*, 26 July 1919).

In August 1920, there was a party for the pupils from the day and Sunday schools at the Church Institute, with a meal followed by sports and games of cricket on the Vicarage meadow (*BFP*, 14 Aug. 1920).

In December 1920, a Christmas party, with a Christmas tree donated by Mr Brabrooke, was arranged at the Church Institute for 150 schoolchildren, funded by a donation from Sir Edward Hulton and profits from a whist drive. During the party, the children were given presents, and prizes for good conduct and attendance (*BFP*, Dec. 1920).

In July 1921, a summer fête on the Vicarage meadow raised £35 for the school. It included a refreshments stall, a tennis tournament, a whist drive, a cake sale, a buried treasure game, hoopla, an auction, a rummage stall and a coconut shy. An aerial trapeze was constructed by Mr Reeve but he fell on the very first trip and injured his shoulder and ankle, so the event was abandoned. Mr Theobald won a fowl in the competition to guess the number of residents in the parish of Great Barton, and the day finished with a dance on the lawn.

In November 1921, there was a party at the Church Institute for the children from the choir and the Sunday school, with a meal, games, dancing and a lantern show (*BFP*, 5 Nov. 1921).

In March 1922, the schoolchildren performed songs, dances, recitations, and a play entitled *The Enchanted Garden* in a concert in the Church Institute (*BFP*, 4 Mar. 1922).

In October 1922, over £8 was raised for the school at an event where
home-made sweets and other items were sold and the pupils performed
songs and dances (*BFP*, 28 Aug. 1922).

Post-war changes in Great Barton

Between 1911 and 1921, the population of Great Barton decreased from
718 to 666, and the number of dwellings from 188 to 178. At least one
person in the village died from Spanish flu, a pandemic, which lasted from
January 1918 to December 1920 and killed more people worldwide than
had died during the First World War.

Unemployment

Before the First World War, men in Great Barton were employed on
farms or as servants, carpenters, wheelwrights, bricklayers, bakers,
butchers, boot repairers, and wagon drivers. Two men were employed in
white-collar jobs, one as a newspaper reporter and another as an insurance
salesman, but these were exceptions. Some of those who returned were
able to pick up their old jobs, but mechanisation during the war years
resulted in a falling demand for farm workers. In 1918, agricultural
labourers were paid 30s. for a 48-hour week in winter, and a 54-hour week
during the rest of the year, with overtime rates of 8½d. on weekdays and
10d. on Sundays (*BFP*, 25 May 1918).

There was a post-war economic boom from 1919 until the early 1920s,
but the number of unemployed workers increased during the 1920s and
1930s and many unemployed men resented the fact that women were
employed in occupations that had been carried out by men before the war.

The situation was slightly alleviated by grants from the United Services
Fund, to which 78 wounded servicemen in Great Barton were entitled. The
Unemployment Insurance Act 1920 created a benefit system, which
covered the majority of manual workers, whereby unemployed men were
eligible to receive cash benefits of 15s. per week and unemployed women
benefits of 12s. per week for a maximum period of 15 weeks.

By 1921, the price of coal had increased to 52s 6d. per ton, so only 45
parishioners received 4 cwt of coal that year from the Poor's Firing Farm
Charity. By 1923, the price of coal had fallen to 43s. so 91 families
received 4 cwt of coal that year.

Electoral reform

The Representation of the People Act 1918 gave the vote to men over
the age of 21, subject to a six-month residency qualification, and to women
over 30 if they were either a member of, or married to a member of, the
Local Government Register, a property owner or a graduate voting in a
university constituency. This tripled the size of the electorate and extended

the franchise to about 13 million men and 8.4 million women. Women accounted for about 43 per cent of the total electorate.

The Parliament (Qualification of Women) Act 1918 gave women over 21 the right to stand for election as an MP, even though those under the age of 30 were not able to vote until the Representation of the People (Equal Franchise) Act 1928. This Act was passed a few weeks after the death of Emmeline Pankhurst, and 21 years after women were granted equal voting rights in the Grand Duchy of Finland, the first European country to do so.

Nationally, 17 women candidates stood in the 1918 election, including Christabel Pankhurst (1880-1958), a co-founder of the Women's Social and Political Union (WSPU). Countess Constance Markiewicz was the only female to be elected, but, as a member of Sinn Fein the Irish republican political party, she refused to take her seat. Viscountess Nancy Astor, an American-born socialite, was elected to represent Plymouth as a Conservative MP at a by-election, held on 15 November 1919, and became the first woman to take her seat in the House of Commons.

In Bury St Edmunds, Eva Paulina Greene, the wife of John Wollaston Greene, a Bury solicitor and great grandson of Benjamin Greene who owned the brewery, was elected as Bury St Edmunds' first woman councillor in November 1921.

In 2015, Jo Churchill was elected as the first female MP for Bury St Edmunds and was the second female MP ever to be elected in the county of Suffolk.

Education legislation

Fisher's Education Act 1918 abolished all fees in state elementary schools, made provision for swimming baths, medical inspections and nurseries and gave more support for pupils with special needs.

It also made provision for school playing fields but there was no room for a playing field at either of the school buildings in Great Barton, so local farmers offered the use of their meadows.

In 1920, the school acquired an acre of land near School Lane for use as a play area. It was a gift from William Norman King [569], who died in April 1914, a week after his ninetieth birthday (*BFP*, 8 Apr. 1914). He had lived at Barton Place, been a manager of Great Barton School, Framlingham College and King Edward VI Grammar School, Bury St Edmunds, president of Suffolk Agricultural Association, a Justice of the Peace for 25 years and on the Board of Guardians of Thingoe Workhouse.

The Lewis Report (1917) proposed that the minimum school leaving age should be raised to 14 and that school leavers should attend day continuation schools for vocational training for at least 8 hours a week or 320 hours a year up to the age of 18. Its proposals were not fully taken up and some schoolchildren were able to leave at the age of 13, or even 12 under certain conditions, until the Education Act 1921 removed these exemptions.

Herbert Albert Laurens Fisher (1865–1940), the president of the Board of Education, was responsible for the Superannuation Act 1918, which granted superannuation allowances to teachers over the age of 60, if they had fulfilled certain criteria.

In 1918, the starting annual salary for a qualified schoolmistress rose from £90 to £150. National salary scales, with a provisional minimum scale, were introduced for elementary school teachers in 1919, with pay and conditions negotiated by the Burnham Committee, which ran from 1919 until 1988, and included representatives from teachers, LEAs and the government.

The National Federation of Women Teachers (NFWT) campaigned hard on the issue of equal pay and, in 1919, called a referendum of NUT members, which approved the principle of equal pay for women teachers. Male teachers, opposed to the principle of equal pay, left the NUT and formed the National Association of Men Teachers. In 1920, the NFWT changed its name to the National Union of Women Teachers (NUWT) and continued to campaign for equal pay.

The changing role of the gentry

By 1922, all that remained of Barton Hall were parts of the walls and a few fragments of masonry. The Barton Estate and most of the land in Great Barton had been sold, and the role of the landed gentry in Great Barton, as in many other parts of the country, had changed irrevocably.

In West Suffolk, Rushbrooke Estate and Livermere Hall were sold in 1919; Rougham Hall was destroyed by a bomb during the Second World War; Fornham Hall was dismantled and sold during the 1950s and Rushbrooke Hall was demolished in 1961. Following the demolition of the Manor House, Mildenhall in 1934, the Bunbury family moved to Naunton Hall, Rendlesham, in East Suffolk.

Great Barton in 1922

In December 1922, Robert Evans retired at the age of 65, after working for 25 years as head teacher of Great Barton Voluntary Mixed School, which was now a very different school from the one he had taken over in 1897. It was now a mixed school with a single head teacher, the LEA was responsible for its maintenance, and the Bunbury family no longer wielded the same influence over the running of the school.

The managers advertised the post of head teacher and interviewed 12 candidates. They offered the post, which no longer included accommodation, to Cecil Frank Channell from Ingham, Suffolk.

12

ECONOMIC AND EDUCATIONAL CHALLENGES

Cecil Channell was the head teacher of Great Barton Voluntary Mixed School during a very difficult period of its history. Its Victorian buildings, sited a quarter of a mile apart, were outdated and in poor condition, and the school found it increasingly difficult to raise sufficient funds to carry out the necessary repairs and improvements.

There was a worldwide economic crisis during the twenties and thirties, which resulted in a reduction in teachers' pay and high unemployment, which created low morale amongst the teaching profession and limited the opportunities for school leavers. In such an educational climate, the new educational ideas promulgated by educationalists in Europe and North America at this time, made very little impact on Great Barton School.

The teachers

In January 1923, Cecil Channell was the only certificated teacher at the school. The Code of Regulations for Primary Elementary Schools 1926 specified that a head teacher must be a certificated teacher, unless an exception to the rule was approved, and must take a definite and substantial share in the actual instruction. It went on to say that neither a clerk in holy orders, nor a regular minister of a congregation, could be recognised as a teacher.

At the lower school in School Lane, Emily Reed taught the infant class and Miss E. J. Ransom, a 'supplementary teacher', the lower junior class (Standards I and II). At the senior school, in School Road, Winifred Evans taught the upper junior class (Standards III and IV) in the single classroom which she shared with Cecil Channell who taught the senior class (Standards V to VII). The classes were named Class I, II, III and Infants, with the oldest children in Class I. The teachers were assisted by pupil-teachers, student teachers, a needlework teacher and a gardening instructor.

In 1924, Winifred Mothersole passed the Pupil Teacher Admission Examination, held at West Suffolk County Secondary School (*BFP*, 7 June 1924). The following year, Doris Robinson and Cicely Bloomfield, both of whom were pupil-teachers, spent a year at West Suffolk County Secondary School training to be teachers, after which they returned to work at Great Barton School. They opted to take the Archbishop Examination in Religious Knowledge, for which textbooks were provided by Polstead Rectory, near Colchester. In March 1925, Cicely passed the Preliminary Examination for the Certificate, but Doris failed. Cecil Channell wrote in the school logbook, 'I think her [Doris'] failure was due to nervousness. She is a very intelligent girl and should make an excellent teacher'. His views were justified, and she passed the examination a year later, with a distinction in music, by which time she was teaching at Fakenham Elementary School. R.J. Farrants joined the staff as a student teacher in 1925. Constance Brown and Rose Mayhew, who were both pupil-teachers, spent a year at West Suffolk County Secondary School and then returned to Great Barton School in 1926 and passed the Preliminary Examination for the Certificate (*BFP*, 20 Mar. 1926).

The Code of Regulations for Primary Elementary Schools 1926 specified that, in rural schools, under 18-year-olds could be employed as a monitor, but not be responsible for the secular instruction of a whole or part of a class. School-age children were no longer to be employed as assistants, and trainee elementary teachers were expected to attend a secondary school on a scholarship and then either pursue a two-year course at a college or work in an elementary school as a student teacher before going to college.

Plan 1. Great Barton Lower School, School Lane (not to scale)

Emily Reed resigned in 1926, in order to teach at Thurston School, which was closer to her home, and received a solid silver Georgian pattern cream jug as a leaving present. She was replaced by Hilda Eleanor Frances Lincoln, who taught Standards III and IV at Walsham le Willows Elementary School. She lived in Bury St Edmunds, where her father was the foreman at a factory, which manufactured grain-cleaning machinery. She was a member of Bury St Edmunds Amateur Operatic Society and was granted leave of absence from the school to perform in *Iolanthe* (1928), *HMS Pinafore* (1929) and *The Duchess of Dantzic* (1930).

In 1927, 57 per cent of all head teachers were female (*TES*, 30 Mar. 2011) but during the 1920s, the number of married women teachers fell as

LEAs gave priority to male teachers. In 1930, Winifred Evans resigned after her marriage to Archie Ainsworth Hunt, one of the school managers, and was replaced by 26-year-old Kathleen Thoburn.

Teachers attended occasional lectures in Bury St Edmunds. In February 1927, Cecil Channell attended a lecture on 'Curricula for children aged eleven-plus' by Professor J. Percy Nunn, MA, Professor of Education at London University. On a Saturday morning in 1929, he and Winifred Evans attended a lecture on 'Experimental Psychology' by J.B. Russell, HMI.

Teachers' pay

In 1923, the average annual salary for certificated teachers in England and Wales was £310 for men and £254 for women. The campaign for equal pay was hindered by the Geddes Report (1922) of the Committee on National Expenditure, which recommended cuts in expenditure on the army, navy, education and public health. Subsequently, a cut of 5 per cent was imposed on teachers' pay, and teachers were forced to contribute a further 5 per cent of their salary towards superannuation and pensions.

Some Local Education Authorities (LEAs) tried to impose even harsher pay cuts. At Lowestoft, Suffolk, the LEA voted to cut salaries by 10 per cent and, as a result, 167 member of Lowestoft National Union of Teachers (NUT) took strike action in April 1923. In response, the council brought in 112 non-union teachers from outside the area, but many parents supported the teachers' action and refused to send their children to school. On 5 May, the *Times Educational Supplement* reported that 'about a thousand small boys and girls, with banners, rattles and flags, were led in procession through the town'. Supported by other trade unions and parents, the NUT members set up strike schools in Lowestoft, called 'welfare centres', which were attended by more than 1,500 pupils; about one in four of all the pupils in Lowestoft. The local authority tried to prosecute a group of parents in June for withdrawing their children from school, but the case was dismissed by magistrates. The strike lasted for 11 months, at the end of which the education authority was forced to stand down and cut salaries by only 5 per cent. Similar strikes in Gateshead and Southampton lasted for about three months.

This was not the first time that there had been school strikes In September 1911, there were a large number of strikes in schools across the country, during which pupils refused to obey teachers, organised mass truancies and marched through the local town.

In April 1914, the children at Burston School in Norfolk walked out of school in support of their teachers, Tom and Kitty Higdon. A strike school was built in the village in 1917, which operated until 1939 supported by contributions from many trade unions and branches of the Labour Party.

During the 1920s, there were frequent strikes in all sectors of the workforce, which culminated in the General Strike, which began on 4 May 1926 and lasted nine days. It was supported by dockworkers, miners, printers, railwaymen, other transport workers, and workers in the iron and steel industry.

The National Economy Act 1931 included proposals by the government to impose a further reduction of 15 per cent on teachers' salaries but, after a lengthy debate in Parliament, this was reduced to 10 per cent.

The pupils

Between 1921 and 1931, the population of Great Barton increased from 666 to 728, and 25 new houses were built. By 1930, there were 150 pupils, many from poor families where the main breadwinner was unemployed or in irregular employment. Poor families no longer lived in fear of the workhouse, after the passing of the Local Government Act 1929, which abolished the workhouse system that had been in operation since 1834.

Each year, about 100 families of poorer parishioners received coal from the trustees of the Poor's Firing Farm Charity. From 1920 until his death in 1928, Arthur Rowell rented the farm at a rent of 77s 10d. but the land was not very productive and he often struggled to pay his rent each Lady Day and Michaelmas. From 1929, the rent was reduced to 56s for C. Parnell, the new tenant, but he was also unable to pay in cash, so paid it in sugar beet in 1934 and 1935, but was unable to pay in cash or crops in 1936 and was given notice to quit.

Charles Johnson and Audrey Osborne-Thomas, who both attended Great Barton School during this time, were interviewed by pupils at the school in 1995. Charles Johnson, the son of a horse keeper, told the pupils that he had taught his father to read and count, and was occasionally asked to wait at table at Barton Manor, where he was told that he should never disclose anything he heard there. Audrey Osborne-Thomas was nearly called Zeppelina, because she was born on a night in 1917 when a Zeppelin dropped a bomb on Billericay, Essex. Charles and Audrey talked to the pupils about the fire at Barton Hall and told them that, during the 1920s, there was a Post Office/shop, a cycle repair shop, a cobblers and a blacksmith's shop in The Street, and the village centre had seven wells and a bus service to and from Bury St Edmunds after 1929.

Pupil attendance was monitored by Mr Wright, the School Attendance Officer, on behalf of the LEA, and the Revd Lipscomb on behalf of the managers. Whenever attendance fell below 60 per cent, the head teacher was expected to justify the absences, in writing, to the LEA.

Most pupils walked to and from school twice each day, and there were often periods of low attendance during wet or snowy weather. One on occasion in 1928, the snow was so deep that Cecil Channell was unable to travel on his motor bike and had to travel by train, bus and on foot. In January 1929, after a heavy snowfall, only five pupils attended the lower school and 16 attended the senior school. In March 1929, only 26 children attended the school after an exceptionally heavy downpour of rain.

The summer holidays were extended in some years so that children could help with the harvest. The village school was closed for a short time in 1923 as a result of an outbreak of influenza (*BFP*, 3 Mar.1923), and again on the afternoon of 27 April 1925 when HRH Princess Mary, the daughter of King George V, visited Bury St Edmunds to open a new hostel. The senior school was used as a polling station for the district elections in April 1925, for a by-election in December 1925, and for the county council elections in April 1928. On each occasion, the whole school was closed.

Pupils with head-lice, ringworm, impetigo or scabies were excluded from school until they were clear of the condition. The school was required to notify the Area Health Authority of any cases of infectious diseases, such as mumps, chicken pox, measles, German measles, whooping cough and scarlet fever, and to inform the district community physician of any outbreaks of food poisoning, dysentery or similar illnesses. Scarlet fever, whooping cough, pneumonia and diphtheria were potentially fatal. In 1924, 11-year-old James (aka Jimmie) Reeve [665], a popular lad with a cheeky smile, died from pneumonia. His coffin was lowered into the grave by his school friends Harry Stiff, Gerald Garwood, Arthur Boreham and Percy Hopwood (*BFP*, 22 Mar.1924). Diphtheria vaccinations were introduced nationally from the 1920s, but were not offered to pupils of Great Barton School until 1941. In 1930, two brothers were diagnosed with the disease, which was the third leading cause of death in children in England and Wales at the time.

The School Medical Service carried out termly medical inspections, during which they monitored the weight, height and sight of each pupil and recorded the results on individual medical cards. The school dentist carried out termly dental inspections and the School Dental Service offered treatment to pupils. Most children had plenty of exercise at home and school. During playtimes, pupils played games with five stones, marbles, jacks, small balls and footballs, conkers, skipping ropes, hopscotch grids, hoops and footballs as well as chasing, hiding and other games.

Some pupils at Great Barton School required extra educational support. In 1925, Donald Backhouse was certified by the Senior Medical Officer as 'mentally deficient'. He attended Barton School for four months in 1926 and then moved away from the village. He returned in 1935 for nine months until he left school at the age of 14. The admission register described him as 'very backward, thus handicapped'. His father, Albert, who joined the Royal Navy after the First World War, was serving on the

Submarine K5 on 20 January 1921 when it went down off the Isles of Sicily *en route* to a mock battle in the Bay of Biscay. All 57 of its crew were killed and Donald was born prematurely, seven months later.

Corporal punishment was used regularly, and Cecil Channell often inflicted three to six cuts on a pupil's back. Mr Philips seemed to have been a popular target for mischievous boys, two of whom received six cuts for stealing from his garden in 1924 and three of whom received three cuts for throwing stones at him in 1925. Another boy bullied a classmate and persuaded him to steal money from his mother's purse.

There were also some successes amongst the pupils. In 1925, the school was very proud of 11-year-old Cecilia Foulger who won a prize for an essay entitled, 'If you were given £500, on what would you spend it?' (*BFP*, 10 Oct. 1925). Unfortunately, the local paper did not reveal any information about the contents of her essay.

In 1928, more than 250,000 schoolchildren nationally, wrote an essay for a 'safety first' competition, organised by the Royal Society for the Prevention of Accidents (RoSPA).

In 1930, 7,305 people in the UK were killed in road accidents [compared with 1,775 in 2014] and there was much concern about road traffic accidents and the poor state of the roads, many of which were unsuitable for heavy traffic. The Road Traffic Act 1930 removed national speed limits for light vehicles, but in 1931, a Cambridgeshire man was fined £4 for driving his Dennis motor van at 40 m.p.h. through Great Barton (*BFP*, 07 Nov. 1931). The Road Traffic Act 1934 introduced a 30 m.p.h. speed limit in built-up areas. In 1935, a driving test was introduced, Belisha beacons (named after Leslie Hore-Belisha (1893–1957), the Minister of Transport) were constructed at zebra crossings, and the cat's eye was patented by Percy Shaw.

Special days
Each Empire Day, 24 May, the children sang the British National Anthem and other patriotic songs. In 1923, they listened to a speech by King George V played on a gramophone loaned by Thomas Nice (*BFP*, 02 June 1923). In 1927, 1928 and 1929, they visited the Church Institute and watched a lantern lecture about the British Empire presented by Robert Evans.

From 1927, Trafalgar Day was celebrated on 21 October each year. Pupils at Great Barton School were taught about Lord Horatio Nelson's naval victory over the combined French and Spanish fleets in 1805.

Armistice Day, 11 November, was especially poignant for pupils, many of whose relatives had died during the First World War. At school, a two minutes' silence at 11 o'clock was followed by the singing of 'O God our Help in Ages Past'. In 1927, 1928 and 1929, Robert Evans gave a talk to the older pupils. One year, the poem 'For the Fallen', written by Laurence Binyon (1869-1943), was read aloud. In 1921, inspired by the World War I poem 'In Flanders Fields', the poppy was used as a symbol to commemorate those who died in the First World War, and from 1928 or possibly earlier poppies were sold each year at the school.

Each Christmas, the staff and pupils performed a carol concert for parents at the Church Institute. In 1923, the cast wore costumes made by Winifred Evans, and Constance Brown and Rose Mayhew, two of the pupil-teachers, performed the popular folk song entitled 'Oh No John' (*BFP*, 29 Dec. 1923).

Pupils were treated to a Christmas party at school, during which they ate a special tea and sat around a Christmas tree to receive books and other presents from Father Christmas.

In January 1932, Cecil Channell and other head teachers were instructed by the Board of Education to read out a message to the senior pupils from the World Disarmament Conference, which called for the reduction and limitation of armaments.

Village activities for the schoolchildren

The Church Magazine (*CM*), which included news about events in the parish of Great Barton, described some of the activities in which the schoolchildren participated.

Pupils were able to join village tennis, cricket and football clubs, and many joined the Anglican or Baptist Sunday schools.

About 50 children attended Holy Innocents' Sunday School, where Abigail Firman was the teacher and superintendent for 30 years until the age of 57, when she resigned in 1928 to look after her terminally ill father.

In 1923, Thomas Nice arranged a 'tea and a wireless concert' at the Vicarage for pupils of Holy Innocents' Sunday school and members of the choir (*BFP*, 11 Aug. 1923).

At the Baptist Chapel, two new classrooms were added in 1923. Members of the Sunday school, taught by Mrs Barton and Miss Johnston, performed concerts, watched lantern shows, and were treated to parties. They were also awarded prizes for attendance and for reciting the Gospel of John, chapter 3, verse 16, which is sometimes referred to as the 'golden text' of scripture.

Whenever a Sunday school summer outing to Felixstowe or Clacton was organised during term time, the whole school was closed for the day.

Queen Alexandra, wife of King Edward VII, died in November 1925, and Cecil Channell and some of the pupils attended a memorial service in Holy Innocents' Church.

The Girl Guide movement was founded in 1910, but there was no group in Great Barton until 1928, at which time it was organised by Mrs Stephen

Cox. In June 1928, the Guides collected 1,521 eggs for West Suffolk Hospital and played tennis on the lawns of the Vicarage with members of the choir (*CM*, June 1928). The following year, they performed in two concerts during Easter week and raised £5 towards Great Barton Guide Company (*CM*, May 1929, p.36).

A troop of the Boy Scouts Association was set up in Bury St Edmunds in 1908, and was one of the earliest ones to be established in England, but there was no troop in Great Barton until 1971. However, in 1928, the Revd Lipscomb hosted a troop of 21 scouts from Rushden, his home village, at the Vicarage for their annual camp on 4 August 1928 (*CM*, Sept.1928, p.74).

The school premises and equipment

The Bunbury family still owned the school buildings, which they let to the school managers for a peppercorn rent.

Most organisations met at the Church Institute, but the parish council and Great Barton Workers' Union held their meetings at the school.

In December 1930, Sir Henry Charles Bunbury, who had signed the tenancy agreement with the managers in 1918, died at the age of 75 [731]. His eldest son, Charles Henry Napier Bunbury (1886-1963) became the 11th Baronet.

In 1923, the board of managers consisted of the Revd Dr William Hatt Lipscomb (Vicar of Great Barton and chair of managers), Archie Ainsworth Hunt (correspondent and vice-chair), Frank Burrell and David Thompson (Foundation Managers), Frank Baldwin (County Council Manager) and William Gillings (Parish Council Manager). Mrs Burrell (wife of Frank) was appointed as a manager in 1926 and Mrs Ruegg a year later, when David Thompson resigned.

The school buildings were in a very poor state of repair and, although Suffolk LEA contributed towards the running costs of the school and general building maintenance, the school managers were expected to find the money for repairs, alterations, improvements and extensions.

The Managers' Fund, set up in 1904, was deposited with Lloyds Bank. It included donations from local benefactors, proceeds from sales or fundraising events, occasional offertories from the parish church, and grants from the Church Schools Defence Fund, the Diocesan Board of Finance, Belton's Charity and Sudbury Voluntary School Association, to which the school paid a subscription.

In 1924, over 100 people attended a church tea, in support of the village school, which included a musical programme and a conjuring show by Ron Bates of Bury St Edmunds (*BFP*, 12 Jan.1924).

In April 1923, the Board of Education recommended the construction of an additional classroom at the senior school so that all of the pupils could be accommodated in a single building. In response, the school managers wrote to West Suffolk Education Committee to explain that this was not financially possible because of the general depression of agriculture, the freehold of the school being the private property of Sir Henry Charles Bunbury, and the need to purchase additional land from the Small Holdings Committee of Suffolk County Council.

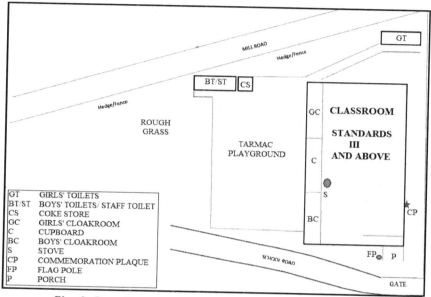

Plan 2. Great Barton Senior School, School Road (not to scale)

In 1924, 16,000 classrooms in England and Wales accommodated more than one class, and His Majesty's Inspector (HMI) sent a report to the managers of Great Barton School, which stated that:

'As all the older children and a number of pupil-teachers are taught in a single room by two teachers, the erection of a partition to secure reasonable teaching conditions is very desirable. Some dual desks to replace old and unsuitable desks without backs are needed.'

Laura Sawbridge wrote to the school, on behalf of Sudbury Voluntary School Association, to advise the managers that she, 'hoped in a short time to submit to them, favourable consideration for dealing with Barton Schools'.

The toilets and stoves always needed attention. In 1925, the school was advised to find a new site for the disposal of toilet pails, and Mr Foster offered part of his field for this purpose. During the same year, a new stove was bought for the senior school and the brickwork of the hearth was secured with an iron band.

In 1927, Robert Fyson, who lived at the Manor House, offered the use of one of his meadows to the school and the village for recreational use (*BFP*, 11 June 1927).

In 1928, the Board of Education recommended the erection of a screen at the senior school to separate the two class groups. Colonel Walter Guinness, MP for Bury St Edmunds, and Messrs Greene King and Co. both gave donations (*CM*, Aug.1928, p.64).

A garden fête was held at Barton Vicarage on 13 September 1928, which raised £39. 6s. 3d. for the Church Institute and the school. It was opened by Winifred Nice, and the children put on a display of English folk dances and played bowls, clock golf and ladder golf. Hilda Lincoln, Miss Ransom and the pupils sold needlework and other goods, Brian Nice set up a bran tub, which raised £1. 4s. and Abigail Firman and Alice Murrell sold eggs and jam. In the evening, a dance was held in the Vicarage gardens.

Archie Ainsworth Hunt, who was an architect and a school manager, was asked by the board of managers to gather specifications and prices for the screen (*CM*, Oct. 1928, p.82). The screen was never purchased but in 1942, a curtain was donated by one of the school managers to separate the two classes.

The playground surfaces were full of potholes and cracks so six loads of clinker were spread on them during the 1925 summer holidays. In 1928, the subject of the playground was raised at a meeting of Thingoe Rural District Council, during which Robert Fyson stated that the children had to walk through puddles to get to school' (*BFP*, 18 Feb. 1928). In 1931, the playgrounds continued to be in a poor state of repair and D. Nye, who lived at Conyers Green, became so incensed that he wrote a letter to *the Bury Free Press* (*BFP*, 21 Feb. 1931):-

'Sir, Do not think you can know the condition of the playground of the Great Barton Junior School. It is not fit for animals to walk through, and yet our little tots have to do so. Their footwear is not worn out; it is rotted by the continually sodden playground, in which they have to play. Just now, the main road is being broken up and, I am told, the old asphalt can be had for the carting away. Why not build the infants' playground with this? It would give work to some, benefiting, not only the children, but also the mothers and the teachers. To build up the playground would also do away with the dangerous tree-roots and stumps. As things are now, what is the use of the school doctor doing his work and the parents doing their best, when the little ones have to sit in wet boots for the biggest half of the day?'

In 1930, the lead roof of the lower school required urgent repairs after water poured into the classrooms in July and November.

A shed at the back of the lower school was converted to a garage, so that it could store a teacher's car under cover.

The school had very few resources, although there was a piano and a blackboard in each building.

In 1922, the British Broadcasting Company (BBC) was formed and Thomas Nice lent his hand-cranked gramophone to Cecil Channell, so that the schoolchildren could listen to recorded speeches on the radio (*BFP*, 2 June 1923). The BBC started to broadcast educational programmes on the radio in 1925.

Educational ideas

At this time, many radical ideas about education were being propounded worldwide. In Europe, Maria Montessori (1870-1952) was an Italian physician and educator, who published *The Montessori Method* in 1912. Jean Piaget (1896-1980) was a Swiss developmental psychologist and philosopher, who published *Language and Thought of the Child* in English in 1927. In America, John Dewey (1859-1952), a philosopher, psychologist, and educational reformer, promoted individuality and the idea that children learn from real life circumstances.

In Britain, these ideas influenced and gave rise to experimental education programmes and the establishment of three progressive schools.

Summerhill School near Aldeburgh, Suffolk, was founded in 1921 by A. S. Neill (1883-1973), a Scottish progressive educationalist, who put freedom of choice for children into practice. The original school was opened in Germany, and a school in Suffolk was opened six years later. Lessons were optional, and pupils were encouraged to make and change the school laws at weekly meetings.

Dartington Hall, Devon, was bought by Leonard Elmhirst (1893-1974) and his wife Dorothy (1887-1968) in 1925, and founded as part of a wider social experiment to revive rural life and the arts.

Beacon Hill, near Harting, West Sussex, was founded in 1927 by Bertrand Russell (1872-1970) and his wife Dora, née Black (1894-1986) as a progressive boarding school. The school reflected the views of Bertrand Russell, a philosopher, logician, mathematician, historian, and social critic, who believed that children should not be forced to follow a strictly academic curriculum.

It was run on the principle that freedom, if understood early enough, would result in maturity and self-discipline. Dora, an author, feminist and social campaigner, emphasized co-operation rather than competition and believed that the best way to teach the benefits of democracy was to operate the school on democratic lines.

The Hadow Reports

During the 1920s and 30s, Sir William Henry Hadow (1859-1937), a leading educational reformer, chaired six important consultative committees, whose reports influenced education at all levels during the next 20 years or more.

Differentiation of the Curriculum for Boys and Girls (1923) suggested that the existing school curriculum was too academic, over-burdened and rigid. It recommended that more attention should be paid to the 'aesthetic side' of secondary education, and domestic subjects (including elementary hygiene) in the girls' curriculum. It listed 24 recommendations, which argued for greater freedom in the curriculum, especially for girls, more time for pupils to develop their own individual interests, and the relaxation of some university matriculation requirements. The report concluded that curriculum subjects should be taught in closer correlation with one another, schoolwork should be more practical, and women should be adequately represented on committees and examining bodies which deal with girls' education.

Psychological Tests of Educable Capacity (1924) considered the use of psychological tests in the public education system and urged the Board of Education to set up an advisory committee to work with university departments of psychology and other relevant organisations, to consider the subject further.

Education of the Adolescent (1926) proposed that education should be a two-stage process with a separation of primary and secondary education. After the age of 11, pupils would either remain at their elementary school for three more years, or transfer to a grammar school for up to five years to follow a predominantly literary or scientific curriculum or to a modern school for four years, to follow a more practical curriculum. It proposed that the minimum school leaving age should be raised to 15.

Books in Public Elementary Schools (1928) urged schools to invest in more books and recommended that every pupil be allowed to retain possession of all the books they needed, at least in school, until the end of term or year during which they were required.

The Primary School (1931) recommended the separation of infant and junior schools, with a break at seven-years-old, and tests in English, arithmetic and intelligence at the age of 11, in order to select pupils for an appropriate secondary school. It proposed that there should be a maximum of 40 children in a primary class, provision for especially bright or 'retarded' pupils, a child-centred approach to learning, collaborative learning and the adoption of the 'project' approach to teaching and opportunities for learning by activity and experience. It advocated the appropriate use of 'look and say', phonics, and sentence methods for teaching children to read, and urged that children should be encouraged to express themselves freely in writing. It recommended the maintenance of a continuous record for each pupil and the production of a termly or annual report for parents. To achieve these aims, it recommended that teacher training courses should 'afford adequate practice in methods of individual and group work' and should train teachers to cope with the special needs of children.

Infant and Nursery Schools (1933) made 105 recommendations, which included appropriate training for nursery teachers with 'helpers' to assist them. It supported the idea that children learn from their surroundings and favoured an 'open air environment' with semi-open-air buildings and garden playgrounds. In London, open-air classes and schools were held in London parks all year round, in an effort to combat tuberculosis and other childhood infections.

In 1928, Cyril Burt (1883-1971), an educational psychologist, published *The Measurement of Mental Capacities*, which was based on his research. It maintained that intelligence was related to 'hereditary or genetic factors', and that children should be segregated, based on results of intelligence tests.

School inspections

In order to keep abreast of some of the new ideas, the Great Barton teachers occasionally attended local lectures, but there was little evidence of any significant changes in the school curriculum. The school was poorly resourced, but pupils were able to borrow books from the library van, organised by Suffolk Library Service to Schools.

The only science teaching was nature study, during which lessons the older pupils were sometimes taken on a walk around the village by their teacher to collect wild flowers and examine birds' eggs. In March 1929, the vicar praised the efforts of schoolchildren, who took care of wild birds during periods of cold weather. He commented that, 'The attention given is an education in itself' (*CM* Mar. 1929. p.20).

His Majesty's Inspectors (HMI) carried out a formal inspection every four or five years, with follow-up visits if necessary. They observed lessons, talked to pupils, looked at pupils' notebooks, studied the syllabuses of work and inspected class and school admission registers, punishment books and the school logbook.

In March 1925, Mr Russell HMI was accompanied by Mr Brotherton, an 'occasional inspector', who questioned pupils about geography, and approved a new geography scheme, prepared by Cecil Channell. They were satisfied with the teaching in the infants and lower standards, but were concerned about the poor speech of the pupils and the low standard of handwriting and arithmetic. For the senior class, they:

> 'were pleased to note the improved relationship between the children and their teacher, but felt that further progress was necessary. They were not satisfied with the progress in arithmetic, reading and spelling, history or geography, where they stated that 'a certain number of necessary facts had been remembered, but important principles were little understood.
> 'While the meagre vocabulary of the children should improve through reading and incidental teaching, suitable questions after interesting lessons should lead to greater facility in both oral and written expression'.

The school was told to complete the school timetable, and include the aims of teaching in each preface to a syllabus of work. English books and arithmetic cards were ordered in 1925, in response to the report.

There were follow-up inspections in July 1925 and 1926, during which HMI noted some improvements and reported that the headmaster had devoted much attention to remedying the deficiencies highlighted in the report. 'He has redrafted and amplified his schemes of instruction, introduced gardening diaries, and insisted upon clearer statement of arithmetic problems worked by members of his class.'

The 1926 inspection was carried out by W. G. Tregear, who reported that the infant teacher had attended a course of training, which he hoped would improve the standard of the work. He was still critical of the work in the senior class and stated that:

> 'The children write fairly neatly, their oral reading as a whole has improved and they are being encouraged to frame plans for their composition exercises. Much of the work lacks depth and there is continued need for the cultivation of speed, concentration on the work in hand and insistence upon effort from every one when oral responses to questions on the subject matter of lessons are required. In this connexion, the adoption of an encouraging attitude would help to kindle the interest that must precede real progress.'

HMI inspected the school again in 1929 and reported some improvement, but stated that much still remained to be done. It mentioned that there were some dull and backward children, two or three years retarded, in the lower school. The report was concerned about the poor spelling, speech and physique of the younger pupils, but admitted that some progress had been made towards the development of the children's vocabulary and handwriting.

It stated that the three-year-old syllabus needed revision, and the teachers could benefit by advice and constructive criticism from the head teacher. It added, 'it is unfortunate that none of the assistants have seen the *Handbook of Suggestions for Teachers* published in 1927. A copy for the junior school is desirable and important recommendations made in Chapters I, V and Appendix A, applicable to this school, might well be discussed at a meeting of the staff'.

In contrast to the HMI inspection, the reports of the Diocesan Inspector in 1925 and 1927 on the non-secular aspects of the school are much less critical. In 1927, the Revd James Scott Vallalley, Vicar of Ingham, carried out an inspection and reported the following:

- 'Infants. In this class, the hymns and home prayers were carefully and reverently taken, and the children showed an intelligent interest both in the work and in that prepared for repetition. They had been taught all the short commandments. There was evidence of good knowledge of the selected portions of the Old Testament and they had covered a fairly large field of work in the New Testament.
- Standards I and II. These classes were especially good in their knowledge of the New Testament and it was clear that the spiritual and moral side of the Old Testament lessons had been brought out as well as the historical. Here again, the repetition of the scripture passage showed careful training. The commandments were well known and the hymns were sung in a very reverent manner. The general tone in these departments in religious subject was distinctly good, certainly above the average and the teachers are to be congratulated on the results.
- Standards III to VI. These classes were taught together for certain portions of the examination. A very wide range of work had been covered in both the Old and New Testaments. The senior class had covered the whole of the four gospels with special emphasis on St Luke and were thus able to give a comprehensive survey of Our Lord's life and teaching. A very large section of the earlier parts of the Old Testament had been taken by both classes and in their work; the children showed a good understanding and marked keenness. The repetition of chosen portions was also carefully done and the musical parts of the work showed in the singing of hymns and the opening exercises, the advantages the children enjoy in the musical ability of the teachers in the senior classes. The written portions of the work were not as uniformly successful as the oral, but this may have been due to lack of time; it is difficult to cover so wide a range of work in one morning session.
- Summary. It was a great pleasure to visit both parts of the school. There was a refreshing keenness shown by the scholars in their work – this is evidence of good teaching. It was obvious that the teachers had given careful attention to the syllabus and had taught with interest and discernment. I should like to congratulate both the teachers and scholars in all departments upon the results of their work.'

The contrasting reports from HMI and the Diocesan Inspectors suggest either that the latter had lower expectations or that the teachers placed an emphasis on the teaching of religious instruction at the expense of the secular subjects.

Transfer to higher education

Many teachers believed that the main purpose of teaching in an elementary school was to train pupils to pass the scholarship examination so that they could attend a secondary school where, at the age of 16, they would be able to take the United Kingdom School Certificate, established in 1918 by the Secondary Schools Examinations Council (SSEC). Pupils were required to pass six subjects, including English and mathematics, in order to earn a certificate, which was often necessary for white collar jobs.

At Great Barton School, between three and eight pupils were entered each year for Part I of the Free Place Examination, which included an intelligence quota (IQ) test. Those who achieved the highest marks were entered for Part II, which took place on a Saturday morning at West Suffolk County Secondary School in Northgate Street, Bury St Edmunds.

Between 1925 and 1928, seven pupils were awarded scholarships and offered places at West Suffolk County Secondary School.

No pupils were awarded a place at King Edward VI Grammar School, Bury St Edmunds, which became a direct grant school in 1925 and offered 14 entrance scholarships in return for financial support from the government.

In 1923, James Symonds was awarded a free place at the East Anglian School for Boys (*BFP*, 26 May 1923), a fee-paying Methodist school, founded in 1873 by a Congregational minister.

In 1924, a mixed school, run by the Roman Catholic Church and taught by the Sisters of St Louis, opened in Bury St Edmunds, but no Great Barton pupils transferred there until 1933.

In March 1929, Cecil Channell was asked to propose pupils for admission to the Lord Wandsworth Agricultural College, which was founded by Sydney Stern (Baron Wandsworth) in 1928 at Long Sutton, Hampshire, for the sons of farmers and farmworkers who had lost one or both parents. The names of four eligible nine and ten-year-old pupils were submitted, but none were successful. In 2015, Lord Wandsworth College was a co-educational independent school with day and boarding pupils aged 11 to 18, and it continues to accept a few 'foundation' pupils. Jonny Wilkinson, OBE an international rugby union player, Julian Sands an actor, and Johnny Johnson the last surviving member of the *Dam Busters* were all ex-pupils, as was Frank Holmes a member of Great Barton History Society.

The new head teacher

Cecil Channell resigned in April 1933 and received a solid silver pedestal clock as a leaving present (*BFP*, 8 Apr. 1935). His new appointment was at Kentford School, near Newmarket, Suffolk.

The managers wrote in the school logbook that they were keen to recruit a 'sound and intelligent man, who was a strict, and yet kindly, disciplinarian'. There were ten applicants for the post, including Robert Gordon Evans, the son of a previous head teacher.

The managers appointed Ernest Edward Reed, a certificated teacher, who was working at St James School, Bury St Edmunds. He was already familiar with Great Barton School, where his wife, Emily, had taught the infant class between 1917 and 1926.

13
NEW TEACHERS AND SCHOOL REFURBISHMENT

Ernest Edward Reed was appointed as head teacher of Great Barton Voluntary Mixed School from April 1933. The school required a great deal of improvement and was in urgent need of refurbishment. Within a short time, there were new teachers, improvements in the standard of teaching, additional resources, and more positive feedback from the government school inspectors. There were some improvements to the school buildings, although these continued to be a serious source of concern and drain on the school's limited financial resources.

The teachers

At the senior school, Ernest Reed taught the senior class (Standards V, VI and VII) and earned a salary of £206. 16s. p.a. He shared a classroom with Hilda Lincoln who taught the upper juniors (Standards III and IV) and earned £117. 11s. p.a. At the lower school, the lower juniors (Standards I and II) were taught by Miss E. J. Ransom, and the infant class by Kathleen Thoburn, whose salary was £123. 2s.

Ernest Reed was the only certificated teacher and, in 1932, the National Union of Teachers (NUT) estimated that there were more than 7,000 uncertificated teachers in service.

By 1935, all three of the assistant teachers had left the school. Miss Ransom resigned at the beginning of the summer term 1933 to take up a post at Herringswell Elementary School, near Newmarket, which was closer to her home. She was not replaced immediately and, although the Local Education Authority (LEA) promised to send a supply teacher, no one arrived for a week so one of the senior girls assisted Kathleen Thoburn at the lower school. For the next few weeks, Miss Creek and then Martha Griffiths were employed as supply teachers until the permanent appointment of Winifred Mothersole, an ex-pupil who had passed the pupil-teacher admission examination in 1924 at West Suffolk County

Secondary School, Bury St Edmunds, and was made redundant from Rougham School in 1933. At Great Barton School, she was paid a salary of £104. 3s. p.a. and taught the lower juniors.

Hilda Lincoln resigned in July 1933 and married soon afterwards. Joan Long, a supply teacher, taught the upper juniors for the first half of the following term, until the appointment of a permanent teacher. There were 20 applicants for this post and Vera Gorham, an uncertificated teacher from Icklingham Voluntary School, was appointed. She was born in Ipswich, but lived in Queens Road, Bury St Edmunds, and travelled to school by bus each day. According to Elizabeth Stalley, who attended the school from 1946 to 1952, Vera Gorham often wore a wide-brimmed hat and resembled Elizabeth, the wife of George VI (later known as the Queen Mother).

In 1933, Kathleen Thoburn wrote to West Suffolk Education Committee to ask whether she would be allowed to continue teaching after she married. She was told that, 'in event of a female teacher getting married, her services would no longer be retained'. In 1925, a Dorset schoolmistress, who had attempted to challenge the marriage bar, was told in a ruling in the Appeal Court that, 'It is unfair to the large number of young unmarried teachers seeking situations that the positions should be occupied by married women, who presumably have husbands capable of maintaining them.' (*Times Educational Supplement*, 22 Dec. 2000).

Although the marriage bar was lifted in London in 1935, it was not removed nationally until 1944 so Kathleen Thoburn resigned her teaching post after her marriage in 1935. By 1938, only 71 per cent of teachers in elementary schools were women, compared with 75 per cent in 1914.

There were 13 applicants to teach the infants' class and Monica Legge, a certificated teacher with 14 years' teaching experience, was appointed as deputy head, in charge of the lower school. She was the daughter of a vicar and travelled to school each day in her Hillman Minx from the Limes, North Lopham, near Diss. As a certificated female teacher, she was paid £100 p.a. more than the other teachers, but £20 p.a. less than that of Ernest Reed, the head teacher.

The four full-time, permanent teachers were sometimes joined by student teachers, who were paid £13. 10s. p.a. from 1933 and £14. 5s. p.a. from 1935. Ellen Crawley filled this post from 1933 to 1935 and Malcolm Cutter from 1935 to 1936. In 1935, Phyllis Reeve joined the staff for six months to gain teaching experience, for which she received a salary of £30 p.a., the same salary as the school caretaker.

In July 1935, the *Bury Free Press* reported that Miss M.F. Frost, a teacher at Great Barton School, had passed the Certificate Examination and been appointed as a teacher at Lavenham Council School (*BFP*, 06

July 1935). However, her name does not appear in the School Staff Record Book of Great Barton School.

Ernestine Bean, an ex-pupil and a student at Avery Hill College, Greenwich, London, had a two-week placement at the school in July 1937, as part of her teacher training, during which she undertook teaching practice and observed lessons.

The school did not have a phone installed until 1962, so all communication with the school was by word of mouth, letter or telegram. In an emergency, the school was able to make use of the public telephone box in the village.

In February 1936, Vera Gorham sent a telegram to the school to inform Ernest Reed that she had influenza and was unable to work. During the following year, she was absent from February until August suffering from a 'tired heart'. If a teacher were absent for only a single day, one of the 14-year-old pupils assisted with the younger children, but a supply teacher was usually employed to cover a longer absence. In 1933 and 1937, Ernest Reed was given leave of absence for a day so that he could accompany a party of British Legion members to the Aldershot Tattoo, in Hampshire.

Physical exercise (PE) instructors sometimes gave demonstration lessons. In February 1938, Mr Curd demonstrated some Scandinavian dances to the senior pupils and, in June 1938, Miss Campbell demonstrated a PE lesson to the senior class in the boys' playground. Mr Creek, a horticultural and gardening instructor, worked with the senior boys in the school gardens.

Occasionally, staff attended courses arranged by the LEA. In November 1933, Ernest Reed attended a conference for head teachers at Shire Hall, Bury St Edmunds, and in September 1937, staff attended a two-day refresher course at one of the Silver Jubilee Secondary Schools in Bury St Edmunds, where Mr Middleton spoke about school gardens and Mr Gunton talked about the teaching of history, reading and written English.

The pupils

Between 1933 and 1939, the school pupil roll fell from 125 to 88. Many pupils came from poor households, as evidenced by the fact that 100 families were eligible to receive coal from the Poor's Firing Farm Charity during that time. Recipients had to be listed on the register of electors for the village and in receipt of a household weekly income of less than £2, with allowances made for children and boarders. After C. Parnell quit the farm in 1936, the tenancy was advertised locally and offered to F. Favell from Norton.

There was no school uniform, but school photographs, taken annually after 1930, show boys wearing short trousers, a shirt with a tie, and a jacket. Girls wore a gymslip with a jumper or blouse, or a dress or skirt with a knitted cardigan, and long socks. Some girls wore a liberty bodice during the winter months and struggled to undo the fiddly buttons.

The School Medical Service made regular visits. The School Dental Service regularly examined the children's teeth and offered dental treatment.   The School Nursing Service carried out regular termly inspections, with occasional ones in between to take throat swabs, eye tests and treatment for pupils who needed spectacles. In 1935, in response to a request from the head teacher and letters of complaint from parents, the school nurse visited the school several times to see the children from one particular family, who lived in a caravan on Bury Road. Their children were unwashed and with head-lice, so some parents requested that their own child should not be seated next to them. On one occasion, the stench was apparently so unbearable that the teacher sent home one of these unkempt children with a message to his mother to wash him and his clothes.

The School Medical Officer regularly replenished the contents of the school's first aid box. In 1938, a girl who had tripped over a stick and cut her head was treated with warm water, boracic lint and iodine, and her head was wrapped with a bandage impregnated with boracic ointment. There was an epidemic of scarlet fever in the school in 1936, of mumps in 1938, and of chicken pox in 1939.

Following the establishment of the Milk Marketing Board in 1933, the National Coalition government launched its 'Milk in School Scheme' in October 1934. This was a public-private partnership, which provided subsidised milk for all British schoolchildren in state elementary schools and free milk for those who were in greatest need. From September 1936, milk was delivered to the lower school each day in one-third pint bottles, but fewer than half of the pupils took advantage of the scheme. This was in spite of the fact that, in 1937, scientific research on nutrition by Sir John Boyd Orr revealed a link between low income, malnutrition and under-achievement, and showed that children's growth could be improved by a daily supplement of milk.

Some of the pupils joined the League of Ovaltineys, a club set up in 1935 by the manufacturer of Ovaltine, a brand of milk-flavouring product made with malt extract, advertised as a means of building up 'resistance to colds, coughs and infection'. To increase the sale of their drink, the manufacturers encouraged children to join the club by sending a cardboard disc from under the lid of a small size tin or a paper slip from the larger tins to Chief Ovaltiney. Members had to make seven promises, to comply with seven golden rules of membership, in return for which they received a membership badge, a book and the chance to take part in competitions and other activities. Ovaltineys recognised one another through a secret password or salute, and could become Silver Star members, with a silver plated star badge, if they introduced three new members. By 1939, the League of Ovaltineys had a peak membership of 5 million children.

The school continued to support local charities, especially West Suffolk Hospital. Pupils donated packages weighing over 200 lbs of goods towards a Hospital Pound Day in 1933, 212 lbs of goods in 1934, and 145.5 lbs in 1935. In 1939, they collected 460 eggs and £2. 18s. for the same cause. A school manager took the money and food to the hospital each time.

The school premises

The school premises were still owned by the Bunbury family, but the buildings were structurally unsound and potentially dangerous. There was no piped water, the heating and lighting were inadequate, the sanitary arrangements were far from satisfactory and the playgrounds were full of potholes. West Suffolk Education Committee was responsible for the general maintenance of the buildings, but the school managers were expected to finance any repairs, alterations, improvements or extensions to the buildings or playgrounds.

In 1933, the board of managers consisted of the Revd Lipscomb (chairman), Archie Ainsworth Hunt (vice-chair and correspondent), Frank Baldwin (County Council Manager), Francis Xavier Patrick Thoburn (the Parish Council Manager), W.D. Catchpole and Mrs Ruegg (Foundation Manager), who was soon replaced by Mr C. E. Whitaker. Ernest Reed attended meetings by invitation only. By 1939, Winifred Nice, Harry Winsor and Mrs Lawther had replaced Francis Thoburn, Mr Catchpole and Mr Whitaker.

Relations were not always good between the managers and the head teacher. In 1937, according to Ernest Reed, Francis Thoburn entered the senior school without knocking, failed to remove his hat, was rude to him in front of the children, and demanded to see the registers, 'in a very aggressive manner'. The LEA investigated the issue, but took no further action.

When the managers needed to raise school funds, they approached families in the village, the wealthiest of whom were the Fairhaven family. In 1925, Urban Huttlesdon Rogers Broughton (1896-1966), who became the first Baron Fairhaven, bought Barton Stud from Sir Edward Hulton, with his brother Henry (1900-1973), who bought Anglesey Abbey, Cambridge, in 1926. In 1937, they leased Barton Stud to Major Harold Murray Fleming (1886-1953), and then to Sultan Muhammad Shah (Aga Khan III) of Pakistan (1877-1957) during the Second World War.

In 1933, water for washing and drinking had to be carried from a well to the sinks each day and stored in jugs and buckets. The lower school used water from a well in the playground, but after it was deemed unsafe by the County Medical Officer in November 1934, an alternative supply had to be found. Francis Thoburn, a school manager, lived opposite the school in what had been the Boys' Schoolhouse, and a deed of his land contained a clause stating that a well on this land should be available to the school. He provided a bucket of water each day, which was then carried by a senior boy to the lower school. In 1933, an application for a piped water supply was submitted to the local authority, who agreed to connect a supply to the senior school at no cost and to the lower school for a small charge. An estimate of £4. 19s. 6d. for carrying out the work was received from Messrs Thompson Bros.

All of the schoolrooms were inadequately heated and during cold spells of weather, the children were sent into the playground to run around and warm up. A kettle was bought for the lower school so that the teachers, and sometimes the pupils, could have a hot drink. Monica Legge was given permission to make hot cocoa with milk and sugar for the children during morning break-time, for which pupils were charged a halfpenny a cup.

The infant classroom was heated by an open fire; the junior classroom (Class I) by a coke stove, bought in 1933 when the LEA contributed 90 per cent towards its cost. Coal and coke were ordered from local suppliers but in April 1936, there was not enough coal for the infant classroom, so the caretaker took some coal into school from her own home. In 1933, a pot-bellied stove was installed in the senior classroom to replace the open fire. On one occasion in 1934, there was a sharp explosion of gas when Ernest Reed stoked the fire. He was shocked but unharmed. In 1935, dense smoke emitted from the fire one day and the village blacksmith was brought in to unblock the pipe.

Regular fire drills were held, which were essential in view of the fact that both schools were heated by fires or stoves and lit by Aladdin paraffin lamps. The Central Electricity Board, created in 1926, began operating in 1933, but no villagers in Great Barton were connected to the grid until 1935, and the school was not connected until 1954.

Both schools used earth closet toilets, housed in sheds in the playgrounds. At the lower school, there were six lavatory pails, which had to be emptied daily by the caretaker into a large hole in the corner of an adjacent wood. At the senior school, there were separate entrances, playgrounds and toilet blocks for girls and boys. The pails from the toilets were emptied into a fenced-off corner of the playground at the back of the school, or into one of the fields adjacent to the school. On 8 March 1938, Ernest Reed wrote in the school logbook:

'A strange man was observed by the head teacher walking round the girls' lavatories. Upon being questioned by the head teacher as to the nature of his business, he stated that his name was Ford and that he was the Sanitary Inspector. He had received a complaint about the state of the school lavatories, so he had come to inspect them.'

In response to a demand from His Majesty's Inspector (HMI) for the removal of tree stumps in the playground, Ernest Reed dug them up with the help of some of the senior boys. They also dismantled some redundant desks and used the materials to build a cycle shelter.

The LEA arranged for the school to be repainted every five or six years. In 1933, the managers received quotes of £139 from Albert Reeve, £132 from Barbrooke Bros, and £121 from William Moyse to carry out the work. They were obliged to accept the lowest quote and William Moyse carried out the work during the summer holidays under the supervision of Frank Baldwin, one of the managers.

In 1935, the school suffered a setback when it learnt that money from the King George V's Silver Jubilee Celebration Fund was to be used to pay for electric lighting at the Church Institute and the Baptist Chapel, but not for the installation of piped water at the lower school.

In 1935, Suffolk County Council bored for water, erected a tank holding 10,000 gallons of water at Conyers Green, and laid thousands of feet of water pipes in the ground. The supply of water was intended for use on the farms of small holders, but several houses also had water laid from this source (*BFP*, 23 Feb. 1935). Great Barton School also hoped to be able to access this water but were unable to pay for the work of installation, so a school restoration fund was set up. Sudbury Voluntary School Association, to which the school paid an annual subscription of 15s., donated £1. 25s. and promised a further £50, the Church Schools Defence Fund donated £25 and the Diocesan Board of Finance gave 12s.

During the summer holidays in 1935, both schools were refurbished. In the lower school, a piped water supply was connected, general repairs made to the building and toilets, and parts of the playground were asphalted. At the senior school, the ceiling, which had collapsed during a lesson, was made safe, windows and doors were adjusted so that they opened and closed properly, the roof was repaired with new slates and ridge tiles, the chimneys were swept and new water pipes were laid. New drains were installed and existing ones cleaned, and the walls were treated with distemper, a type of paint mixed with water and glue.

The Revd Lipscomb wrote in the monthly magazine of the local churches that, 'one could not help noticing how greatly appreciated these alterations were by both the teaching staff and the pupils. Everything looked beautifully clean' (*CM*, Oct. 1935, p.92).

However, an additional classroom or a partition was required at the senior school, both schools needed electric lighting and more asphalt was needed on both playgrounds. Some money was raised at a summer fête in 1936, opened by Laura Sawbridge, secretary of the Sudbury Voluntary School Association, who donated two boxes of articles for sale.

Albert Reeve often carried out general repairs and maintenance such as sweeping the chimneys, clearing blockages in the boys' urinals and repairing windows that were smashed accidentally by boys' playing football. In June 1938, a gale broke a window and blew slates off the school roof.

The surfaces of the playgrounds continued to be unsatisfactory. The lower school playground had a rough potholed surface with holly trees, brambles and nettles around a patch of grass. In 1938, 21 mothers of pupils signed a letter, which they sent to West Suffolk County Council, at Shire Hall.

'We, the undersigned mothers of Great Barton, beg to call attention to the disgraceful condition of the playground in the junior school. We are asking if something cannot be done to improve the condition, as the children's boots and clothes are always wet and covered with mud directly they step inside the playground. We find the children's health is suffering through sitting in school with damp clothes and boots.'

In response, various people from the LEA visited the school in February 1939 to inspect the playgrounds. They included Mr Curd and Miss Campbell, who were both PE Instructors, Mr R. F. Carter, who was Secretary to the West Suffolk Education Committee, and Mr Creese the County Architect.

In 1939, a joint meeting was held between the school managers and the Parochial Church Council to discuss how to raise funds for repairs to the schools and an extension to the Church Institute.

A fête was held on 8 July 1939 in the grounds of Manor House, with an entrance fee of 3d. for adults and 1½d. for children. The programme included a fortune teller, a tennis tournament, a clay pigeon shoot, various sports, a gymnastic display by the First Bury St Edmunds troop of Boy Scouts, a keep fit display by members of the YWCA of Bury St Edmunds and a display of country dancing. Other events included a balloon race, bowling for a pig, target bowls, clock golf, a sale of work, a treasure hunt, darts, a coconut shy, a baby show and a competition to guess the weight of some coal (*CM*, July 1939, p.14).

The school curriculum

In 1933, the school was poorly furnished and inadequately resourced. West Suffolk Education Committee was responsible for the running costs of the school and all requisitions had to be channelled through them.

In May, the secretary of West Suffolk Education Committee visited the school and decided that it should be provided with new furniture. The senior class was given a head teacher's desk, two large cupboards and a cutting out table.

The infant class was given a small cupboard. The school was also provided with 106 chairs of different heights, 35 table desks, 18 smaller desks for pupils in Standards I and II, 15 small folding table desks for the infants, 6 other infant desks and 2 adult chairs. Two new chalkboards were bought in 1935.

There was already a piano and a wind-up gramophone in each building, and Ernest Reed took his own radio from home to school when necessary. The BBC started television broadcasting in 1936, but the school did not purchase a TV for another 32 years.

To brighten up the walls, the school was given a large map of the Isle of Man and pictures of *Rydal Water, The Old Water Mill* and *Cattle at Drinking Time* to add to the pictures of Exeter and Worcester cathedrals, and portraits of Queen Victoria and King Edward VII.

In 1937, at the age of four, Jean Boreham joined the infants' class taught by Monica Legge. She recalled that there were posters on the walls displaying the alphabet and simple words. Pupils were taught to read and write with the aid of square bricks with letters, a slate and slate pen, and a sand tray with a stick for tracing the letters. The only teaching equipment was an abacus and a globe. Jean had covered much of the infant stage work at home with her foster mother before she started school, so she already knew the alphabet, could recognise colours, tell the time and was able to count. Consequently, she became bored and frustrated and, on one occasion, she was so fidgety that Monica Legge tied her to the chair with a skipping rope.

Perhaps Monica Legge should have read the school's copy of *Handbook of Suggestions for the Consideration of Teachers and Others Concerned in the Work of Public Elementary Schools*, published in 1937 by the Board of Education, which emphasised the need for child-centred primary education.

In 1935, Marion Richardson published *Writing and Writing Patterns*, which was widely adopted as a handwriting scheme, and the new *Missionary Service Book* was made available to Church of England elementary schools. From the age of seven, pupils sat monthly and termly tests and, from 1936, they took *Burt's Mental Tests*, which were marked externally.

Mathematics lessons in the senior class included practical activities, such as measuring the school gardens and the classroom, the length of a road, and the dimensions of a field. During science lessons, pupils were taken on nature walks to look for wild flowers. Jean Boreham won a book about trees when she found the widest variety of flowers.

Many lessons involved learning by rote, and copying from the board or text book, but the school timetable was occasionally livened up by visiting speakers and trips to places outside the school. From 1933, Ernest Reed escorted senior pupils to the County Agricultural Show, which was usually held at Ipswich, but was held in Bury St Edmunds in 1937, so the school was closed for the day to enable all of the pupils to attend. In July 1938, the head teacher took the senior boys to the Royal Air Force Station at Honington, which had opened in 1937 with 77 *Audax* and *Wellesley*, and 102 *Heyford* aircraft.

During music lessons, pupils stood by their desks to sing hymns or traditional folk songs accompanied by a teacher on the piano. A wind-up gramophone was used for country dancing lessons in the playground, which would cause great amusement when it ran down before the teacher could rewind it.

In 1936, a sewing machine was purchased for the senior class and pupils contributed pieces of needlework and watercolour paintings, created during art and craft lessons, to the West Suffolk Elementary School Work Exhibition. In 1938, pupils contributed three rugs, wool tapestry pictures of a ship and a dog, a lemonade basket carrier and a willow shopping basket.

PE lessons were usually held in the playground. They mainly consisted of keep fit sessions, leapfrog and marching activities. Hockey was introduced to the senior girls in 1934. A new PE syllabus was introduced in 1935, after which the activities became more varied. The school purchased four bats for stoolball, two cricket wickets, a bladder football, a large India rubber ball, a skipping rope, six large mats and 50 cord gymnastic mats. Both Mr Gill and Mr Clarke made their meadows available for organised games, and the senior boys played cricket in Major Fleming's private grounds.

In 1937, Monica Legge took some pupils to a County Dance Festival at Woodbridge, where they won second prize. Outside school hours, pupils could join the village football and cricket clubs.

Ernest Reed was particularly enthusiastic about athletics and, from 1933, the school was closed for an afternoon each June, so that pupils could compete at the Bury and District Schools' Sports Day at King's Road, Bury St Edmunds. Pupils, teachers and parents paid 5d. to travel on an Eastern Counties double decker bus to the competition, where boys and girls competed in separate races, which included sack races, caterpillar races and long jump. In 1935, there were two challenge cups to commemorate King George's Silver Jubilee (*BFP*, 18 May 1935) and in some years, some pupils performed folk dances.

Ernest Reed was a keen horticulturalist and gardener and, during their gardening lessons, the senior boys transformed waste areas of the playgrounds into flower beds. In 1935, the Sudbury Voluntary School Association bought rose trees for the school flower gardens. In 1936, three boys and Ernest Reed prepared the greenhouses at the Vicarage to raise seeds. In 1937, there were eight school gardens in various locations in the village.

In November 1936, R. Pemberton recommended that senior boys over the age of 11 should enrol in manual instruction (woodwork) classes and senior girls should attend classes in domestic science at West Suffolk Secondary School. In January 1937, 13 boys started manual instruction classes. They travelled each Wednesday morning by bus from Great Barton to Bury St Edmunds, using travel vouchers provided by the LEA. However, during that year, four of these boys were caught stealing from Woolworth Store in Bury St Edmunds. The manager was persuaded not to prosecute them but allow them to be dealt with by the school and at home. The weekly woodwork lessons continued in 1938, attended by 16 boys, some of whom constructed a corner cupboard for their classroom.

The senior girls received extra tuition in domestic science from Miss Chalmers at the Church Institute. In 1937, two girls who had passed the minimum school leaving age of 14 attended domestic science classes at Thurston and at the Church Institute.

School discipline

Corporal punishment was liberally used at the Boys' School, where Ernest Reed caned boys for misdemeanours such as punching, bullying, interfering with other children's clothing, disobedience, swearing and immodest conduct. He administered between one and four strokes each time, depending on his view of the seriousness of the offence. In 1934, a boy who had been fighting received four cuts on the buttocks and his mother complained to Ernest Reed about the severity of the caning.

Girls were punished by being made to stand in the corner with their hands on their head, smacked, shaken, slapped, hit with a ruler or kept in at playtime. For some offences, 'lines' were given, which involved the writing of the same sentence many times. Sometimes mothers were summoned to the school for an interview with the head teacher, as happened when two junior girls were heard using 'obscene language'.

Jean Boreham was a quiet and timid child. On one occasion, her class was copying pictures by tracing over them and scribbling on the back of the tracing paper with a black crayon. During the lesson, Jean touched her paper with her hand and then touched her nose so that it had a black smudge. When the other children laughed at her, she was distressed when Monica Legge admonished her for causing a disturbance and smacked her in front of the class. When she was a little older, she was slapped for standing up to look through the window at the chickens outside the building. She said that she and others were often so scared of the teacher that they were too frightened to learn.

School inspections

The school logbook mentions only one formal inspection by HMI during this period, although HMIs made occasional visits to the school. In October 1935, R. W. Pemberton, HMI, carried out an inspection of both schools, during which he looked at text and exercise books and talked to pupils. He told the head teacher that, 'there was a considerable improvement all round, and work in school was proceeding on the right lines, although much remained to be done.'

Between 1933 and 1938, Diocesan Inspections, which inspected the non-secular aspects of the school, were carried out by the Revd Henry Carey Dobree (1933), the Revd Francis H Simms, the Rector of Honington and Sapiston (1934 and 1935), the Revd Henry Dobree (1936), the Revd Canon Herbert Henry Baker Ayles, Vicar of Barrow (1937 and 1938).

Most Diocesan Inspectors gave glowing reports and were particularly complimentary about the quality of the singing, suitability of the prayers, discipline, relationship between the staff and pupils, examination results and the teaching of church history throughout the school.

In 1934, the report by the Revd Simms stated that:

'This school has done excellent work in all classes. At various times, I have inspected different schools, but I do not remember ever being so full of admiration as I was when I listened during the opening of the school to the hymns and canticles, which were being well rendered with real feeling and reverence. I should like to congratulate the scholars upon their behaviour and the keen answers they gave, also the headmaster and his staff for the efficiency of their instruction.'

In 1937 and 1938, the inspector stated that the school needed more pictures and suggested that the school should apply for a grant.

In February 1935, Archie Ainsworth Hunt visited and inspected both schools, on behalf of the managers, and pronounced them to be in good order. On the evidence of his report, additional wages were awarded to the caretaker for cleaning the toilets. However, in July 1935, Ernest Reed wrote a letter to Ethel Stiff, who had just taken over as caretaker from Mrs P. Clarke, in which he complained about the state of the toilets and the cleanliness of both schools.

School closures

The school was closed on special occasions. On Ascension Day, celebrated 40 days after Easter, pupils attended a short morning service at Holy Innocents' Church, Great Barton, and enjoyed a holiday from school for the rest of the day.

The whole school was closed one day each summer term, so that some pupils could go for a trip to Felixstowe with Great Barton Sunday School. On 14 July 1933, Winifred Mothersole, who taught at Great Barton

Sunday School as well as the village school, accompanied a group of 67 adults and children on three coaches, where they ate tea at the Regal Café (*CM*, Aug. 1933, p.72). On 13 July 1934, there was a party of 70 (*CM*, August 1934, p.78). In 1935 Phyllis Reeve, who was at the school for work experience, accompanied the vicar and 30 children (*CM*, Aug. 1935, p.75). In 1938, 35 children went to Felixstowe.

On 6 April 1933, both schools were closed for stocktaking purposes. They were closed again on 10 October 1935, so that the teachers could attend a retirement presentation to Mr F.R. Hughes, secretary to West Suffolk Education Committee.

Whenever the senior school was used as a polling station for a general or local election, both schools were closed. However, the school remained open when some pupils went for a day trip arranged by the Baptist Sunday school, in 1934 when a large number of pupils visited Bertram Mills Circus, in Bury St Edmunds, and in 1938 when some pupils went on a Conservative Party outing to Felixstowe.

Special days and festivities

In 1935, Monica Legge and Ernest Reed donated flagpoles, which were erected by the entrance doors of each school building.

Thereafter, on Armistice Day 11 November, both Union Jacks were flown at half-mast. Each year, the children sang 'The Supreme Sacrifice' and the British National Anthem, listened to a talk by their teacher or a visiting speaker, and heard the roll call of the men who had fought and died in the First World War. In 1933 and 1934, the senior pupils listened to a 20-minute talk by Lt Col. G.B. Astley-Cooper, OBE, from Thurston, on the meaning of the armistice. In 1934, he shared some of his experiences about his trip to Canada, made even more memorable by pupils being allowed to taste some Canadian maple syrup, which he had brought with him. Many pupils were particularly interested to learn more about Canada, as they had befriended five Canadian children, who had joined the school for a month in February 1934 before returning to Canada.

After 1936, Ernest Reed took his own radio set into school so that the pupils could hear the service broadcast from the Cenotaph in London.

On 24 May each year, the Union Jacks were hoisted to commemorate Empire Day, after which the head teacher gave the pupils a suitable talk, and the children read out appropriate poems, performed country dances and sang patriotic songs such as the British National Anthem and 'Jerusalem'.

To raise money for the Children's Christmas Festivities and Sports Fund, a social evening was held at the Church Institute each November. Ernest Reed and the teachers organised games and competitions, Eleanor Fleming distributed prizes, Mrs Catchpole and her helpers prepared the food, and Kenneth Lomax accompanied the dancing on a piano accordion. The social evening raised £14. 15s. in 1934 and £13. 15s. 9d. in 1935.

On 20 December 1934, Christmas festivities for the parents and the children of the elementary and Holy Innocents' Sunday School were held at the Church Institute. Mr J Schofield donated a huge Christmas tree, which was transported and erected by Albert Reeve. The children ate a Christmas tea before their parents joined them for a party, which included a conjuring show by Mr S Hubble followed by carol singing and dancing, accompanied by a piano accordion. The climax of the party was the arrival of Father and Mother Christmas who, according the monthly magazine of the local churches, 'came down a chimney and distributed oranges, sweets and presents to all the children' (*CM*, Feb. 1935, p.12). The children went home at nine o'clock, but many parents stayed for a dance, which lasted until 11 o'clock.

In 1935, 110 children attended a similar party and, for the next three years, a Christmas party was held on the last afternoon of term at the school or in the Church Institute, with a tea party, presents and sweets. There are no specific details in the school logbook of the type of sweets, but several new ones came onto the market during the 1920s and 1930s, all of which were still available in 2015. These included Milky Way (1923), Crunchie (1929), Snickers and Freddo (1930), Mars Bar (1932), Whole Nut chocolate (1933), Aero and Kit Kat (1935), Maltesers and Blue Riband (1936) and Smarties, Rolo and Milky Bar (1937). The ice lolly was invented in 1923; Jaffa Cakes went on sale in 1927; Twiglets in 1929 and Penguin biscuits in 1932.

In May 1935, nationwide events were organised to celebrate the Silver Jubilee Anniversary of the reign of King George V and Queen Mary. In Great Barton, Ernest Reed sat on a committee which organised a whole day of entertainment, but unfortunately there was an epidemic of measles so some pupils were unable to join the festivities. In the morning, some villagers listened to a service, broadcast from St Paul's Cathedral, London. During the afternoon, there was a decorated cycle parade, a fancy dress competition and a six-a-side football contest, in addition to sports events and side shows. After a special tea, during which each child received a Jubilee mug, there were sports for the adults until half past seven, when prizes were awarded. In the evening, there was a free dance in the Church Institute until midnight. The occasion was marked with the planting of a tree and the presentation of a teak bench (*BFP*, 11 May 1935).

In September 1935, each class was given a copy of the *King's Jubilee Message to the Children of the Empire*.

The school was closed on 6 November 1935 for the wedding of Henry, Duke of Gloucester, to Lady Montagu Douglas Scott (1901-2004), who became Princess Alice, Duchess of Gloucester.

King George V died on 20 January 1936 and on the day of his funeral eight days later, Great Barton School was closed and the school flags were flown at half-mast.

Two days later, King Edward VIII was proclaimed as the new king and the senior school pupils listened to a wireless broadcast and a special talk by Commander Stephen King Hall.

On 11 December 1936, King Edward VIII abdicated and was succeeded by his brother, Albert, Duke of York, who was crowned as George VI on 12 May 1937.

In June 1938, HRH The Duke of Kent, a brother of King George VI and president of the Rural Community Association (RCA), visited the 400-year-old smithy at Great Barton owned by Albert Reeve, the village blacksmith, who was on the executive committee of the RCA. The Duke looked at, and possibly ordered, some hand-wrought iron gates for himself. The pupils wore red, white and blue rosettes and were taken down the road to stand opposite the smithy so that they could wave union flags, but it was an uncomfortable experience for one pupil. Jean Boreham was reprimanded for not standing still but what her teacher did not know at the time was that poor Jean was standing on an ant hill and was being bitten all over!

Educational reorganisation

During the 1930s, pupils remained at Great Barton School until the minimum statutory leaving age of 14 unless they passed an examination and were offered a place at a secondary school at the age of 11. The minimum leaving age was raised to 15 by the Education Act 1936, but not implemented until 1947.

Three girls and two boys transferred to secondary schools in Bury St Edmunds without scholarships. In 1935, Eleanor Abrey, of Vicarage Farm, passed the Free Place Examination and was awarded a scholarship at West Suffolk County School (CM, June 1935, p.52). This was the first time that a pupil from the school had obtained a free place since 1928.

In 1933, two sisters transferred to the St Louis Roman Catholic School at Bury St Edmunds.

In 1934, one boy was awarded a place on *HMS Arethusa*, which was a Royal Navy light cruiser.

No pupils transferred to Culford School, which moved into new premises at Culford Hall in 1935 on the site of a house built by the family of Nicholas Bacon, the first English landscape painter.

In 1935, elementary education in Bury St Edmunds was re-organised into junior and senior schools. This gave those 11-year-old pupils from Great Barton School who were not awarded a scholarship to a grammar

school, the opportunity to transfer to one of the Silver Jubilee Secondary
Schools, which were opened in March 1936.

In 1938, seven pupils passed Part II of the Free Place Examination,
including Margaret Foster, who achieved 86 per cent in the examination,
and was invited to Shire Hall for a special interview.

Between 1902 and 1938, the Church of England lost 2,620 schools to
the state system, mainly because it could not afford their upkeep. By 1938,
three and half million children were educated in council schools, and one
and a quarter million in Church of England schools.

The Education Act 1936 authorised building grants of up to 75 per cent
for new denominational senior schools so that the Church of England
could reorganise its schools into primary and senior ones with the age of
transfer at 11. Nationally, the Church of England submitted proposals for
230 schools and the Roman Catholic Church for 289 schools.

In 1938, the churches were concerned that when children transferred to
a senior or secondary school outside their village, they would drift away
from organised religion.

The Diocesan Board of Education issued a report proposing that
'church children' should be withdrawn from their senior schools once or
twice a week to receive religious instruction from a clergyman in each
deanery, to be arranged by the Sudbury Voluntary School Association.

In 1939, a meeting, attended by 21 parents, was held in the senior
school at Great Barton to hear a presentation on the controversial subject
of the reorganisation of schools in West Suffolk. It was addressed by Lord
Loch, the chairperson of West Suffolk Education Committee, Mr R. F.
Carter, the secretary of the West Suffolk Education Committee, and Miss
Lee, who was a member of the Education Committee.

The Association of Assistant Masters and other unions favoured a
system of comprehensive schools, attended by secondary pupils of all
abilities.

However, a consultative committee of the Board of Education
published the Spens Report (1938), which recommended that pupils should
take intelligence and other tests at the age of 11 to determine whether they
should transfer to a grammar, technical or secondary modern school.

The Second World War

In spite of Ernest Reed's determination to improve the quality of
teaching, refurbish the school buildings and enhance the school resources,
many more improvements were required.

However, the Second World War, which took Ernest Reed away from
the school for nearly four years, interrupted further progress.

14

EVACUEES AND RATION BOOKS

Declaration of war

On Friday 1 September 1939, six-year-old Jean Boreham, a pupil at Great Barton School, was playing with her friends in her garden in School Road, when her neighbour, Mrs Shinn, came round to her house and told Jean's foster-mother that she had just heard on the radio that Britain was at war with Germany. Jean's mother's response was to tell the children to stay in the garden and keep safe, and everyone wondered how soon there were going to be Germans marching down School Road, or bombs falling from the sky.

In fact, within a year, four Germans fell from the sky and landed in Great Barton. On 30 July 1940, a *Dornier* bomber landed in a sugar beet field near Holy Innocents' Church and burst into flames. By the time help arrived, the aircraft was completely burned out and two parachutes were found entwined in a nearby oak tree. The four dead German airmen, who were eventually named as J. Berlage, W. Bohlke, B. Glaser and F. Krause, were buried in plain coffins in Great Barton churchyard on 1 August 1940 (CM, Feb. 1941), where they remained until 3 December 1962, when their bodies were exhumed and removed to a special German War Cemetery in Cannock Chase, Staffordshire.

This was not the first time that a plane had crashed in the village. On 7 August 1938, the Royal Air Force (RAF) was engaged in home defence carrying out night exercises above the air force base at RAF Mildenhall. At 12.45 p.m. the next day, a *Harrow* bomber, returning to RAF Feltwell, crashed into some trees at Vicarage Farm, hit the ground, disintegrated and burst into flames, which resulted in the deaths of five crewmen, aged 23 to 27. An inquest was held in the senior school at Great Barton and the airmen were buried with full military honours at RAF Feltwell, Norfolk.

The evacuees

On 1 September 1939, all schoolteachers were recalled early from their summer holiday, but pupils did not return to school until 11 September.

In April 1939, in response to a letter from the Ministry of Health about the proposed evacuation, Great Barton School was informed that, since the current school roll was 88 and the school could accommodate 144 pupils, there were 56 available places for evacuees.

Operation Pied Piper began on 1 September 1939 under the Government Evacuation Scheme, which was developed by the Anderson Committee and implemented by the Ministry of Health.

During the first four days, nearly 1.5 million people, about half of whom were children of school age, were transported to the countryside away from those towns and cities that the government considered to be in greatest danger from aerial bombing.

Evacuees were met at Bury St Edmunds railway station by members of the British Red Cross, the Women's Institute, or the Women's Voluntary Service, which was founded in 1938 by Stella Isaacs, the Marchioness of Reading. Evacuees arrived with a label round their neck, or attached to their clothing, on which was stated their name and age. They carried a gas mask and hand luggage containing a change of underclothes, nightclothes, shoes, spare stockings or socks, a toothbrush, towel, soap and face cloth. At the station, the children were sorted into groups before being taken to their new homes, where the host families were paid 10s. 6d. a week for the first child and 8s. 6d. per week for each subsequent child.

The evacuees at Great Barton School came from London, south Essex, Surrey and west Kent. No teachers were evacuated to Great Barton in 1939, although about 100,000 teachers and other helpers were evacuated at this time. There were two further waves of evacuation. One from June 1940 after the Fall of France, and another in June and July 1944 to avoid further attacks from German V-1 flying bombs (known as buzz bombs or doodlebugs) and V-2 rockets (the first ballistic missiles).

During the war, 64 evacuees were enrolled at Great Barton School. They stayed for varying lengths of time and, in one case, up to four years, but the majority stayed for one, two or three terms. Where possible, siblings boarded together, and several families took in three siblings, whilst one brave family hosted five siblings, who stayed for six weeks. The Vicarage accommodated some elderly evacuees from London.

The first evacuees to enrol were William and Samuel Iskad. They came from the East End of London and registered at the school on 13 September 1939. Village life and a village school was a cultural shock for city children and many preferred to return to London, viewing the terror of war in a city or town as less terrifying than life in the countryside away from their families. In July 1942, two brothers were so unhappy after their first morning at the school that they tried to hitch-hike back to their home at Kings Cross, London, at lunchtime instead of returning to their billet for lunch. The 13-year-old managed to hitch a lift, but was later taken back to the village. It was soon apparent that neither boy would settle in Great Barton, so they were allowed to return to London in August.

The children's welfare was monitored and two health visitors from London County Council visited the school in March 1941. Irene Edith Grace Forsdike, from West Ham Local Education Authority (LEA), joined the teaching staff in June 1944.

Jean Boreham recalled that most of the evacuees integrated well into the school and village, and enjoyed playing with the local children and sharing their favourite past-times. They made perfume with rose petals, collected eggs, watched the cows being milked, rode the carthorses and carts and helped with the harvest. One popular running game involved poking a stick into a cowpat, swirling it around and letting it go, in the hope that it would hit one of the other children who had not run away fast enough.

The teachers

In 1939, at the start of the Second World War, Ernest Reed was the head teacher assisted by Monica Legge (deputy head teacher), Vera Gorham and Winifred Mothersole.

In contrast to the previous decade during which the pay of teachers had been cut twice, the salaries of teachers increased during the 1930s. By 1939, the salary of Ernest Reed was £302 p.a., of Monica Legge was £258 p.a. and of Vera Gorham and Winifred Mothersole, neither of whom was certificated, was £114 p.a.

Vera Gorham married Benjamin Reeve during the 1939 summer holidays, and Winifred Mothersole married Henry Bridge in December that year. The LEA permitted them to continue their employment as married women, but on a monthly instead of a permanent contract. This discrimination continued until the Education Act 1944, which stated that no woman could be disqualified or dismissed from her employment by reason only of marriage.

Ernest Reed taught the seniors (Class I) in a room he shared with Vera Reeve, who taught the upper juniors (Class II). At the lower school, Winifred Bridge taught the lower juniors (Class III) in the larger room, and Monica Legge taught the infant class in the smaller one.

However, as soon as war was declared, Ernest Reed was called up to serve in the National Defence Corporation Territorial Army Reserve, but he obtained permission from his commanding officer to postpone his military duties for two days so that he could supervise the re-opening of the school at the start of the school year. He then served in the Royal Navy and manned guns on a convoy escort ship for almost four years.

Monica Legge, the deputy head, was promoted to acting head teacher and given two additional incremental salary points.

Mrs Ozanne, the wife of the Vicar of Rougham, had previously worked at the school on a supply basis. She was now given a temporary contract to teach the senior class in place of Ernest Reed.

Monica Legge suffered from a duodenal ulcer and was often absent. Miss H. Brand, a supply teacher, was put in charge of the senior school, and Mrs Percy Hopwood was offered a temporary post to teach the infants.

When Mrs Hopwood rejected the offer, pressure was put on Monica Legge to resign. She retired on 18 April 1941 after teaching for 20 years and received a travel rug as a leaving present.

In June 1941, Mrs E Winsall took over as acting head teacher until January 1942, when Zoe Esther Ward was appointed for five terms. Mrs M. W. Mayes, a supply teacher, joined the staff in March 1943 on a salary of £100 p.a. Initially she was employed to cover for the absence of Mrs Ozanne, who contracted influenza and bronchitis, but was retained on a temporary contract after Mrs Ozanne returned, and worked at the lower school until the end of February 1944.

Ernest Reed returned to work on 5 July 1943 and wrote in the school logbook:

'Having been released from military duties, I re-assumed control of the school via instruction received from R. F. Carter M.A., secretary to the West Suffolk Education Committee.'

Rose Mayhew was appointed, on a permanent contract on 1 May 1944. She had previously taught at Hitcham School for two years and then at Exning School for 15 years. After the death of her mother, she moved to The Hawthorns at Great Barton to look after her father, who had been badly wounded in the First World War. Rose was a neat, slim lady, who was very committed to the job and had high expectations of her pupils. She had a calm temperament, smiled a lot and was rarely cross. She never married but her four-year-old nephew from Croydon lived with her for a year from May 1946, during which time he attended Great Barton School.

In 1944, Winifred Bridge left at the end of July and was replaced by Mrs H. E. Lovett, a supplementary teacher, who left after only one week and returned to Essex. In 1946, the infants were taught by Miss A. N. Rolfe during the spring and early summer term, until she resigned in June and moved to Flempton, Suffolk, and then by Mrs Pickering for the remainder of the summer term.

The female teachers were granted leave of absence whenever their husbands were home on leave from the armed forces. During their absence, their classes were taught by Miss Kirklan, Miss Rowe and Miss Howe, who were all supply teachers.

The McNair Report (1944) recorded the findings of a committee, which looked into the Supply, Recruitment and Training of Teachers and Youth Leaders. It recommended that:
- there should be one grade of teacher, i.e. qualified;
- teachers' salaries should be substantially increased, with a basic salary scale for certificated or qualified teachers, and an additional allowance for special qualifications or experience.

The *Burnham Agreement*, signed in 1945, set out a single national pay scale for primary and secondary teachers.

In 1946, Ellen Wilkinson (1891-1947), the first female Minister of Education in Britain, introduced measures to reduce the number of uncertificated teachers in maintained schools. Uncertificated teachers with more than 15 years' service were given a teachers' certificate, subject to a satisfactory report of their work; those with between five and 15 years' service could take a short course leading to the certificate; and those with less than five years' service had to take the normal two-year course. By September 1946, all of the teachers at Great Barton School were classified as qualified. By 1953, there were only 2,000 uncertificated teachers in the country.

In September 1946, West Suffolk Education Committee decided that Great Barton School needed only three teachers. From that time, Rose Mayhew taught the infants (Class III), Vera Reeve taught the juniors (Class II) and Ernest Reed taught the seniors (Class I) and no longer shared the room with another teacher. By 1949, the salary of Ernest Reed had risen to £610 p.a., that of Rose Mayhew to £297 p.a., and of Vera Reeve, who had worked for two years longer, to £318 p.a.

The caretakers

In 1935, Ethel Stiff was appointed as the caretaker and cleaner. In June 1940, she was paid a salary of £30 p.a., plus an extra £5. 4s. p.a. for cleaning and emptying the lavatory pails twice a week. In response to her application for a pay rise, the managers increased her basic annual salary to £33 p.a. from November 1940, in the hope that it would encourage her to be more conscientious.

It was not an easy school to maintain or keep clean, especially during the blackout, and there were frequent complaints from parents and managers about the inadequate state of cleanliness. The caretaker applied for a torch and batteries to help her to manage during dark mornings, and was provided with a storm lantern.

One of her most difficult jobs was to light the anthracite-fuelled stoves, which were often defective and rarely warmed the school above 42°F / 5.5°C. In January 1942, the temperature in the classrooms fell below 37°F / 2.7°C. To increase the daytime temperature in the classrooms, the stoves were sometimes filled and banked up so that they burnt all night, but the glow from the chimneys infringed the blackout regulations.

In January 1942, Mr R. F. Carter, secretary to the West Suffolk Education Committee, and Mr Creese, the County Architect, inspected the school and stated that it was not clean enough. Ethel Stiff faced repeated criticism for the dirty state of the schools and eventually gave in her notice in October 1943. Her replacement was Mrs Miller, who was paid an additional £1.1s. per month to take account of the extra work entailed whilst the schools were being redecorated.

However, on the first day of the spring term 1944, both schools were dirty, and the fires were unlit. The vicar, with the help of two pupils, lit the fires, and some of the girls dusted the rooms. As an interim measure, Ernest Reed was advised by the LEA to find volunteers from amongst the pupils to undertake these tasks. Eileen Colthorpe and Peggy Clarke, who were both due to leave school at the end of the term, cleaned the floors during January for a monthly wage of £1.14s. 1d.

Ethel Stiff was re-employed in April 1944, but resigned in December, leaving the keys of the main doors on Ernest Reed's desk, together with 'one tin of floor polish and one tin of Brasso', as he recorded in the school logbook. At the senior school, pupils kept a duster in their desks and Jean Boreham remembers Ernest Reed coming round with a tin of polish every Friday afternoon so that each pupil could clean their own desk. Ethel Stiff remained living in the village until her death in 1952 (*BFP*, 8 Feb. 1952).

When Mrs D. R. Stebbing, who lived at No. 1, Council House, Great Barton, took over as caretaker on 12 January 1945, at a starting salary of £78 p.a., and remained in the post until 1960.

The school premises

In 1939 the board of six managers consisted of the Revd Lipscomb (chairman), Harry Winsor (correspondent), Archie Ainsworth Hunt, Winifred Nice, Mrs Lawther (Parish Council Manager) and Eleanor Fleming (County Council Manager). Mr W. J. Williams was appointed as a manager in 1944, and Mrs Peck and Mrs Schofield in 1946.

The school buildings and outbuildings were in a very poor state of repair, and the managers were expected to finance the cost of repairs from the Managers' Fund, which, in December 1941 stood at £2. 18s. 2d. In January 1942, Mrs Lawther and others organised a fundraising social, which raised £18. 2s. 6d. for the school. Appeal letters were sent to 200 potential benefactors, including Lord Fairhaven, to request annual contributions to the school.

An inspection by Mr R. F. Carter and Mr Creese in 1942, found that the guttering on the roof of the lower school was in a serious condition, the toilets on both sites were unsafe and in need of immediate work, and the playgrounds required improvement. The report stated that if the repairs were not carried out, the LEA would consider closing the school. Albert Reeve, a local builder, estimated that the work would cost £10, which exceeded the amount in the Managers' Fund at that time.

On 6 January 1942, there was a very serious incident in Mrs Ozanne's classroom. It was caused by a stove, which had previously been reported as faulty. Following an unpleasant smell, 19 of the 25 children in the classroom either fainted or were sick, so they were taken outside and given a hot drink. They were then allowed to walk home, or driven home by Mr and Mrs Kay if they were unfit to do so. The School Medical Officer was called in straightaway and diagnosed carbon monoxide poisoning. He recommended the closure of the junior school for a few days, whilst the classroom and the stove were made safe.

Some funds for the building repairs were received and in January 1943, the hole in the floor of the junior classroom was repaired, but none of the other work, including the repair of the broken window in the junior classroom, was carried out. The problems were exacerbated on 7 April 1943 when the roof of the boys' lavatory at the senior school was blown off and the toilet wall collapsed a week later. Until the toilets were restored, the senior boys were escorted to the junior school each playtime, to use the facilities there. In 1943, after an application for funds from the Bishop of Dunwich, the school received 10s. from Sudbury Voluntary School Association and £5 from the Diocesan Board of Finance.

In August 1944, the managers agreed to employ someone to repair the floorboards, improve the playground at the junior school, cut the hedges, clear the ditches around the junior playground, lime-wash the toilet walls at both schools and remove the anti-blast substance from all the windows.

School opening hours

During the war, school opening hours changed in response to the hours of daylight and the blackout regulations. From 1 October 1939, the morning session operated from 9.00 a.m. until noon and the afternoon session from 1.30 p.m. until 3.40 p.m. but the start of the morning session was postponed to 10.00 a.m. if there had been an air raid warning during the night, which happened quite frequently. From 14 October 1939, the afternoon session ran from 1.00 p.m. until 3.10 p.m.; from 11 November 1939, the sessions operated from 9.30 a.m. until 12.30 p.m. and 1.30 p.m. until 3.40 p.m. During the summer months, the end of the afternoon session was 20 minutes later.

In 1940, the government shortened the Whitsun half term by a day. In 1941, the school had a split summer holiday, closing for two weeks at the beginning of July and three weeks in September, to enable children to help with the harvest or take part in a 'harvest camp'. In 1942, the holidays were split again, with one week at the beginning of June and four weeks from 21 August. In response to an appeal from the Government's War Agricultural Committee, 12-year-old Dennis Meadows (1930-1997) volunteered to work for Mr Borley at Vicarage Farm.

From 1943, the school was closed each year during August for the summer holiday but in September 1943, the Agricultural Executive Officer at Bury St Edmunds asked schools to grant leave of absence to volunteers from amongst the older pupils who were willing to help with the harvest. Three girls and two boys were released from the school for two weeks, during which time they picked potatoes at Barton Place Farm.

In 1944, after a request from the War Agricultural Committee, the LEA issued employment cards for boys to undertake Juvenile Agricultural Employment at East Barton Place for a week in May but at the end of the week, their employer, Mr D. Gough, said that, 'they were more trouble than they were worth'.

Air raids and safety precautions

Although the village of Great Barton was not a specific enemy target, it was surrounded by RAF and United States Army Air Force (USAAF) bases. Furthermore, it lay on the route between Germany and the industrial targets of the English midlands and German bombers sometimes dropped any unused bombs on Suffolk and Norfolk on their return to their base.

In Suffolk, the town of Lowestoft was a target because of its docks and schoolchildren from Lowestoft Secondary School were evacuated to Worksop. In Norwich, the cultural heart of East Anglia, was bombed on 27 and 29 April 1942, as part of the Baedeker raids, which targeted cities with historical significance.

Villagers were advised by the authorities to take precautions against potential bomb damage. In the schools, there was a bucket of sand and a stirrup pump for water in each classroom to use in the event of damage or fire, and all of the windows were criss-crossed with brown and white, gummed paper strips to reduce damage from broken glass.

In 1938, the Imperial Tobacco Company issued a series of 50 cigarette cards on the subject of Air Raid Precautions, which were collected by many pupils.

Between July and September 1938, the government distributed about 40 million gas masks across Britain. The pupils at Great Barton School were supplied and fitted with one each in September 1938 at the Church Institute. The black, rubber face mask was fitted with a Perspex eyepiece and a grid to allow breathing and was carried in a brown cardboard box with a string handle. From September 1939, the school held weekly gas mask practices, during which the teacher blew a whistle and everyone donned their mask as quickly as possible. However, it was not always easy for the children to take the practice seriously after they discovered that they could make rude noises when they exhaled. From time to time, the local air-raid warden visited the school to inspect the children's masks and replace damaged or dented ones.

Jean Boreham's family shared an Anderson air raid shelter with their next-door neighbour. These were built in back gardens and cost £7 each, but were issued free to householders who earned less than £5 a week. The shelter had a corrugated iron roof, covered with sand bags or soil, to give some protection from shell fragments. They were often full of creepy crawlies, and some children preferred to stay indoors during a raid, rather than venture into them at night. Other families bought a Morrison shelter for indoor use, which was a cage-like construction and came in a self-assembly kit, consisting of 359 parts and three tools. On a morning following an air raid, the school opened an hour later than usual. One day in February 1942, 65 pupils were absent, including 35 who suffered from a cold, cough or flu, and 18 who had had no sleep as the result of an air raid.

A popular pastime of some of the children was collecting bullets and other objects as keepsakes. In 1943, Police Sergeant Bigmore visited each class and gave a short talk about the dangers of interfering with, or removing, incendiary devices, bombs or any other strange objects that they might find.

On one occasion, as Ernest Reed and the children walked down School Road to the Church Institute for lunch, a German plane flew so low that the children claimed they could see the pilot in his leather hat, and the tail-end gunner. The plane fired bullets towards the ground and Ernest Reed told the children to climb through the hedge and lie down in the ditch. When the plane had flown off, the children stood up to continue on their way, but the plane returned and strafed the road again before it flew back to Germany. Fortunately, nobody was hurt but, in spite of Sergeant Bigmore's advice, some children returned to the scene in the evening to collect the bullets as souvenirs.

Rationing and shortages

On 29 September 1939, a National Registration of the population of the United Kingdom was organised to enable the government to plan for conscription and provide the relevant information for the production of identity cards and ration books, issued in October 1939.

Before the Second World War, Britain imported over 20 million tons of food a year, much of it from North and South America, but, as the result of attacks by German U-boats in the North Atlantic Ocean, food convoys were often delayed or destroyed and many goods were in short supply.

In 1940, the Ministry of Food introduced a system of rationing for essential foodstuffs. From 8 January 1940, adults were issued with a buff-coloured ration book, pregnant mothers and children with a blue one, babies with a green one. Families had to register with a grocer or butcher and purchase all rationed goods from them. Bacon, butter and sugar were rationed first, followed by meat, tea, jam, biscuits, breakfast cereals, cheese, eggs, milk and canned fruit. By 1945, a weekly allowance per person consisted of 8 oz sugar, 4 oz marmalade or jam, 8 oz butter or other fats, 2 oz cheese, 4 oz bacon, 2 oz tea, two pints of milk and one egg.

For non-essential goods, a points system operated with each person allocated 16 points a month. These could be used at any shop to buy other foodstuffs such as sweets, which could be bought for 6d. a quarter plus one rations point. Rationed goods were subject to availability and some fruit and vegetables, including onions, were in short supply, and many children did not see a banana or an orange, until after the war.

Gardening became an even more important part of the school curriculum when the Ministry of Agriculture launched its 'dig for victory' campaign to encourage families and schools to grow vegetables in their gardens and grounds. In 1940, Miss Barton, His Majesty's Inspector (HMI), visited the school and suggested that Winifred Bridge should take the senior boys for gardening lessons with help from Mr Creek, the gardening instructor, whilst Vera Reeve taught needlework to the senior girls. Each boy was allocated a small plot in the school gardens, in which to grow peas, beans, onions, lettuces, radishes and other salad crops. In 1943, the school received a gift of seed potatoes, delivered by the School Attendance Officer. The vicar gave permission for all the pupils and teachers to go out during afternoon school to pick wild blackberries, and pupils were able to buy produce, which included blackberries and fruit from the cordon fruit trees, grown in the school garden. The school did not keep rabbits, as suggested by the government in 1942. Prizes were awarded each year for gardening and, in 1945, James Foster won 9s. 6d. and the Gorham Cup, Brian Porter won 6s. 6d. and Robin Doel won 4s.

In 1940, the Welfare Food Scheme was introduced to protect pregnant women and children under the age of five against wartime food shortages.

Pupils whose family income fell below a certain level were eligible for free school milk, and subsidised milk, in bottles containing one-third of a pint, continued to be available for pupils at Great Barton School. The milk was ordered from Bury St Edmunds Co-operative Society, which endeavoured to maintain a regular delivery, although on one occasion it was unable to do so because there had not been enough time to wash the empty bottles and refill them. The School Milk Act 1946, overseen by Ellen Wilkinson, stated that all pupils under the age of 18 were entitled to a third of a pint bottle of milk, at no charge.

In 1941, the Ministry of Food set up an Agricultural Pie Scheme, which was operated by the Women's Voluntary Service from 1942. At the peak of the scheme, 120,000 pies were delivered to the public each week.

It must have been a great relief for parents when the Education Act 1944 made it a statutory duty, rather than optional entitlement, for local authorities to provide school meals with legal nutritional requirements.

In 1945, school meals were described by the Ministry of Education as having 'a vital place in national policy for the nutrition and well-being of children', and 1.6 million school meals were served each day to one-third of the pupil population. The shortage of fat and sugar meant that wartime children had a healthier diet than those born before or after the war, and school meals were as nutritious and varied as possible, given the limitations of rationing.

At Great Barton School, meals were cooked in West Suffolk Schools Canteen, located at one of the secondary schools at Bury St Edmunds, and delivered in large metal containers, called Grundy tins, to the Church Institute, where there was running water, flushing toilets and enough room to accommodate all the pupils in a single sitting. Until 1951, a senior pupil walked or cycled to the lower school every day to find out how many children had ordered a school lunch, and then to the Church Institute to give the numbers to the canteen helpers. Each week, 50 to 60 pupils ate a school lunch, sitting on benches. Free school meals were available to children from low-income families, and the local authority subsidised up to 90 per cent of the actual cost, so that the remainder of the pupils were charged 4d. or 5d. per meal. The money was sent by registered post, each week, to West Suffolk Education Office, in Bury St Edmunds.

There were frequent problems with school meals. On several occasions Mrs J. Reeve, who was in charge of the canteen, had to enter the Church Institute through a window because she had not been given the key. When she was ill, three of the senior girls assisted. There was no choice of menu, and pupils were expected to eat all their food, hold their cutlery correctly and behave with good manners throughout lunchtime. Offal and minced beef, made of fat, skin and gristle, was often served, along with boiled potatoes and a vegetable, and desserts were usually a milk or sponge pudding served with thin custard. Jean Boreham enjoyed school lunches, in spite of finding a boiled green caterpillar in her cabbage one day. Her favourite dessert was sponge pudding with raspberry sauce.

Children took turns to serve the meals to the others on their table, but some pupils disliked doing this. In 1944, after the vicar was summoned to talk to a boy who refused to wait on table when it was his turn, the boy was banned from having any more school meals. When lunches were delivered late, the start of afternoon lessons was delayed. On one occasion, lunches were delivered for only 37 instead of 72 children, and the shortfall was made up with tins of spam, bought from the local shop. On one particular day in January 1944, no school meals were cooked at all, due to the absence of so many staff at the central kitchens, so most children went home for lunch that day. Mrs Horsfall provided bread, butter and minced beef for those who could not get home and back in time for afternoon school.

In October 1945, Mrs W. Mills took over the canteen responsibilities until she was replaced in March 1946 by Mrs E. Hart and Mrs L. Wardley, who were paid 19s.7d. per week during the winter months and £1. 4s. 7d. during the summer months.

Various people talked to the pupils about how they could support the war effort. In April 1940, Sir Ralph Griffiths, Governor of the North-west Frontier in British India from 1932 to 1937, talked to the children about the importance of avoiding waste, and asked them to collect silver paper. Some children entered a scrap-collecting competition, organised by *BBC Children's Hour,* in which the winners collected a total of nine tons of scrap. Children were also asked to collect wild rose hips, which could be used to make vitamin C syrup.

In February 1941, a representative from the National Savings Association visited the school and encouraged the children to save money in various government accounts, including war bonds and savings certificates. He was a representative of Bury St Edmunds War Weapons Week Campaign, which was the second branch to be set up in Britain and raised over £300,000. He presented one pupil at the school with an award for giving the best answer to the question, 'Why I should save and lend all I can to the country' in a competition, open to boys over the age of 11, organised by the *Bury Free Press.* The school itself managed a school savings club, so that families could save up for Christmas.

By 1942, there was a serious shortage of paper, which was controlled under the No 48 Paper Control Order and managed by the Ministry of Production. In Great Barton, Jean Boreham and her friends collected waste paper in a large cart on pram wheels and took it to the garage of Cynthia Oakes at The Cottage, where it was sorted and collected. There were limited supplies of writing and drawing paper, pencils, pen holders, rubbers and books and at school, pupils were taught not to waste paper and how to make exercise books with string binding. The children in the infant class used slate boards and chalk, sand trays and sticks for learning to write, and the older pupils wrote in pen or pencil, but not ballpoint pen, patented in 1938 by Laszlo Biro. Michael Nash, who attended the school from 1948 to 1952, was naturally left-handed, but Miss Mayhew did not force him to become right-handed as many teachers did at this time. Elizabeth Stalley, who was in the junior class in 1949, recalled her time as an ink monitor, when she had to mix black powder with water and replenish the inkwells of the double desks.

Paper shortages meant that shops were unable to wrap goods unless the customers provided their own wrapping paper. Newspapers became smaller and a broadsheet consisted of a single sheet of paper, folded into four pages. Children in the senior class at Great Barton cut up old newspapers and threaded the pieces onto string for use in the school toilets. As a result, many children went home with black bottoms.

From 1 June 1941 until 15 March 1949, new clothes were rationed. Everyone in the United Kingdom was issued with a pink ration book containing coupons for clothing, and all clothes were listed with a price plus the required number of coupons. At first, the annual allocation was 66 points per adult, which were enough points for one new outfit each year as long as you also had sufficient money. In 1941, a skirt, blouse, cardigan and coat for a girl required 23 coupons; short trousers, a shirt and a jumper for a boy required 22. From 1942, children were allowed an extra 10 points each, to take account of the fact that they were growing and needed to buy new clothes more often. During the war, the annual number of coupons per adult was reduced to 42 in 1942, 36 in 1943 and 24 from September 1945 until April 1946.

Utility clothes, with fewer pockets, buttons or pleats, were produced from 1943. These were price controlled and generally well designed and hard-wearing. Second-hand clothes were not rationed, although the prices were fixed. The government produced posters which encouraged people to 'make do and mend'.

In October 1943, Ernest Reed applied for 20 supplementary clothing coupons for 26 pupils aged 14 to 16. In the same year, a question was raised in the House of Parliament, directed at the President of the Board of Trade, asking what should be done about parents who used children's coupons for themselves and whose children were unable to go to school because they had no shoes.

It became more difficult to keep clothes and children clean after 1942 when soap and soap powder were rationed, and there were limited supplies of hot water as the result of fuel shortages.

Children were permitted to have only one bath a week, using no more than five inches of water, and were expected to share this with their siblings.

From 1942, first-time house buyers, and families made homeless by the bombing, were able to purchase utility furniture. This was produced under a government scheme, designed to cope with the shortage of raw materials.

The school curriculum

The school curriculum continued to be stereotyped. After Ernest Reed returned to the school from military service in 1943, the boys from the junior class went up to the senior school to be taught art by him. The senior girls went to Vera Reeve at the lower school for sewing and knitting lessons, during which they made iron-holders and shoe polishers for their family, and khaki socks and mittens for the soldiers.

In June 1944, Ernest Reed took the senior boys to watch an acetylene welding demonstration in Albert Reeve's smithy, in association with the Rural Arts and Craft Association.

The library van from Suffolk Library Service to Schools still made termly visits. Some of the fiction, written for children during the first half of the twentieth century, includes *The Wonderful Wizard of Oz* (L. Frank Baum), *Peter Pan* (J. M. Barrie), *The Secret Garden* (Frances Hodgson Burnett), *The Lost World* (Sir Arthur Conan Doyle), *Doctor Dolittle* (Hugh Lofting), *Five Children and It* and *The Railway Children* (Enid Nesbit), *The Wind in the Willows* (Kenneth Grahame), *The Hobbit* (JRR Tolkien), *Just So Stories* (Rudyard Kipling), *Peter Rabbit* and other books by Beatrix Potter, *Rebecca of Sunnybrook Farm* (Kate Douglas Wiggin), *Winnie the Pooh* and *The House at Pooh Corner* (AA Milne) and *Swallows and Amazons* and the other books by Arthur Ransome. Many of these were subsequently adapted for television or the cinema and continued to be popular.

One of the books that Jean Boreham recalled reading in school was *Her Benny* by Silas K. Hocking, a novelist and Methodist minister from Cornwall. It was written in 1879 and was the first book to sell more than one million copies during the lifetime of the author. It is a classic tale of two youngsters who battled to survive in Victorian Liverpool. Although the title is no longer a favourite, the story was performed on the stage in Liverpool in 1993, and again in 2008, when it was adapted by Anne Dalton as a musical and performed at the Liverpool Empire during Liverpool's year as the City of Culture.

Physical education (PE) lessons usually took place in the playgrounds, but several pupils had accidents when they tripped on the uneven surface or a pothole. In May 1940, a boy broke his leg during a PE lesson. As an interim measure, until money could be found for repairs to the playground, the school asked Mrs Jenkins, who owned a field adjacent to the school, whether she would allow her field to be used for PE lessons, but she refused because the grass was often long and wet. Shinty, an Irish form of hockey, was played in 1943, using sticks lent to the school by Miss Campbell, a PE instructor.

Religious instruction (RI), known also as Religious Knowledge (RK), followed the Cambridge Examination Board syllabus and included a study of the Bible with an emphasis on the teaching of the catechism, the Ten Commandments, the Lord's Prayer and the life of Christ.

Petrol was rationed and there were no coaches available for school trips. However on 1 September 1941, Vera Reeve and 20 children from the senior class travelled by bus to Bury St Edmunds, where they walked round the town to study its history.

On Empire Day, 24 May, the children sang patriotic songs and either listened to talks by their teacher or to a wireless programme, which was broadcast at 11 o'clock in the morning. In 1945, Mrs Reeve, who was in charge of the canteen, devised an Empire Quiz for the pupils.

On Ascension Day, pupils were expected to attend a children's service at half past nine at Holy Innocents' Church or the Mission Church, constructed 40 years earlier on Conyers' Green. It no longer exists, but its position is marked by a red chestnut tree. Children from Nonconformist families attended the Mission Hall, the Baptist Chapel on Conyers Green.

The only reference in the school logbook to a Christmas party during the war was in 1940. Occasionally the children were treated to a film show at the Church Institute but, in order to comply with the blackout regulations, very few events were held in the evening. In June 1944, 75 of the 82 pupils went for afternoon tea at The Cottage, hosted by Cynthia Oakes.

After the war, school visits resumed, although evidence of the war lingered for some time and, when they visited Felixstowe for a school trip in 1946, landmines and jumbled rolls of rusting barbed wire were still heaped up on the beach.

School inspections

There are no references to official inspections from HMI during the 1940s, although Mrs Barton HMI, paid regular visits to the school.

In August 1944, Ernest Reed reported to the school managers that on his return to the school in July 1943, he found the standard of education to be extremely poor, and a lowering of the moral standard as the result of inadequate supervision. The difficulties of the year had been aggravated by being under-staffed and without a school cleaner for the first three months of the year.

However, the Diocesan Inspections in July 1942 and 1943, carried out by the Revd Fanshawe, were very complimentary. The older pupils were given a written test, whilst the younger pupils were questioned orally by the inspector. The Revd Fanshawe was impressed with the teaching and the learning of RI throughout the school, and wrote that, 'the prayers were reverently conducted and the singing was good'.

School discipline

Most children were well behaved, but the punishment book lists 32 occasions between 1941 and 1949 when senior boys were caned. The reasons given in the punishment book included blotting or having an untidy arithmetic book, throwing stones, breaking a pane of glass and misbehaving in class. On most occasions, one stroke of the cane on each hand was recorded, but some of the ex-pupils recall receiving several strokes, some of which broke the skin and made it very difficult to write for a few days afterwards. There are no records in the girls' punishment book, but some pupils recall that girls were smacked.

The name of one boy appears many times. He received two strokes of the cane for bullying, and then for swearing, had his ears boxed for interfering with another boy's clothing, and one stroke on his left hand for misbehaving in Vera Reeve's class. He received two strokes for interfering with a girl and striking her on the head, but persisted in annoying her and received two strokes on each hand for interfering with the same girl on the way home from school. This same boy was accused of 'corrupting the minds of other little boys by indecent conversations'. The Revd Lipscomb went into school to talk to him and a letter was sent to his parents. A few months later, he was in trouble for stealing some toys, a door key and a bunch of cupboard keys. An officer from the National Society for Prevention of Cruelty to Children and the School Attendance Officer talked to him at the school, the head teacher visited his mother, and the matter was reported to the school managers. Following this incident, bolts and catches were fitted on all doors and windows at the school. In January 1945, the same pupil was allegedly involved in an incident when a fellow pupil's face was burned and his eyebrows and hair singed whilst using matches to light a cigarette lighter full of fuel.

During very cold weather, according to Derek Mothersole, a pupil from 1933 to 1942, boys took it in turns to leave the classroom during lesson-time to pour a bucket of water on part of the playground to make an icy slide. However, as soon as the slides were discovered, they were immediately covered with fire ash.

In 1944, there was a complaint about three boys who wilfully damaged some gates belonging to Thomas Nice and Mr Clarke, and a fence owned by Miss Smith, by sawing and chopping pieces off the top. Ernest Reed investigated the allegations and it was agreed that the three boys concerned would be punished by the school rather than the police. They each received two strokes of the cane on each hand, wrote notes of apology, which they delivered personally to Thomas Nice and Miss Smith, and paid 7s. 2d. in compensation to the owners.

At the lower school, the range of misdemeanours included the failure to bring a clean handkerchief to school or to hold a knife, fork or spoon correctly. Teachers usually made pupils stand in the corner and face the wall, or stay indoors during playtimes. Misdemeanours such as climbing up a drainpipe or throwing another boy's cap over the hedge were punished with a smack with a ruler across the hand or on a bare leg. The threat of washing out a pupil's mouth with carbolic soap was mentioned, but no ex-pupil recalled it being used.

Pupil health

Medical inspections were carried out by the School Medical Officer, the School Dental Service and the School Nursing Service. The government implemented a mass immunization programme to eliminate diphtheria, an infection that was associated with poverty, poor sanitation and water supply. Two vaccinations were needed, one month apart. During the spring term of 1941, Dr Clayton and a nurse inoculated 90 of the 104 schoolchildren, 31 pre-school children and two members of staff.

There was a fatal accident in March 1942, when 12-year-old Eric Stiff [24] and his brother Victor were playing on an icy pond on their way home from school to East Barton. Eric fell through the ice and drowned, and was buried in Great Barton churchyard.

Attendance

In an effort to improve pupil attendance, the LEA issued a low attendance certificate to a school whenever the weekly attendance fell below 60 per cent. This often occurred during cold weather, especially if there were heavy falls of snow, but there were no advanced warnings of inclement weather because forecasts were banned during the war. In January 1940, there was a heavy fall of snow and many children stayed at home. The 41 children who did venture to school were sent home early and the school was then closed for nearly a week because the classrooms were so cold. During the following year, the school was closed for a few days after heavy snowfall, because half of the children were unable to travel to school. Only 43 children arrived on a very cold morning in January 1942, and 68 on a cold and icy day in January 1944.

Career advice

Career advice for school leavers was minimal and most of those from Great Barton School were expected to find employment on a farm, in domestic service, or in a shop. When Jean Boreham left school at the end of January 1947, just after her fourteenth birthday, Ernest Reed and asked her what she wanted to do. She wanted to be a nurse, but would not be able to start her training until she was 17-years-old. Instead, she worked for a doctor and his family, helping with the housework and looking after their children. She then worked for Bury St Edmunds Co-operative Society as a sales assistant until the age of 18, when she got married and was asked to leave, because they did not employ married women.

Use of the school buildings outside school hours

The school was officially closed when the senior school was used as a polling station on 29 February 1944 and 4 July 1945.

In March 1942, there was a break-in at the lower school. A number of soldiers broke a small window in the cloakroom, unlatched another window, climbed in, slept in the school overnight and refused to let the caretaker clean the room on the Monday morning. Zoe Ward, the acting head teacher, found the room filthy, muddy and covered with bacon fat and breadcrumbs. The clean towels in the cloakrooms were dirty and the lavatory pails were full. When the soldiers left, they stole some cups, and a suede coat and coat hanger belonging to Vera Reeve. Despite these problems, the vicar gave the military authorities permission to occupy both schools during the Easter holidays, but, once again, the rooms were left in a filthy state.

From September 1943, the lower school was used each Friday evening from five o'clock until six o'clock by Dr Cory as a consulting room for Great Barton patients. The classroom was repainted and Mrs Lawther provided some blackout curtains for the windows.

The Women's Land Army, Prisoners of War (POWs) and the United States Army Air Force (USAAF)

Members of the Women's Land Army were employed on the farms, and three of them boarded at Manor Farm. Jean Boreham remembers that her foster-mother was shocked when she sang, 'Roll me over in the Clover', which the land girls had taught her on the way home from church. The Women's Land Army continued until it was disbanded in 1952.

In 1939, there were two POW camps in the United Kingdom (UK) but, by 1945, there were 600 camps housing more than 155,000 Italian and 400,000 German POWs. They could be identified by their uniform with a round patch on the back of their jacket, and were allocated the same food ration as British servicemen and given access to medical care. In Suffolk, there were permanent camps at Bungay, Botesdale, Newmarket, Bury St Edmonds and Mildenhall, in addition to many temporary camps. Italian POWs were housed in a temporary camp at Vicarage Farm, Great Barton, where some carved toys for the village children in their spare time. From 1943, they helped on the farms, especially with the sugar beet harvest. German POWs lived in Nissan huts on the road to Fornham St Martin.

From September 1942, American servicemen from the 8th USAAF were based nearby at RAF Bury St Edmonds, on Rougham Airfield – Station No. 468, which was built by the Costain Group, and was one of 34 airfields in Suffolk used by the RAF and USAAF. The 47th Combat Bombardment Wing of the 3rd Bomb Division was the first to be stationed there.

In November, in response to a suggestion made by the Board of Education, Captain J F Rooney from the US Army visited the school. He told the pupils about the origin of Thanksgiving in the United States of America, and gave each child an American coin. From 1 December 1942 until January 1943, 322nd Bombardment Group was based at Rougham Airfield until replaced by the 94th Bombardment Group in June 1943.

From 1943, the tanks of the US army were often parked near the Bunbury Arms and at the junction of School Road and The Street. The American servicemen were very popular with the children. Some of the older girls would lean over the hedge of their playground and call out to passing Americans to 'give us some chew gum, chum', and, if they were lucky, the Americans would throw them packets of chewing gum, dates and other goodies over the hedge from the back of their lorries.

Jean Boreham remembers that one year the Americans gave a party at Rougham to the children who lived in Great Barton and the surrounding villages. Those children unable to get to the party were given a shoe-box filled with treasures that were difficult to acquire during wartime, such as soap, tooth-brushes, beads and broaches.

By 1944, there were 426,000 US airmen in Britain, the majority of whom were stationed in Norfolk and Suffolk. In Suffolk alone, with a population of about 400,000, there were 71,000 US airmen.

On 5 January 1945, two *B-17 Flying Fortresses* collided and crashed over Bury St Edmunds, killing 16 airmen and scattering wreckage over a wide area. The following day, an aircraft lost one of its engines during take-off from Rougham Airfield and crashed at Mount Farm. Its impact could be felt at Great Barton, several miles away.

On 28 January 1945, another *Flying Fortress* crashed at East Barton and young souvenir hunters swarmed all over it. Later, at Thingoe Juvenile Court, 20 local schoolboys were charged with the theft of various small parts of the plane and its contents. Their parents argued that the Americans should have put a guard on the site. The boys were 'bound over to keep the peace' and required to refrain from certain activities for a stipulated period.

In 1946, Rougham Camp was used to manage the demobilisation and discharge of Polish soldiers and airmen who wished to return to Poland.

Great Barton men who died during the Second World War

Private Charles Kitchener Stiff, the son of James and Elizabeth Stiff, served with the Cambridgeshire Regiment, 2nd Battalion. On 5 March 1942, he died at the age of 25 from a fever, whilst a prisoner of war in Malaysia, and was buried in Cheras Road Cemetery, Kuala Lumpur, Malaysia.

Arthur Edmond Allen was a telegraphist on *HMS Dasher*, a British Royal Navy aircraft carrier of the Avenger class, converted from an American merchant ship. His ship successfully escorted one convoy across the Atlantic Ocean, but on 27 March 1943, shortly after leaving with the second convoy, developed engine trouble, turned back and suffered a major internal explosion, as a result of which she sank in the Firth of Clyde, Scotland. There were 149 survivors, but Arthur Allen, who was aged 22, was amongst the 400 navy personnel who drowned or burned to death. He is commemorated on the naval memorial at Chatham.

Flight Sergeant (Pilot) Richard Alderton, VR served with the RAF Volunteer Reserve and was the son of Spencer and Elsie Alderton, who lived at Conyers Green. He died on 10 July 1943 at the age of 20. He was buried in Grave 18, in the Eastern Portion of the military cemetery at Port of Spain, St James, Bermuda, West Indies.

Lieutenant Simon Denis St Leger Fleming was the only child of Eleanor and Harold Murray, a retired army major, who lived at Barton Stud. He was killed on 13 June 1944, whilst serving with the RHA in the Long Range Desert Group, and was buried at Foiano della Chiana, Provincia di Arezzo, Toscana, Italy. He was only 23 years-old.

Flying Officer Brian Kinder Nice, VR, regimental number 181051, was a graduate of Trinity Hall, Cambridge. He was the son of Thomas Hale and Winifred Audrey Kinder Nice, who lived at Trelawne, Great Barton, both of whom were involved with Great Barton School. Brian Nice died on 28 December 1944, at the age of 22 and is remembered at the Malta Memorial Part II, panel 13, column 2.

The end of the Second World War

The Second World War ended in Europe on 8 May 1945, and the day was declared a public holiday. In Bury St Edmunds, an enormous crowd gathered in Abbey Gardens, and many people danced on Angel Hill.

On 9 May, Great Barton held a Village Fête and some of the schoolchildren decorated bikes and prams with crêpe paper and painted a Union Jack on their carts.

On 8 June 1946, every schoolchild in Britain received a personal message from King George VI to celebrate the victory. It included the statement that 'I know you will always feel proud to belong to a country which was capable of such supreme effort'.

Education questionnaire to members of the Women's Institute (WI)

In 1943, the WI sent out 5,800 questionnaires to its members and received 4,000 responses. It asked members for their views on the raising of the school leaving age from 15 to 16, state boarding schools, compulsory part-time education for students up the age of 18, and whether country and town teachers should be paid the same salary.

The majority of the responses favoured the raising of the school leaving age to 16, broader subject teaching, and an extension of vocational training.

Many members were concerned about the state of rural schools and their ability to educate students up to the age of 16.

Butler's Education Act, 1944

In 1944, the debates, which had been triggered, by the Hadow Reports, the Spens Report (1938) and the Norwood Report (1943) were brought together in the Education Act 1944, which was amended in 1946. The Education Act 1944 replaced the Board of Education with the Ministry of Education, created a universal tripartite education system with free secondary education for all and an end to fee-paying in local authority schools. The Education Act 1946 laid down arrangements for the management of voluntary and controlled schools.

The new system was a partnership between the state and church, and voluntary schools could either hand over control to the local authority and become a 'community school', or apply for 'voluntary aided' or 'voluntary controlled' status. In community schools, the local authority took over responsibility for all aspects of the school. In voluntary aided and controlled schools, the Instrument of Government included a 'Church of England Statement of Ethos'; and the vicar or priest-in-charge of a parish was automatically appointed as a foundation manager. Where schools opted for voluntary controlled status, the local authority took responsibility for the building and running costs, and controlled the admissions policy and appointment of all staff and managers, with the exception of foundation managers, who were appointed by the Church of England (C of E). Where schools opted for voluntary aided status, the local authority took responsibility for the running costs, but not the building costs, of the school. The governing body had a majority of foundation managers, controlled the admission policy and staff appointments, and shared the capital costs with the diocese.

Both the government and the Archbishop of Canterbury assumed that no more than 500 of the 9,000 C of E voluntary schools would opt for voluntary aided status, but they underestimated the determination of the Diocesan Education Committees (DEC) to retain control of voluntary schools.

In fact, about 3,000 schools applied for voluntary aided status. This included some C of E schools and nearly all Roman Catholic and Jewish schools. More than half of the C of E schools eventually applied for voluntary controlled status.

No decision was made by the managers of Great Barton Schools until 1946, when they 'unanimously agreed that the best interests of Great Barton schoolchildren would be served if the managers surrendered their rights, and requested the West Suffolk Education Committee to be completely responsible for Great Barton Schools as from the earliest possible date'. A resolution to this effect was sent to the Chief Education Officer of the West Suffolk County Council, with a copy to the DEC.

In February 1947, the DEC informed the managers that they deemed this extreme course to be inadvisable. They explained that the managers could retain their rights, without being responsible financially, if they applied to become a voluntary controlled school instead of a community school.

In April 1947, the managers received a letter and circular from St Edmundsbury and Ipswich DEC, which explained that aided status relieved the managers of certain financial liabilities, whereas controlled status relieved the managers of all financial responsibility. In view of the poor condition of the buildings, outbuildings and playgrounds, as well as the lack of school finance, the managers did not seek aided status. They informed West Suffolk Education Committee and the DEC that the managers wished 'to rescind the resolution, whereby the managers surrendered their rights, and applied 'for Great Barton Schools to become controlled school under the Education Act 1944'.

In December 1947, the managers applied to the Ministry of Education for voluntary controlled status and, three months later, received a reply from the Ministry of Education, which granted it to Great Barton School.

The Education Act 1944 stipulated that trust deeds for educational purposes should be recorded with the Minister of Education. In December 1949, the LEA gave Great Barton School permission to use £10 from the Managers' Fund to pay legal expenses in connection with the drawing up of a new Trust Deed. The Bunbury family, who claimed the freehold of the two school premises, agreed to the school having a 99-year lease, with the Diocesan Board of Finance as the trustee.

In September 1946, the board of managers received a letter from the LEA, with details of the future *Development Plan for Primary Schools in West Suffolk*. It proposed the construction of a new two-class primary school for 64 pupils, aged 5 to 11, on a new site in Great Barton, and secondary school accommodation, for pupils aged 11 and over, at a grammar school in Bury St Edmunds, or a secondary modern school at Ixworth. The plan was approved by the Minister of Education in July 1949.

The end of the 1940s

The Revd William Hatt Lipscomb [88], who had been Vicar of Holy Innocents' Church for 33 years, died in August 1948 and the Revd David Duval was appointed as the new vicar in 1949.

Ernest Reed died in July 1949, at the age of 60, following a surgical operation at West Suffolk Hospital.

Mr Bartholomew was appointed as acting head teacher until the appointment of a permanent head teacher.

SECTION IV SCHOOL REORGANISATION

15
RENOVATE OR REPLACE?

In April 1950, Elsie Evelyn Carter was appointed as head teacher of Great Barton Church of England Voluntary Controlled (CEVC) Primary School.

At the end of 1953, Dr Ray, Her Majesty's Inspector (HMI), reported that she had 'thrown herself into the task with zest and vigour and has already affected many improvements'. Elsie Carter retired in 1960, after 33 years in the teaching profession.

She was replaced by Ron Ceurstemont, the 42-year-old deputy head teacher of Guildhall Feoffment School in Bury St Edmunds who was keen to make further improvements.

Both head teachers had to work in school buildings which were structurally unsound, seriously outdated and no longer fit for purpose.

By the early 1960s, some of the new families in the village were choosing to send their children to more up-to-date schools with indoor toilets and good facilities.

The Local Education Authority (LEA) recognised that it was time that the school buildings should be either totally renovated, or replaced by a brand new building, as originally planned in the *Development Plan for Primary Schools in West Suffolk (1946)*.

The teachers

The teaching staff in 1950 consisted of Elsie Carter, Vera Reeve and Rose Mayhew, all of whom were able to benefit from the recommendations of the Royal Commission on Equal Pay (1946), officially agreed in 1955 and phased in during the following five years.

At the School Road building, Elsie Carter taught the senior class (Class 1), whilst at the School Lane building, Vera Reeve taught the junior class (Class 2) in the larger room, and Rose Mayhew taught the infants (Class 3) in the smaller room.

Vera Reeve retired in December 1952 after teaching at the school for 19 years, and moved to Harwich, Essex. At her leaving assembly, Gillian Mills, the Head Girl of the school, presented her with a bouquet and a handbag (*BFP*, 26 Dec. 1952).

Her replacement was Mrs C.J. Jones, who kept corgi dogs and lived at West Stow, Culford. Her husband, who had played football for Swansea and Wales, worked as a forester in King's Forest, Thetford.

The Education Act 1944 limited class sizes in primary schools to 40 pupils, so Great Barton School with only 60 pupils on roll in 1953 was entitled to employ only two teachers. Mrs Jones was originally given a temporary contract but because of the difficulties of managing a school on two separate sites with only two teachers, she was given a permanent contract in 1954. By 1960, there were 100 pupils on roll.

In 1960, Mrs Jones resigned when her husband was relocated by the Forestry Service. She was replaced by Margaret Mildred Huggins (née Clarke), who lived in Great Barton and cycled to school each day from her home at Ellan Vannin in Bury Road. She had qualified as a teacher in 1949 from Hockerill College, Bishop's Stortford, and had previously taught at Elmswell Primary School for two years and St Edmundsbury Primary School for nine years.

The non-teaching staff, advisory staff and School Medical Service

Mrs Nice from Thurston was appointed as the school clerk from 1950 to 1951. On 2 February 1952, she was replaced by Miss M.W. Thoburn, who worked for 30 hours a month until 1954, when her hours were reduced to 15. There was no office so they both worked at a desk in the corner of the senior classroom. After 1962, a telephone was installed in the classroom, which delighted the pupils each time it rang during a lesson.

Miss Thoburn died in October 1964 and Doris Mayhew, who had worked at the school as a lunchtime supervisor since 1960, was appointed as the new school clerk. Born and educated in south-east London, she moved to Great Barton in 1956 from Middlesex, where she had operated a comptometer, a mechanical calculator. Doris Mayhew was employed at the school for six hours a week, during which time she collected the registers and dinner money, paid in the cash at Great Barton Post Office and dealt with paper work. She administered the school savings scheme, originally set up as a Christmas club, where pupils took 3d. or 6d. to school each Monday morning, to be returned as a lump sum when it reached 10s. or £1.

Mrs Stebbing was employed as the school caretaker until she retired in 1960. She was replaced by Mrs J. A. Chapman. From 1946 to 1960, Mrs E. Hart and Mrs L. Wardley helped at lunchtimes, being described in the School Staff Record book as domestic helpers at first, and then as canteen helpers. They were replaced by Mrs K Curtis and Mrs Heath.

During the 1960s, a Primary Schools Advisor made periodic visits to the school, and an educational psychologist gave advice about support and remedial treatment for pupils with additional needs, who were in those days termed 'backward readers'.

The School Medical Officer, School Dental Service and School Nursing Service continued to monitor the health of the children.

Undernourished pupils were given a daily spoonful of malt but in spite of efforts to improve children's health there were several cases of scabies and many cases of measles, which the school were officially obliged to report to West Suffolk Education Office.

The school managers

Great Barton School was entitled to elect six managers. In 1950, the board of managers consisted of the Revd David Duval (Chairman), Mr W. J. Williams (Foundation Manager), Mrs Schofield and Albert Reeve (Parish Council Managers) and Winifred Nice and Mr Ashen (County Council Managers). Between 1950 and 1967, Mr Gooding, Cecil Aldous, Mr Garnham, Audrey Osborne-Thomas, Mr Humphrey, Mr F. Clarke and Colin Winsor also served as managers. In 1960, the Revd David Duval was replaced by the new vicar, the Revd Harold Grayson. Managers' meetings always began and ended with a prayer, and were held at the Vicarage or Conyers Green Farm during the 1950s and at the school during the 1960s.

The LEA controlled the school budget, but the managers were permitted to make recommendations about the employment of staff and submit requests for funding. Requisitions for books, teaching materials and equipment were sent from the school to the LEA, which had the power to veto items before goods were ordered centrally on behalf of all the schools within its authority.

The school no longer had to rely on donations from village landowners, the wealthiest of whom was Lord Fairhaven, who still owned Barton Stud and Manor Farm in Great Barton, but had donated Anglesey Abbey to the National Trust in 1966.

The Managers' Fund, which was deposited with Lloyds Bank, had a regular balance of less than £30, which was used to purchase items outside the remit of the LEA. These included prizes for summer sports, an annual Christmas party, subsidies for school visits and the purchase of hymn books and copies of the *Book of Common Prayer*. After Great Barton Parent Teacher Association (PTA) was set up in 1964, the use of this fund declined, although it was used in 1965 as a float for the purchase of school blazer badges, which were resold to parents.

School managers regularly checked the registers and attached great importance to pupil attendance. In 1958, the use and abuse of holiday forms were discussed at a meeting of the school managers, where concerns were expressed about pupils who were taken on holiday during term time.

The school premises

The LEA was entirely responsible for the maintenance of the school buildings, which were more than 100 years old and in a very poor state of repair with leaking roofs, missing roof tiles, rotten floorboards, ill-fitting windows, damp walls and crumbling ceilings.

Furthermore, the toilet, washing, heating and lighting facilities were in urgent need of modernisation. Classroom heating was provided by big, round, black coke-burning stoves, surrounded by playpen-type fireguards.

Toilets

Both schools had toilet blocks sited away from the school buildings. At the lower school, they were accessed by a path which was overgrown with stinging nettles.

Debbie Williams, who started at the school in 1958, described the toilet blocks as being 'cold and smelly and crawling with spiders and daddy-long-legs'. Each block had a corrugated roof and each toilet consisted of a wooden seat on top of a rusty bucket, which was emptied by the caretaker each evening.

At first, newspaper was used as toilet paper, but during the 1950s it was replaced with Izal toilet paper, which was kept on a roller in the classroom and handed out by the teacher, one or two sheets at a time, depending on one's need! Penny Slade, who attended the school between 1965 and 1971, recalls being told how to rub two sheets together to soften it and make it less harsh.

At the senior school, boys and girls used separate toilet blocks and, at each school, one toilet was kept locked and reserved for use by the staff. In 1959, the bucket toilets were replaced by Elsan chemical toilet closets with plastic seats. These were less smelly and unpleasant, but still needed to be emptied daily. The school applied for flushing toilets with septic tanks, but the LEA preferred to wait until a mains sewerage scheme was installed in the village.

Washing facilities and electricity

According to Elizabeth Stalley, the washing facilities at the lower school consisted of a green enamel bowl on a stand, filled with cold water from a jug each day, and bars of red carbolic soap.

At the senior school, there were three sinks with cold running water in the boys' cloakroom, and a sink, filled by an urn with a ladle, in the girls' cloakroom. There was a roller towel in each cloakroom, until individual paper towels were provided in 1956.

The village was connected to the National Grid during the early 1950s, and electricity was installed in both schools in 1954. Electric lights replaced the Aladdin paraffin lamps, and drying racks and an electric hot air heater were installed in the cloakroom at the lower school, so that wet clothes could be dried out during the day. A hot water system was installed in 1964.

Great Barton Lower School c1960

School journeys

Most children walked to and from school. The school day started at 9.15 a.m. and finished at 3.15 p.m. at the lower school and 3.45 p.m. at the senior school. Keith Mills started school in 1959 and recalls being taken to school on his first day by his Dad, arriving late and being stared at by the class. He was so embarrassed that he ran all the way home, arriving there before his Dad did and starting school on the following day.

Pupils who lived over a mile from the school were allowed to cycle to and from school, and a new cycle rack was built at the school in 1960. Michael Nash lived near Barton Stud and when he started school in 1948, he was taken there and back in a carrier on his mother's bicycle. When he was seven-years-old, for the price of one penny, he was able to catch a bus for the short distance to the end of School Road, although he still had to walk home because there were no return buses at the end of the school day.

Pupils who walked to the lower school in School Lane had to pass the Crown Beerhouse and Fisk's Farm, where mink and pigs were reared.

Many pavements in the village were in a poor state of repair, and the managers wrote to the local authority to request improvements to the paths between the senior school, the Conyers Green crossroads and the Bunbury Arms public house.

School discipline

Elsie Carter was very strict and only needed to raise her voice to convey her displeasure. At the end of each lesson, she insisted that pupils stood at the side of their desks before walking (not running) in an orderly line, in silence, to the door. She smacked naughty children with a slipper but used use the cane on two occasions: when a pupil disobeyed Mrs Jones and when a pupil took a knife into school and threatened fellow pupils.

Ron Ceurstemont did not use the cane, but occasionally smacked a child with his hand, a ruler or slipper.

In September and October 1956, Elsie Carter wrote to three families, to complain that their children had been playing in the lower school playground at weekends and evenings, had dropped litter and knocked down the house martins' nests. In January 1957, the father of one of these pupils wrote to Elsie Carter, accusing her of victimising his son, and to the managers to make a complaint against her. She forwarded the letter to the Chief Education Officer, who suggested that she arranged a meeting with the father and Mr Grove, a representative of the LEA, but, when she tried to do so, the father informed the LEA that he no longer wished to receive any letters from Elsie Carter, but to communicate directly with the LEA. She was so upset by the allegation of victimisation that she considered consulting the National Union of Teachers, but there is no record of how the issue was resolved and the children continued to attend the school until 1963.

School milk

Until 1968, free milk was available to all pupils under the age of 18. At Great Barton School, pupils drank it just before morning playtime but did not always appreciate it. If left outside too long in cold weather, the milk froze in the bottle, expanded and pushed the lid up, and in hot weather, it tasted warm and creamy.

Debbie Williams, who attended the school from 1963, recalled that she disliked the milk so much that she took chocolate powder to school to flavour it, but this practice was discouraged because she made such a mess when she stirred the powder into the milk bottle.

School meals

Each day, about half of the pupils ate a school meal, which continued to be cooked at West Suffolk Schools Canteen in Bury St Edmunds and delivered to the Church Institute in Grundy tins. Lunch cost 7d per meal in 1953, and 1s. per meal in 1957. It was served in two sittings, with the younger children eating first. The children walked in pairs, hand in hand, to and from the Church Institute, escorted by the school clerk.

Meals became more varied as new foods came on the market, and rationing was lifted from bread in 1948, sugar and sweets in 1953, and meat and the remaining foodstuffs in 1954. Fish fingers became widely available from 1955. During the 1960s, meals included cheese flan with tinned tomatoes, chocolate crunch with chocolate or pink custard, and sticky cornflake tart.

One wintry day, the school lunches could not be delivered to the village, so a lady who lived in The Street made sandwiches, free of charge, for the few pupils who had managed to travel to school.

Playgrounds and playtimes

Great Barton Senior School c1960

At the senior school, the boys' playground was surrounded by two or three large chestnut trees and was resurfaced with tarmac in 1958. The girls' playground had some grassy areas. In 1959, a climbing frame, which consisted of two A-frames with a ladder across the top, was installed in the playground, but there was no safety surface beneath it. In May 1963, a pupil fell off the frame and damaged his teeth and head, and in February 1966, Angela Bryant, fell off the frame and broke her collarbone.

The windows of the junior classroom were low enough for a teacher to be able to supervise the playground from the warmth of the classroom, whilst enjoying a warm cup of tea or coffee from a flask. Jane Slade, who attended the school between 1966 and 1973, recalled that Margaret

Huggins used to bang her rings on the window if she saw anyone misbehaving in the playground.

The playground at the lower school was composed of loose gravel and hardened earth until it was resurfaced with tarmac in 1958. There was a wooded spinney at one end of the playground, where children could shelter from the cold and wet, if necessary. On another side was a farm, and Julie Wright and Jane Slade both recalled an occasion, when a bull managed to come into the playground through a broken fence.

At playtimes, football and cricket were most likely to be played by boys, whilst hopscotch and two-ball were more likely to be played by girls, as were skipping games accompanied by the words of 'On the Mountain', 'In and out the Dusty Bluebells' and 'Teddy Bear, Teddy Bear'. Boys and girls played Fox and Hounds, Hide and Seek, 'Please Mr Crocodile', Oranges and Lemons, 'Farmer's in his Den', 'Lucy Lockett', 'Farmer, Farmer, May I Cross your Field' and 'What's the Time, Mr Wolf?'

School uniform

There was no school uniform until 1960. The Education (Miscellaneous Provisions) Act 1948 empowered local authorities to provide clothes for pupils who were unable to take full advantage of the education provided as the result of a lack of suitable clothing.

In 1960, Ron Ceurstemont introduced a school uniform, with an optional blazer, cap, tie and scarf, which were available from W.H. Cullen, in Bury St Edmunds.

For the girls, it consisted of a grey skirt or pinafore dress, white blouse and grey jumper with white socks and black shoes, or a summer dress during warm weather.

For the boys, it consisted of a white shirt and grey jumper, short grey trousers for the younger boys and long grey trousers for the older ones, and grey socks with black shoes.

In 1964, a school competition was organised

School badges, 1964 to 1991

to design school badges, which could be sewn onto the blazer or cap. The winning designs were based on the Bunbury family coat of arms and were created by David Stearn.

The school curriculum

The school logbook makes no mention of any in-service training for teachers until September 1960, when the school was closed for two days so that all the staff could attend a teaching course at Bury St Edmunds. In 1961, Ron Ceurstemont attended a meeting of primary school head teachers in Bury St Edmunds and, in 1964, spent a day at the Education Office in Bury St Edmunds to learn about a new record card system.

The infants were taught by Rose Mayhew, who was described in the 1953 inspection by HMI as 'patient and hardworking'. The walls of her classroom were brightened up with pictures of the months of the year, letters of the alphabet, and nativity pictures at Christmas. The few toys included a doll's house with furniture, and a wooden 'stacker' clown called Joey. In 1955, an electric gramophone was bought for the infant class to replace the wind-up one.

Pupils used copybooks, which contained examples of words and numbers to be copied in the space on the page below. They were taught to read using the 'look and say' method, based on the *Janet and John* reading scheme, which featured a white, suburban, middle-class, two-parent family and contained key words for building up a basic reading vocabulary.

In 1953, the inspectors reported that pupils in Class 2, taught by Mrs Jones, 'read with understanding by the age of eight or nine'.

At the senior school, the head teacher sat at a large desk, purchased in 1933, which was still in use by Sue Spiller in 2004. The partition for the room, which had been suggested by Her Majesty's Inspectorate (HMI) in 1924, had never been built but in 1955, the room was partitioned by a curtain in 1955. There was a chalk board at each end of the room, and pupils of different age groups were taught in two separate groups for English and maths and a single group for other subjects.

Mathematics consisted mainly of arithmetic lessons. Helen Ellis attended the school from 1965 and recalled having to copy sums from the board and chant tables, but not having any practical lessons.

Elsie Carter widened the scope of the work so that 'pupils would take an interest in their immediate surroundings and in happenings past and present throughout the world' according to the inspection report. She often took her class on nature walks around the village. A globe was bought in 1953 as a souvenir of the coronation of Queen Elizabeth II.

During the early 1950s, the older girls occasionally had cookery lessons and home-craft lessons.

The boys worked in the school gardens until July 1953, when it was decided that the gardens were no longer needed.

After the appointment of Ron Ceurstemont, the curriculum for the older pupils involved more practical and hands-on activities. He adopted a child-centred and topic based approach to teaching, and endeavoured to make his lessons interesting and varied. Several pupils recall making hovercrafts and carrying out experiments during science lessons. Helen Ellis remembers walking down to Great Barton Church to do some brass rubbing, and to the pond in Church Road to study pond life.

On one or two afternoons a week, boys from the junior class went to the senior class for drawing and craft lessons, and girls from the senior class went to the junior class for sewing and knitting lessons, where they learnt how to hem a handkerchief, knit a square for a blanket and use a sewing machine. Val Mayhew recalled doing some simple embroidery on binca fabric in the infant class. Jane Slade, who attended the school between 1965 and 1971, recalled knitting dishcloths from white cotton yarn.

Ron Ceurstemont purchased more books, but was unable to persuade the LEA that the school needed a separate room for use as a library. The school continued to borrow books from Suffolk Library Service to Schools. After a 'Banda' duplicating machine was purchased, worksheets in various colours gradually replaced copybooks.

Occasionally, outside speakers or entertainers were invited into school. Amongst them were Mr Scott, who lived at Rickinghall and represented the Dumb Friends League, PC Scarf from Bury St Edmunds Traffic Department, who showed road safety films, Mr Stride, from the Dr Barnardo's charity for children, Major Arnott from the Royal Society for the Prevention of Cruelty to Animals, and actors from an educational puppet theatre.

In 1964, the Schools Council for Curriculum and Examination was set up to bring about reforms and 'uphold the principle that each school should have the fullest possible measure of responsibility for its own work and teaching methods'.

Religious instruction (RI)

The Education Act 1944 stated that it was the duty of LEAs to 'promote the spiritual, moral, mental and physical education of pupils' in their schools. It required all schools, whether community, voluntary aided or voluntary controlled, to begin with a daily act of collective worship (assembly), which 'must not be distinctive of the traditions and practices of particular religious denominations, but must be wholly or mainly of a broadly Christian character'.

Community and voluntary schools were obliged to provide non-denominational RE lessons, but the Education Act 1944 reiterated the 'conscience clause,' introduced by the Elementary Education Act 1870, which permitted parents to withdraw their child from school assemblies and RE lessons on conscientious grounds.

At Great Barton School, a daily assembly of the whole school was impracticable, so on most days, each class held its own assembly, which always included a recitation of the Lord's Prayer and the singing of a hymn. However, from time to time the younger pupils carried their chairs up to the senior school for a whole school assembly led by Elsie Carter.

Most of the 18 Baptist and Roman Catholic pupils who attended the school during this period sat in the cloakroom during school assemblies and in the classroom with alternative work during RI lessons. In 1957, Elsie Carter sent a letter to the Chief Education Officer, with reference to children from one Roman Catholic family. She wrote that these children had been separated from church teaching since September 1956, and went on to say that 'we are always careful to separate the children from the goats during our scripture period', a remark which reflected the attitudes and language of the time.

In voluntary controlled schools with two or more teachers, one teacher was delegated as a 'reserved' teacher. This person was deemed competent by the school managers to give religious instruction, but could not be the head teacher, or selected by the LEA, without the consent of the foundation managers. In larger schools, there could be more than one 'reserved' teacher, but the number could not exceed a fifth of the total teaching staff. At Great Barton School, Mrs Jones was the 'reserved' teacher between 1955 and 1960, and Margaret Huggins between 1960 and 1986.

At this time, the teaching of religion was variously known as religious education (RE), religious instruction (RI) or religious knowledge (RK). At Great Barton School, it was referred to as RI, and pupils studied an adapted version of the *Cambridge Examination Board Syllabus*.

In addition, once a week, the vicar prepared some of the senior pupils who attended the Church of England for the Bishop's Examination, which was passed by about 20 pupils in total during the 1950s, some with a credit and a few with a distinction.

On 17 May 1955, the school was inspected by the Revd Beaton, the Diocesan Inspector, whose report stated that the school owned 38 Bibles, 50 prayer books, 50 hymn books and 28 religious pictures. Of the 66 pupils on roll, 50 received church instruction and none was withdrawn from religious education. The inspector commented that there was a 'happy atmosphere and that good work was being done'. In 1962, the school managers purchased 20 copies of the *New English Bible*.

Music, art, dance and drama

Margaret Huggins, who played the piano and sang in a choir, encouraged children to develop their musical abilities and took the school choir to Bury St Edmunds to participate in the Schools' Music Festival each year. In 1960, the children performed a Christmas show for their parents in the Church Institute, during which Class I performed a play, and Classes 2 and 3 a nativity story.

In 1962, the pupils performed a concert in Great Barton Village Hall, which was built in 1952 for the residents of Great Barton as a Thanksgiving Memorial to villagers who had served in the Second World War. The Village Hall was managed by a Management Committee, which consisted of representatives from village organisations which used the hall. The members of the committee were also Managing Trustees of Great Barton Thanksgiving Fund.

Until 1960, there was only one radio for the whole school, and this had to be transported between the two buildings by a child on a bicycle. Val Mayhew, the daughter of Doris Mayhew and niece of Rose Mayhew, attended the school between January 1958 and July 1964, and recalled listening to *Music and Movement* on the radio and joining in the singing of traditional folk songs, broadcast in *Singing Together*. In 1960, the school acquired a radio from a school that was closing down, and purchased a new High Fidelity radio and an Essex Grey speaker. Two record players were purchased in 1962, but the school did not buy a television (TV) until 1968. The BBC had launched a pilot television scheme for schools in 1952, and Associated Rediffusion and the BBC started to broadcast TV programmes for schools in 1957. In 1964, the school purchased a kiln for the children to fire the objects they made out of clay.

Ron Ceurstemont was very keen on arts and drama and, in 1961, took the top class to a performance of the Minerva Ballet, and to Beyton Secondary Modern School to see a performance of *Toad of Toad Hall*. He often wrote or adapted plays for the children and, in 1964, his class performed extracts from Shakespeare's *A Midsummer Night's Dream* in the garden at the lower school, and a nativity play in Great Barton Village Hall. The senior pupils watched a performance of Benjamin Britten's *Noyes Flood* in Bury St Edmunds Cathedral, and went to Ixworth Middle School, in March 1967, to hear a programme of music by the London Gabrielle Brass Ensemble. Later that year, all of the pupils were taken to Ixworth Middle School to watch a puppet show.

Physical exercise (PE) and sport

During PE lessons, pupils removed their outer clothes, wore their vests, knickers or underpants, and went barefoot for indoor sessions.

On wet or very cold days, lessons took place indoors with the desks moved to the side of the classroom. David Pearce, who attended the school between 1955 and 1960, recollects that he played a game in the junior class where two teams stood opposite each other in two lines and tried to knock a balloon behind their opponents, using their hands or their head. However,

David was injured, when his head hit the iron frame of a desk, so this activity was discontinued.

Pupils wore plimsolls (pumps) for outdoor PE lessons, which were held in the playground and included keep fit exercises and activities with hoops, balls and other small pieces of equipment. Colourful woven mats, for the perfection of forward and backward rolls, were bought in 1947. Country dancing lessons were held outside, but they were not popular with everyone and Elizabeth Stalley recalled that, on one occasion, she deliberately forgot her plimsolls so she could get out of the lesson, and was made to dance in wellington boots instead.

From the 1950s, the school used the recreational ground adjacent to Great Barton Village Hall. The boys played cricket and football, and the girls played netball, stoolball or rounders. The pupils competed against teams from other primary schools and when matches were played away from the village, the team members cycled to the relevant venue. Elsie Carter refereed football matches.

Annual sports days were held at the recreational ground. They included running, skipping, sack, egg and spoon, potato, flowerpot, three-legged and slow bicycle races, in addition to the popular mothers' race. Sometimes pupils were treated to an ice cream afterwards. Pupils may have been inspired by the 1948 Summer Olympic Games, held in London, with Wembley Stadium as the main venue. Over 4,000 athletes participated in 19 sports, and represented 59 nations, although neither Germany nor Japan was invited to the games, and the Soviet Union declined to take part.

In 1964, Great Barton School competed in the Bury and District Schools' Sports Day with 12 other schools, and won the cup for the smaller schools. During the same year, Margaret Huggins took a group of children to Stanton Primary School to participate in a dance festival, and to St Edmundsbury School to take part in a dance evening.

Pupil reports

In 1951, the end of year reports for senior class pupils recorded marks out of 100 and a class position for reading, recitation, composition, writing, arithmetic, mental arithmetic, geography, history, English, nature study and art. There were comments, without marks, for scripture, handcraft, general progress and attendance.

In 1952, marks were given for spelling and, in 1953, pupils in the senior class received marks out of ten, and a comment for the same subjects as the junior pupils, plus literature and dictation. After 1960, the format of reports changed and only contained a general remark and comments, not marks, for English and mathematics.

At the end of each year, the school managers presented certificates and prizes to pupils for English, maths, RI, art, general progress and the Bishop's Examination.

School visits

In 1951, the government organised a Festival of Britain to celebrate Britain's contribution to science, technology, industrial design, architecture and the arts. The senior class were taken to see a provincial arts festival, held in Norwich from 18 to 30 June, which featured theatrical and musical performances, lectures and dances. In the same year, pupils were taken to Bury St Edmunds to see West Suffolk Schools Art Exhibition.

During the 1950s, pupils walked to Holy Innocents' Church to look at the architecture, Manor Farm to see a model dairy and Albert Reeve's blacksmith shop to see a working smithy and receive a tiepin in the shape of a horseshoe. They visited Pakenham windmill and were taken by bus to Bury St Edmunds to look round St Mary's Church and Abbey Gardens. In June 1952, they visited Bury Fire Station, and pupils who owned bicycles were allowed to cycle to Bury St Edmunds.

Pupils were taken by coach to Cambridge and Ely in 1955, and the Norfolk Broads and Yarmouth in 1962. In 1952, they visited Castle Rising, Sandringham, Kings Lynn and the beach at Hunstanton before the North Sea flood of 31 January 1953, which devastated parts of the Norfolk, Suffolk and the north Essex coasts. It was an unprecedented flood, caused by a combination of a high spring tide, a deep depression and a tidal surge in the North Sea, which raised the local water level to 5.6 meters above mean sea level. It resulted in the deaths of 1,835 people in the Netherlands and 307 in Britain, including 58 people on Canvey Island, 37 at Jaywick, near Clacton, and 38 at Felixstowe, when wooden prefabricated homes in the West End area of the town were flooded.

From 1953 to 1973, the senior pupils were taken to London for a day, travelling by train from Bury St Edmunds and accompanied by three adults. They toured at least three sights each year and during this period visited the Festival Hall, London Heathrow Airport, Windsor Castle, London Zoo, the Tower of London, St Paul's Cathedral, Hampton Court, the London Planetarium, Madame Tussauds, the Children's Gallery of the Science Museum, the Natural History Museum, the Royal Exchange, the Guildhall Museum, Trafalgar Square, Buckingham Palace and Westminster Abbey. Several visits included a boat trip on the River Thames to Greenwich to see the *Cutty Sark* or the Tower of London.

The whole school was taken to the cinema at Bury St Edmunds to watch *A Queen is Crowned* in June 1953, and *The Conquest of Everest* in 1954.

According to Ann Last, who left Great Barton School in 1955, it was assumed that boys would work on the land when they left school, and girls would marry and raise a family, or do domestic work. One year, four senior girls were taken to visit a mobile nursery exhibition at Silver Jubilee Secondary Modern School.

Between 10 and 20 June 1959, a Magna Carta Pageant was held in Abbey Gardens, Bury St Edmunds, to celebrate the town's association with the Magna Carta. In 1214, the English barons met in the Abbey Church, Bury St Edmunds, and forced King John to accept the Charter of Liberties, the document that influenced the creation of the Magna Carta. Benjamin Britten wrote the *Fanfare for St Edmundsbury* and the pageant involved thousands of people from West Suffolk. There were 12 performances of the pageant, each of which commemorated ten events in the history of Bury St Edmunds, including the death of St Edmund and the town's links to Magna Carta.

Mark Williams, a pupil between 1961 and 1968, recalled a class visit to West Stow Anglo-Saxon Village, which existed from 420-650 AD. Archaeological excavations were carried out between 1956 and 1972, and an Anglo-Saxon village was reconstructed with original building techniques.

Special days

Penny Slade, who was in Class 3 in 1966, has fond memories of her birthday at the lower school, when she received a small bar of chocolate from Rose Mayhew and stood on her chair whilst the class sang 'Happy birthday' to her.

On Empire Day, 24 May, a Union Jack was hoisted at each school, the British National Anthem was sung, and pupils listened to an Empire Day service which was broadcast by the BBC from the Royal Festival Hall, London. Colonel Oborne, of the Suffolk Regiment, was sometimes invited into the school to talk to pupils.

An annual harvest festival was held in the senior schoolroom, which was decorated with fruit, vegetables, flowers and eggs. Pupils read the lessons during the service, which was conducted by the vicar. In 1952, a collection of 13s was donated to the Dr Barnardo's Fund, and the produce was donated to West Suffolk Hospital (*BFP*, 24 Oct. 1952). After 1964, the produce was distributed amongst the pensioners of Great Barton.

During the 1950s, an annual Christmas concert, attended by school managers, parents and pupils, was normally held in the Mission Church. However, in 1956 it was held at the school when the roof of the Mission Church leaked, and it was cancelled in 1959 because the village was without a vicar.

In November each year, a fund-raising event was arranged to raise money for the Christmas parties for the schoolchildren. The Christmas parties were held in the Church Institute, with tea and entertainment. In 1951, tea was prepared by Cynthia Oakes and a team of ladies, as it had been for many years. In 1952 and 1953, it was provided by Palmers' Restaurant in Bury St Edmunds, and in 1954 by Mrs Hart and Mrs Wardle, the canteen helpers.

After rationing was lifted on sweets in 1953, children were given these as a treat to take home. The party included a Punch and Judy Show and a conjuror in 1952 and 1954, and entertainment by the Funnelly Funsters in 1955 (*BFP*, 30 Dec. 1955).

When the death of King George VI was announced on the radio on 6 February 1952, both of the school Union Jacks were flown at half-mast. Nine days later, the vicar conducted a short service in the senior school for Classes 1 and 2, followed by the observance of two minutes of silence.

Closure days

Schools were permitted to arrange three discretionary closure days. At Great Barton School, these always included Ascension Day, when Anglican children attended morning service at half past nine at either Holy Innocents' Church or the Mission Church on Conyers Green.

The school also closed on Suffolk Show days in 1951, 1958 and 1959, on 2 June 1953, for the coronation of Queen Elizabeth II, and on 6 May 1960 for the wedding of Princess Margaret to Anthony Armstrong-Jones.

On 23 February 1950, 25 October 1951, 26 May 1955 and 8 October 1959, the school was used as a polling station. In 1950, the Conservative Party used a small cattle float, drawn by a pony, to take electors to the polling station, and a bath chair to take aged electors (*BFP*, 24 Feb. 1950).

Parents

From 1952, parents were invited into school for an afternoon at the end of each school year, to look at their child's work and see examples of some of the class activities. This annual event was always described in the school logbook as being 'very successful'.

On 12 November 1964, a Parent Teachers Association (PTA) was set up, with a committee composed of all the teachers and seven parents. It aimed to provide an opportunity for educational liaison, raise funds for additional educational equipment, and organise social events.

At the first meeting, it was decided to 'prepare a scheme to provide a swimming pool for the school'. In November 1965, Ron Ceurstemont estimated that £1,000 was needed to build a learner swimming pool, 40 foot by 20 foot in size, with a heater and filtration plant. The LEA agreed to contribute to the cost of the pool and the PTA planned to raise £500.

Each Monday morning, 37 parents donated at least 6d. each, which raised 30s per week. However, by November 1966, the estimated cost had risen to £1,200.

The PTA held a dance and concert in 1964, and a dance, jumble sale, summer fête, whist drive, autumn concert, bingo evening and tea afternoon in 1965. The following year they organised a sale of work, sausage supper, jumble sale, summer fête, coffee evening, car treasure hunt and a sale of Christmas cards.

Reorganisation of secondary education in Bury St Edmunds area

The Education Act 1944 set up a tripartite system of secondary education, with grammar, secondary modern and technical schools.

From 1946 onwards, 11-year-old pupils in West Suffolk sat a Transfer Test Examination, more commonly known as the Eleven Plus, which tested their knowledge of mathematics and English and their ability to solve problems using verbal and non-verbal reasoning. Based on this test, taken on a single day, pupils were selected for a place at either a grammar or a secondary modern school, since no technical schools were built in the town.

Schools in the Bury St Edmunds area were reorganised into a bipartite system. West Suffolk County Secondary School became the County Grammar School for Girls, and King Edward VI Grammar School for Boys became a voluntary controlled grammar school, with places for 170 boys including 50 boarders. St Louis Convent School became a state-run Catholic School.

In addition, there were two single-sex Silver Jubilee Secondary Modern Schools, each of which had accommodation for 500 pupils.

Secondary education for pupils from Great Barton School

Between 1947 and 1970, 22 girls and nine boys from Great Barton School passed the Eleven Plus examination and went to one of the grammar schools in Bury St Edmunds.

Seven pupils transferred to St Louis Catholic School. Several others went to Culford School, which was originally the East Anglian School for Boys, or to its sister school, the East Anglian School for Girls, both of which were fee-paying schools.

The remainder either stayed at Great Barton School until the minimum school leaving age of 14, increased to 15 in 1947, or transferred at the age of 11 to one of the Silver Jubilee (secondary modern) Schools in Bury St Edmunds until 1953 when Beyton Middle School was opened.

In 1959, the Crowther Report, entitled 15-18, recommended the raising of the school leaving age to 16, but this was not enacted until 1973.

Great Barton village

Between 1931 and 1951, the population of Great Barton grew slowly from 728 to 813.

In 1948, William John Cook took over the tenancy of the Poor's Firing Farm, which was also known as Paltry Farm. Colin Winsor was appointed as clerk of its board of trustees, which consisted of D. Borley, Albert Reeve, F.B. Clarke, H. Gooding and the vicar as an ex-officio trustee. The farm rent was raised to £100 p.a. and villagers received a fuel allowance in wood instead of coal. When the charity was closed down forty years later, the remaining funds of £1,493 were transferred to Great Barton Thanksgiving Fund.

By the 1960s, West Suffolk was the fastest growing county in the country, recording a 27 per cent increase in population as the result of the relocation of London's overspill population and the expansion of towns to revitalise the local infrastructure. In Great Barton, private housing estates were built at Conyers Green and Hall Park, bringing the parish population to 1,495 by 1971.

In June 1963, the senior class carried out a village survey and delivered a short questionnaire to every household. Only the replies from 42 households in the Mere Close and Icepits Close areas of the village have survived. These show that those houses had flushing toilets, but not all were connected to mains water, drainage and sewerage systems, although Thurston Sewage Works had been built in 1945. The five houses in the Cattishall area relied on well water until 1979, when piped water from the mains became available.

In Mere Close and Icepits Close, 38 households used electricity for cooking, four relied on solid fuel, every home had a wireless, 39 had a television and 13 a telephone. Nationally, in 1950, just one per cent of the population owned a television set; by 1965, 75 per cent owned one, many of which were bought by means of hire purchase arrangements. The questionnaire did not mention ownership of refrigerators, although, nationally, 33 percent of households owned one in 1962, and 69 per cent owned one in 1971.

The responses expressed concerns about the behaviour of teenage boys and gangs on street corners, the amount of litter, untidy gardens and poorly maintained hedges and grass verges. They also made many positive suggestions about improving the bus service between Great Barton and Bury St Edmunds, building a by-pass around the village, increasing the frequency of car speed checks, providing more activities for young people, increasing police supervision of the bus shelter, and improving the playing fields and road signage. They also suggested that the village would benefit from having more houses in the Cattishall area, more shops, a 'decent' pub, more street lights and telephone kiosks, a parking space outside the

Post Office and a guard rail by its door and a bus shelter on Elms Close. Only one person suggested that the rates should be reduced.

From this part of the village, at least two children who were eligible to attend Great Barton School attended schools in Bury St Edmunds. Several people suggested enlarging or modernising the village school or building a new one.

A new school building

By 1960, the schoolrooms were in a very poor state of repair and the sanitation arrangements and facilities were totally inadequate. The distance between the two school buildings and between both school buildings and the canteen and playing fields made it difficult to manage the school efficiently.

In 1961, the managers suggested that a new school be built on land next door to the senior school on Mill Road, but access would have been from a busy road.

Later that year, John Hill, the County Education Officer, who lived in Great Barton, attended a meeting of the managers of Great Barton School. He spoke about the provision of a new four-class school in the village, on a site at Elms Farm in School Road that was owned by Suffolk County Council and rented out to a small holder. The new school was agreed in principle by Suffolk County Council, but the actual building work was postponed until after Great Barton was connected to a mains sewerage system in 1964.

On 10 April 1964, John Hill wrote to the managers to advise them that the Secretary of State for Education and Science had approved the building of a new Great Barton School to accommodate 150 pupils. Its estimated cost was just over £43,000, and it was to be built during the year beginning 1 April 1966.

16
BRAND NEW PREMISES

In 1966, Suffolk County Council approved plans for a five-class school to be built in Great Barton, and recommended that it should be a 'transferred controlled school' and retain its voluntary controlled status.

The new school and school bungalow were sited in School Road on a piece of land owned by Suffolk County Council, and built by R. Hogg & Son; a building company based ten miles away at Coney Weston. A loan for the estimated gross cost of £43,044 was sanctioned by the County

Finance Committee and Suffolk County Council, and building work commenced in November 1966, with E.M. Stow as the project manager.

The County Architect for West Suffolk Council was Jack Leonard Stanford Digby, ARIBA, AILA (1924–2006), a qualified landscape architect, who encouraged his staff to exploit the local topography, flora and views. Consequently, the single-storey, timber framed school buildings and the adjacent bungalow were built of light grey, Ibstock Alpine White facing bricks and block cavity walling with timber window frames, to blend in with the construction of houses in the surrounding rural landscape. Jack Digby's own house, Matsudana, in The Park in Great Barton, was also built with light-coloured bricks.

On 10 October 1967, Ron Ceurstemont wrote in the school logbook:

> 'Today we occupied the new school. The children met at their old schools and were brought to the new building by their teachers.'

On the day of the move, Angela Bryant, who attended the school from 1962 to 1968, recalled that:

> 'It was a breezy day and my walking buddy, Claire Blades, and I were still wearing summer dresses. We were cold and shivering but, at the same time, we were very excited to be officially seeing our new school. When we reached the bottom of School Lane, we met up with Miss Mayhew and Mrs Huggins and their classes, and we all walked together to the new school. We went straight into the assembly hall where Mr Ceurstemont talked to us. I remember everyone was so excited that we now had a kitchen for hot school meals. What a thrill that was! Once that was over, we were free to roam around and I showed my classmates where our classroom was, before taking advantage of some extra playtime. We ran into the playground and some of us played on the new climbing equipment, which was a real treat for us.'

Penny Slade recalled that the school was blessed by the Revd Harold Grayson, the Vicar of Holy Innocents' Church, Great Barton.

The centre of the building comprised a large hall with a high ceiling, which was surrounded on two sides by five classrooms, each of which opened out onto a brick paved, covered veranda. Each classroom was linked to the hall by a small room, which provided additional teaching space, and was separated from the hall by one of three open-air courtyards. Most of the walls between the hall and the classrooms were glazed so that it was possible to see into four of the classrooms from the hall. On the third side of the hall was a kitchen and an entrance hall that led into a school office and staffroom. On the fourth side was the caretaker's cupboard and cleaning area, and a double door that led onto the playing field.

In an article in *Architectural Review*, Ron Ceurstemont stated that 'I am somewhat suspicious of open planning, but at Great Barton, we have the best of both worlds. It goes far enough in terms of openness and flexibility, and we can see through the glazed panels, across courtyards - a feeling of one large family.'

Plan 3. Great Barton CEVC Primary School, School Road, 1967

►	External entrance	
W	WCs	
Ch	Changing room	
C	Coats	
St	Store room/cupboard	
	Carpeted areas	

Key to Planning Ingredients

E	Enclosed room
H	Home base
V	Covered area

In 'Village schools in West Suffolk', published in *ERA: Journal of the Eastern Region of the Royal Institute of British Architects*, Ron Ceurstemont was quoted as saying:

'The provision of furniture and equipment is generous, and the ample pin up (from floor to ceiling, and covering most surfaces) is very, very good and extensively used. The low-level chalkboards are popular with the children, and the heater, standing in the centre of one side of the teaching space, makes a very useful metal, magnet board; we make full use of the moveable cloak trolleys, which pull out into the classroom and cut down congestion in the cloak area.'

The pupils were especially delighted with the indoor toilets, a school kitchen, and a large hall for school assemblies, lunches and indoor PE lessons. Angela Bryant expressed the view that, 'We were all proud of our new school and it was wonderful to have everything new and modern and, most of all, heat in the wintertime.'

Whilst the teachers were delighted with the new building and particularly appreciative of having a staffroom, they had reservations about:

- noise from the school entrance foyer and the kitchen, which disturbed lessons and assemblies in the hall:
- a lack of storage facilities for electrical and physical education (PE) equipment, lunchtime tables and chairs, all of which all had to be stored in the main hall;
- insufficient sockets, especially in the staffroom, where the only socket was located in the wrong place;
- the design of the tall cupboards in each classroom, which were covered by a curtain that attracted dust, and had a top shelf, which was beyond the reach of most teachers.

'However,' Ron Ceurstemont stated, 'these complaints fade against our pleasure in our new surroundings, and the children seem particularly happy with their school.'

In 1968, inside one of the courtyards, an aviary was built with Barbary doves, lovebirds, Java sparrows and budgies, which were looked after by various pupils during the holidays. A second courtyard housed a sand pit and a goldfish pond, and the third contained the plaque, which had formerly been built into the wall above the entrance to the Boys' School.

A door was erected between the entrance foyer and the hall soon after the opening of the school, and extra electric sockets were added later, but the problem of inadequate storage facilities was still unresolved in 2004. During the 1990s, the asbestos in the ceilings and other parts of the building was removed and new ceilings were erected.

In 1972, Ron Ceurstemont asked Great Barton Parent Teacher Association (PTA) if it would raise money for blackout curtains for the hall, but whilst it was agreed in principle, the curtains never merited top priority. However, the PTA did provide carpet squares so that children could sit on the floor more comfortably, vases for each classroom, and an electric cooker for cookery lessons.

There were various problems with the design of the building. A low wall near the entrance to the kitchens was knocked over by visiting cars on at least four occasions, the floor of the boiler house was regularly flooded, and there were leaks in the ceilings of a classroom, the hall and around the windows of one of the small teaching rooms.

The premises were hired by village groups and clubs. On one occasion, the Girl Guides left the school in a very dirty state and scratched the hall floor whilst playing hockey with school hockey sticks, borrowed without permission.

In 1971, 1972 and 1973, the local branch of the British Red Cross organised a summer holiday camp for handicapped children and made use of the school's facilities, and sports and other equipment.

The growth of the school

In October 1967, there were seven age groups of pupils at the school, aged 4 to 11, who were taught in three classes by Ron Ceurstemont, Rose Mayhew and Margaret Huggins.

Table 13. Pupil roll of Great Barton Primary School, 1967-72

September	Pupil roll	Number of classes	Average class size
1967	106	3	35.3
1968	125	4	31.3
1969	146	5	29.2
1970	175	5	35.0
1971	184	6	30.7
1972	191	6	31.8

Source: *Great Barton School class registers*

Between 1967 and 1972, there was a huge increase in the pupil roll. In October 1967, there were 106 pupils on roll and 32 more were expected to join during the year, so the managers wrote to the Chief Education Officer to set out the case for the appointment of an additional teacher.

At the end of October 1967, Mrs Trodden was appointed as a full-time teacher to teach a fourth class, and Mrs Jones as a part-time teacher to give the head teacher some non-teaching time.

During the year, the pupil roll rose to 138, which included 11 children from traveller families who had set up a camp in the village.

In April 1969, there were 144 pupils at the school, and Mrs Gladwell was employed to teach a fifth class. Each class contained children from at least two age groups, with the juniors in Class 1 and Class 2, the upper infants in Class 3 and 4 and the lower infants in Class 5.

In July 1969, Rose Mayhew retired and was presented with a gold watch and a cheque, Mrs Trodden resigned, and Ron Ceurstemont took advantage of a teacher exchange programme and taught for a year in a school at Malaga, California, United States of America. Margaret Huggins and Mrs Gladwell were joined by Mr J. Nock, from Stoke-by-Nayland, who was appointed as the temporary head teacher, with Mrs Davis as his deputy and Mrs Edwards as an assistant teacher.

A year later, Mr Nock recorded in the school logbook that it had been 'a very happy year' and Ron Ceurstemont recorded that: 'Mr Nock had left everything in good order, and it gave me great satisfaction to return to the school after a most interesting year, teaching in Malaga, California.'

After his return to Great Barton School, Ron Ceurstemont gave an illustrated talk to the pupils and parents about his time in California.

In 1970, Mrs Haytack, Mrs Aldous and Mrs Hill, the wife of the Education Officer, replaced Mrs Davis and Mrs Edwards. Pat Barratt was appointed as deputy head teacher from January 1971. Pat had trained at Keswick College, Norwich, and taught at Ilford in Essex, Cranleigh in Surrey, Earl Shilton in Leicestershire, Whitstable in Kent, Tripoli in Libya and Wattisfield in Suffolk.

By April 1971, there were 195 pupils on roll, so it was necessary to set up a sixth class. However, the school buildings had space for only five classrooms, so the LEA provided a mobile classroom, which was sited between the school and the playground and was occupied by Mrs Hill and 34 of the older pupils from 20 April 1971.

A year later, there were 217 pupils on roll, the highest number ever recorded in the school's history. The teaching staff consisted of Ron Ceurstemont, Margaret Huggins, Mrs Hill, Mrs Haytack, Pat Barratt and Jennifer Barber. Mrs J. Gladwell, who had left in December 1970, was re-employed in September 1971 to replace Mrs Aldous. Sally Bulbrook was employed as a part-time teacher from September 1972 and Wenda Pennells replaced Mrs Hill in May 1973. The classes were numbered 1 to 6, with the oldest children in Class 1.

External support and advice was available for children with learning difficulties from Suffolk Educational Psychology Service, a speech therapist, the School Remedial Service and Bury Remedial Day Centre.

The staff photograph for 1973 shows Julia Briggs, Mrs Haytack, Jennifer Barber and Wenda Pennells (back row from left to right) and Doris Mayhew, Pat Barratt, Ron Ceurstemont, Margaret Huggins and Mary Ceurstemont (front row from left to right).

Staff photograph 1973

Fall in the school roll from 1973, as the result of school reorganisation

Primary schools in West Suffolk were part of a two-tier education system, and pupils transferred to a grammar or secondary modern school at the age of 11, after taking the Eleven Plus examination.

In August 1963, Sir Edward Boyle, the Minister of Education, asked the Central Advisory Council for Education (England) to 'consider primary education in all its aspects, and the transition to secondary education.' When a Labour government was elected in 1964, about 20 per cent of all pupils were awarded a place at one of the 300 grammar schools, and the remainder were offered a place at a secondary modern school. The government was concerned that secondary schools were not performing well, and believed that the system of selection at the age of 11, based on a pupil's performance on a single day, was an unfair system and should be replaced by a comprehensive one.

Nationally, various ways of organising comprehensive education were discussed. Boyle's Education Act 1964 permitted the creation of middle schools as part of a three-tier system, which had been proposed in 1963 by

Sir Alec Clegg, the Chief Education Officer of the West Riding of Yorkshire. Circular 10/65 invited LEAs to submit proposals for the provision of comprehensive education in their area.

John Hill, the Education Officer for West Suffolk from 1961 to 1973, and Suffolk from 1973 until 1979, was an enthusiastic supporter of a three-tier comprehensive system. Under his leadership, the Conservative-led Suffolk County Council approved plans for the introduction' of a three-tier system in Suffolk. In June 1966, West Suffolk Education Committee voted in favour of its adoption *(Suffolk Record Office: 3077/2: Minutes of Secondary Education Sub-committee of West Suffolk County Council Education Committee, 14 June 1966, p13; Education Committee 29 June 1966, p.3).*

In 1970, a Conservative government was elected, under the leadership of Edward Heath. It was keen to reverse the comprehensive system of education and issued Circular 10/70, which permitted local authorities to retain a selective system. However, Suffolk County Council continued with its plans to create comprehensive schools.

In February 1970, Mr T. R. Cornthwaite, Suffolk County Council Assistant Education Officer, spoke to the managers of Great Barton School about the proposals for the reorganisation of schools in central and northern Suffolk. Two months later, John Hill addressed 100 parents at the school on the subject of 'Going Comprehensive'. He stated that purpose-built schools for the new age groupings (i.e. middle and upper schools) would bring facilities almost unheard of in an agricultural area, where the task of modernising outdated schools could only be regarded as long term. He explained that in West Suffolk, pupils would no longer take the Eleven Plus, but would leave primary school at the age of nine and transfer to a middle school for four years. At the age of 13, they would transfer to an upper school until at least the minimum school leaving age, which was raised to 16 from 1973.

In the Great Barton area, the schools would form part of the Thurston pyramid of schools, and pupils from 22 primary schools would transfer to one of three new middle schools at Stanton, Ixworth and Beyton at the age of 9, and then to Thurston Upper School at the age of 13.

From 1971, the secondary schools in Bury St Edmunds became comprehensive and co-educational. The County Grammar School for Girls remained on the same site that it had occupied since 1964, and became County Upper School. King Edward VI Grammar School for Boys was relocated on the site of the Silver Jubilee Secondary Modern Schools and renamed as King Edward VI Upper School.

In 1972, Culford School, founded in 1881, amalgamated with the East Anglian School for Girls and became one of the first fully co-educational schools to belong to the Headmasters' and Headmistresses' Conference, an association of the headmasters and headmistresses of selected independent schools in the United Kingdom.

By 1974, more children, nationally, attended comprehensive schools than selective ones. More than 1,000 middle schools had been set up in the 44 counties which had adopted a three-tier system. In April, East and West Suffolk Councils were merged with Ipswich Council to become a unified Suffolk County Council, but the school system in Suffolk was never unified and some areas retained the two-tier system.

The Education Act 1976 empowered LEAs to plan for comprehensive, secondary education. It was repealed by the Education Act 1979, which enabled LEAs to retain selective schools.

The changes for pupils at Great Barton School were introduced gradually. From 1971, pupils no longer sat the Eleven Plus examination but transferred to the comprehensive school at Beyton at first, and then to Thurston Upper School when it opened two years later. From 1973, pupils transferred at the age of nine instead of 11, and there was a consequent decrease in the number of pupils at Great Barton School. By September 1975, there were only 127 pupils at the school in five age groups, so it was no longer possible to justify six full-time teachers.   Miss Gray, a probationary teacher, who had replaced Mrs Haytack in 1974, moved to Tollgate Primary School, Bury St Edmunds, and the number of teaching hours for part-time staff was reduced.

Table 14. Pupil roll of Great Barton First School, 1973-1978

September	Pupil roll	Number of classes	Average class size
1971	169	6	28.2
1974	155	6	25.8
1975	127	5	25.4
1976	127	5	25.4
1977	117	5	23.4
1978	110	5	22.0

Source: *Great Barton School class registers*

The non-teaching staff

From April 1971, Ron Ceurstemont's wife, Mary, worked as an ancillary classroom helper and school nurse for 20 hours a week. Her job included listening to children read, managing the library, looking after children who were unwell and contacting parents.

Doris Mayhew, the clerical assistant, worked at the school until October 1983 for 15 hours a week. She and the head teacher shared an office, which was equipped with a manual typewriter, a filing cabinet, a telephone, and a Banda duplicating machine. In addition to her clerical duties, she recorded radio programmes for each class.

Mrs J.A. Chapman continued as caretaker, unlocking and locking the school, managing the heating system, preparing the hall for meetings held out of school hours, and maintaining the school swimming pool.

R. Hill, who taught at another school but whose children attended Great Barton School, occupied the school bungalow until 1968. Ron Ceurstemont hoped that the bungalow could be used as an inducement to attract a prospective teacher, but it was decided that, since Ron Ceurstemont was going to America for a year on a Teacher Exchange Scheme, the school needed an on-site caretaker.

Mrs Chapman resigned in March 1969 and her replacement, Fred Arbon, moved into the school bungalow with his young family. His wife, Sylvia, was employed as the school cleaner and helped out as a canteen assistant and lunchtime supervisor. She rarely had a day off work and even when her second son, Neil Paul, was born in September 1969, she worked the night before and cleaned the school the next afternoon, having given birth at 10.50 a.m. that morning. She always dressed very smartly and often cleaned the school in high-heeled shoes and a pretty frock. On one occasion in the mid-1970s, she fell over in a classroom and hit her head on the corner of a table. Ron Ceurstemont insisted that she went to hospital, where she had 12 stitches but refused an x-ray because she was pregnant with her third son, Giles, and was back at work the next day.

Non-teaching staff were sometimes employed as lunchtime supervisors, especially after the School Meals Agreement (1968) removed the obligation on teachers to supervise children at lunchtime.

The school managers

The board of managers consisted of Mr G. A. Garnham, Colin Winsor, Mr Clarke, Mr M. J. Humphrey and Audrey Osborne-Thomas. The Revd Harold Grayson was the chair until he left the village in September 1969. He was replaced as vicar by the Revd B. Vaughan Parry.

In 1968, the school managers were advised by letter that 'in the opinion of the Diocesan Director of Religious Education, and the lawyers of the Diocesan Registry at Ipswich, the managers have no responsibility in law with respect to the old school buildings.'

The properties and sites reverted to the ownership of the Bunbury family. The school buildings in School Lane were demolished and a new house, known as Woodlands, was built on the site in 1976. The school building in School Road was converted into a private residence.

School uniform

Most pupils wore a school uniform, which was slightly adapted in 1973 to match the uniform of Ixworth Middle School. A pale blue t-shirt replaced the white one, and a grey jumper and black blazer were optional, as were the black and grey ties and the school badges on sale at the school office.

The PTA organised a school clothing exchange, which raised a small amount of money for the school.

A school photographer made an annual visit each autumn term to photograph each class and the netball, skittle ball and football teams.

School discipline.

Corporal punishment was still legal, but there were no entries in the punishment book recording the use of the cane after 1960. However, one pupil recalled being smacked after he threw a brick into the swimming pool to break the ice. In May 1968, a boy was 'severely reprimanded' after he stabbed another boy with a sharp pencil and drew blood. In July 1968, Ron Ceurstemont recorded in the logbook that he had smacked a boy on his bottom after he threw a stone at a girl, bruising her and injuring her head. The perpetrator, who was often accused of attacking other children, also had to report daily to the head teacher for lessons in anger management. Three years later, when another child was hit in the face by a stone, the boy who threw it, who was normally well behaved, was given a 'severe reprimand'.

Pupil safety

Pupils travelled to school on foot, by bicycle, by car or on a school bus from the Bunbury Arms. Ron Ceurstemont was unwilling to lay down rules about who should be allowed to cycle, since he believed that the decision should be made by parents, not the school.

Suffolk Constabulary administered the Cycling Proficiency Test at the conclusion of a training course, organised each summer term by staff and parents, who were trained by a Road Safety Officer. A police officer visited the school to inspect bicycles and, in 1969, 11 children were presented with road safety awards.

From 1967, staff and parents were concerned about the congestion outside the school at the beginning and end of the school day. This became an even greater problem when the parents of children who attended Park Croft, a small private school in the Park run by Mrs Valentine, parked in School Road. In 1970, the school wrote to the Highway Authority of West Suffolk County Council to request the erection of a barrier in front of the school to prevent parents parking on the school side of the road. In February 1971, a pupil was knocked down by a car outside school and was taken to West Suffolk Hospital by ambulance. Fortunately, her injuries were minor.

Suggestions for easing the parking problems included:
• the creation of a lay-by in School Road;

- the painting of yellow zigzag lines outside the school;
- the employment of a school crossing patrol (more popularly known as a lollipop man or lady);
- the acquisition of land for a car park;
- the erection of a chain link fence between the gate and the Church Institute;
- the imposition of a one-way system in School Road.

They did not suggest the employment of traffic wardens, who had been deployed by West Suffolk Police since 1963. NO PARKING signs were placed outside the school but these were frequently damaged by parents who parked too close to them, and were removed in 1977 because they had been run over so often that they were beyond repair. West Suffolk Road Safety Officer and Eldon Griffiths (1925-2014), Member of Parliament for Bury St Edmunds, were both involved in trying to resolve the issue, which was compounded in 1975 when the 30 m.p.h. speed restrictions, imposed throughout much of the village, were not applied to School Road.

A School Liaison Police Officer visited the school each term to teach pupils about safety issues and he often illustrated his talks with a 16 mm film, including one entitled *Green Cross Code.*

In 1969, a man was seen standing outside the school gate handing out sweets to children, so PC Oakes talked to pupils about personal safety and showed them a film called *Never Go with Strangers.* In 1971, children were taught about safety with the help of two clowns named Roland and Shandy.

School milk, meals and water

In 1968, free milk was withdrawn from pupils in secondary schools, and the Education (School Milk) Act 1970 ended free milk for 7 to 11-year-olds, unless they were designated as being 'in need' by school medical officers. Margaret Thatcher was the Minister for Education at the time, so it led to the jibe of 'Thatcher, Thatcher, milk snatcher'. The Department of Education and Science estimated that free milk for primary school children in 1971 cost £14 million a year, twice as much as the amount spent on school books, and that the new act would save £9 million.

In 1971, as the result of parental concern about the need for children to have access to a drink at playtime, the LEA agreed to the provision of a water drinking fountain outside one of the classrooms.

In 1977, the European Economic Community School Milk Subsidy Scheme was introduced. This permitted local authorities to claim funding for secondary and primary milk sales and from 1978, free milk was available for 7 to 12-year-olds whose families were dependent upon Income Support.

During the 1970s, over 90 per cent of the pupils ate a school lunch, which cost 25p. Up to ten people were employed each day at the school to assist with lunches, in either the canteen or the dining hall. The ovens in the kitchen were powered by gas and, in December 1970, there was a gas explosion, which could be heard throughout the school. Fortunately, Miss Hawes, the school cook, was unharmed, although she was understandably upset. In order to accommodate all of the pupils, there were two sittings for lunch each day. Grace was said at the beginning of the meal, and food was served by two pupils from each table. Water glasses had numbers on the bottom, and pupils competed with each other to see who had the highest number. In 1973, Ron Ceurstemont was seriously concerned about the amount of food wastage, which he blamed partly on the quantity of snacks eaten by children at morning break, so he wrote to parents to request that each child was provided with no more than one piece of fruit a day.

Pupil health

The School Medical Service carried out individual health inspections for new entrants and others, and the School Nursing Service continued to carry out regular vision and hearing tests, and head-lice inspections. The School Dental Service carried out dental inspections and, in 1968, showed a film about dental care to pupils, entitled *Eskimos don't have Toothbrushes*.

The school curriculum

To update their knowledge, skills and understanding, teachers from Great Barton School attended courses run by Suffolk Advisory Service on the teaching of religious education, spelling, maths, drama, history, country dancing, reading, PE, music, French and 'gifted children'.

According to the school logbook, the school received regular visits from Her Majesty's Inspectors (HMI), including Mr Read, Mr Husband, Mr Jary, Mr Simonds, Mr Simon, Mrs Brook and Mr Chapman. There are no references to any official inspections by either HMI or a Diocesan Inspector but in 1968, R. Sheppard, a schools' advisor for West Suffolk Education Committee, stated in a letter of reference for Ron Ceurstemont that Great Barton School was efficiently run and the children were happy and made good progress.

In 1967, a committee chaired by Lady Bridget Plowden (1910-2000), a British educational reformer, published the Plowden Report (1967) entitled *Children and their Primary Schools*. It was strongly influenced by the work of Jean Piaget (1896-1980), a Swiss developmental psychologist who advocated a child-centred approach to education. The second chapter of the report opened with the oft-repeated statement that, 'at the heart of the educational process lies the child' and endorsed the ideas of individual learning, a flexible curriculum, the importance of play, the value of collaborative learning, the use of the environment, learning through discovery and exploring, and the importance of evaluating all round pupil progress. It supported the expansion of nursery schooling for children from the age of three, the introduction of educational priority areas and the nurturing of home-school relationships. It recommended the abolition of corporal punishment in schools, the replacement of the term 'educationally sub-normal' by the term 'slow learner', and the need for more male teachers in primary schools.

Religious education (RE) and collective worship
A school assembly was taken by Ron Ceurstemont each Monday and Tuesday, and by the Revd B. Vaughan Parry, Vicar of Holy Innocents' Church, Great Barton, each Thursday. Each Wednesday morning the junior classes listened to a recorded BBC religious service, and on Friday afternoons, the whole school congregated in the hall for a longer assembly, often with music or stories provided by the children. Margaret Huggins, who was the 'reserved' teacher, taught hymns to the children and accompanied the singing on the piano.

The school followed the Suffolk *Agreed Syllabus for Religious Education*, which was non-denominational and recognised that 'the religious traditions in Great Britain were Christian, whilst taking account of the teaching and practices of other principal religions practised in Great Britain'. RE was taught in each class by the class teacher, and the Revd Parry taught Bible studies to the top class once a week. Every school day ended with a prayer.

In June 1975, Margaret Huggins and Julia Briggs took Class 1 and Class 3 to Walsham-le-Willows to look at an exhibition of biblical material. In 1977, the head teacher was asked to submit a report on *Worship and Religious Education* to the school managers.

Early year's education
Children attended school from the start of the term during which they celebrated their fifth birthday, and some benefited from having a nap after lunch. Consequently, in the reception class, the double wooden desks with drawers were pushed aside at the beginning of each afternoon session, and the children lay on small mats on the floor.

English
At Great Barton School, a mixture of approaches was used for the teaching of reading. Every pupil began by reading the books in the *Janet and John* reading scheme, after which independent readers chose books from amongst the colourful new reading books, including those bought by

the PTA or on loan from Suffolk Library Service to Schools. The *Sound Sense* series [now out of print] and *Objective English Books-Levels 1 to five* were used throughout the school to teach spelling and grammar, and pupils were given weekly spelling tests.

In 1972, there were articles in the national and local press about falling standards in reading, so Ron Ceurstemont analysed the reading results of the pupils at Great Barton School from 1963 to 1971. He found that average standards at the school were rising, which he attributed to improved teaching and changed demographics of the school intake. In 1976, he attended a conference, organised by the LEA, on the Bullock Report (1975) entitled *Language for Life,* which included recommendations about how to raise reading standards.

Head teachers of the primary and middle schools in the Thurston Pyramid agreed that cursive handwriting would be taught in the middle, but not the primary, schools.

Mathematics

Pupils were expected to chant and memorise their times tables. Decimalisation of the British currency was introduced on 15 February 1971, and Paul Downing, an ex-pupil, remembers being shown a little blue plastic wallet with the new decimal coins.

Larkcom's Arithmetic Series [now out of print] a popular scheme for teaching mathematics, was used until 1977 when the Ixworth cluster of schools agreed to use a common mathematics syllabus, after which pupils followed a scheme of work based on the *Scottish Heinemann Maths* series.

Special Educational Needs

Pupils with special educational needs (referred to at this time as 'remedial pupils') were given extra help by one of the part-time teachers.

The Warnock Report (1978) of the Committee of Inquiry into the Education of Handicapped Children and Young People suggested that there was a continuum of educational needs from the most severe and permanent to the relatively minor and remediable. It proposed that children with moderate learning difficulties who were in mainstream schools should be identified and their needs met.

Cross-curricular topic work

At this time, the school curriculum was determined within each school. At Great Barton School, geography, history, science, art and craft were often taught within a single topic or theme, rather than as separate, or discrete, subjects. Each year, topics were determined by the teachers, most of whom adopted a child-centred approach and aimed to make the children so interested in the subject that they wanted to find out more for themselves.

Whilst this method of determining what was taught usually ensured that teachers were enthusiastic about their chosen topic, there was not always curriculum progression within the school. Furthermore, pupils who changed schools could find themselves repeating a topic they had already studied.

The variety of topics taught at Great Barton School is illustrated by the range of 16 mm films and television programmes shown to the children. Topics included Norway, North Sea gas and oil, Sioux Indians, animal habitats, a tree as a living thing, rabbits and hares, reptiles, flowers, how animals move, *Ship to Shore* and *The Little Shepherdess*. Angela Brook, who attended the school between 1971 and 1976, remembers learning about dinosaurs, New Zealand and Tristan da Cunha, where a volcano erupted in 1961 and most of its occupants moved to Britain.

Jane Slade recalled that pupils who finished their classwork were allowed to sit in one of the small rooms outside the classroom, where the library books were displayed, and use some of the new books to do independent topic work.

The only TV in the school was a black and white set and, in July 1969, the whole school assembled in the hall to watch a televised broadcast of Neil Armstrong and Buzz Aldrin, the Apollo II spacemen, who were the first human beings to walk on the surface of the moon. In 1976, the PTA paid £199 for a colour television. During the Easter holidays of 1977, broadcasts for schools were shown on Anglia TV so that teachers could evaluate the programmes before deciding whether to use them in school.

The Electrical Appliance Regulations (1969) resulted in significant changes to the colour coding of electric cables. The core colours of flexible cables of electrical appliances changed to brown for the live, blue for neutral, green and yellow for the earth conductor, and each pupil in Class 1 made a post-card, which illustrated the old and new colours, which they took home to show their family.

During nature study lessons, pupils explored the school grounds for plants and mini-beasts, examined things under a microscope, grew plants, and hatched chicken eggs. On one occasion, the Lecture Service from Linton Zoo brought a salamander, a boa constrictor, an Amazon parrot and a skunk to show the children.

Art and craft

There was a pottery kiln in one of the classrooms. In 1969, 1971, 1973 and 1975, pupils were taken to Henry Watson's Potteries at Wattisfield to learn more about ceramics. Sewing machines from the old school were still in use and, in May 1971, Rosemary Sawyer, an advisory teacher, taught machine embroidery in the hall to some of the nine-year-olds. The PTA bought art materials and a boiler for tie-dyeing, and pupils contributed work to the West Suffolk Schools Art Exhibition held in Bury St Edmunds. In 1977, Great Barton pupils exhibited their art work in an art show at the school for parents and ex-pupils.

Physical education (PE) and sport

Gymnastic lessons were taught in the school hall all the year round, using climbing apparatus, a rope ladder, PE benches for balance, a bright blue vaulting horse and agility equipment.

Games lessons took place on the playground or playing field, with football, skittle ball and netball lessons during the autumn and spring terms, and athletics and games of rounders during the summer term. In spite of concerns about the potential problems of cats using it as a toilet, a sand pit was constructed so that pupils could practise long jump.

A traditional school sports day was held each year in July. It usually took place on the school playing field on a school day, but in 1975 and 1976 it was organised by the PTA on the recreation ground next to Great Barton Village Hall and on a Saturday, so that more parents could attend. Pupils competed in the Bury and District Schools' Sports Day, where Great Barton School won the Rural Cup in 1967, 1968 and 1969. Sixty pupils went to Norton Primary School in 1972 to compete against pupils from eight other primary schools.

Country dancing lessons included folk and maypole dances, using the newly acquired maypole, which required four children to sit on the base to prevent it from toppling over when the ribbons were pulled.

Some pupils joined after-school clubs. The boys' football team and the girls' netball and skittle ball teams, whose kit was bought by the PTA, played matches against primary schools at Ixworth, Pakenham, Thurston, Elmswell, Stanton, Rougham, Cockfield, Moulton, Kedington and Westgate School in Bury St Edmunds. Members of the gym club, trained by Miss Maude, competed annually in county gymnastics competition held at different venues each year, including Scaltback School in Newmarket, in 1973. A chess club, run by Mrs Voice, competed in tournaments at Bury St Edmunds and Thurston in 1977 and 1978.

Music, dance and drama

Two pianos and a variety of tuned percussion instruments were available for music lessons. Margaret Huggins ran the school choir and a poetry-reading group, and Wenda Pennells ran a recorder group. In 1974 and 1977, pupils were entertained by Suffolk County String Quartet and Suffolk County Wind Quintet, and a few pupils took part in the Breckland Music Festival. In 1978, the choir and recorder group contributed to a music morning at Tollgate Primary School, Bury St Edmunds. In 1975, parents attended the end of year assembly to watch their children sing, play music on the recorder, ring hand bells and receive certificates.

The pupils often performed concerts and plays in school, and up to 200 parents watched the Christmas productions. Jane Slade can still recall the first few lines of 'Night Train', by W.H. Auden, which she had to learn by heart and recite at a concert. In 1972, Mrs Haytack's class performed *The Wizard of Oz* to the rest of the school, and two years later, Pat Barratt and Sally Bulbrook invited the parents of the youngest pupils into school to watch their children perform a play and buy sweets and cakes from the children to give them an opportunity to practise using money.

In Bury St Edmunds, in 1970, on the 1,100th anniversary of St Edmund's death, a pageant depicting the *Life and Martyrdom of St Edmund* was staged to celebrate the completion of the Cathedral extension. In 1974, Class 2 performed *Snow White* in the cloisters in Abbey Gardens during a Magna Carta Festival.

In 1972, Mrs Haytack took Class 4 to a drama morning at Sexton's Manor Primary School in Bury St Edmunds, and in 1973, 1974, 1975 and 1976, to a drama morning with pupils from Ingham, Norton and Barrow primary schools. In 1973, Class 4 performed *Beauty and the Beast* and in 1974, Class 2 performed *Snow White*. In 1975, 171 children attended a drama morning at Great Barton School, during which Class 6 performed the story of *Goldilocks* and Class 1 acted out the verses of the *Pied Piper of Hamelin*.

In 1971, the children visited the Bury St Edmunds Theatre Royal, built in 1819, which is the only surviving Regency theatre in the UK. The top class watched an evening performance of a ballet performed by Cambridge Ballet. During the next three years, pupils participated in a theatre workshop, watched a puppet version of *Snow White*, and puppet shows performed by the Hogarth Puppets and Tinder Box.

In 1976 and 1977, pupils from Great Barton School watched a performance at school by the East Anglian Dance Company and the East Anglian Dance Puppet Theatre Company. In 1971, 1975 and 1976, pupils were joined by pupils from Norton, Rougham and Pakenham schools to watch a performance by the Polka Dot Theatre Company.

Tests

From 1968 until 1975, in addition to taking the Eleven Plus examination, pupils at Great Barton School took some of the Moray House Tests, devised at Edinburgh Provincial Teacher Training Centre.

In 1975, the Department of Education and Science (DES) set up the Assessment of Performance Unit (APU) to develop methods of assessing and monitoring pupil achievement and identifying under-achievement.

In 1976, Suffolk County Council introduced Educational Guidance Tests. These consisted of the D. Young's Group Reading Test for pupils who attained the age of eight during the academic year; the National Foundation for Educational Research (NFER) Reading Test, for those who attained the age of nine during the academic year; and a verbal reasoning test, for those who attained the age of 11 during the academic year.

Playtimes

The grounds of the school were described by Ron Ceurstemont, in an article in a magazine entitled *Village Schools in Suffolk, Building Appraisal No.5*:

> 'The site is bounded on south and west by hedgerows and trees, and careful thinning and replanting, combined with generous new planting around paved areas, has been carried out. The intention is to achieve a pleasantly smooth integration with the rural environment.'

Boys and girls usually chose to play separately. There was not enough room to play football safely on the playground, but posts were available for netball and basketball, and there was room to practice skittle ball. There was a climbing frame, although it did not have a safety surface beneath it. All pupils played running games, whilst girls used the wall at one end of the playground to do handstands, play games of two-ball, or 'sevensies', which involved throwing and catching a tennis ball against the wall in seven different ways. Clapping games, hop scotch, skipping, French skipping and chasing games were enjoyed throughout the whole year; games with conkers, marbles and jacks during the appropriate season.

During the summer term, pupils played on the playing field, where they made daisy chains, created nests and dens from newly mown grass, or played chasing games, including 'kiss chase', often hiding in the bushes at the side of the field, which were theoretically out of bounds.

In 1972, a pest officer visited the school on at least three occasions to destroy wasp nests in the field. In 1975 and 1981, a tree surgeon was employed to fell elm trees that were infected with Dutch elm disease.

Parents

In November each year, parents were invited into school for an Open Evening. In 1967, it was attended by 150 parents, who listened to a short account of the founding of Great Barton School by the Revd Grayson. In 1968, they watched displays of country dancing and gymnastics and a film entitled, *I do and understand*. In 1970, they watched *Children of China, Notes on a Triangle, River Pilot* and *Animals in Winter*.

From May 1970, children who were due to enrol at the school during the following academic year, together with their parents, were invited to spend an afternoon in the infant class during the summer term. In December 1971, Pat Barratt, Jennie Barber and Mrs Haytack arranged a meeting to explain their teaching methods to the parents of the children in their classes.

From 1971, almost every parent attended a ten-minute interview with his or her child's class teacher, once a year. On this occasion, the school managers gave permission for the pupils to be sent home at 2.45 p.m. so that interviews could be held from 3.00 p.m.

In 1975, some parents requested an additional evening during the year, but the head teacher rejected the idea and assured parents that they could request an individual meeting with their child's class teacher at any time.

Great Barton Parent Teachers Association (PTA)

The PTA, set up in 1964, included some mothers who had been involved with fund-raising activities before their child started school, through the local playgroup, which was started up in Great Barton, in 1968, by Joyce Lord and Joyce Jackaman, and held in the Church Institute.

From 1970, PTA activities were advertised on a notice board, made by Mr Wright, a parent. A dance was arranged each term at the school or the Village Hall, a jumble sale was held at the Victoria Mission in Bury St Edmunds in 1970, a Harvest Supper in 1973, a Gilbert and Sullivan evening in 1974, and a fashion show during the spring terms of 1972, 1975, 1976 and 1977. Between £150 and £500 was raised each year. The PTA also arranged non-fund raising activities. At the end of each summer term, up to 200 parents and children attended a country dancing and barbeque evening, arranged by the PTA, and, in 1973, Mr Christopher Bunbury, the youngest brother of Michael William Bunbury, 13th Bt, spoke to a meeting about the history of the Bunbury family.

The PTA continued to raise money for the building and maintenance of a learner swimming pool. It was built on the playing field and officially opened in 1968 at the summer fête, which was attended by children in fancy dress costume and their parents. Two rooms next to the caretaker's cupboard were converted to changing rooms with showers. The pool was maintained by the caretaker and Mr Slade, chair of the PTA, until Suffolk County Council took over responsibility on 10 November 1970.

In 1971, wooden benches were erected around the pool, and a vacuum pool cleaner was purchased the following year. A Calor gas heater, bought in 1972, proved to be unsatisfactory, so an electric one, housed in a small wooden hut next to the pool, was installed in 1974. The PTA contributed £400 towards its cost of £625. The school considered enclosing the pool so that it could be used all year round, but the estimated cost of £2,700 was prohibitive, so the PTA bought a plastic cover for the pool at a cost of £148.

There were ongoing problems with the swimming pool. Poor drainage from the showers resulted in the shower cubicles being covered with soapy water and becoming slippery; the rough surface of the concrete bottom of the pool caused swimmers' feet to bleed; and cracks gradually appeared around the pool, as the soil in the field dried out. Furthermore, it was necessary to repaint the swimming pool each year and, on one occasion, the Paints Division of Imperial Chemical Industries, based at Stowmarket 17 miles away, donated some tins of paint for this purpose.

In spite of these problems, every pupil received a weekly swimming lesson in the school pool during term-time between the end of May and September, and most earned one of the four levels of West Suffolk Education Committee's swimming certificates. Some pupils took part in 'Bury Standards Day', where they could qualify for bronze, silver and gold medals. In order to have deep-water experience before the competition, pupils were taken to practise in a deeper pool at another school. The more confident swimmers took part in swimming galas at Sudbury in 1971 and 1972. In some years the pool was used at weekends and during the school summer holiday under the supervision of parents.

Special events during the school year

On Ascension Day, the older pupils attended a service at Holy Innocents' Church, Great Barton. but the rest of the day was no longer given as a school holiday.

Children donated flowers to decorate part of the church during a biennial Flower Festival, during which the school choir, and sometimes the recorder, hand bell and poetry recital groups, performed at an evening service. The Christmas carol service was usually held in the school, but was held in the church in 1974. Most years, members of the school choir sang at an evening service in the church, and a few children formed a tableau at the annual carol singing evening at Manor Barn.

Members of Great Barton Over 60 Club were invited into school for an afternoon during the spring term each year to watch an entertainment by the children and eat afternoon tea, prepared by the pupils. At the end of the autumn term, they were invited to the school to watch a dress rehearsal of a concert, after which they were served with a cup of tea and mince pies, made by the children.

In December 1973, as a token of their appreciation, the club gave the school a flowering cherry tree, which was planted near to the school entrance. The following spring, May Barnard fixed a commemorative plaque to the tree.

Between 1974 and 1977, children in Class 1, accompanied by parents, delivered school-made Christmas cards and puddings to the homes of about 75 pensioners in the village.

Harvest festivals, attended by up to 140 parents, were held at the school, during which items of food donated by pupils were displayed before being delivered to elderly village residents by children in the top class, accompanied by parents.

A Christmas party was arranged for the pupils each year, when the school was decorated with paper chains made from coloured pieces of paper. Until 1969, children were given sweets to take home at the end of the party. These may have included Polo mints (1948), Bounty (1951), and Twix (1967). In 1970, the PTA contributed £30, so that each child could have an ice cream during the party and a balloon and Ladybird Book to take home. In 1971, the PTA contributed £180, and each child was given a 15p set of felt-tipped pens. From 1972 to 1974, the PTA contributed £50, raised to £65.50 in 1975, towards the costs of the party. From 1976, it decided to subsidise a visit by a professional entertainer instead of the Christmas party.

Fund-raising for charity

Between 1970 and 1978, the school raised about £250 each year for various charities, which included the Royal British Legion, the Church of England Children's Society, the National Institute for the Blind, the Spastic Society, OXFAM, Shelter and Help the Aged. In 1970, programmes for sports day were sold in aid of the Multiple Sclerosis Society. A sponsored swim in July 1975 raised £162. 61s. for Suffolk Red Cross, and money was raised at a toy sale in 1975 in aid of Great Barton Village Hall car park.

Publicity for the school

There was great excitement in October 1969, when the BBC interviewed some of the pupils about their views on gambling and horse racing for a BBC2 programme called *Children Talking.* When it was screened in June 1970, it included interviews with Paul Downing and Ross Donovan, two pupils from Class 1.

In October 1969, a reporter from the *East Anglian Daily Times* visited the school to collect information for an article on the village of Great Barton, and published a photograph of the top class and a view of the school from the playing field. In January 1970, the Chief Education Officer for West Suffolk visited the school with a journalist, but the school logbook does not mention whether a follow-up article was published.

Three years later, following a visit from a journalist and photographer from the *Bury Free Press,* a report appeared in the paper in February 1973, in response to which, the mother of a prospective pupil informed Ron Ceurstemont that she would not be sending her children to the school, because she 'had had enough of this progressive mumbo-jumbo'.

Class visits and the jubilee celebrations

At least one annual educational visit was arranged for each class until 1976. In 1969, 1971, 1972 and 1973, the 10 and 11-year-olds were taken by train from Bury St Edmunds to London, where they visited tourist sights and ate fish and chips for lunch.

In Suffolk, pupils visited the dairy farm at Manor Barn in Great Barton (1968), Norton Pet Centre (1970), Devils' Dyke, near Newmarket (1970), Melford Church (1970), Bury Cathedral (1975) and Bury Fire Station (1976). In 1968, some of the pupils visited West Stow, an Anglo-Saxon village, which was excavated between 1965 and 1972 and reconstructed from 1973.

In Norfolk, visits were arranged to the nature trail at Kings Forest, Thetford (1968), Norwich Castle and Great Witchingham Wild life Park (1969, 1973 and 1975), Bressingham Steam Museum and gardens (1973), Kilverstone Wild life Park (1974 and 1975), Banham Zoo (1975), Strangers Hall and the Bridewell Museum at Norwich (1975) and Castle Rising, Thetford (1975).

In the adjacent counties of Essex, Cambridgeshire and Bedfordshire, children visited the Botanical Gardens, Fitzwilliam Museum and Kings' College, Cambridge (1970), Colchester Castle, Museum and Zoo (1970 and 1972), the headquarters of the Royal Society for the Protection of Birds Nature Reserve at Sandy, Bedfordshire (1971), Ely Cathedral (1973 and 1975), the Scott Polar Expedition Institute at Cambridge (1973), and Saffron Walden (1974).

Although Queen Elizabeth II acceded to the throne in February 1952, her Silver Jubilee was celebrated in June 1977, her official birthday, and 7 June was declared an additional public holiday. All schools were closed and a street party was held in School Road, Great Barton.

On 1 June 1977, the school choir sang and recited poems at a village concert. Two days later, every pupil was given a jubilee spoon and a jubilee badge. Two weeks later, on Saturday 18 June, the school took part in the Village Family Fun Day at Great Barton Village Hall. It opened at 2.15 p.m. with a grand parade, which included children with their bicycles decorated in red, white and blue. Pupils put on a display of maypole dances and gymnastics, and sold second-hand toys. The PTA provided a tug of war team and organised a wheel of fortune, a wheelbarrow event, and a coconut shy, in spite of a national shortage of coconuts. Games and competitions included traditional games such as an Aunt Sally, which involved players throwing sticks or battens at a model of an old woman's head, and a welly-hurling event, in which participants competed to see how far they could throw size eight wellington boots.

On the afternoon of 14 July 1977, special events were organised at the school on the theme of patriotism. Parents watched short plays and displays of maypole dancing and gymnastics, and listened to the choir and the recorder group. After the singing of the British National Anthem, everyone went outside to watch a traditional sports day event with races. At the end of the day, each child was presented with a jubilee crown, provided by the PTA.

On 14 November 1973, Princess Anne married Captain Mark Phillips and, although it was not declared as a national holiday, the school was closed for the day.

Industrial action

During the early 1970s, the school was affected directly and indirectly by industrial action. Electricity generation was severely restricted as the result of industrial action by coal miners, and, in December 1970 and December 1971, the school borrowed an emergency generator, in case there was a blackout as the result of industrial action by the Electrical, Electronic and Telecommunications Union and Plumbing Trades Union.

In June 1971, Pat Barratt's class were sent home for the day, when she went on strike in support of the pay claim by the National Association of Schoolmasters and the Union of Women Teachers. Following recommendations of the Houghton Report (1974) on teachers' salaries, teachers won a substantial pay rise, which brought the average salary of a nursery or primary school teacher, to £3,220 p.a. from March 1975.

In November 1971 and February 1972, the school only had 50 gallons of heating oil in the tank, so the LEA advised the school to switch off the heating in the school until the next delivery.

Retirement

Ron and Mary Ceurstemont both retired at Easter 1978. Coincidentally, a memorandum issued by Suffolk County Council, dated 18 April 1978, included a statement that 'Head teachers are reminded of the decision of the Education Committee, whereby the spouse of a head teacher may not be appointed to any post on the teaching or non-teaching staff of the same school.'

During his 18 years as the head teacher of Great Barton School, Ron Ceurstemont taught 700 children and oversaw a significant number of changes. In 1960, he took over an antiquated Victorian school, housed on two separate sites, which was part of a two-tier system of education, within which each pupil transferred to a single-sex grammar or secondary modern school. In 1978, he handed over a new school building, housed on a single site, which was part of comprehensive, co-educational system, within a three-tier system of education.

Map 6. Old and new school buildings in Great Barton

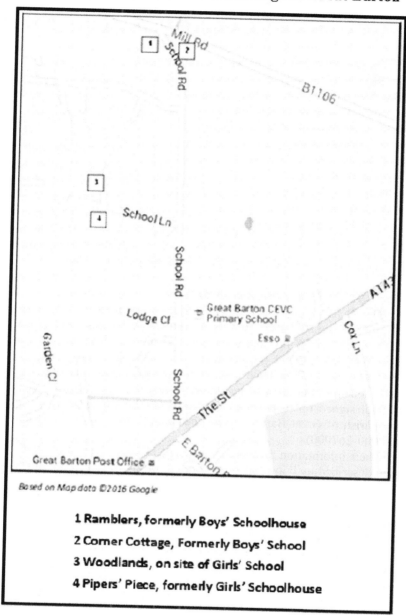

Based on Map data ©2016 Google

1 Ramblers, formerly Boys' Schoolhouse

2 Corner Cottage, Formerly Boys' School

3 Woodlands, on site of Girls' School

4 Pipers' Piece, formerly Girls' Schoolhouse

17

A FALLING ROLL AND THE BALANCE OF POWER

Between 1980 and 1988, the government passed a series of laws, which increased the power of the Department of Education and Science (DES), school governing bodies and parents at the expense of Local Education Authorities (LEAs) and professional educationalists. New legislation imposed the National Curriculum, set up a more rigorous school inspection system, increased the involvement and power of parents, encouraged the integration of pupils with special educational needs, introduced an appraisal scheme for teachers, and transferred financial management from LEAs to school managers (renamed governors in 1980) under a system known as Local Management of Schools (LMS).

John Dawkins, the head teacher of Great Barton School from 1978 to 1990, had to manage not only the implementation of this new legislation, but also the introduction of new technology and the consequences of a dramatic fall in the pupil roll at the school during the 1980s.

The *BBC Domesday Project (1986)*

The *Domesday Project* marked the nine hundredth anniversary of the original *Domesday Book*. It was a partnership between the *BBC*, Acorn Computers Ltd, Philips and Logica, with some funding from the European Commission's ESPRIT programme.

The project divided the country into blocks, and 1 million volunteers provided information for one or more blocks. Pupils from Great Barton School signed up to cover D-block GB-588000-267000, which included the parish of Great Barton (www.bbc.co.uk/history/domesday/dblock/GB-588000-267000).

Their information provided a snapshot of Great Barton in 1986, which was described as lying 'on rising ground on the A143, three miles NE of Bury St. Edmunds, in the administrative Borough of St Edmundsbury. It is a main road village with flint and stone cottages (original Estate cottages) on both sides of the village street.'

During the 1960s and 1970s, new housing estates were built at Hall Park and Conyers Way and the population of the village grew from 979 in 1961 to 1495 in 1971. The *Domesday Project* described the occupants of these new estates as 'middle class, middle management, owner occupier, car owners, often with both parents commuting to work, and liable to move frequently for employment reasons'.

Employment opportunities within the village were limited to the village Post Office, Great Barton Service Station, one of three building companies or on one of the seven farms, which varied in size from 90 to 430 acres. Three of the farms grew barley, wheat, oil seed rape, potatoes, and sugar beet for the British Sugar Corporation factory at Bury St Edmunds, two raised chickens, one fattened bullocks and pigs, and one was a market garden.

Villagers were asked to state what they liked about living in the village and to suggest improvements. Most people considered that it was a friendly, quiet, clean, good-sized village, with plenty of trees and big gardens, set in attractive countryside with open skies. Whilst being near a town, it was not too far from the coast. Villagers praised the school, the shops, the clubs and church life. Families with young children appreciated living in a village with a large number of other young families.

Many villagers regretted the lack of a unifying feature in the village, such as a public house, green or church, and some people suggested that a new public house should be built in the centre of the village. Several villagers suggested that a health centre, teashop and service station with full garage facilities would be good additions, as would a better bus service, a village police officer, a village roadman, some public benches and connection to town gas.

The building of a by-pass, the enforcement of existing speed restrictions, a ban on cars in Elms Close and the installation of rumble strips, additional street lighting and a pedestrian crossing were all suggested as ways of alleviating traffic problems through the village.

The demography of Great Barton

The census statistics from the Ward and Civil Parish Monitors 1991 revealed that the population decreased from 1,991 in 1981 to 1,967 in 1991. During the same period, there was a reduction in the number of children of primary school age in the village, as they had gone on to middle schools, and fewer new families moving into the village.

At the same time, an increasing number of families in Great Barton were choosing to send their primary-aged children to one of the private, fee-paying schools in the locality. These included Culford School (a co-educational public school), South Lee School (a charitable trust school founded by a group of parents in 1961), Park Croft School (a small private school in The Park at Great Barton), and Cherry Trees School (a Montessori school, which opened at Risby in 1982).

Changes of staffing levels at Great Barton School

1978 to 1982

In April 1978, there were 110 pupils, taught in five classes by John Dawkins (head teacher), Pat Barratt (deputy head teacher), Margaret

Huggins, Wenda Pennells and Reinhild Raistrick (full-time class teachers), and Julia Briggs (a part-time teacher).

Reinhild Raistrick was appointed to the teaching staff in January 1978. She was born and brought up in Tanzania, in East Africa, of German missionary parents, and qualified in art and teaching at Cheltenham, Gloucester. She taught in East Africa and in primary schools in various parts of the UK, and moved from Northumberland to Great Barton in 1976. She was a talented botanical artist and she inspired her pupils to develop their artistic abilities.

In January 1981, John Dawkins presented Margaret Huggins with a bouquet of flowers, in recognition of her 20 years' service to the school. That same year, he discussed the building of an extension with the County Architect and, during the next few months, organised fund-raising events to finance the new building. A cake, candy and coffee sale raised £64, a sale of bricks raised £40 and an Easter Fair raised £110, but the extension was never built.

1982 to 1988

In 1982, there were 91 pupils on roll, and in spite of John Dawkins' best efforts to protect staffing levels, the LEA decided that the school could no longer justify the employment of so many teachers. Wenda Pennells signed a part-time contract for 15.5 hours a week and Julia Briggs accepted redundancy and devoted her time to fund-raising for the Children's Society, for which she was subsequently awarded an Order of the British Empire (ØBE). After the number of classes was reduced from five to four, the empty classroom was used as a library and for practical lessons.

Doris Mayhew, the clerical assistant, retired in October 1983. She was replaced by Janet Cobbold, a canteen assistant at the school, who was contracted to work for 12 hours a week.

In July 1984, Wenda Pennells resigned for personal reasons. At the end of the following term, Pat Barratt, the deputy head, retired and was replaced as a class teacher by Sandra (Sandie) Williams. Reinhild Raistrick was promoted to deputy head teacher.

On 26 June 1986, Margaret Huggins [476], a well-loved and highly respected teacher, died at the age of 57, whilst conducting a concert of the Meade Singers in Great Barton Village Hall. Her death came as a great shock and, for many of the children, it was the first time that someone close to them had died. On the day of the funeral at Holy Innocents' Church, Great Barton, one teacher remained at school to look after the pupils whilst the remainder joined family and friends of Margaret for the service. In May 1987, a small plaque in her memory was erected at the edge of the school playing field. A 'Margaret Huggins Award' was created, which was awarded to Allan Gladwell in 1986, Julie Austin in 1987, and no-one in 1988, owing to a lack of agreement about who should receive it.

During the remainder of the summer term, Pat Barratt returned from retirement to teach the top class. From September 1986, it was taught by Sylvia Taylor, who had previously worked at Drinkstone Primary School, which closed earlier that year.

In 1986, parents at the school were so concerned about the possibility of further staff reductions, that they contacted Sir Eldon Griffiths, MP, who spent an hour at the school in May and offered to investigate the situation.

At this time, the Bury Area Review examined the viability of small village schools in the Bury St Edmunds area. Following the *Report of the Small Schools Working Party*, which examined the viability of very small schools, primary schools were closed at Whepstead, Chedburgh, Chevington, Horringer, Eastgate, Ingham, Hepworth, Icklingham, Little Bealings and Charsfield. Various options were considered for the relocation of their pupils, including the transfer of children from Ingham School to Great Barton School. Their head teacher, chair of governors and some of the parents visited the school with Tom Scherb, the newly appointed Western Area Education Officer, but the Ingham parents were unenthusiastic about their children transferring to a school in a village with which they had no community links (*BFP* 5 Sept. 1986). It was ultimately decided that pupils from Ingham School would transfer to Barnham School.

In November 1986, Dr Platts and a group of people from County Hall, Ipswich, visited Great Barton School in connection with Suffolk's Small Schools' Review, to examine the school's viability. A week later, 16 members of the Small Schools' Working Party spent 45 minutes at the school, and ten days later Tom Scherb and Sir Macdonald Miller, chair of Suffolk Education Committee, spent an hour at the school in connection with the same review. Although the LEA decided to keep Great Barton School open, it remained at risk of closure.

In 1987, it was decided to close Pakenham School and there was a suggestion that its pupils could transfer to Great Barton School. In March 1987, three parents of pupils at Pakenham School visited Great Barton School and, during the same month, Jane Coleman, the Assistant Area Education Officer, attended a governors' meeting of Great Barton School to listen to their views on the subject.

In January 1989, more than a dozen parents from Pakenham School looked round Great Barton School. However, when the head teacher of Pakenham School was appointed as the new head teacher of Norton School, most pupils transferred there.

In 1987, Reinhild Raistrick resigned in order to pursue a career as an artist. She exhibited her botanical pictures in the cloisters of Bury St Edmunds Cathedral and 20 years later published her first book, *African Violets,* a study of all the known African species of the genus *Saintpaulia,* many of which are now severely endangered in the wild. Rosemary Roe replaced Reinhild Raistrick as deputy head teacher, Liz Chapman was appointed as a part-time teacher, and Shirley Hissett replaced Wenda Pennells as a classroom assistant.

In 1988, the school had to reduce further the number of teaching staff, so Sandie Williams was redeployed to Paddocks School, Newmarket. Rosemary Roe used the second empty classroom as an additional teaching area for the younger children.

1988 to 1990

In September 1988, there were 70 pupils on roll, three full-time teachers and one part-time teacher. Fred Arbon was made redundant as full-time caretaker after nearly 20 years. He was presented with a carriage clock and gardening token, in recognition of his service to the school, and was able to continue living in the caretakers' bungalow, because his wife, Sylvia, was appointed as cleaner-in-charge, with some caretaking duties. Two weeks later, the caretakers' supervisor visited the school to measure up the building in consideration for the privatisation of the cleaning services.

The Education Act 1981 gave parents the right to be consulted on and to appeal against decisions that concerned their child. It recommended that children with special educational needs should be taught in mainstream schools wherever possible. Each pupil who needed additional help to access the school curriculum was issued with an individual 'statement', which outlined the details of the required support.

From 1981, Great Barton School received assistance with assessment and support for pupils with special educational needs from Suffolk's Learning Support Service, members of the county medical team, educational psychologists, speech therapists, education welfare officers and remedial advisory teachers. In 1989, Sue Manning, who had been a lunchtime supervisor since 1983, was employed to give one-to-one support for a pupil with special educational needs.

In 1989, Lynn Andrews replaced Shirley Hissett as a classroom assistant and, in July 1990, Liz Chapman was made redundant.

The school curriculum

The 'Great Debate' about the nature and purposes of education was launched in 1976 by Jim Callaghan (1912-2005), the Labour prime minister, in a speech at Ruskin College, Oxford. It was followed up by the publication of 15 discussion documents by Her Majesty's Inspectorate (HMI), between 1977 and 1984. A survey of primary schools by HMI, published in 1978, criticised the teaching of mathematics and science and found that schools that performed best in the basic subjects did so in the context of a broader curriculum.

Teachers at Great Barton School attended courses on reading, art, language, testing, mathematics, preparing for spring, RI, special needs, health education, media, multicultural education, management and child abuse. They received support, advice and training from members of Suffolk Advisory Service, who presented model lessons in school and gave ideas for follow-up sessions.

During the 1980s, the teaching curriculum at Great Barton School was determined within the school. Each year, each teacher liaised with the rest of the teaching staff in order to plan their teaching programme.

Religious education (RE) and collective worship

Great Barton School followed the Suffolk *Agreed Syllabus for Religious Education* and Margaret Huggins was the 'reserved' teacher, responsible for the teaching of RE. From 1988, schools were permitted to delegate the head teacher as 'reserved' teacher, in contrast to the terms of the Education Act 1944.

During a daily school assembly, held in the school hall, pupils no longer had hymn books, but the words of hymns were projected onto the slanted ceiling from an overhead projector, and one of the older children pointed to each word as the hymn was sung. On Monday and Tuesday mornings the head teacher or another member of staff led the assembly, on Wednesday mornings the three older classes listened to the BBC Service for Schools, and on Thursday mornings the Vicar of Great Barton led an assembly, after which he taught Bible studies to the top class. On Friday afternoons, pupils listened to music or stories presented by pupils.

In 1984, the Revd Derek Hill accompanied John Dawkins to a meeting on 'Our Church Schools in the 1980s'. In 1987, the Revd Hill was replaced by the Revd Alan Beardmore, and the Revd Clare Sanders made regular visits to the school, on behalf of the Diocesan Education Committee, from 1989 onwards.

English

Reading was taught by a variety of methods, which included for a short time the use of the *Initial Teaching Alphabet* (ITA), invented in the early 1960s by Sir James Pitman, the grandson of Sir Isaac Pitman, inventor of a system of shorthand.

Sound Sense books were used for teaching English grammar and spelling, and pupils were given weekly spelling tests. Six and eight-year-old pupils were given a standard reading test and parents came into school and listened to children read.

The carpeted area between two of the classrooms and the hall was used as a school library, which was kept up-to-date with books from Suffolk Library Service to Schools, which visited the school each term with a mobile van, from which the school could purchase or borrow books.

In November 1978, 1979 and 1980, parents were invited to buy books from a book exhibition and sale in the school hall, with books provided by Suffolk Bookshop, from which the school received a percentage of the sales in the form of books for the school library.

Mathematics

John Dawkins and Reinhild Raistrick attended a meeting, during which Peter Reynolds, County Mathematics Advisor, spoke about the Cockcroft Report (1982) entitled *Mathematics Counts*, which described the state of maths teaching in primary and secondary schools.

Pupils still used the *Scottish Heinemann Maths* books, and seven and eight-year-old pupils at the school took mathematics tests, produced by the National Foundation for Educational Research.

Topic work

Geography, history and science were taught as cross-curricular subjects through topic work. The interim school development plan, written in 1990, stated that, 'It was felt that the thematic approach offered advantages in planning and understanding and was a particularly appropriate way of teaching science and the humanities since, of necessity, it involved the extensive use of English.'

Local people and organisations with special interests were invited into school. Bury St Edmunds Fire Service demonstrated two fire appliances to the infants; members of Suffolk Constabulary brought a 'front-line' police car and two police dogs, and members of the School Dental Service talked to the pupils each year about dental hygiene.

One local resident took her fox cub to show the children; another brought his collection of snakes, frogs and lizards, and a third talked to pupils about education in Kenya. Rosemary Roe was particularly enthusiastic about gardening and nature study and, in April 1989, she and six pupils took part in a recording of *Looking at Nature*, broadcast on *BBC Schools Radio*.

Class visits were regularly arranged to Charity Farm and the Post Office in Great Barton. Elsewhere in Suffolk, pupils visited Aldeburgh (1978), Framlingham Castle (1978), USAF Lakenheath (1979), GPO general sorting office in Bury St Edmunds (1980 and 1986), Bury St

Edmunds Fire Station (1981), RAF Mildenhall (1985), Ickworth House and Park (1987), Ipswich Museum (1989) and Southwold (1989).

In Norfolk they visited Norfolk Wild Life Park at Great Witchingham (1980 and 1984), Kilverstone Zoo (1984, 1987), Banham Zoo (1986), Cockley Cley (1986), Thursford Steam and Fairground Museum (1987 and 1989) and the Sea Life Centre at Hunstanton (1990).

In Essex and Cambridgeshire pupils visited the Colne Valley Railway at Castle Hedingham (1983), Colchester Museum and Heavy Horse Centre (1984), Mole Hall Wildlife Park (1988), the Imperial War Museum at Duxford (1987) and the Polar Museum, Cambridge (1988).

Art and pottery

After 1978, Reinhild Raistrick taught arts and crafts throughout the school. On one occasion, the whole school was involved in creating a huge stegosaurus out of boxes, wire and papier-mâché, a photograph of which was published in the *Bury Free Press.*

The school regularly contributed to West Suffolk Schools Art Exhibition and participated in an art competition organised by the Co-operative Wholesale Society, in which a group entry achieved a distinction for their art project in 1987 and three pupils won cash prizes for their entries in 1990.

Pupils made pottery items, which were fired in the school kiln.

Physical education (PE)

Each class had weekly lessons of indoor PE and outdoor games. In 1985, Godfrey Bancroft, a PE advisory teacher gave demonstration lessons to each class, which included activities using the floor and PE apparatus. In July 1990, new roll-out PE apparatus was fitted in the hall to replace the old free standing equipment.

During the second part of the summer term, pupils had a weekly swimming lesson in the school pool and earned awards each time they achieved certain standards.

In July 1981, 1989 and 1990, pupils performed country dances, including Morris and maypole dancing at the annual garden party of Great Barton Over 60 Club. In 1988, Rosemary Roe took the younger children to a dance festival at St Edmundsbury School, Bury St Edmunds, and other children to the Great Barton Church Fête. Each May, parents watched and participated in country and maypole dancing.

Each July, a sports afternoon was held on the school playing field and winners were given ribbons by a teacher from another school, an ex-teacher, or a member of Great Barton Parent Teacher Association (PTA).

In July 1981, to mark the Royal Wedding of Charles, Prince of Wales, and Lady Diana Spencer, pupils were presented with a commemorative coin at the end of the sports afternoon and a royal wedding mug at the start of the following term.

Football and skittleball matches were arranged with other primary schools, and both teams played friendly matches against primary schools at Hopton, Thurston and Badwell Ash. Boys played in six-a-side football tournaments at Wattisfield recreation ground each year, a seven-a-side football competition organised by the British Sugar Corporation in Bury St Edmunds, a nine-a-side football tournament at Tollgate Primary School, Bury St Edmunds in 1989, and five-a-side football rallies at Bury St Edmunds Sports and Leisure Centre, which was opened by Sir Alf Ramsey in 1975. The girls' skittleball team wore red t-shirts and skirts and took part in an annual skittleball rally with other primary schools at Blackbourne Middle School, where they came first in 1982, 1987 and 1989. Pupils took part in the annual Ixworth and Stanton Area Sports Competition, where they won the Larger Schools Cup and a relay trophy in 1982.

Two parents ran an after-school gymnastic club, where pupils could earn *Coca-Cola* gymnastic badges.

From 1977, the LEA refused to pay the cost of heating the swimming pool during the school holidays, so the costs were borne by the school budget and the PTA. Between 1978 and 1986, the school swimming pool was used during the summer holidays and children were supervised by parents who had received some training in resuscitation techniques.

Music and drama

The school owned two pianos and a wide range of percussion instruments. Pupils from the top class joined the school choir and learnt to play the recorder. Geoffrey Wright, a composer whose work had been performed in the West End of London, retired to Suffolk in 1975. He wrote *Sir Eglamore,* based on an old English ballad, especially for Great Barton School in 1980, and the choir, accompanied by Geoffrey Wright on the piano, made a recording of the ballad.

The older pupils took part in annual music mornings at Ixworth Primary School. Pupils heard performances by Suffolk County Guitar Duo in 1979, 1982 and 1987, Suffolk County Wind Quintet in 1979, and Suffolk County String Quartet in 1982.

In 1978, 1979 and 1980, Ray Dyer, Suffolk Drama Advisor, organised a drama morning at the school for pupils from Great Barton and other local primary schools. In 1985, some of the parents set up a school drama club. In addition, pupils were able to watch professional performances at the school by the East Anglian Dance Theatre, Wolsey Theatre in Education, Motion Theatre Company, the Brockley Puppets, and Phil Spellacy, a puppeteer with the Norwich Puppet Theatre, founded in 1979 by Ray and

Joan Da Silva. In 1981, the whole school went to the Theatre Royal in Bury St Edmunds to watch *Toni Arthur's Music Box* and, in February 1985, the youngest children saw *Mr Merlin,* but the school logbook records that 'some found it frightening'.

In 1981 and 1982, Margaret Huggins took the top class to Ixworth Middle School to see the Polka Children's Theatre and, in 1985, the two top classes went to Stanton Primary School to watch a performance of Roald Dahl's *James and the Giant Peach,* performed by the Norwich Puppet Theatre. The top class watched various performances by the students of West Suffolk College and Ixworth Middle School.

Information Technology

In 1982, the government embraced information technology and presented every school with a computer. Countywide meetings were held to disseminate facts about this new technology and in November 1983 John Dawkins attended a meeting entitled 'Computers in First Schools', which he described in the school logbook as 'very amusing, informative and useful'. In April 1984, the school took delivery of a brand new, stand-alone, RM Nimbus PC-186, a 16-bit microcomputer produced by Research Machines Limited, Oxford. In October 1985, the school acquired a second RM Nimbus PC-186 and bought a printer, which was set up with the help of a parent who worked for a computer company.

Margaret Huggins and John Dawkins attended one-day, two-day and after-school training sessions, during which they learnt how to use a disc drive and printer, manage the computer, use databases and software, and write simple computer programmes. In September 1987, teachers from Great Barton School were joined by staff from three other primary schools for a 'Computer Familiarisation Day'. During 1989 and 1990, Jim Owers, an advisory teacher for computer education, worked with teachers in school, and led four additional morning training sessions for teachers of the primary schools at Great Barton, Walsham-le-Willows and Barnham.

School correspondence was typed on an electric typewriter and duplicates made on carbon paper or a Gestetner duplicating machine, bought in 1979. A photocopier was acquired from Orwell Junior School, Ipswich, in June 1985.

Special events during the school year

In 1978 in England, Wales and Northern Ireland, the first Monday in May became an additional bank holiday.

In 1983, 1985, 1986, 1988 and 1990, there was an Easter Bonnet Parade and a cake sale, which made a profit of between £60 and £105 each year. In 1985, a draw was organised, which raised £75 towards the purchase of a computer printer. In 1990, the Easter Bonnet Parade was followed by an afternoon of dancing, singing and poetry recitations by pupils.

A Christmas carol service was held at the school in most years but in the parish church in 1985 and 1988, to which children either travelled with parents in cars, or walked from the school with their teachers.

In 1978 and 1979, Father Christmas distributed a gift of a book to every pupil. From 1982, pupils were given a free Christmas lunch, funded at first from the Managers' Fund, now known as the School Fund, and from PTA funds after 1983.

A Christmas concert or play was held in the school most years and, from 1982, pupils performed on new staging in the hall. Parents were invited to watch evening performances, after which donations were collected for the Royal National Institute for the Blind (RNIB) each year between 1983 and 1989, except for 1988, when money was donated to the Armenian Earthquake Disaster Fund.

Fund-raising for charity

Pupils were encouraged to contribute to charities and disaster funds throughout the year. Representatives from Help the Aged and the Church of England Children's Society visited the school to talk to the children about the work of their societies. Pupils raised money for charities associated with the International Year of the Child (March 1979), Cambodian refugees (September 1979), a Christmas charity (November 1980 and December 1981), the Columbian Volcano Disaster Appeal (1985), and St Nicholas Hospice (1988). In 1985, the pupils collected more than 100 lbs of food, including split peas, lentils, sugar and flour, for the Live Aid appeal for Ethiopia. Poppies were sold each November to raise funds for the Royal British Legion.

School milk and meals

The Education Act 1980 limited free meals to families who were in receipt of Family Income Supplement, and removed the obligation of the LEA to provide school milk or a lunchtime meal of a nutritional standard. LEAs were permitted to provide free milk for children in nursery, primary and special education, and obliged to open school meal services to compulsory competitive tendering and award contracts to the most competitive offer.

The cost of a school lunch increased from 25p per day in 1977 to 40p per day in 1980, which pupils paid weekly. In 1988, the number of assistant cooks was reduced from two to one, after a decrease in the uptake of school lunches following the increase in cost, removal of minimum nutritional standards and reduction in the number of children entitled to a free school meal.

The weekly menu was displayed on the main entrance door and the pupils ate lunch in a single sitting. Five minutes before the end of the morning session, pupils from the top class helped the canteen staff to move and set out the hexagonal tables for lunch.

School discipline

The Education Act 1986 abolished corporal punishment in state-funded schools, but its use was permitted in private and public schools in England and Wales until 1999. The Elton Report (1989), which enquired into discipline in schools in England and Wales, made recommendations about group management skills and gave positive examples of ways of enforcing pupil discipline.

At Great Barton School, staff imposed discipline by the use of an 'evil-stare', a raised voice or depriving the pupil of playtime. Rachel Patterson, who was called Rachel Chatterson by John Dawkins, recalled that Margaret Huggins was very strict and arranged the tables in her classroom in single rows, with no desk touching another, to discourage children from talking during her lessons.

When two of the eight-year-old boys left school, without permission, during the lunchtime break, they were quickly found, returned, reprimanded, and given a letter to take home to their parents.

This contrasted with an incident in about 1970, when Kate Downing and Elizabeth White ran away from home, at the age of four, and tried to join the school.

Pupil safety

During the 1980s, an increasing number of pupils were brought to school by car. Tragically, the four-year-old brother of a pupil at the school was killed in a road traffic accident in 1980 and two years later a nine-year-old boy, who had recently left Great Barton School, was killed.

Less than a month later, Pat Barratt, the reception class teacher, was involved in a car accident on her way to school and was unable to teach for six weeks.

A representative of the Royal Society for the Prevention of Accidents (RoSPA) visited the school at least once a year to show a film, talk to the children and exhibit some of the RoSPA teaching materials to staff, for use in subsequent lessons. Rollo and Shandy, two safety-first clowns, made a return visit to the school, and pupils continued to train for the Cycling Proficiency Test.

A School Liaison Police Officer made a termly visit to each class to talk about all aspects of safety. PC Farthing was the officer from 1980 to 1982, WPC Jackson from 1982 to 1984 and PC Depper from 1984 to 1991.

School closures

Pupil attendance was good and the registers were regularly inspected by the Educational Welfare Officer and school governors.

The school was closed on a few occasions because of inclement weather or industrial action. In 1979, after heavy snowfall, Suffolk County Council postponed the start of the spring term and the end of the February half-term by a day. However, on most occasions during a period of bad weather, the school was kept open, and when snow made the roads impassable, pupils who managed to walk to school were taught by teachers who lived locally, including those from other schools who were unable to drive to their own school. Those teachers, who lived outside the village but managed to arrive later in the day when the roads were clearer, were allowed to leave early.

On 22 January 1979, during the 'winter of discontent', the school was closed to pupils when members of the National Union of Public Employees (NUPE), including some of the non-teaching staff, went on strike for the day.

Almost all schools in Suffolk, including Great Barton School, were closed on 16 October 1987 after a hurricane hit the south-east of England. The school buildings were undamaged, but four trees in the grounds, including three beautiful horse chestnut trees, were so seriously damaged that they had to be felled.

Working with Great Barton Playgroup

Before starting full-time school, many pre-school children attended Great Barton Playgroup for at least one year. This met in the Church Institute at first, and later moved to Great Barton Church. The reception class teacher regularly liaised with the playgroup, where mother-helpers assisted the full-time staff on a rota basis, which enabled the provision of at least one adult for every six children. During the 1980s, on one day a week, the two playgroup instructors worked in the school with the pre-school children who were due to begin school the following term.

Thurston Upper School Pyramid

Great Barton School belonged to the Thurston Upper School pyramid of schools.

Pupils from the primary schools at Great Barton, Ixworth, Norton, Barnham, Bardwell and Honington transferred to Ixworth Middle School at the age of nine, and Thurston Upper School at the age of 13. John Dawkins attended regular meetings with head teachers from other schools within the Thurston pyramid of schools and elsewhere in West Suffolk. He was the secretary and then the chair of the meetings of the group of head teachers from the primary schools in the Ixworth and Stanton clusters.

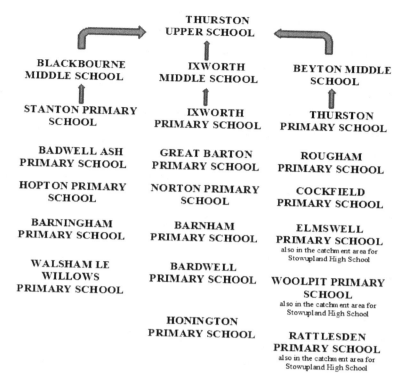

THURSTON
UPPER SCHOOL

BLACKBOURNE
MIDDLE SCHOOL

IXWORTH
MIDDLE SCHOOL

BEYTON MIDDLE
SCHOOL

STANTON PRIMARY
SCHOOL

IXWORTH
PRIMARY SCHOOL

THURSTON
PRIMARY SCHOOL

BADWELL ASH
PRIMARY SCHOOL

GREAT BARTON
PRIMARY SCHOOL

ROUGHAM
PRIMARY SCHOOL

HOPTON PRIMARY
SCHOOL

NORTON PRIMARY
SCHOOL

COCKFIELD
PRIMARY SCHOOL

BARNINGHAM
PRIMARY SCHOOL

BARNHAM
PRIMARY SCHOOL

ELMSWELL
PRIMARY SCHOOL
also in the catchment area for
Stowupland High School

WALSHAM LE
WILLOWS
PRIMARY SCHOOL

BARDWELL
PRIMARY SCHOOL

WOOLPIT PRIMARY
SCHOOL
also in the catchment area for
Stowupland High School

HONINGTON
PRIMARY SCHOOL

RATTLESDEN
PRIMARY SCHOOL
also in the catchment area for
Stowupland High School

Class teachers of nine and ten-year-olds from Ixworth Middle School held joint meetings with those of the seven and eight-year-olds from the first schools in their cluster, to agree the school curriculum and record keeping system for their years. The Year 5 Co-ordinator from Ixworth Middle School spent a morning at Great Barton School each July, in order to meet the pupils who were due to transfer there in September, and to discuss each pupil with their current class teacher.

During their final term at their primary school, pupils visited the middle school to which they were due to transfer, to meet their new teachers and familiarise themselves with the layout of the school.

The staff of the schools at Great Barton, Barnham and Walsham-le-Willows arranged joint training sessions, including a visit to Ipswich Museum in 1989. Each year, one or two pupils from Thurston Upper School spent two weeks at Great Barton School to gain work experience. On the night of 15 March 1984, vandals broke into the grounds, overturned the climbing frame and damaged a bird table. When the woodwork teacher at Thurston Upper School learnt of the damage, he and some of his pupils made a new bird table, which was erected two weeks later

Parents

From 1978, bi-annual meetings were arranged for parents so that they could discuss their child's progress with the class teacher.

Evening meetings were organised so that parents could listen to talks by advisors and other educational specialists. John Marsh, an advisory teacher for Computer Education, outlined some of the uses of computers in the classroom; Giles Job, County Science Advisor, talked about science teaching in primary schools; Barbara Pointon from Homerton College spoke about the teaching of music, and David Evans, the head teacher of Tudor Road School, Sudbury, Suffolk, described the teaching of mathematics. Helen Arnold, co-author of books for the *Reading Together* series, spoke about the importance of listening to children read aloud and reading alongside the child.

The PTA organised summer barbeques, country dances, harvest suppers, jumble sales, wine-tastings, family discos, a toy and cake sale, autumn and Christmas fayres, a plant and cake sale, a table-top sale, cake sales, video mornings, a spring dance, a treasure hunt, and a 'Suffolk Wild-life Evening'.

In 1979 and 1985, the swimming pool was emptied during the spring and repainted by a working party, which consisted of the head teacher and members of the PTA. Parents and other volunteers were sometimes invited into school for a buffet lunch during the last week of term.

The National Curriculum (England, Wales and Northern Ireland)

In 1977, the government published a green paper, entitled *Education in Schools: a Consultative Document,* which asked LEAs to review their school curriculum.

The *LEA Arrangements for the School Curriculum (1979)* required local authorities to publish their curriculum policies. HMI published a *Framework for the School Curriculum (1980)*, which set out preliminary views on the form that a framework for the proposed National Curriculum should take and the ground it should cover.

The DES published *The School Curriculum (1981)*, which outlined their approach to the curriculum, and required LEAs to consult school governors and teachers in order to frame policies, consistent with this approach. In 1983, the DES requested each LEA to report on its progress in drawing up a curriculum policy in its primary and secondary schools and, in response, Suffolk County Council produced *The Suffolk Curriculum (1983)*.

Between 1984 and 1989, HMI published a series of 17 discussion documents, entitled *Curriculum Matters from 5 to 16,* which included documents on English, mathematics, history, classics, geography, environmental education, information technology, craft, design and technology, drama, modern languages, music, physical education, health education, personal and social education, home economics and careers. In 1985, the DES published *Better Schools: A Summary*, in which the government announced that it would take the lead in promoting agreement nationally about the purposes and content of the school curriculum and *Science 5 to16: A statement on Policy.* HMI published *History in the Primary and Secondary Years. An HMI View.*

In July 1987, the DES published a consultation document entitled *The National Curriculum 5-16.* The Kingman Report (1988) on *The Teaching of the English Language,* and the Cox Report (1989) entitled *English for ages 5 to 16,* both influenced the National Curriculum for English.

The Education Reform Act 1988 set out the details of the National Curriculum that was to be taught in all maintained schools. Its aim was to standardise the content taught across schools and ensure continuity. The curriculum was divided into four key stages. Key Stage 1 applied to pupils aged 5 to 7, Key Stage 2 to pupils aged 8 to 11. Key Stage 3 to pupils aged 12 to 14, and Key Stage 4 to pupils aged 15 to 16. The National Curriculum consisted of three core subjects (English, mathematics and science), six foundation subjects (history, geography, technology, music, art and physical education), and a modern foreign language at Key Stages 3 and 4.

For each key stage, it set out:

- attainment targets - the knowledge, skills and understanding which children would be expected to have by the end of each key stage;
- programmes of study to be taught during each key stage;
- arrangements for formal assessment of pupils at the end of each key stage, the results of which were to be published.

The Education Reform Act 1988 also stated that the basic school curriculum should include provision for religious education.

The Schools Council for Curriculum and Examination, in which teachers had played a significant role, was disbanded in 1984. The Education Reform Act 1988 set up the National Curriculum Council (NCC) and the School Examinations and Assessment Council (SEAC) in its place.

Duncan Graham, who had been County Education Officer in Suffolk between 1979 and 1985, became the first Chairman and Chief Executive of the NCC. This organisation was required to review all aspects of the curriculum, give advice to the Secretary of State for Education, carry out programmes of research and development, publish and disseminate information relating to the curriculum and perform 'such ancillary activities as the Secretary of State for Education may direct'.

From 1988, in addition to the 190 teaching days they were already contracted to work, teachers in state schools were required to attend five IN-SErvice Training (INSET) days each year, in order to prepare for the National Curriculum. These were known as Baker Days, named after Kenneth Baker (1934-), the Minister for Education at the time. In addition to these days, teachers attended other training courses and received regular assistance from members of Suffolk Advisory Service. In September 1988, the teachers from all the primary schools in the Thurston pyramid attended a training session on National Curriculum mathematics. In January and March 1989, the teachers from the primary schools at Great Barton, Barnham and Walsham-le-Willows planned teaching strategies together and devised common documentation for keeping records.

Local Management of Schools (LMS)

Until 1988, the budget of Great Barton School was controlled and managed by the LEA, although the governors controlled a small fund of money, banked with Lloyds Bank, which was used to buy small items outside the remit of the LEA. This fund was closed during the 1980s and replaced by the School Fund, which was managed by the school secretary and controlled by the head teacher and governors. School budgets came under scrutiny during the 1980s, and in 1982, the school logbook mentions, for the first time, a visit from an auditor.

The Education Act 1986 required LEAs to provide school governors with financial information about their school, but the Education Reform Act 1988 went further and set up the Local Management of Schools (LMS), which transferred financial management from the LEA to school governors. Meetings were arranged by the LEA to inform head teachers, school secretaries and governors about the new arrangements. From 1989, schools managed their own budget and determined how much to spend on staff, premises and teaching materials. At Great Barton School, 85 per cent of the school budget was required to cover staffing costs.

In February 1989, Mr Barnes, an auditor from Suffolk County Treasurer's Audit Section, spent the morning in school and, according to the school logbook, 'was generally very satisfied with what he found'.

Arrangements for determining teachers' pay and conditions

In March 1978, the average salary for a teacher was £4,410 p.a. but £280 million was cut from the education budget the following year. In 1982, Sir Keith Joseph, the Secretary of State for Education and Science, stated that, 'ineffective teachers should be sacked', and followed up his remarks by a proposal that teacher's pay should be linked to performance; an idea which had been strongly opposed by teachers and managers in the past.

When the government tried to remove the Burnham Committee, which had negotiated teachers' pay since 1919, members of the National Union of Teachers (NUT) and the National Association of Schoolmasters/Union of Women Teacher (NAS/UWT) took part in long-running industrial action, in support of a pay claim and the retention of the Burnham Committee.

During 1984, Pat Barratt's class was sent home early when she took part in industrial action. During two weeks in May 1985, she worked a five-hour day in further support of the action by the NAS/UWT.

In 1985, the DES published *Quality in Schools: Evaluation and Appraisal*, which reported on HMI surveys of a small number of schools that had trialled teacher appraisals. Subsequently, the Education Act 1986 required governors of state-funded schools to ensure that there were arrangements in place for the appraisal of qualified teachers and support staff, within a two-year performance management cycle. Governors were given responsibility for undertaking the performance management of the head teacher.

In spite of the teachers' protests, the Teachers' Pay and Conditions Act 1987 abolished the Burnham Committee. From 1987, teachers' pay and conditions were determined by the Secretary of State for Education, and teachers were contracted to work for 1260 hours a year.

On 1 October 1987, the top of the basic salary scale was increased from £12,700 p.a. to £13,300 p.a., and five levels of incentive allowances, from £500 to £4,200, were introduced. By March 1990, the average salary of a full-time, qualified teacher in a primary school was £14,500 p.a.

Increase of parental power in schools

School managers, renamed governors in 1980, were responsible for the general and strategic management of the school, whilst the head teacher was responsible for the day-to-day management.

The governing body at Great Barton School included one foundation governor, two parish council governors and two local authority governors, in addition to the Vicar of Great Barton and the head teacher, who were both ex-officio members. Each term, a meeting of the whole governing was held, and two governors spent a morning in school.

The Education Act 1986 set out a new formula for determining the composition of a governing body, which included representation from parents. From 1988, the newly constituted governing body at Great Barton School consisted of one foundation governor, one governor appointed by the parish, two local authority governors, one teacher governor and two parent governors. The Vicar of Great Barton and the head teacher were entitled to serve as ex-officio members, but John Dawkins chose not to do so.

Governors were elected for four years and had responsibility for the curriculum, RE, sex education, school terms, pupil discipline, finance, admissions, appointment and dismissal of staff, premises and health and safety.

This legislation also gave parents the right to obtain information from the governors about the teaching curriculum, policies, exam results and criteria for admission, and introduced the concept of educational law, as a consequence of which, there was an increase in the number of legal challenges by parents. The Education Reform Act 1988 gave greater freedom to parents to select the state-funded school of their choice, and took steps to ensure that schools could not artificially limit the number of pupils. As a result, parents were able to choose to send their child to a school outside their catchment area and head teachers spent an increasing amount of time showing prospective parents round their school.

From 1986 until 2013, school governing bodies were required to produce an Annual Report and hold an annual meeting for parents. The first meeting, held in July 1987, was attended by 23 parents and lasted 15 minutes. In March 1988, the second one began with a talk on current education legislation by Tom Scherb, the Area Education Officer. The school logbook recorded that the annual parents' meeting was attended by 'very few parents' in October 1988 and 'only one parent' in 1989.

Accountability and support

Schools were inspected by HMI, who reported to the Secretary of State for Education. According to the school logbook, Mr Husband, HMI, found 'no serious defects' in 1979, and Mr Chapman, HMI, spent a day at the school in 1982, in connection with one of the five major surveys carried out by HMI into the quality of education, and considered it to be 'a very successful and very pleasant school'. In 1986, Mr Lewis, HMI, 'was pleased with what he saw and was particularly complimentary about the quality of social education'.

During this time, schools in Suffolk were also regularly reviewed and monitored by representatives of Suffolk Advisory Service, employed by the LEA. These included up to 40 specialist educational advisors, advisory head teachers, pastoral and primary schools advisors and Special Educational Needs advisors. After each review, they reported their findings verbally to staff and governors of the school, provided a programme for improvement, and wrote a report, which was retained by the school, but not published.

In 1981, Great Barton School carried out a self-appraisal exercise with the help of a primary schools advisor; a role which was filled by Miss Rowe during the early 1980s, Jocelyn Woods from 1987, and Mike Ingham from 1990.

In April 1988, some parents from Great Barton School wrote to the LEA with a series of complaints. This prompted an investigation by the Western Area Education Officer, followed by visits from HMI and Suffolk Advisory Service. A formal school review was carried out by five LEA advisors during two weeks in June 1988; their findings were confirmed by HMI and reported orally to staff and some governors.

In 1990, an 'Interim School Development Plan' was drawn up, which identified priorities for the following academic year.

Retirement

In 1990, John Dawkins applied for early retirement. On the penultimate evening of the summer term, he was presented with a word processor from the staff, governors and the PTA. On his last afternoon, he wrote in the school logbook that:

'there was another light-hearted and delightful assembly, when the children and teachers performed some surreptitiously practised items, featuring Wales and cricket - even a phonetically-learned Welsh national anthem. They presented the headmaster with a specially engraved glass to mark his 12 years at the school.'

On 21 June 1990, a panel of three county councillors, three governors and two LEA officers interviewed four applicants for the post of head teacher of Great Barton School. They appointed Sue Spiller from Eye Church of England Voluntary Aided Primary School, Suffolk. She had had 20 years' teaching experience, mostly in Suffolk, during which time she had taught in upper, middle and primary schools, and had worked as an advisory teacher for information and computer technology.

18
THE RAINBOW ROOM

The 1990s was a decade of educational initiatives and acronyms. The Local Education Authority (LEA) devolved financial autonomy to schools through a scheme called Local Management of Schools (LMS). Personal, social and health education (PSHE) and information and computer technology (ICT) were added to the primary school timetable. The National Curriculum Council (NCC) specified numerous attainment targets (ATs), devised programmes of study (PoS), and developed Statutory Assessment Tests (SATs) for seven, 11 and 14-year-olds. The National Foundation for Educational Research (NFER) devised reading, spelling and mathematics tests for pupils in Years 3, 4 and 5.

The Department for Education and Science (DES) was set up in 1964. It was renamed the Department for Education (DfE) in 1992, the Department for Education and Employment (DfEE) in 1995, the Department for Education and Skills (DfES) in 2001, the Department for Children, Schools and Families (DCSF) in 2007, and the Department for Education (DfE) in 2011.

The Education (Schools) Act 1992 implemented the requirements of the Education Reform Act 1988 to reform the inspection system. It led to the creation of the Office for Standards in Education (Ofsted), with inspections by independently contracted, centrally trained school inspectors, who were guided by *The Framework for School Inspection*. Schools were to be inspected at least once every six years, the inspectors were to report directly to the government and their reports were to be published. Schools that they judged to be 'failing' would be placed in 'special measures'.

The Education Acts of the 1980s, the *Parents' Charter - Rights, Responsibilities and Choices,* published by DfEE in 1991, updated in 1994, and the white paper entitled *Choice and Diversity: A New Framework for Schools (1992)* formed the basis of the Education Act 1993, which supported the right of parents to choose the most suitable school for their child. School prospectuses, Ofsted reports, and school performance tables helped parents to make an informed choice.

The Education Act 1993 replaced the NCC and the Schools Examination and Assessment Council (SEAC) with the School Curriculum and Assessment Authority (SCAA). In 1997, the National Council for Vocational Qualifications (NCVQ) was merged with the School Curriculum and Assessment Authority (SCAA) to become the Qualifications and Curriculum Authority (QCA), which was renamed the Qualifications and Curriculum Development Agency (QCDA) and was replaced by the Standards and Testing Agency (STA) in 2010.

The challenges – 1990 to 1996

Sue Spiller saw her principle tasks as the implementation of the new educational legislation and securing the long-term future of the school.

She identified five major challenges.

1. To increase the number of pupils on the school roll and avoid the threat of school closure by the LEA.
2. To implement the National Curriculum and ensure the best possible standard of teaching and learning for all pupils.
3. To work closely with the governing body, manage the powers devolved to the school under LMS, and oversee an effective teacher appraisal system.
4. To make more efficient use of the school building
5. To steer the school through its first Ofsted inspection.

1. To increase the number of pupils on the school roll and avoid the threat of school closure by the LEA

In September 1990, there were 52 pupils on the school roll, taught in three classes, each of which contained pupils from more than one age group. Rosemary Roe (deputy head teacher) taught the four to six-year-olds, Sue Spiller (head teacher) the six to seven-year-olds, and Sylvia Taylor, the seven to nine-year-olds. They were supported by Lynn Andrews and Sue Manning, the teaching assistants (TA).

Rosemary Roe resigned in December 1990 to take over the headship of another school. She was not replaced by another deputy head teacher, because a school of this size could no longer justify one. Susan Smith was appointed as a class teacher to teach the youngest children from January 1991.

Janet Cobbold, the clerical assistant, was employed for only 15 hours a week. When the office was unstaffed, the head teacher answered the phone in her classroom or left the children with another teacher or TA if she needed to meet a visitor.

The government's policy of parental choice resulted in an increase in the number of parents who considered sending their child to a school outside their catchment area. Consequently, from the start of the autumn term 1990, much of the head teacher's time was taken up with showing prospective parents around the school.

From January 1991, the school employed a supply teacher, known as a head's relief, for one afternoon a week, so that the head teacher could meet visitors by appointment, show prospective parents around the school and carry out some administrative duties. Rosemary Scales, Diane Grimes, Chris Overy, Linda Panayi and Cathy Hiscox fulfilled this role at various times.

Four-year-old pupils, referred to as Rising Fives, started school at the beginning of the term during which they were due to celebrate their fifth birthday. In September 1990, there were no Rising Fives on roll, but five were due to join later in the school year. In September 1991, after pupils in Year 4 transferred to middle schools, there were only 41 pupils on roll but there were positive indications that more parents wanted to enrol their children in the future. By January 1993, there were 73 pupils on roll, and a fourth class taught by Christine Holden on a part-time basis. By April 1994, there were 100 pupils on roll and four full-time classes.

During the autumn term, 1994 Sue Spiller was on sick leave, and Liz Donnelly from Sebert Wood Primary School, Bury St Edmunds, was appointed as acting head teacher. Trudy Lindsay was employed as a part-time teacher to share the teaching of the head teacher's class.

By September 1995, there were 130 pupils on roll, of whom 31 lived outside the catchment area. Most of the under five-year-olds from the village were enrolled at Great Barton School, and it was anticipated that by April 1996, there would be 148 pupils on roll. From September 1995, a fifth class was set up, taught by Hilary Bilonick the deputy head teacher, Trudy Lindsay was given a full-time contract, Lynda Mulley and Liz Baker were employed as additional TAs, and the head teacher no longer had a responsibility as a class teacher.

By 1995, the school was no longer at risk of closure, and it enjoyed an excellent reputation. So many parents were keen to enrol their children that there was a waiting list. One parent even tried to register her child at birth. This success was the result of a combined team effort by staff and governors, who enthusiastically worked with the head teacher to:-

a) raise the school's profile and build up its reputation;
b) integrate the school more closely with the village;
c) liaise with Great Barton Under 5s and parents of other pre-school children in the village;
d) enlarge the school's catchment area.

a) Raising the school profile and building up its reputation

In order to win back support for the village school from those local families who currently sent their children to a private or state school outside the village, it was important to make local people aware of what Great Barton School could offer their child.

In November 1990, a colour photograph of all the pupils at Great Barton School appeared in the *East Anglia Daily Times (EADT)* as part of a general article about schools in West Suffolk. From that time onwards, all school initiatives, newsworthy activities and achievements were mentioned in the school newsletter and, whenever possible, the local media.

The school appeared regularly in the *EADT,* the *Bury Free Press (BFP)* and the *Citizen,* often with a photograph, and occasionally on *BBC Look East* and *ITV Anglia News.* Interviews with staff and pupils were broadcast on *Saxon Radio (SGR Radio)* and *BBC Radio Suffolk,* which went on air for the first time on 12 April 1990.

The school developed its links with Barclays Bank, which had begun in 1990 when the school arranged an impressive floral display in its Bury St Edmunds branch. In January 1991, Barclays Bank opened a branch in the school, managed by Sue Manning with help from pupils in Year 4.

The school raised hundreds of pounds for charity each year, donating money to Save the Children Fund, Blue Peter appeals, Comic Relief, OXFAM, Children in Need, and the Tearfund, a UK Christian relief and development agency. In October 1990 and June 1992, pupils from 30 families took part in a sponsored walk at Ickworth Park, in aid of the

World Wildlife Fund (WWF). In December 1990, a representative from the WWF visited the school and presented pupils who had participated with toy pandas, and the school with a shield. After 1993, children raised money for a charity at harvest time instead of taking produce to school, and delivered cards to older people in the village after the harvest festival.

Two pupils won a prize in the 'Design a Pantomime Cover' competition, run by Bury Theatre Royal, in association with the *Bury Free Press*. A seven-year-old pupil won a prize in the Bury Rotary Club Prose and Poetry Competition and her poem was included in a book produced by the Rotary Club.

Each year, the pupils performed in a play, written or adapted by members of staff. They performed it to their parents and members of the Great Barton Over 60 Club. The plays included *Three Wise Space People* in December 1990, *Christmas Storyland* in December 1991, *Tell Us the Way to Christmas* in 1992, four shadow-puppet plays in February 1994, and *The Smallest Angel* in December 1994.

Pupils received national as well as local publicity. In 1991, 1992 and 1993, the top class wrote a poem for *Wordplay*, a *BBC Radio 5* programme, and were delighted when they heard it read aloud on the radio in 1991 and 1993. In May 1992, the top two classes took part in a *BBC* recording of *Together*, a religious broadcast for schools, at County Upper School, Bury St Edmunds.

To promote environmental studies, a piece of ground at the side of the school building was fenced off as a conservation area, with a pond, mini-beast area and wild-flower garden. Susan Smith, a keen conservationist, led the conservation project. On 15 October 1991, the conservation area was officially opened by Barbara Morris from Wildlife Watch, the junior branch of The Wildlife Trusts, and Susan Smith, some Year 4 pupils, and Peter Fisk, an ex-pupil and governor, were interviewed by Chris Opperman from *BBC Radio Suffolk* for a programme called *Country Matters.* The day was designated as a 'green day', and every pupil and teacher wore green clothes, studied environmental issues and ate a lunch, which was mostly green and included green mashed potatoes. During the afternoon, prizes for environmental achievements were awarded to pupils by Barbara Morris, Chris Opperman, Sam Grey from the WWF, and Peter Hayman, an ornithological artist.

In October 1992, the school celebrated the twenty-fifth anniversary of the occupation of the new school premises, by recreating some of the aspects of the school as it had been in 1967. Every pupil and member of staff wore clothes typical of those worn in 1967. The school borrowed a mannequin from a shop in Bury St Edmunds to dress as a 1967 schoolchild, which attracted odd looks from passers-by who saw the head teacher carrying what appeared to be a naked child through the town centre. Ron Ceurstemont, who had been the head teacher in 1967, addressed a special school assembly, and pupils studied life in Britain in 1967. The lunch menu was the same as one served in 1967 and included roast pork and chocolate pudding. At the end of the school day, there was a party with a magnificent cake in the shape of 25, which was shared amongst the staff and pupils.

In the evening, Ron Ceurstemont, John Dawkins, 15 ex-teachers, and 30 ex-pupils who had attended the school in 1967 attended a wine and cheese party at the school. Unfortunately, Elsie Carter, the head teacher from 1950 to 1960, was not sent an invitation, because no one knew her contact details. During the evening, the visitors looked around the school, and at various exhibitions in the hall.

To commemorate the twenty-fifth anniversary, a new play area with play equipment was created on the playing field. £1,000 was raised at the 'Twenty-fifth Anniversary School Fête', held on Sunday 9 July 1992, which was opened by David Hoffman, from *Saxon Radio*. The remainder was raised by Great Barton Parent Teacher Association (PTA) through sales of draw tickets and school tea cloths, which featured a hand-drawn self-portrait of each pupil. PC Stanford, the School Liaison Police Officer, officially opened the play area in April 1993, at the start of a PTA mini-fête, which raised £325 for a new cover for the swimming pool.

In 1995, students from King Edward VI Upper School, Bury St Edmunds, donated a giant chess set to the school and created a giant ceramic chessboard adjacent to the play area. To limit the number of children on the play equipment at any one time, children from Key Stage 1 and 2 used it during different playtimes according to a rota displayed nearby. Some years later, a pupil revealed that many children did not understand the meaning of a key stage and were consequently confused by the rota.

In July 1993, the school celebrated the foundation of the original school. Staff and pupils produced an exhibition, entitled *One Hundred and Fifty Years of Education in Great Barton,* to which parents, villagers, friends of the school and people who had been associated with the school in the past were invited. Visitors were able to talk to pupils, observe special lessons, look at displays of arts and crafts, study old school documents and follow an environmental and mathematics trail around the school.

Four of the oldest children dressed as a Victorian head teacher, assistant teacher, vicar and squire, and the rest of the class dressed as Victorian schoolchildren. They talked to visitors about school life during the nineteenth century, based on what they had learned in the classroom and during their visits to Great Barton church and rectory, the remains of Barton Hall, the old Smithy, the Bunbury Arms and Suffolk Record Office.

The lessons for the top class included handwriting, arithmetic and nature study. Some of the pupils cooked biscuits according to a recipe by Mrs Beeton (1836-1865), the author of *Mrs Beeton's Book of Household Management*. Canon John Eley, the 'cooking canon', interviewed some of the pupils for his daily programme on *BBC Radio Suffolk*. The seven to nine-year-olds dressed in the school uniform of 1967 and produced a display of the school that year. During the morning, they were taught by Ron Ceurstemont and Sally Bulbrook, both of whom had taught at the school during the 1970s. The six and seven-year-olds produced displays of recent events, and the five and six-year-olds demonstrated aspects of the modern science curriculum, using mirrors, magnets and magnifying glasses.

In November 1993, Richard Spring, the local Member of Parliament, looked around the school and was very impressed, as was a local member of Suffolk County Council who visited five months later.

Each July, the school held an extra-curricular prize-giving event, to which parents and the local press were invited.

By publicly celebrating achievements, the school's profile in the Bury St Edmunds area was raised, and pupils felt a sense of pride in their school and themselves. Most of the parents who visited the school decided to enrol their child at the school, including some who commented that they believed that Great Barton School could offer their child as good an education, if not better, as that available at a private school.

In April 1994, the school enrolled Laura Happs as its one-hundredth pupil. The chair of governors presented Laura with a certificate, and staff and pupils shared a cake, which was in the shape of 100. That afternoon, every child in the school stood on the playing field to form the number 100, whilst local reporters took aerial photographs from the roof of the school.

b) Integrating the school more closely with the village

In 1990, the village had two churches, a post office and shop, public house, service station, Village Hall and Church Institute. The school saw itself as the heart of the village and endeavoured to forge closer links with people and organisations in the village.

The school worked closely with Holy Innocents' Church, Great Barton. It held the school Christmas carol services in 1991 and 1993 and the harvest festival in 1994 in the parish church. The school ran a stall and organised children's races at the Church Fête each year, and each class visited the church as part of its RE studies.

The top class sang carols for the residents and staff at Montana, a residential and nursing home in Great Barton run by the Benedictine Sisters of Our Lady Grace and Compassion.

Each Friday morning, the school invited people from the local community to take a school assembly. These included church wardens from Holy Innocents' Church, the pastor of Great Barton Free Church, teachers from Great Barton Junior Church, members of Great Barton Mothers' Union, one of the 'Sisters' from Montana, a representative from Barton Players (an amateur dramatics group) and the Mayor of Bury St Edmunds. Assemblies were also addressed by local Church of England clergy, including the Revd David Underwood and the Revd Clare Saunders, who were both Diocesan Education Officers, the Revd Peter Barham from Bury St Edmunds Cathedral, the Revd Jonathan Ford from Christchurch Moreton Hall, and the Revd Sally Fogden from Honington Church. Representatives from Bury Christian Youth, the Salvation Army, the Roman Catholic Church, and the Religious Society of Friends also shared some of their ideas with the children.

School badge from 1991

In 1991, the school changed its badge from one, which featured part of the coat of arms of the Bunbury family, to a multi coloured one featuring the village sign as shown here.

Blazers were no longer worn, but this badge was emblazoned on the school sweatshirt, cardigan and sun hat and featured on the school brochure, headed paper and other school documents.

Members of Great Barton Over 60 Club were encouraged to come into school as helpers. At Easter and Christmas, they were invited into school to watch entertainments performed by pupils, and during the summer term, they invited the pupils to perform maypole and other country dances at their summer tea party, which was held inside the school if the weather was inclement.

The school lent staging and the maypole to organisations in the village, and hired the school hall to Great Barton Parish Council, Great Barton History Society, Great Barton Crusader Group, Great Barton Brownies, Christian Mission, Slimming World and a yoga group. Some of the pupils joined Great Barton Brownies and Cubs, and took part in the village pantomime. In May 1995, the school and village organised a joint street fair.

c) ***Liaising with Great Barton Under 5s and parents of other pre-school children in the village***

The school name was changed from Great Barton First School to Great Barton Primary School to bring it into line with other local primary schools. The school brochure was updated, improved and made more comprehensive, and copies were distributed to parents of pre-school children, village organisations and local estate agents.

The school used information from the local health authority to identify pre-school children who lived in the catchment area, and sent birthday cards to each child on their fourth birthday. Their families were invited to an annual 'open morning', which was attended by 25 families in 1991 and 15 in 1992. Most visitors stayed for a school lunch prepared by Carol Elsey, the school cook, who was nominated by the pupils for the Best Kitchen Award in 1991.

The reception class teacher, and sometimes the head teacher, spent a morning each term at the village playgroup, known as Great Barton Under 5s, which organised daily sessions at Great Barton Free Church. However, this was not an entirely satisfactory venue because their equipment had to be stored in a shed and carried into and out of the room at the start and end of each session. The two supervisors of the Under 5s attended first aid and other courses run by the Pre-school Providers Association. Up to 16 children attended each Under 5s session, during which the room was arranged with a home area, a book corner, a practical area and a space for ride-on toys. The children listened to music and stories, cooked biscuits, buns or pizzas to take home, were taken on trips to local gardens, West Stow or Banham Zoo, and enjoyed teddy bears' picnics in a park.

On one or two mornings each week, the supervisors of the Under 5s provided more structured learning for the Rising Fives in one of the empty classrooms in school and, during the term before they started school, these new intake pupils joined the infant class for four mornings and stayed for a school lunch.

The parents or guardians of all pre-school pupils were offered an individual interview with the head teacher and given the latest school brochure. During the term before their child was due to start school, parents were invited to school events, including a meeting at the school, addressed by the head teacher and the staff of the reception class. The head teacher's talk covered a wide range of subjects, including the subject of head lice, which was illustrated with a magnified photograph of a louse, which usually produced audible gasps of horror by the parents. After the meeting, parents were offered coffee, a tour of the school and an opportunity to meet members of staff and other parents.

Each pre-school child was given a hand-written, illustrated booklet [these were pre-computer days], which contained photographs of the staff, child-friendly information about the school and suggestions of personal things that the school hoped pupils would be able to do before they started school, which included dressing themselves and using a knife and fork correctly.

The school was keen to house Great Barton Under 5s within its school grounds so that they could be more closely integrated with the school and would have their own building. In 1995, the head teacher was offered a redundant, 54-foot portable building from Whittle Laboratories, Cambridge University. Personnel from the United States Airbase at RAF Mildenhall initially agreed to transport it from Cambridge to Great Barton School by helicopter. However, when they saw the condition of the portable building, they were afraid that the downdraft from the rotor blades would cause it to break up and scatter debris over Cambridgeshire and West Suffolk, so the idea had to be abandoned. The Under 5s continued to meet at Great Barton Free Church for another 15 years.

d) Enlarging the school's catchment area

In 1991, the head teacher investigated the possibility of enlarging the school's catchment area by incorporating the village of Great Livermere, an adjacent parish that had no school of its own but had historic associations with Great Barton. Children from Great Livermere currently attended Ixworth Primary School, but, after consultation with Ixworth Primary School and the LEA, it was agreed that from September 1992, the catchment school for the Great Livermere children would become Great Barton Primary School.

These children were provided with school transport in the form of a taxi at first, and then a mini-bus when the numbers increased. From 1993 onwards, a 'happy hour' was organised, once a term during the last hour of a school day, for parents from Great Livermere and others, who did not collect their child from school. During this time, they were invited to look round the school and talk to governors and other parents over a cup of tea.

2. To implement the National Curriculum and ensure the best possible standard of teaching and learning for all pupils

The National Curriculum was introduced in 1988, but not fully implemented until 1991. It met with some resistance, especially amongst older teachers, who were at the end of their teaching career and were reluctant to adopt a new curriculum or adapt their teaching methods.

From 1990, ring-bound folders containing the details of the National Curriculum for each single subject were delivered to the school, with enough folders for each member of staff and governor. Folders for the core subjects of English, mathematics and science were delivered first, followed by those for the foundation subjects of history, geography, technology, music, art and PE. There were no documents for RE but in 1991, the NCC published *Religious Education: a Local Curriculum Framework* to give advice to LEAs, and then a discussion paper entitled *Spiritual and Moral Development* in 1993. In Suffolk schools, RE was taught in accordance with the Suffolk *Agreed Syllabus for Religious Education*. From this time, each subject was taught as a separate entity, and the content of the syllabus followed the guidance laid down in the appropriate document.

Until September 1995, there were five age groups in the school but only three or four teachers, so each class included pupils from more than one year group. The National Curriculum stated what should be taught to each year group in each subject, so mixed-age classes presented additional challenges for teachers and schools in deciding what needed to be taught in each class and how to plan a whole school curriculum which guaranteed continuity and progression throughout the school.

The school's curriculum plans were rewritten but, in order to teach all of the programmes of study, teachers found that there were insufficient hours during any school year to teach the whole of the curriculum. In 1992, Robin Alexander, Jim Rose and Chris Woodhead (The Three Wise Men) reviewed the National Curriculum at the request of Kenneth Clarke, the Education Secretary, and produced a report entitled *Curriculum Organisation and Classroom Practice in Primary Schools*.

The Dearing Report (1993) entitled *The National Curriculum and its Assessment*, published by SCAA, concluded that teaching and learning were being damaged by the new curriculum. The report recommended that there should be a reduction in content, less time spent on testing, and 20 per cent of teaching time available for discretionary use by schools. Subsequently, the National Curriculum was revised at a cost of £744 million, schools revised their curriculum plans, teachers rewrote their lesson plans, and the new National Curriculum was in use until 2000, when it was revised again.

Staff meetings and IN-SErvice Training (INSET) days were used to discuss curriculum planning and share ideas about teaching methods, record keeping, assessment techniques and curriculum policies. The school benefited from the advice and support of Mike Ingham, a General Advisor with responsibility for Great Barton School, and of Suffolk Advisory Service, which arranged courses for teachers and offered in-school support.

Primary schools worked together to share ideas. In 1991, Sue Spiller wrote an *Early Years Policy* as part of a pyramid assessment project. In 1993, the primary schools in Thurston Pyramid adopted a common format for pupil reports.

The reception class teacher discussed a 'baseline entry profile' with the parents when their child started school, continually assessed each child throughout the year, produced an amended profile at the end of the year, and discussed the new targets with parents.

The standard of reading continued to be measured every term, using one of the *Salford Sentence Reading Tests*. Pupils whose reading age fell below their chronological age were targeted for additional support. The school also continued to administer *Suffolk Reading Scale Tests* to six and eight-year-olds, the results of which were collated by Suffolk LEA.

National Curriculum tests and tasks were piloted in 1991 and from 1992, Year 2 pupils were required to undergo a battery of tests, known as SATs, in English, mathematics and science. During the first year, one of these tests required the use of a fresh coconut, the sales of which must have increased exponentially that year.

Parents and guardians of all the pupils received an annual written report on their child's progress. From 1993, some members of staff used computer software, produced by SPARKs, to help them to plan work, assess results and record pupil's progress. Eventually, SPARKs was replaced by more sophisticated assessment software.

Trudy Lindsay was the Special Educational Needs Co-ordinator (SENCo), with responsibility for the day-to-day operation of the school's special needs policy, in line with the *Special Education Needs: Code of Practice* set out in the Education Acts of 1993, 1994 and 1996. She managed the 'record of support' system for pupils who were identified as having additional needs, and when a child reached stage four, indicating that their needs could no longer be met satisfactorily by the school, she made an application to the LEA for a formal assessment of the pupil's needs. At the end of this assessment, a 'statement of special needs' was issued. This outlined the details of the extra support to which the child was entitled. Parents who wished to challenge the 'statement' could appeal to a Special Educational Needs Tribunal.

In Suffolk, support for pupils with additional needs was available from an army of specialists. These included an educational psychologist, a community nurse, a school medical officer, an occupational therapist, a speech therapist, advisory teachers for special needs, visual impairment and 'learning support', and staff at Bury St Edmunds Child Development Centre. When a five-year-old German pupil who spoke no English joined the school, she received support from an advisory teacher for English as a Second Language for two hours a week for two terms and, within a year, spoke English fluently.

In 1992, the school purchased two additional classroom Research Machine microcomputers, bringing the total to four. By 1995, Microsoft had launched Windows 95, compact discs had replaced vinyl records, and videos had replaced filmstrips and slides.

To extend the school curriculum and compensate for having only three or four teachers, offers from outside organisations were always welcome. A School Liaison Police Officer spent one day each term working with each class in turn. A Road Safety Officer, members of the School Dental Service and Suffolk Fire Service, a shepherdess, an ornithological artist, a wild flower artist and a local author were amongst others who spent time with pupils. Pete Cunningham and Liz Bonner ran a folk music morning and accompanied maypole and country dancing. Representatives of Fit Kids, organised by St Edmundsbury Leisure Department, helped pupils to improve their fitness, and those from 'Pass Soccer' helped pupils to practise football skills. The New Venture Music Club taught music to each class, and children studied fossils for a whole day under the guidance of an expert geologist. Professional puppeteers taught every child to make a puppet and create a puppet show for villagers and parents. Club Française ran an after-school club to give pupils a chance to learn a second language. The top class attended a concert in St Edmundsbury Cathedral, performed by a children's choir from Ramenskoye, Russia, which had won the 'All Russia Folk Festival'.

Most of the school budget was allocated to staff employment, leaving insufficient funds to purchase all the necessary school resources. To relieve the budget, Sue Spiller used her own Amstrad computer in the school office until the school could afford to buy one.

In February 1991, she joined three other members of staff in a six-week sponsored slim, to raise £100 for new reading books for Key Stage 1 SATs. The PTA organised discos, ceilidhs, book fairs, cake sales, Christmas fairs, summer fairs, car treasure hunts, quiz evenings, jumble sales, a race night, a beetle drive, a Tupperware party and the sale of home-made Christmas cards, which together raised thousands of pounds for the school. It also arranged non-profit-making events including an annual summer barbecue and swimming party for pupils in Year 4.

In 1990, very few mothers of the pupils at Great Barton Primary School were in paid employment, and the school actively encouraged them to volunteer in school. Teachers took advantage of any special knowledge, talent or skill of local people and up to ten volunteers per week listened to children read or helped during mathematics, science, music, recorder, art and craft lessons.

In 1995, with the help of one of the parents, four of the oldest pupils entered the Anglia Heritage CD-ROM competition, organised by Lindis Getting IT Right. This included a presentation about the school badge, village sign and Sir Henry Edward Bunbury. The pupils were highly commended for their entry and were presented with certificates at Lindis Computer Carnival at Norwich on 10 June 1995.

The school swimming pool was used during the second half of the summer term. Parents who volunteered to help with swimming lessons were offered training in resuscitation by someone trained in first aid. Members of the PTA ran evening and holiday swimming sessions during the summer months, and parents accompanied pupils in Red and Orange classes to a weekly swimming lesson at Bury Leisure Centre during the rest of the year.

Parents accompanied staff and pupils on school visits to Charity Farm and Holy Innocents' Church in Great Barton, Mole Hall Wildlife Park in Saffron Walden, Pentlow Farm in Cavendish, Wimpole Hall in Cambridgeshire, the Norfolk Show, and exhibitions of clocks and of toys at Moyse's Hall Museum, Bury St Edmunds.

Parents made costumes for school plays, ran chess, violin, craft, football, gymnastics and country dancing clubs, accompanied children on school visits, helped with cycle proficiency training, and transported the older children around the village to deliver cards after the harvest festival and at Christmas.

Volunteers were invited to a special event at the end of each term as a small token of the school's appreciation.

3. **To work closely with the governing body, manage the powers devolved to the school under LMS, and oversee an effective teacher appraisal system.**

In 1990, the governing body was composed of one foundation governor, nominated by the local church, two governors nominated by Suffolk County Council, one governor nominated by Great Barton Parish Council, two parent governors, and one teacher governor. The Vicar of Great Barton and the head teacher both served as ex-officio governors.

From 1993, governors were required each year to consider whether to opt out of LEA control and apply for grant-maintained status, and were empowered to organise a secret ballot of the parents to ascertain whether there was a majority in favour of a change of status.

The whole governing body met once a term. In addition, two governors spent a morning in school each term, on a rota basis, during which they read the school logbook, inspected the registers, observed lessons and talked to staff and pupils.

Some governors chose to take a particular interest in one of the classes or a curriculum subject, and most governors attended school events and gave active support to the school. The Vicar of Holy Innocents' Church took the school assembly each Thursday morning and taught Bible studies to the children in the top class.

The *Education (School Teacher Appraisal) Regulations (1991)* required that the performance of each teacher should be assessed annually by a more senior staff member or another teacher, and the head teacher by a head teacher of another school.

From April 1993, the school governors took control of staffing and personnel matters, as well as financial ones, and set up sub-committees composed of three or four governors. Finance, personnel, premises and health and safety committees met at least once a term, whilst hearings, appeals and staff salary committees met only when necessary.

The governors were required to produce an annual report for parents and invite them to an annual meeting to discuss matters contained in the report. In 1995, the governors worked extremely hard to produce a comprehensive and imaginatively laid-out report, which they entered into a competition organised by the *Times Educational Supplement*.

The head teacher consulted parent governors and PTA members about school hours and the school uniform. Circular 7/90 *Management of the School Day* recommended that, in addition to the time for registration, collective worship, playtimes and the lunch hour, five to seven-year-olds should work for 21 hours a week and eight and nine-year-olds for 23 hours a week. From September 1991, in response to the wishes of parents not to have staggered opening hours, the school day began at 9.00 a.m. and finished at 3.15 p.m., and the younger children were given an afternoon playtime and an extended lunch break. Parents requested that the school uniform should be as inexpensive and easily sourced as possible, so white polo shirts replaced blouses and shirts, and the school sold royal blue sweatshirts embroidered with the school badge.

4. To make more efficient use of the school building

Until 1995, one of the spare classrooms was used as a library and the other for teaching practical subjects. However, they were both needed as classrooms after the fourth and fifth classes were set up. As more and more equipment was required by all age groups for the teaching of art, science, DT and ICT, it made sense for all those resources to be housed in a central area, and for practical subjects to be taught in this area. Ideally, they needed to be accommodated in a single, designated area with access to running water. The school also required a library, separate offices for the secretary and head teacher, and a quiet room for staff to study, mark books and prepare lessons.

There was insufficient money in the school budget to extend the school building, and the LEA was prevented by national guidelines from funding such an extension. However, the LEA did offer to carry out planning and architectural work on behalf of the school, and the County Architects' Department agreed that it was feasible to convert two courtyards and the room in between them into a resources area, and to adapt the building elsewhere to create a library, office and quiet room.

To make this dream become a reality, the school launched a Redevelopment Appeal Fund for £35,000, to which Sir Michael Bunbury, 13th Baronet, lent his name but made no further contribution. After a few months, it was evident that it was going to be an uphill struggle to raise the whole sum, so the appeal total was reduced to £16,000; the amount needed to create the resources area.

The school appeared on *BBC Look East,* in a feature about the involvement of parents in fund-raising for school buildings. The PTA, staff and pupils raised £8,342, which included £2,700 from an 'auction of promises', £50 from a sale of sweets and toys by pupils, and £400 from a staff sponsored, six-week slim, during which ten members of staff, collectively, lost 83 lbs in weight. Further activities included weekly sales of cakes and home-made produce, plant and jumble sales, sponsored walks, tea parties with paying guests, a country and western dance, a book and bottle party, the sale of aluminium cans and Webb Ivory goods, a Christmas fair and a summer fête. A sponsored matchbox competition raised £700, during which the joint winners each succeeded in filling their matchbox with 190 different things, including an eyelash and a nail clipping.

Great Barton Parish Council and the LEA each donated £2,000, local businesses and organisations donated £2,107, and £4,259 was used from the school budget. The final cost of the resources room was £18,708, of which the roof cost £10,000. It represented the fruits of a huge fund-raising effort by parents, governors, pupils, staff and friends of the school.

In July 1995, workers from Calor Gas donated their services free of charge and dug the foundations in a single day. The resources room was completed in time for the start of the autumn term and, although the official opening was not planned until November, the room was in use from September.

There were however some teething problems. At lunchtime on 15 September 1995, there was a huge thunderstorm. Water from under the sink area rose up through the floor and flooded the new room, two adjacent carpeted classrooms and one end of the school hall. Sylvia Arbon and all the staff did their best to mop it up, but the water level continued to rise and the caretaker slipped and hurt her head and arm. Anglia Water, Suffolk Fire Service and an ambulance were called. Anglia Water turned off the water and Sylvia was sent home to bed. Parents were contacted and asked to collect the children and, whilst one member of staff looked after the uncollected children, everyone else cleaned up with help from the crew of the Fire Service and a parent who brought in a pneumatic machine to suck water out of the carpets. The builders and a representative of the County Architects' Department discovered that the problem had been caused by blocked gutters, which were full of leaves.

The five classes were named Red, Orange, Yellow, Green and Blue so the new resources area was named the Rainbow Room, because it was to be used by all of the classes. On 17 November 1995, the Rainbow Room was officially opened. All of the pupils wore clothes the colour of their class, which produced a wonderful rainbow effect when they assembled in the hall. Lunch was composed of seven items, each of which was a different colour of the rainbow and, at the end of the day, an enormous cake, made by a parent and decorated with a rainbow, was shared amongst the staff and pupils. During the day, Canon John Eley from *BBC Radio Suffolk* interviewed staff, parents and pupils. During a special event in the evening, Graham Mothersole, who had acted as building consultant, and Graeme Kirk, who had organised the appeal, cut a ribbon and formally opened the Rainbow Room. Visitors looked at displays and photographs, took part in a school quiz, and listened to piano music, played by a parent who was a professional pianist.

In April 1996, the small carpeted rooms on each side of the hall were equipped as mini-libraries, with fiction books in the Silver Library, and non-fiction books in the Gold Library, with Lynn Andrews as manager of both libraries. Books were still borrowed each term from Suffolk Library Service and out-of-date books, which included *Bob and the Knockers*, *Kate Crackernuts* and *Little Freddie and his Fiddle,* were withdrawn and new books purchased.

In 1995, a food technology area, with an electric cooker, was set up between the staffroom and Blue Class, but was relocated to the Rainbow Room in 1997. There was no money for a new office or study area for staff, but the staffroom was made more comfortable by the purchase of new furniture and the removal of a huge table that had dominated the staffroom for many years.

5. To steer the school through its first Ofsted inspection

In June 1995, the school was informed that, under Section 9 of the Education (Schools) Act 1992, it had been selected by Ofsted for an inspection, scheduled to take place at some time between Easter 1996 and Easter 1997.

In October 1995, two auditors from Suffolk County Treasurer's Audit Section spent two days in school, during which they gave financial advice and support to the head teacher and secretary. In February 1996, the school received a formal notice of the date of the inspection to be held during the week beginning 30 September, carried out under Section 9 of the Education (Schools) Act 1996. This was the first experience of an Ofsted inspection for all of the staff and governors and although the long notice gave the school plenty of time to prepare, it also allowed more time for everyone to become increasingly anxious.

The Ofsted inspectors collected paperwork from the school 11 days before the inspection. The documentation included the school brochure, the school development plan, schemes of work, teachers' planning documentation, and 25 policy statements for National Curriculum and other subjects. In advance of the inspection, questionnaires were sent to all the parents to seek their views of the school.

An inspection under Section 13 of the Education (Schools) Act 1992, which reported on the 'collective worship and the social, moral, spiritual and cultural development of the pupils', was scheduled for the same time.

On 30 September, five Ofsted inspectors began their inspection. They observed two school assemblies, watched 41 lessons, scrutinised teachers' lesson plans and records, looked at children's work, listened to pupils read, observed children at lunchtime, playtime and before and after school, reviewed the provision for pupils with special educational needs and examined attendance records, the school budget and minutes of meetings of the whole governing body and its committees. They interviewed the head teacher, teachers, non-teaching staff, pupils and governors, and held a meeting to hear the views of parents.

The Section 9 inspection report stated that, 'Great Barton CEVC School is a school with many strengths. Amongst these are successful whole school development, a positive ethos which supports the pupils' personal development, the support of the parents and governors and the leadership of the head teacher'. Three-quarters of the lessons were satisfactory, better than satisfactory, good, very good or excellent, with 'particularly good teaching in science in Key Stage 2, and in music and religious education throughout the school'. The report congratulated the school on all aspects of its social, moral, spiritual and cultural education.

The Section 13 inspection report stated that, 'the school has established a clear, confident and caring ethos, which provides a very positive context for collective worship and the development and education of its pupils.' It judged the acts of worship to be of a high standard, and reported that the school had established a clear set of principles and values, expressed through its aims.

Great Barton Primary School in 1996

By 1996, the school was no longer in danger of closure. It had increased the pupil roll, successfully implemented the National Curriculum and LMS, and had sufficient space to teach every subject. It was in a good position to move forward, build on the strengths and address the weaknesses highlighted by the Ofsted inspection team, and deliver an excellent standard of education throughout the school.

19

BROADENING HORIZONS

From 1996, the staff and governors of Great Barton Primary School were determined to build on the successes of the past.

In order to prepare pupils for the next stage of their education, the school aimed to teach, not only the basic knowledge, skills and understanding in every subject, but also the study skills that would enable them to work towards independent learning and self-reliance. To equip pupils for life in a pluralistic and digital society, the school encouraged tolerance and open-mindedness, provided opportunities for pupils to broaden their horizons, and helped them to become confident users of the internet and the latest technology.

The teachers – 1996 to 2004

In September 1996, there were 125 pupils, five classes and five full-time class teachers. Blue Class (reception) was taught by Susan Smith, Green Class (Year 1) by Liz Babbedge, Yellow Class (Year 2) by Trudy Lindsay, Orange Class (Year 3) by Hilary Bilonick (deputy head teacher) and Red Class (Year 4) by Christine Holden. Staff changes were infrequent and usually only occurred as the result of personal promotion or relocation of a partner.

The staff appointment policy was to employ teachers with different strengths and interests to ensure that all areas of the National Curriculum were covered. In addition to their class teaching responsibilities, each teacher co-ordinated at least one curriculum area and was given the opportunity to develop her own interests and enthusiasms, as long as they benefited the pupils. The school actively encouraged professional development of teaching and non-teaching staff.

Liz Babbedge

Liz Babbedge co-ordinated music and religious education (RE) and became a highly respected teacher in the world of RE. In July 1995, Lisa Williams from Carlton TV, spent a whole day in the school making a recording for a 45-minute programme entitled *RE - In-service Training*. It included a discussion between Liz Babbedge and Christine Holden about the teaching of RE in the school and the materials used in lessons, an RE lesson with Red Class, taught by Liz Babbedge, during which pupils composed and performed music and songs, produced art work and discussed symbols in African pictures. The programme was shown on *Channel 4 TV* on 16 January 1996.

In 1997, Liz Babbedge received a Millennium Award, which granted her a term away from school to study the subject of 'spiritual development in the primary school'. In 1998, she studied for a Master in Education (M.Ed.), a postgraduate academic degree. Her lessons were observed by students from the Farmington Institute, Oxford, and by Geoff Hundleby, the RE Advisor for Suffolk, who shared some of her ideas in a publication by Suffolk Local Education Authority (LEA). In May 1998, her work was reported in an article in the *Times Educational Supplement*, and, in July 1998, Her Majesty's Inspectors (HMI) filmed an RE lesson, taught by Liz Babbedge, for a training video for Ofsted inspectors.

She served on the committee of Qualifications and Curriculum Authority (QCA), which dealt with the teaching of RE, contributed to courses for trainee teachers at Homerton College, Cambridge, and the Farmington Institute, Oxford, and was asked to represent East Anglia on the Professional Council for Religious Education. In 1999, she and the Farmington Institute received an award, and she was one of 200 award winners who attended the launch of the Millennium Awards in Whitehall with the Prime Minister, Tony Blair. She was amongst 50 award winners who were invited to spend 31 December 1999 at a reception in the House of Lords, followed by the official opening of the Millennium Dome, London. She became involved with a team from the Stapleford Centre, an independent Christian education charity, which produces teaching materials for schools.

Liz Babbedge resigned in 1999 after her marriage to Gary Mills, a lecturer at Oxford University, who formerly taught at Thurston Upper School. They wanted to be married in Holy Innocents' Church, Great Barton but because neither of them lived in the parish, they were required to apply for a special marriage licence. Unbeknown to Liz Babbedge, the 145 pupils at the school wrote letters to the Archbishop of Canterbury in support of her application, which were all sent without correction, except in the case of one, in which a pupil had written, 'Miss Babbedge helps us with our sinning'. Liz and Gary were granted their special licence, and many of the staff and pupils attended their wedding on 24 July 1999.

Liz Babbedge continued to teach in primary schools and, in 2002, published *Opening Windows: Spiritual Development in the Primary School.*

French

During the summer term, Sue Spiller taught French to pupils in Years 3 and 4. The school successfully applied for a French assistant through the Socrates programme, an educational initiative of the European Commission, organised by the British Council. In September 1999, Julie Goury, a French trainee teacher from Lille in northern France, joined the school for eight months. She lodged with Freya Smith (generally known as Miss S.), taught French and lessons about life and culture in France to pupils in Years 3 and 4, joined in school activities, ran an evening class for parents and staff, and became a fully integrated member of staff.

New Opportunities Fund

In 2001, money from the National Lottery Fund was used to finance the New Opportunities Fund (NOF), which was a government initiative to provide training in information and computer technology (ICT) for teachers in the United Kingdom. From September 2001, training sessions were held at the school on two evenings a week, over the course of two school terms. All of the teaching and some of the non-teaching staff took advantage of this opportunity and produced impressive folders of work, for which they were awarded a certificate at the end of the course.

Sue Spiller was appointed as a NOF advisor to another school. She contributed to county-wide courses on ICT at Belstead House, Ipswich, ran ICT courses for teaching assistants in the Thurston pyramid of schools, and represented Suffolk LEA at a National Learning Support Programme conference in London, where she spoke about Suffolk's good practice in the teaching of ICT.

In 2001, she managed a project, funded by the Department for Education and Science (DfES), which involved Ixworth Middle School and its six feeder primary schools. The aim was to improve the standard of teaching and learning in ICT in each school, and to ensure that there was continuity and progression from each primary school to Ixworth Middle School. The schools drew up a common assessment transfer form for ICT and agreed on a joint scheme of work, which consisted of seven lessons, four of which were taught at the end of Year 4 at each primary school and three of which were taught the following September at Ixworth Middle School.

Teacher training and work experience

The Education Act 1994 set up the Teacher Training Agency for England and Wales and encouraged schools to become involved in the in-service education and training of teachers and governors.

At Great Barton School, Hilary Bilonick managed the teacher training programme for Postgraduate Certificate in Education (PGCE) students from Homerton College, Cambridge, each of whom spent one or more terms on teaching practice at the school.

She also managed the work experience students at the school, who came from Thurston Upper School, King Edward VI Upper School, County Upper School, West Suffolk College, Culford School, University College Ipswich, and Purse School, Cambridge.

Staff photograph, mid-1990s

The staff photograph for the mid-1990s shows Liz Baker, Lynn Andrews, Christine Holden, Lynda Mulley, Sue Denny, Mary Presland and Janice Clennell (back row from left to right), and Trudy Lindsay, Susan Smith, Liz Babbedge, Hilary Bilonick, Sue Spiller, Janet Cobbold, Sylvia Arbon, Sue Manning and Louise Colclough (front row from left to right).

Teacher appraisal and performance-related pay

During the 1990s, the salary of most teachers was static in real terms. However, performance pay and an upper pay scale were introduced in 2000. Three teachers at Great Barton Primary School submitted lengthy application forms for a threshold payment, which each of them claimed took ten hours to complete. All were successful and received a salary increment.

Also, that year, salaries for newly qualified teachers increased by 6.6 per cent, more than double the rate of inflation.

In 2000, the government announced the establishment of a National College for School Leadership to provide leadership training for prospective head teachers.

The non-teaching staff

In 1995, Lynn Andrews, Sue Manning, Lynda Mulley and Liz Baker were employed as teaching assistants (TAs), but the school's financial situation meant that there was a risk that the total number of TA hours per week would need to be reduced in the future. The budget share per pupil at Great Barton Primary School fell from £2,022 per pupil in 1991, to £1,504 in 1995, and there were further threats of education funding cuts in 1996. The school governors, together with those from other schools, lobbied Members of Parliament to explain the effects that future cuts would have on their school. In 1996, school budgets were cut by less than anticipated and in 1997, after the Labour Party came to power, the annual national expenditure on education increased from £38.6 billion in 1997/1998 to £65.1 billion in 2004 and £88.6 billion in 2009/2010 *(Source: Nominal expenditure figures from HM Treasury (2011b), Table 8.a)*. Consequently, the school was able to maintain, and eventually increase, the number of TA hours each week.

On 1 September 1998, Janet Cobbold, the school secretary, died from breast cancer. Her funeral at West Row Church, Bury St Edmunds, was attended by 500 people, and the school created a small memorial garden by the front door of the school. Janet Cobbold was replaced by Lynda Mulley, who immediately attended courses on financial management and SIMS Management Information Systems, and was replaced by Linda Borley as the fourth TA.

In 2000, David Cianciola was appointed as a nursery nurse; the only male member of staff. Subsequently, Hazel Ellis and Tracey Manning were employed as TAs and all of the non-teaching staff members were assigned new grades in 2002.

Non-teaching staff were encouraged to develop their special strengths and skills, and attend LEA and other courses. Tracey Manning and Hazel Ellis worked with pupils who struggled with numeracy or literacy, Sue Manning was given more responsibility for teaching swimming and games, and Linda Borley and Sue Manning supervised RE lessons. Liz Baker studied for a General National Vocational Qualification (GNVQ) in Learning Support in 1997.

In January 2003, school workforce unions, local government employers and the Government signed a national agreement, entitled *Raising Standards and Tackling Workload*, which was followed up with *Developing the role of school support staff – What the National Agreement means for you*. It introduced important changes to teachers' conditions of service, and called for workforce 'remodelling', to enable teachers to focus more effectively on teaching, and increase the role of support staff.

Great Barton School, which placed great value on TAs as a means of reducing the workload of teachers and offered them relevant training and additional responsibilities, was selected as one of a small group of schools in Suffolk, invited to share with other schools, their innovative ways of deploying TAs.

Sylvia Arbon, the caretaker and cleaner, employed at the school since 1969, retired in November 2003 after her sixty-fifth birthday, and the school organised a huge party for her. She was replaced by Keith Stringer, who worked at the school until 2012.

The pupils

In September 1996, there were 125 pupils on the school roll, with 17 more pupils registered to start later in the year. By April 2000, 132 pupils were registered, 33 of whom lived outside the catchment area and seven of whom were American pupils, whose families were stationed at the United States Air Force Base at RAF Mildenhall or RAF Lakenheath, .

The school endeavoured to restrict the number of pupils in each class, in line with the School Standards and Framework Act 1998, which imposed a statutory limit of 30 pupils in infant classes. However, this became difficult when a new family moved into the catchment area with seven-year-old triplets, whose appropriate class already had 28 pupils.

The school continued to arrange an annual 'open morning' for parents of pre-school children, and the supervisors of Great Barton Under 5s ran sessions in school for the Rising Fives.

The Nursery Education Regulations (1996) introduced inspections for maintained nursery schools, and obliged their supervisors to undertake further training. The Nursery Education and Grant-Maintained Schools Act 1996 introduced nursery vouchers, which allowed pupils to attend the school on a full-time or part-time basis from the start of the term in which their fifth birthday fell. The school accepted vouchers from April 1997, but the voucher scheme ended in September 1997. It was replaced with free nursery education for all four year olds, and was based on a partnership between the voluntary, private and education authority sectors.

In 1998, Sure Start was introduced to provide a quality service for pre-schoolers and their parents.

On the day that children started at Great Barton School, their parents were offered coffee in the staff room, where they could talk to other parents and stay until they were sure that their child had settled happily into school.

The Education Act 1996 repealed the Education (Miscellaneous Provisions) Act 1948 so that LEAs were no longer empowered to provide suitable clothes for needy pupils.

In April 2000, half of the pupils regularly ate a school lunch, but fewer than five children were entitled to a free school meal.

During the second half of each summer term, the head teacher ate lunch in one of the libraries with groups of five or six pupils from Red Class, who provided a tablecloth, decorated the table and carried the food from the school kitchen. This gave pupils an opportunity to talk to her about their school experiences and their hopes for the future.

Almost every child was transported daily by car, to and from school, and the parking problems continued.

The school tried to encourage parents to walk or cycle to school with their children and, for a short time, there was a 'walking bus' from Elms Close. Even during the annual Walk to School Weeks, more than half of the pupils still travelled by car.

The school curriculum

After the Labour Government came to power in 1997, Tony Blair's mantra of 'education, education, education' presaged an even greater plethora of educational directives, and schools became frustrated when they were expected to respond to new initiatives before they had had a stable period of time during which to consolidate and evaluate current practices.

In 1998, David Peachey, Suffolk's Education Officer, told a meeting of head teachers that he received between five and ten pieces of correspondence each day from the Department for Education and Employment (DfEE).

A white paper entitled *Excellence in School (1997)* set out the government's educational objectives for the next five years. In 1998, English, mathematics, science, ICT and RE were made compulsory, but there was a degree of flexibility with the other subjects. Whilst this reduced the pressure on the timetable, it risked the loss of other subjects essential for a balanced education.

The DfEE and QCA jointly published *National Curriculum: A Handbook for Primary Teachers in England (1999),* which was available to parents and governors and set out the legal requirements of the National Curriculum in England for pupils aged 5 to 11.

In 1999, the government created an Early Years Foundation Stage for children aged three to five, which was incorporated into the National Curriculum in 2002.

A green paper entitled *Schools - Building on Success (2000)* set out the achievements of the education service over the previous years and its plans for the years ahead, and a consultative document entitled *Schools - Achieving Success (2001)* set out the future proposals of the government for the maintenance of high educational standards. These were included in the Education Act 2002.

English

Reading was monitored each term using one of the *Salford Sentence Reading Tests*. From these and other tests, it was evident that the reading level of boys was below that of their female peers, so the reading progress for all pupils was monitored more closely, more non-fiction, boy-friendly reading books were bought, and fathers were invited to a meeting to discuss ways of encouraging their sons to be more enthusiastic and proficient readers.

The National Literacy Strategy: A Framework for Teaching (1997) gave detailed guidance to teachers on the teaching of literacy. It was very prescriptive and required pupils to have a daily hour of literacy teaching and, whilst it contained many good ideas, there was a risk that lessons could become dull, predictable and lack spontaneity. The National Literacy Trust delivered the National Year of Reading, which was a key part of the government's drive to raise standards through the National Literacy Strategy. It was launched on 16 September 1998 by David Blunkett, the Secretary of State for Education and Employment, on the set of *BBC TV EastEnders.*

Learning to read and write through phonics was a central part of the literacy strategy. Pupils were expected to be able to read and spell words from lists appropriate for their age group. In 1998 the school adopted *THRASS (Teaching Handwriting, Reading And Spelling Scheme)*, a structured multi- sensory literacy programme, which taught 44 phonemes, 20 vowel sounds and 24 consonant sounds, to help pupils to read and spell.

ERIC (Everyone Reading In Class*)* was adopted throughout the school, during which the teacher and each child read in silence.

In 1995, the United Nations Educational, Scientific and Cultural Organization (UNESCO) introduced World Book Day to promote 'reading, publishing and copyright'. Subsequently, it was celebrated annually in the UK on the first Thursday of March and each schoolchild received a £1 book token. At Great Barton School, every pupil and member of staff dressed up as a character from a book, the timetable that day was devoted to the study of literature, and professional poets and writers were invited to the school to work with pupils.

Sue Spiller was very enthusiastic about poetry and, in 1996 and 1997, gave a weekly poetry lesson to each class, during which pupils learnt poems by heart, and wrote their own poems, some of which were collated into a school publication, entitled *Rhyming Rainbows.*

Freya Smith used a *Reading Together* project with Orange Class, which was observed by Swedish educationalists who visited the school in 2000. Her class also visited the offices of the *East Anglian Daily Times*.

In 2000, the school made use of *Catch Up*, a learning programme created by a not-for-profit charity, to help pupils who were behind their peers in literacy and numeracy. TAs were given appropriate training so that they could provide structured teaching to small groups of pupils twice a week, in 15-minute sessions.

The Education Act 2002 enabled certain schools to apply to the authorities for permission to innovate.

Mathematics

The National Numeracy Strategy: Framework for Teaching Mathematics from Reception to Year 6 was published in 1999. This placed a strong emphasis on mental arithmetic. Maths Year 2000 was modelled on the National Year of Reading, and was a government initiative tied in with the National Numeracy Strategy, which aimed to demonstrate the importance of mathematics in daily life. During Maths Year 2000, the school organised a Maths Day throughout the school, devoted to the study of shape.

Information and computer technology (ICT)

In November 1997, the government published *Connecting the Learning Society: National Grid for Learning*, which outlined their plans for information and communication technology (ICT) in schools and required all schools and colleges to be connected to the internet by 1998.

In 1998, the government funded the National Grid for Learning (NGfL), which provided high-quality, up-to-date, educational materials for teachers and pupils. However, the school had no internet access until June 1999, when it could only be accessed via the school phone landline, which blocked the use of the phone whilst in use. An ISDN2 line was installed in February 2000, which cost £395 p.a., for 15 hours a week and was only available between 8.00 a.m. and 6.00 p.m.

In 2000, ten new computers were bought with the help of a grant of £13,360 from the NGfL and were housed at one end of the Rainbow Room. The ten old computers were distributed around the school, so that each classroom had two computers and one printer. By September 2002, the school owned 26 computers.

In 2001, 77 per cent of the households of pupils at Great Barton School owned a home computer, and 64 per cent could access the internet at home. When optional ICT homework was given, pupils without a home computer were given supervised access to the school computers during lunchtime and after school.

Sue Spiller devised a scheme of work for ICT, with the objective that every child would be able to use information technology safely and effectively to develop their knowledge, skills and understanding in other areas of the school curriculum. She taught ICT to each class, with assistance from teaching assistants and trained adult volunteers. Pupils were taught how to carry out research, interpret and check information, process and present text, tables and graphics, manage data, produce designs, and write simple computer programmes using *Logo*, an educational programming language that moved a robotic turtle around the floor. Pupils were given 'Chip Awards' when they achieved certain basic competences and Sue Spiller ran a lunchtime computer club for the older pupils.

Religious education (RE) and collective worship

In 2000, the school aims for Great Barton Primary CEVC School included the statement that, 'This school seeks to be a place where there is no ideological pressure or indoctrination, but is firmly based on Christian principles.'

The School Standards and Framework Act 1998 reinforced the requirement that, 'each pupil in attendance at a community, foundation or voluntary school, shall on each school day take part in an act of collective worship'. At Great Barton School, Anglicans, Nonconformists, Roman Catholics, Hindus and 'those of no faith' participated in school assemblies and RE lessons, but Jehovah's Witnesses opted out of both.

RE was taught in accordance with the Suffolk *Agreed Syllabus for Religious Education*. Pupils were encouraged to be open-minded, and were given a sense of their own value and self-esteem so that they had confidence in themselves, and respect for and tolerance of others.

QCA produced the *Non Statutory National Framework for Religious Education (2004)* with guidelines for teaching RE, which they hoped could eventually replace each locally agreed syllabus.

Geography, history and science

Geography, history and science were no longer taught as cross-curricular subjects, but as discrete subjects following the guidance in the National Curriculum documents.

To support classroom-based studies, members of Bury St Edmunds Fire Service and the School Liaison Police Officer visited the school, as did an actor dressed as a Roman soldier on one occasion.

Each class went on educational visits. Green and Red Class both walked around Great Barton to study local geography and history. Blue Class went to Ixworth Thorpe, Wimpole Hall, Bury St Edmunds, the 'Enchanted Forest' at Bradfield Woods run by Suffolk Wildlife Trust, and for a teddy bears' picnic. Green Class went to Felixstowe, Yellow and Orange classes to Thetford Forest, Yellow Class to Framlingham or Mountfitchett Castle, Orange Class to Bury St Edmunds and the Fitzwilliam Museum at Cambridge, and Red Class to Christchurch Mansion at Ipswich, Foxburrow Farm and Colchester Castle. Two-day residential visits for Red Class were organised once a year at Kings Lynn from 1997 to 1999 by Christine Holden and at Thornham Field Centre from 2000 to 2003 by Karen Rees and David Cianciola.

The science curriculum was supplemented by two whole days devoted to the study of flight and recycling. In March 1998, during a science, engineering and technology week, each class visited a workplace in Bury St Edmunds and the school received a commendation for its entry in 'Today's Engineers' competition.

Physical education (PE) and sport

Hilary Bilonick co-ordinated the teaching of PE and games, and provided 'Top Sport' training to teachers in the Thurston pyramid of schools.

Each class had three PE sessions per week and pupils in Red Class took part in sports afternoons with other primary schools in the Ixworth cluster.

Swimming lessons at the school continued each year, using the school pool from May until September. The school took advantage of local experts and initiatives, and arranged for instructors from 'Pass Soccer' and the 'Bodycare Roadshow' to work in school.

From 1994 to 1997, a trained instructor ran an after-school fitness class. During the autumn and spring terms, teams from the netball and football clubs, both run by parents, played matches against other local schools and participated in tournaments. During the school assembly each Monday morning, team members stood up and one of them presented a verbal account of the weekend's match to the rest of the school. Photographs of the teams and reports of the matches were collated in a book displayed in the Rainbow Room.

Music, singing, dance and drama

Music lessons made use of a wide selection of percussion instruments, and older pupils were able to join the school choir and learn to play the recorder. A guitar club, hand-bell ringing club and country dancing club were run by volunteers after school and the LEA provided violin lessons at the school from September 2003.

In 1997, every pupil in the school studied Kodaly's Viennese Musical Clock during a music week.

A Circus Skills Workshop was arranged as part of the school's joint project with the Theatre Royal.

There were opportunities for all pupils to dance, sing and act in Christmas performances, which were written or adapted by members of staff. These were entitled *Baboushka* (1995), *The Bright Lights of Christmas* (1996), *The Smallest Angel* (1997), *The Bossy Christmas Fairy* (1998), *Mother Christmas's Journey* (1999), *A Boy is Born* (2000),

Hosanna Rock (2001), *Jack and the Beanstalk* (2002), and *Hoity Toity Angel* (2003). Between 1996 and 2003, Red Class usually sang carols at St Edmundsbury Cathedral and Montana Retirement Home, Great Barton.

In 2000, the drama club, run by Sally Whatling a parent and aspiring teacher, put on performances based on *A Midsummer Night's Dream* during the summer term, and *Harry Potter and the Philosopher's Stone* and a pantomime entitled *Beauty and the Space Beast* during the autumn term.

The older pupils were taken to Ixworth Middle School each year to watch a play performed by some of the middle school pupils.

Multicultural education

During the 1990s, the majority of pupils were of white British ethnicity. The school believed that it was important to teach children about other cultures and customs to equip them for life in a pluralistic society. From 1995, as part of this policy, the regular timetable was abandoned for one week each year during which pupils studied the people, culture and religion of a country or group of countries. Pupils studied West African countries in 1995, India in 1996, Peru in 1997, Japan in 1998, France in 1999, Ghana in 2000, Australia in 2001, Caribbean countries in 2002 and Russia in 2003. People with a special knowledge or interest in that country or region were invited to the school to share their expertise and, on one day during the week, pupils and staff dressed in a relevant costume and ate a school lunch which consisted of food served in that part of the world.

During the first multicultural week, introduced by Derek Merrill, Suffolk's advisory teacher for multicultural education, visitors introduced pupils to the music, games, dances, storytelling, language, art and ceramics of West African countries. On the Wednesday, the children sat down on the hall floor and ate bowls of rice, sweet corn and chicken stew, followed by fruit salad composed of fruit, grown in Africa and prepared and assembled by the pupils. Some pupils cooked peanuts over an open fire and cleaned their own classroom at the end of a school day, as some children in Ghana were expected to do. On the Friday, the whole school wore African-style clothes and visited the Aklowa Heritage Centre, a reconstructed Ghanaian village near Bishop's Stortford, Essex, where they took part in drumming, dancing and cooking activities, and experienced some aspects of life in a traditional West African village.

In 1995, Christine Holden arranged for a group of 22 Romanian students and three of their teachers to visit Great Barton and stay with pupils' families. They spent a day in school during which they put on a colourful concert of singing and dancing, which was screened on *ITV Anglia News*. In the evening, they attended an evening garden party with pupils and the host families at Great Barton Lodge, owned by Graham and Linda Mothersole.

In 1998, the International Voluntary Service organised an East-West Dance Camp at East Bergholt, Essex, and Sue Spiller took 12 pupils from Red Class to perform dances with children from countries in East Europe.

Citizenship

In 1998, the Crick Report, entitled, the *'Teaching of Citizenship and Democracy'* was published. In advance of this report, the oldest pupils received citizenship lessons from Sue Spiller during 1997. On the day of the general election organised a non-party political, mock election for the whole school, which resulted in a win for The Smarty Party.

The older pupils contributed to a booklet about traditional playground games so that everyone could entertain themselves better at playtimes.

From 2000, there was a suggestion box in the Rainbow Room. Pupils were encouraged to post sensible suggestions, which could be discussed by the staff. One proposal was for a 'Friendship Stop' in the playground, where children could stand if they had no-one to play with. To the children's credit, no child ever stood there for more than a minute before another child invited them to join in their game.

Support for pupils with additional needs

Trudy Lindsay was the special educational needs co-ordinator (SENCo) until 2001, when Carolyn Cooper took over the role. Between 1996 and 2004, up to 20 children each year had a 'record of support', and one or two had a 'statement of special needs'. A green paper, entitled *Excellence for All Children: Meeting Special Educational Needs (1997),* reappraised existing provision for children with additional educational needs.

In response to a suggestion in the school's Ofsted Report (1996), a register was kept of gifted and talented pupils. Some were enrolled on a course for mathematically gifted pupils on Saturday mornings in Bury St Edmunds; others attended extra art, music, French or problem-solving classes at Great Barton School.

Performance targets

The Education (Schools) Act 1997 required all primary schools in England to carry out National Baseline Assessments during the first seven weeks of a pupil's attendance in the reception class, and assess 32 aspects of language and literacy, mathematics, and personal and social development. This legislation also gave powers to Ofsted to inspect LEAs.

In addition, the *Education (School Performance Targets) (England) Regulations (1998)* required schools to set annual performance targets for each pupil, monitor the results, and take appropriate action where the performance did not match the target. This data contributed to a value added project, through which the effectiveness and quality of the teaching and learning in a school could be measured. Not only were these targets a useful monitoring tool for teachers and head teachers, they also enabled the government and other outside agencies to quantify and compare schools, and make judgements.

Extracurricular activities

From September 1997, there was an after-school club for primary and middle school pupils, which had 48 children on its register at first, but was discontinued in 1999 as the result of a lack of support.

From January 1999, Lynn Andrews and David Cianciola ran a breakfast club from 8.15 a.m. until 8.50 a.m.

In addition to the sports, music and other clubs previously mentioned, there were clubs for chess, handicrafts, British Sign Language, rocks and fossils and the natural world.

Pupils who belonged to clubs or organisations outside school were encouraged to demonstrate their skills and knowledge to their class or the whole school. One such pupil was Alice Laidler, a talented dancer, who trained at the Hazelwood Dance Studios in Bury St Edmunds, and occasionally agreed to give a demonstration of her latest dance to her fellow pupils. She continued her training at the Central School of Ballet, graduated with BA (Hons), and joined Phoenix Dance Theatre in August 2013, at the age of 20, as an Apprentice Dancer under the Northern School of Contemporary Dance apprentice scheme, performing classical, neoclassical, contemporary, modern and jazz ballet.

Some pupils entered local and national competitions. In 1998, Fiona Mulley, Charlotte Sallis and Amy Bucknell, three talented singers in Red Class, made a recording of 'Il est Né', a French Christmas carol, for a competition organised by *Classic FM*.

Many pupils entered a competition organised by *BBC Gardeners' World*, which involved growing a Busy Lizzie (*Accent Impatiens*) with the maximum number of flowers. In 1998, six-year-old Oliver Lindsay, the son of Trudy Lindsay, was a finalist and invited to the National Exhibition Centre in Birmingham. In 1999, he came first when he grew a plant with 27 blooms and beat 42,000 other young horticulturalists. He won £750 and a trophy for his school, and a replica trophy, certificate, crystal glass globe, stainless steel trowel, cap and t-shirt for himself.

In 1999, a five-year-old pupil won a prize of £25 in a colouring competition organised by Wyevale Garden Centres.

In 2001, a pupil won a drawing competition run by the Cheltenham and Gloucester Building Society.

School certificates for a variety of achievements were awarded during an extracurricular assembly, held at the end of each summer term.

Up to £2,500 was raised by the school each year for a diverse range of charities, which included causes highlighted by UNICEF, Comic Relief and the Blue Peter appeals. They donated to the Poppy Appeal, Save the Children Fund, the National Society for the Prevention of Cruelty to Children, Water Aid, Harvest Help, the Rainbow Appeal for West Suffolk Hospital, the Marie Curie Cancer Trust, Bury St Edmunds Hospice, Shoebox, Samaritan's Purse, Denim Day, Jeans for Genes and National Children's Home Action for Children. Pupils participated in sponsored spelling and swimming events, and Readathon, a sponsored reading event, which donated money to Sargent Cancer Care for Children and the Roald Dahl Foundation. David Cianciola raised £170 for Shelter when he took part in the Thetford Chase Charity Walk.

The school premises and grounds

There was an overnight break-in at the school in November 1995, when a computer and a speaker system valued at £1,500 were stolen, and £700 worth of damage was caused. School security was reviewed and additional measures put in place. All members of staff were expected to wear a name badge and visitors were asked to sign in and out and wear a badge whilst on the premises. Additional smoke and fire alarms were installed, equipment was security-marked by the police, a keypad was fitted to the front door, an external letter box replaced the internal one, the site was surrounded by a £3,000 security fence, and closed-circuit television (CCTV) cameras were installed.

In 2002, alterations were made to the offices of the head teacher and administrative assistant, and a glass barrier was erected between the entrance hall and the offices.

In 1997, a grant from the Schools Access Initiative was used to improve the accessibility for disabled children, parents and visitors. The staff toilet was made wheelchair-friendly, ramps were built at two of the entrances, and one of the parking places in the car park was allocated for a disabled driver or passenger.

In addition, all of the classrooms and small teaching rooms were carpeted and redecorated, and internal doors were positioned between each classroom and the adjoining cloakroom areas where air fresheners were installed. Some ceilings and pin-boards, and the original boiler were replaced, additional electric sockets were installed, the kiln and sinks were removed from classrooms, sun blinds were fitted on classroom windows, blackout curtains were put up in the hall and computer room, and smoke alarms were placed in each room. An air conditioning unit was installed in the computer suite.

Hilary Bilonick worked with Great Barton Parent Teacher Association (PTA) to develop the facilities in the school grounds. A quiet area and an additional adventure play area were created, the playground was painted with markings for playtime activities, a grassed play area for the reception class was created outside their classroom, and sunshades and pergolas were bought to provide shade on the playing field during the summer months. A new cycle shed was erected, and a shed was placed near the swimming pool to store staging, surplus furniture and PTA equipment. The fence around the swimming pool was replaced, and a new cover bought for the pool. In 2002, the playground was resurfaced, a beach area with wooden boats was created at the end of the playing field, and a 'trim trail' was built.

In 2004, a new room to store the dining room tables and chairs was built between the hall and the playing field.

Building Schools for the Future (2004) committed the government to invest in the rebuilding and renewal of secondary and primary schools.

The governing body and parental involvement

In September 1999, the governing body was increased to 12 members, to take account of the increased number of pupils. Henceforth, there were four parent governors, two local authority governors, two foundation governors, two community governors (nominated by Great Barton Parish Council) and two members of staff, who represented the teaching and the non-teaching members of staff respectively. The parish vicar and head teacher were ex-officio members.

The governors held an annual discussion about whether to opt out of LEA control and apply for grant-maintained status, and they unanimously rejected the idea each year.

Under the School Standards and Framework Act 1998, foundation schools were set up to replace grant-maintained schools. This legislation also required schools in England and Wales to have a signed home-school agreement, to be signed by parents when their child was admitted to the school. At Great Barton School, the document outlined the school's aims and values, the responsibilities of the school and the parents, and the school's expectation of its pupils.

Parents and governors were kept well informed about school events and achievements by means of a regular school newsletter. Class teachers held at least one meeting per year to talk to the parents of all the pupils in their class, held one-to-one interviews with parents at least twice a year, and produced a detailed and informative report for every child at the end of the year.

The PTA raised up to £3,500 each year for the school. It organised discos and ceilidhs, sales of cakes, toys and clothes, jumble and nearly new sales, fêtes and fairs, ladies' nights, fashion shows, quiz nights, beetle drives, an Ascot race night, a cookie walk, car treasure hunts, after-school video shows, leavers' barbecues, matchbox competitions and Easter egg hunts. It sold school calendars and tea cloths, sweets and ice creams in the summer and inexpensive items in Santa's Secret Shop at Christmas, where children could buy presents for their parents. The Big Wow, a family fun day, raised £70. At Christmas, it organised a craft fair, and members ran a stall at night markets at Ixworth and Bury St Edmunds. It sold Webb Ivory goods and ran the Red House Book Club to raise money for the school, and organised the 100 Club, a lottery fund, which paid out 50 per cent of the fund each month in prizes, with the remainder donated to the school for school library books.

Debbie Williams, a parent and ex-pupil, competed in the Great North Run and raised £200 for playground games. Hilary Bilonick and some parents took part in a sponsored abseil at Stowmarket fire station.

Front entrance of Great Barton CEVC Primary School, 2000

The PTA not only bought equipment for the school, but also paid for a visit from a theatre group each year. Between 1995 and 2003, pupils watched performances by the Booster Cushion Company (1995, 1999), Norwich Puppet Company (1996), Tollhouse Theatre Company (1997, 1999), the Garlic Theatre Company (1998, 2002) GNVQ students from King Edward VI School (1999), the Barking Dog Theatre Company (2001) and Golden Egg Productions (2003).

From September 1999, parents were invited to a coffee morning once a year, in support of the 'World's Biggest Coffee Morning' to raise money for Macmillan Cancer Support. Parent-helpers and other volunteers continued to be invited to a special event at the end of each term as a token of the school's appreciation of their support.

The Millennium and the Queen's Golden Jubilee

In 2000, the school participated in 'On the Line'; a joint project between the World Wild Life Fund, Oxfam, *Channel 4 TV* and Voluntary Services Overseas, initially devised by television broadcaster, Jon Snow, to link people who lived on the zero degree meridian line and raise public awareness of the interdependence of people all over the world. It included the UK, France, Spain, Algeria, Mali, Burkina Faso, Ghana, and Togo. Red Class collaborated with a school in Ghana, with whom they exchanged letters and presents.

In January 2000, the PTA organised a well-attended millennium party, during which staff, parents and pupils released many helium-filled balloons with labels stating the name and address of the school. Several labels were returned to the school from where they were found, including one from Holland.

On 1 March 2000, the school buried a time capsule in the playing field, two metres under a newly planted oak tree, which was surrounded by a hexagonal bench. The capsule was 33cm in diameter, 53cm deep, and filled with argon gas, before being sealed with a watertight PTFE seal and screwed down. It contained artefacts and documents that gave a snapshot of Great Barton Primary School at the end of the twentieth century, to be opened in 2050 by either the head teacher of the school or the chair of Great Barton Parish Council if the school no longer existed. As far as possible, documents were written on high quality, acid-free paper, and newspaper items were de-acidified with milk of magnesia and soda water (reputed to preserve them for up to 200 years). However, the school brochure, a village newsletter and details of the National Curriculum were written on ordinary paper. The artefacts, selected by the pupils, included items of school uniform, postage stamps, coins, a metal pencil sharpener, a millennium mug, a teapot, Pokémon cards, some pieces of Lego, a credit card and an audio-tape. Its site and contents were registered with the International Time Capsule Registry, Oglethorpe University, 4484 Peachtree Road, Georgia, USA, and with the Public Library and Record Office at Bury St Edmunds.

In July 1999, the school received a bequest of £250 from the will of Jill Plant, a volunteer at the school between 1996 and 1998, to thank the school for making her so welcome. Her money was used towards the purchase of a carved story seat, which the Grounds Millennium Committee, composed of members of staff and the PTA, commissioned from Ben Platts-Mills, a local wood sculptor.

Staff and pupils contributed to a school booklet entitled *Photos for the Future*, which was part of a local history project organised by *The History Channel*, an American cable and satellite broadcaster, which produced documentary programs and historical fiction series until 2008. On each page of the booklet, there was a photograph from a family album, which reflected an aspect of life in the twentieth century, with an explanation by each family describing its significance.

Five pupils had a poem included in *Our World 2000*, published by Macmillan Children's Books, an anthology of children's writing and artwork about the millennium.

At a Millennium Service in Holy Innocents' Church, Great Barton, 25 pupils sang and played hand bells.

In 2001, the PTA arranged for five class videos to be made for sale, which included an interview with each pupil in a class, the class teacher, a teaching assistant and other adults who worked with the class.

In 2002, the school celebrated the Queen's Golden Jubilee and some pupils in Red Class produced the *Jubilee Times*, which was on sale for 10p and featured articles about Queen Elizabeth II and a supplement with a drawing of a royal coach to 'colour, cut out and keep'. On 24 May, the school was adorned with bunting and flags, and everyone wore red, white and blue clothes. During the morning, parents watched a display of maypole and country dancing by the pupils, who then ate lunch at long tables on the playground, in the style of a street party. After lunch, members of Great Barton Women's Institute and Sylvia Arbon, the school caretaker, talked to the pupils and shared their memories of life at the time of the Queen's coronation in June 1953. At the end of the day, each pupil wore a paper crown to a school assembly, during which they sang songs from the 1950s, and were presented with a mug, a gold-plated commemorative coin, and a Jubilee Certificate, produced by the school.

Ofsted inspection – 2000

In May 2000, the school received notice of an inspection to be carried out under Section 10 of the School Inspection Act 1996, which was scheduled for the week beginning 3 July 2000. The Section 13 inspection, which reported on collective worship, was planned for the same week. The senior management team of Sue Spiller, Hilary Bilonick and Trudy Lindsay were well prepared for the inspection, having recently completed an Ofsted-endorsed course on 'Helping Schools to Carry Out Self-Evaluation', which was part of Suffolk's School Improvement Project.

Unfortunately, Hilary Bilonick was absent on sick leave for a few weeks before and during the inspection, but Cathy Hiscox, who was one of the school's regular supply teachers, volunteered to teach Yellow Class in her absence.

The School Inspection Act 1996 aimed to make school inspections more manageable and less bureaucratic, but the school was required, nevertheless, to provide a large number of documents. These included policy statements for each National Curriculum subject, early years education, life skills, special education needs, more-able pupils, citizenship, economic and industrial understanding, assessment, multicultural education, collective worship, homework, school security, health and safety, equal opportunities, drugs, sex education, child protection, pupil attendance, pupil discipline, teacher appraisal and spiritual, moral, social and cultural education.

Other documentation included the school brochure, details of staff and governors, the home-school agreement, and school development and improvement plans.

During the inspection week, the inspectors scrutinised schemes of work, lesson and termly teaching plans, samples of work from three pupils in each class, and examples of school reports. They looked at the school budget, minutes of meetings and sub-committees of the governing body and interviewed teachers, governors and parents.

The Section 10 inspection report stated that the school 'has made a considerable improvement in all the key issues, and the overall quality of teaching'. It also stated that the school was judged a 'very effective school', which achieved standards that were 'well above the national average in English, mathematics and science at the end of Key Stage 1' and gave 'good value for money'. Teaching was good or very good throughout the school, and the head teacher was described as a very effective manager, well supported by well-informed governors and a strong school team. The Section 13 inspectors were impressed by the high quality of collective worship.

Other memorable events and personal memories – 1996 to 2004

Pupils and staff have various memories from these years which Susan Smith recalled as being a time of very hard work, but with a great deal of laughter, mutual support and a strong sense of togetherness.

Susan has a special memory of a very helpful five-year-old girl in her class, who, when asked to do just one more thing, responded, 'Oh, Mrs Smith, you've had me up and down like a whore's drawers!'

Some children in Blue Class remember the escape by Maud, one of their class guinea pigs. The children were told to sit in a circle on the grass in their play area and ensure that that there were no gaps between them, so that the guinea pigs could play securely inside the circle. Unfortunately, one timid child leapt in the air when a guinea pig ran towards her, with the inevitable result. Maud was found the following day, shivering and hungry under a hedge.

Children in Red Class built an amazing structure on the edge of the playing field. It was constructed from natural materials, populated with plastic dinosaurs and named Dinocity. It occupied their playtimes for several weeks and even received publicity in the local press.

The pupils enjoyed celebrating April Fools' Day, and the teachers joined in. One year, Trudy Lindsay and David Cianciola created a dummy tree in the Blue Class play area, by decorating a tree with a colourful array of rubber dummies, which delighted the children and were still there several years later.

Another year, the secretary handed a telegram to the head teacher at the end of a school assembly. It stated that baby tortoises had escaped from a lorry whilst it was refuelling at Great Barton Service Station that morning *en route* from Banham Zoo, Norfolk, to Broadcasting House, London, where the tortoises were due to appear on *BBC TV The Really Wild Show*. The telegram warned the school that the baby tortoises might attempt to reach the school pond to find water. During morning playtime, every pupil walked on tiptoe around the school playing field in almost total silence, looking for the thirsty tortoises. It was a peaceful playtime, during which every child had some exercise, the pupils shared a common purpose, and no child was bored, friendless or involved in an argument.

Andrew Buttress, the minister of Great Barton Free Church from 1998, has a vivid memory of an assembly on the subject of creation, which did not go according to plan. He took animals as his theme, through which he hoped to explain God's attention to detail. He used an overhead projector to display some live insects, including woodlice and earwigs, and made a sticky frame to keep them in place. His *pièce de résistance* was a small dead newt, which he had found under a stone. He placed it on the screen and started to describe its amazing structure. However, after a few minutes, the 'dead' newt came to life as the heat from the projector brought it out of hibernation. When the newt threatened to leap onto the laps of the children in the front row, there was uproar amongst the pupils and as their screams subsided, Andrew switched his theme from creation to resurrection.

Kori Buttress, Jade Rutterford, Daisy Henwood, Jess Smith and Roisin Evans remember being delighted when they were sent to the head teacher to show her some good work, and being rewarded with a coloured sticker, which read 'Mrs Spiller says well done'.

They recall their pleasure when it was their turn, at the end of an assembly, to blow out the candles on the fake birthday cake to celebrate their birthday, and their shock when a child in their class was sent to the head teacher for bad behaviour. In their words, 'the whole class was, like WOAH', because that only happened on rare occasions.

They also remember the end of year assembly, where the head teacher spoke about each leaver in turn and made some predictions about what he or she might do in the future. These pupils later commented that they had a feeling that, 'she may have got it pretty accurate for most of us'.

Retirement

In April 2004, Sue Spiller applied for early retirement, after working for almost 14 years at the school. She received letters from West Suffolk Education Office, Suffolk County Council and Charles Clarke (the Secretary of State for Education) to thank her for her contribution to education and her outstanding service. One letter read that, 'a school in danger of failing when you took over is now a top-quality primary school'.

A week before the end of the spring term, she and her husband were invited by David Peachey, Suffolk Education Officer, to join him and Tom Scherb, Western Area Education Manager, for an evening at Snape Maltings to watch *Peter Grimes* by Benjamin Britten, performed by Suffolk schoolchildren.

On the penultimate day of term, a special assembly was arranged at the school, attended by many well-wishers, local clergy and others who had contributed to school assemblies. The pupils sang some of her favourite assembly songs, and Tom Scherb presented her with an astronomical telescope from the parents, pupils and governors of the school, and a book on astronomy from the staff in West Suffolk Education Office. She also received a large ceramic plate decorated with the school logo and signed by every child in the school, place mats with a self-portrait of every pupil, and a folder from each class containing pupils' memories. After assembly, she was presented with a large cake, made by one of the parents, which she shared with staff and pupils later that day. It was beautifully decorated with a drawing of six children, surrounded by a globe, a planet, the sun and a crescent moon.

On the last day of term, she was amazed to see a cream-coloured, chauffeur-driven Rolls Royce motor car outside her house in Bury St Edmunds to transport her to school. When she arrived at the school, she was cheered by a crowd of flag-waving parents and pupils, and walked into school on a red carpet, past members of staff, who all wore t-shirts emblazoned with her photograph and messages of good wishes. She sat down to coffee and croissants in the Rainbow Room, after which she was escorted to her office, where she found a beautiful bouquet of flowers and dozens of gifts from parents and children, which included a caricature of herself, in which she held a telescope in one hand and a bottle of '*chateau plonkeau*' in the other.

After school, the PTA organised a party on the playing field, during which she was presented with a magnificent hand-made quilt, composed of squares that had been beautifully decorated by pupils and staff.

The school governors invited applicants for the post of head teacher of Great Barton Primary School and suggested that applicants visit the school because 'only by meeting the staff and children and looking at the buildings, equipment and resources can you get a genuine idea of the happy and caring atmosphere, the quality of the learning environment, the standard of work, and the behaviour and positive attitudes of those who work here.'

Sue Spiller retired and moved to south-west France. She was confident that the school would continue to prosper under the leadership of her successor, Sarah Rees.

20
AN OUTSTANDING SCHOOL

Great Barton Church of England Voluntary Controlled (CEVC) Primary School (URN 124697) was judged as 'good' in 2006 and 'outstanding' in 2009 by school inspectors who carried out inspections under Section 5 of the Education Act 2000.

As a Church of England school, it was also subject to inspection by representatives of the Church of England. It was judged as 'outstanding' by the Statutory Inspection of Anglican Schools in 2006 and 2009 and a Statutory Inspection of Anglican Schools and Methodist Schools in 2014.

School reorganisation in West Suffolk

Following a School Organisation Review carried out by Suffolk County Council and begun in 2007, it was decided that the three-tier system would be replaced by a two-tier one. Suffolk closed its middle schools, in common with much of the rest of England where the number of middle schools fell from 1,800 in 1981 to 550 in 1999.

In 2012, Great Barton Primary School formed a partnership with Thurston Community College and the other primary schools in the Thurston Pyramid to ensure a smooth transition from a three-tier to a two-tier system. From September 2013 and 2014, pupils in Years 5 and 6 at Great Barton School were accommodated in a new building, which was erected between the school and the playing field. In August 2014, the middle schools at Ixworth, Beyton and Stanton closed, and all pupils in the Thurston Pyramid of Schools transferred directly to Thurston Community College or another school at the end of Year 6.

Some 11-year-old pupils from Great Barton Primary School transferred to Ixworth Free School set up by the Seckford Foundation Free Schools Trust following the closure of Ixworth Middle School in September 2014.

Free schools were authorised under the Academies Act 2010, which permitted their establishment by a charity, university, independent school, community group, faith group, teacher, parent or business. They received government funding and were no longer under the control of the Local Education Authority (LEA). Free schools were permitted to appoint their own staff, and teaching staff were not necessarily required to have qualified teacher status. They could set their own terms of pay and conditions, determine the length of the school day and the dates of the school terms and were not obliged to follow the National Curriculum.

The teaching and non-teaching staff at Great Barton CEVC School

In September 2014, in addition to Sarah Rees the head teacher and Jane Green the deputy head teacher, there were six other full-time teachers, all of whom had qualified teacher status.

Table 15. Teachers and teaching assistants

Year group	Class name	Teachers	Teaching assistants
Early Years Foundation Stage	Owl	Jane Green	Tracey Manning Suzanne Smalley Sam Cunningham
1	Robin	Ruth Larke	Linda Borley
2	Fox	Kate Scales	Tina Campan
3	Squirrel	Suzie Deeks	Jo Barry
4	Badger	Kate Pizzey	Wendy Coe
5	Hare	Rachel Power	Leanne Heath
6	Osprey	Claire Riley	Ros Betts

Source : http://greatbartonprimaryschool.co.uk

Table 16. Non-teaching staff

Job title	Non-teaching staff
Office manager	Lynda Mulley
Office assistant	Shane Hales
Cook in charge	Tracy Moss
Assistant cooks	Lisa Hudson Shirley Woods
Senior midday supervisory assistant	Linda Borley
Midday supervisory assistants	Wendy Bolero Tina Campan Tracey Manning Suzanne Smalley Shirley Woods
Caretaker and cleaner	Peter Woods

Source: http://greatbartonprimaryschool.co.uk

The school employed additional teachers for three days a week to enable the leadership team to meet and teachers to have non-teaching time.

In 2014, the *Bury Free Press* named Kate Pizzey as Teacher of the Year and awarded £750 to the school.

The Education Act 2011 abolished the General Teaching Council for England, the professional body for teaching. From 2012, some of its functions were performed by the Teaching Agency, an agency of the Department for Education.

The pupils

Between 2001 and 2011, there was a slight increase in the village population from 1512 to 1600. By September 2015, there were 202 pupils on roll, two-thirds of whom lived in Great Barton or Great Livermere. Almost all of the pupils were classified as 'white British', and those pupils for whom English was an additional language were competent, bi-lingual speakers.

Pathways

Great Barton Under 5s, renamed Pathways, moved from Great Barton Free Church to a brand new, purpose-built building next door to the school. The Education Act 2011 extended the duty of LEAs to provide 15 hours of nursery education, free of charge, for all three and four-year-olds.

In addition to providing pre-school education, Pathways also offered breakfast, after school and holiday clubs for three to nine-year-olds.

The school governors

In 2015, the governing body included five parent governors nominated and elected by parents, and two members of staff nominated and elected by the teaching and the non-teaching members of staff respectively. It also included two governors appointed by the LEA, two community governors appointed by Great Barton Parish Council and two foundation governors who were appointed by the local church. The head teacher and the Vicar of Holy Innocents' Church, Great Barton were both ex officio members of the governing body.

The Education Act 2005 removed the requirement for school governors to produce an annual report, or to hold an annual meeting with parents.

In 2009, the school attained the Financial Management in Schools Award, in recognition of the efficiency of the financial systems and the effectiveness of oversight by the governing body.

In addition to his role as Vicar of Great Barton, the Revd Alan Gates was appointed as Vicar of St Peter's Church, Thurston, in 2012. Consequently, he became an ex-officio member of the Board of Governors of Thurston Primary School. In August 2014, he and his wife retired to

Majorca. In 2015, the Revd Manette Crossman (known to the pupils as Revd Manette) was appointed as Vicar of Great Barton and Thurston.

The school premises and grounds

The premises underwent several changes inside and outside the building.

The swimming pool was filled in and incorporated into the school playing field. A canopy was fitted over part of the area outside the classroom of the youngest children. The school car park was enlarged to provide sufficient accommodation for 22 cars.

Inside the building, part of the changing rooms was converted into a study room for staff. The secretary's office was enlarged so that there was room to accommodate an office assistant.

The school also improved many aspects of the environment and entered the Eco Schools Award.

In 2014, it installed solar panels on the school roof to reduce the electricity bill, and renewed ceilings and lighting.

The school curriculum

As a voluntary controlled school, it was obliged to follow the National Curriculum. The National Literacy Strategy and the National Numeracy Strategy were regularly amended and adapted, and the National Strategies website was closed in June 2011.

The new National Curriculum, introduced in September 2014, contained the programmes of study and attainment targets for all subjects at all key stages.

After 2004, one of the main curriculum developments at the school was the introduction of the *Philosophy4Children* programme, which aimed to develop pupils' inquiry and reasoning skills. It was based on work in Australia so Sarah Rees and Jane Green visited Buranda School in Brisbane, Queensland, with a small group of Suffolk teachers to observe the teaching programme in action. Subsequently, all of the teachers at Great Barton School were trained to teach philosophy.

The school supported the Great Barton Community Woodland project, set up in 2007, whose logo was designed by a pupil in Year 6.

In 2008, Reinhild Raistrick, an ex-teacher at the school, produced four tree illustrations for the group.

Jane Green and Suzanne Smalley became fully trained Forest School leaders. They managed the programme, which offered regular opportunities to children, young people and adults to achieve and develop confidence through hands-on learning in a woodland area. Happy Wood, an area of woodland, was given to the school by the council, and pupils spent time there and in Downing Wood.

From 2010, peripatetic music staff taught class instrumental lessons (including trombone and tenor horn lessons) to pupils in Year 4.

Great Barton Parent Teacher Association (PTA) raised money to purchase a set of African drums for children in Years 3 and 5 to play during their class music lessons. Optional violin lessons, for a small charge, were available to pupils in Years 3, 4, 5 and 6.

In 2012, 100 percent of pupils attained level two or above in the Key Stage 1 assessment tests in reading, writing and mathematics. Nationally, Great Barton School was in the top 20 per cent of schools.

By 2014, this had fallen to 89 per cent in writing, 81 per cent in reading and 89 per cent in mathematics. Great Barton School was in the bottom 40 per cent of all schools and was selected as one of twelve schools in Suffolk to be funded for participation in a mathematics project with the Primary Advantage Federation in Hackney, London, which used an innovative maths programme.

Great Barton School achieved Activemark in recognition of its work in sports and physical education (PE). Increased funding allowed the school to employ a sports coach to support high quality PE teaching.

In September 2014, information and computer technology was renamed 'computing'. At Great Barton School, there were 15 desktop computers in the computer room, and older computers and an inter-active white board (SMART Board) in each classroom. Mini iPads and 30 laptops were shared between the classes.

Each member of staff had a tablet computer, each teacher had a lap top computer, and all of the staff had the use of desktop computers in the staff study room.

Academies

The Academies Act 2010 allowed all existing state schools to become academies. These were run by trusts, funded by central government and free from LEA control. They were required to follow the same rules on admissions, special educational needs and exclusions as other state schools, and were required to teach a 'broad and balanced curriculum' and follow the National Curriculum in the core subjects of maths, English and science, with freedom to innovate in the other subjects.

By November 2014, according to figures produced by the DfE, 21.6 per cent of all mainstream state-funded schools were academies or free schools.

Academies were monitored by regional schools commissioners (RSC) on behalf of the Secretary of State for Education.

On 1 July 2015, Tim Coulson, previously director of education at Essex County Council, was appointed as the RSC for the east of England and north-east London.

Thedwastre Education Trust

On 31 December 2015, Great Barton CEVC Primary School closed and reopened on 1 January 2016 as Great Barton Church of England Primary Academy; the beginning of a new chapter in the history of the school. It joined with primary schools at Thurston, Rattlesden and Woolpit to form Thedwastre Education Trust, a multi-academy trust, teaching almost 700 pupils. The schools at Great Barton, Thurston and Rattlesden were CEVC primary schools, whilst Woolpit Primary School was a community primary school, but all four schools shared a common philosophy, which focused on effective teaching. In a statement to the *East Anglian Daily Times*, Sarah Rees stated that, 'The pupils will notice no immediate difference. In the long term, we will be able to benefit from working closely together and sharing resources' (*EADT*, 09 Nov 2015).

Great Barton CE Primary Academy

Rattlesden CE Primary Academy

Thurston CE Primary Academy

Woolpit Primary Academy

SECTION V REFLECTIONS

21
RECURRING ISSUES

The British education system has experienced many radical upheavals since the formation of the 'National Society for Promoting the Education of the Poor in the Principles of the Established Church'. During that time, many of the same educational issues have recurred, in spite of attempts by each generation of politicians, educationalists and other interested parties to resolve them.

Susan Kerry, the first head teacher of Great Barton School, witnessed a huge improvement in the provision of education for working class children. At the time of her birth in 1825, education for poor children was available at a Sunday school, dame school, or one provided by a voluntary society or charity. Teachers were unqualified and pupils were taught to read, mainly using the *Holy Bible* as their textbook. By the time of her death in 1894, every school-age child in England and Wales had the opportunity to receive elementary education in a building of reasonable quality, and to be taught, in most cases, by a qualified head teacher. Elementary education was largely free and consisted of religious instruction, reading, writing and arithmetic, and a widening range of other subjects.

During the late 1890s, Sir John Gorst, the Minister for Education from 1895 to 1902, wanted to introduce further reforms but was frustrated by the problems he faced when he attempted to do so. In an article he wrote in 1896, entitled *'Prospects of Education in England'*, he stated that, 'The chief obstacles to the progress of education in England are party spirit and religious intolerance. Proposals for educational reform are discussed and decided, not in a philosophical spirit, but with all the acrimony of partisans.' (Gorst J.E. *Prospects of Education in England*. North American Review 163. Oct. 1896. pps 427-437).

Educational provision improved significantly during the twentieth and twenty-first centuries, but ideological and religious battles between political parties, and the church and state have continued throughout that time.

Consequently, many of the issues discussed during the 1890s by the Board of Education, the National Union of Teachers (NUT), the Church Teachers' Association (CTA) and the teachers and managers of Great Barton School often reappeared on the agendas of their equivalent organisations during the following 120 years.

A fragmented education system

The British education system has developed in a piecemeal way and has never been a cohesive national scheme. The tenacity of the church to retain control over schools has contributed to the fragmentation of the system.

In July 1833, Mr John Arthur Roebuck, the Whig Member of Parliament (MP) for Bath, tried to introduce a national education system that would offer a non-denominational religious curriculum for the poor, but his motion was withdrawn. From 1833, government funding was channelled through religious societies. The *Education Census of Great Britain* (1851) divided all schools into private and public ones, and subdivided public schools into 4 categories and over 50 subcategories, the majority of which related to different religious denominations.

During the nineteenth century, the National Education Union, supported by members of the Conservative Party and the Church of England, wanted education to be Anglican in nature, whilst the National Education League, supported by members of the Liberal Party and Nonconformists, believed that it should be non-denominational and free from Anglican doctrine. In 1870, religious organisations took advantage of the grants available under the Elementary Education Act 1870 to extend existing schools and build new ones.

By 1900, elementary education in England, Wales and Scotland was provided by 2,500 board schools managed by school boards and attendance committees, and 14,000 voluntary schools administered primarily by the Church of England. In addition, poor law schools, truant and industrial schools, industrial and reformatory schools and day industrial schools were managed separately, and involved several different government departments. In 1901, the Fabian Society published The *Education Muddle and the Way Out*, in which Sidney Webb described the fragmented education system as an inefficient use of government resources.

The Education Act 1902 brought most providers of state-funded education under the control of Local Education Authorities (LEAs), but permitted the churches to retain control of schools.

In 1944, the government eschewed the opportunity to unify the education system and, judging by Great Barton School's experience, diocesan education committees went to some lengths to persuade each existing voluntary school to become a Church of England Voluntary Aided (CEVA) or Church of England Voluntary Controlled (CEVC) school instead of a community one. From 1948, community and church schools coexisted within a dual system.

In 1984, 24.7 per cent of schools in the United Kingdom (UK) were associated with the Church of England and by 2010, over one-third of all state-funded schools were faith schools, including 6,776 Christian schools, and 54 Muslim, Hindu, Jewish or Sikh schools (www. gov. uk/government/publications/maintained-faith-schools). Great Britain was the only western democracy that required collective worship in non-religious publicly funded schools, and the teaching of religious education (RE) in all state-funded schools.

In 2015, primary education was provided by community schools, faith schools (including CEVA, CEVC and RC schools), foundation schools, academies (including faith academies), multi-academies, free schools, state boarding schools (with free tuition, but charges for boarding), pupil referral units and special schools (offering individualised education for students with special educational needs).

This system created problems for LEAs, which were responsible for ensuring that there was sufficient school accommodation for all eligible pupils in their area but had no control over the number of schools under their management.

In 2015, Russell Hobby, the general secretary of the National Association of Head Teachers (NAHT), reiterated the views of Sidney Webb when he stated that, 'We operate in a highly autonomous and fragmented system' (www.bbc.com/news/education-31044929 - 30 Jan. 2015).

The defenders of a fragmented system argue that it offers a choice to parents. However, not all parents have a realistic choice. For example, in Suffolk in 2015, there were 246 local authority maintained schools including 214 primary schools, 4 middle schools, 9 secondary schools, 4 special schools, 14 pupil referral units and 1 nursery school. In addition, there were 75 academies and 6 free schools. However, 43 per cent (93 out of 214) of state-funded, non-academy primary schools were church schools, most of which were the only school in the village.

Inequalities of the British education system

During the 1890s, the Fabian Society and others were concerned about the inequality of the education system that 'favoured the children of wealthier parents, wasted the abilities of working class children, and resulted in economic inequality'. At this time, it was almost impossible for those who did not attend a grammar or private school to gain a higher qualification or obtain employment in one of the more highly paid or influential occupations.

There were a few notable exceptions. James Keir Hardie (1856-1915), a self-educated man who started work at the age of seven, became a Member of Parliament (MP) at the age of forty. He campaigned for an education that was 'free at all stages, open to everyone without any tests of prior attainment at any age' (*Westminster Gazette,* 1 Aug. 1896).

The Education Act 1902 established local authority higher elementary or secondary schools, which enabled some academically gifted, working class pupils to receive a secondary education if they qualified for a place. However, they were only able to take up the offer if they received a scholarship or their parents could afford the school uniform and the other costs involved.

The Education Act 1944 gave all children access to free secondary education at a secondary modern, technical or grammar school, with selection based on an examination at the age of 10 or 11. Pupils who passed were awarded a place at either a state-funded grammar school or a direct grant grammar school, both of which offered an academic education. Very few technical schools were built so the majority of pupils attended a secondary modern school, which offered a more practical curriculum and fewer opportunities to study for those examinations needed to achieve higher paid jobs.

Table 17. Secondary schools in England and Wales, 1964

Type of secondary school	Number of schools
Secondary modern schools	3,906
Grammar schools	1,298
Direct grant grammar schools	179
Technical schools	186
Bi- and Multi-lateral schools	69
Comprehensive schools	195
Other secondary schools	240
All-age schools	411

Source: Statistics of Education 1964 HMSO 1965 p.12

Circular 10/65, issued by the DES in 1965, requested but did not compel LEAs to convert secondary schools into non-selective comprehensive ones.

Some counties retained some of the existing grammar schools but 90 per cent of state secondary schools in England were comprehensive and co-educational by 1975.

Some LEAS provided a two-tier system, within which pupils changed from primary to secondary schools at the age of 11, whilst others organised their schools into a three-tier system in which pupils attended a middle school for three or four years between a primary and a secondary school. Suffolk LEA operated a mixture of the two systems.

The School Standards and Framework Act 1998 prohibited the building of grammar schools and provided the mechanism for their abolition, so that, by 2015, only 164 grammar schools remained. However, in October 2015, the Conservative Government granted permission for a new grammar school site to be opened as an 'annexe', nine miles away from an existing grammar school.

In the UK in 2012, 88 per cent of schoolchildren attended comprehensive schools, 5 per cent grammar schools and 7 per cent independent (private) schools.

In 2014, the Social Mobility and Child Poverty Commission found that a disproportionate number of people in influential jobs had been educated at an independent school.

Table 18. Percentage of people in influential occupations in 2014, educated at an independent school

Occupations	% educated at an independent school
Senior judges	71
Senior armed forces officers	62
Commons select committee chairs	57
Permanent Secretaries	55
Diplomats	53
Newspaper columnists	43
Public body chairs	45
Members of the House of Lords	50

Source : www.gov.uk/government/publications/elitist-britain

In May 2015, 17 per cent of Labour Party MPs and 48 per cent of Conservative Party MPs were educated at independent schools, 19 per cent of all MPs at grammar schools, and 49 per cent at comprehensive schools (Sutton Trust analysis).

The subject of comprehensive schools remains controversial and it is highly likely that the current policy will be overturned in the future.

Disparity of educational funding

In 1901, Sidney Webb wrote that, 'An excellent system of education is one of the best forms of public investment'. Few people would disagree with this statement but this investment has always been distributed unevenly amongst state-funded schools in the UK. In 1850, an education return, which compared 60 of the best schools in various counties, reported that the average annual amount per school spent on books was £10. 2s. 8d in Surrey, compared with £3. 1s. in Suffolk.

During the nineteenth century, voluntary schools were funded less well than board schools, and the Education Act 1902 tried to address this issue by increasing funding for voluntary schools.

The proportion of government income spent on education rose from 5.9 per cent in 1901 to 7.7 per cent in 1950 and 13.3 per cent in 2010, although not all schools benefited equally.

Governments used various formulae to determine school budgets and, during the twenty-first century, the Dedicated School Grant was dependent on the characteristics of a school and the number of pupils eligible for a free school meal.

In 2011, the Department for Education (DfE) published its report entitled *Consultation on School Funding Reform: Proposals for a Fairer System*, which stated that, 'it is almost impossible to explain why a particular school receives the budget that it does.'

According to figures on school funding during the 2013 to 2014 financial year, produced by the DfE, the funding per pupil ranged from £7,800 in Southwark to £3,885 in Suffolk and £3,591 in Cambridgeshire. In 2015, the government allocated an additional £390 million to boost school budgets in 69 of the worst funded areas of the country, but the disparity continued with the average spend per pupil being £6,858 in Tower Hamlets and £3,718 in Cambridgeshire.

In 2015, schools received a pupil premium to provide additional financial support for poorer pupils, but the Public Accounts Committee stated that, 'some schools received about £3,000 a year more than others per disadvantaged pupil' (www.bbc.com/news/education-34476163 - 9 Oct. 2015). In October 2015, 111 MPs called for the implementation of a new national funding formula to reduce the level of inequality (http://www.f40.org.uk/news/111-mps-petition-prime-minister - 23 Oct. 2015).

Recruitment of qualified teachers

In 1839, the Committee of the Privy Council on Education made provision for teacher training schools known as 'normal' schools, the first of which was set up at Battersea in 1840 and was subsequently attended by two future head teachers of Great Barton School.

In 1846, the Committee of the Privy Council on Education offered teachers financial incentives for the training of pupil-teachers.

In 1870, the government lowered the pass standard and allowed students to qualify after only one year at a teacher training college. HMI were permitted to recommend experienced teachers for a teaching certificate even if, like Susan Kerry, they had received no formal training.

By 1895, there were 53,000 qualified teachers in England and Wales, but an increasing number of unqualified teachers, many of whom were employed in small rural voluntary schools.

The Census of England and Wales 1901 recorded that there were nearly a quarter of a million qualified and unqualified teachers, of whom nearly three-quarters were female.

To cope with the teacher shortage at the end of the Second World War, the Fleming Report (1944) recommended the setting up of emergency teacher training colleges to recruit ex-service personnel. The scheme was limited at first but was opened up in 1945 to all men and women who had served in HM Forces for at least one year. By December 1947, 55 emergency colleges offered a one-year crash course of intensive study, often with a grant, and by the time the programme finished in 1951, 35,000 additional qualified teachers had been trained.

After the Second World War, state schools were expected to employ certificated staff, and the rules for enabling existing teachers to qualify were relaxed. By 1953, there were only 2,000 uncertificated teachers in the country.

After 2010, free schools and academies were permitted to employ non-qualified staff. In 2012, there were 24,372 schools in England, attended by 8.2 million pupils including 4.2 million primary pupils. In 2013, according to the DfE, 400,000 children in state-funded schools were taught by 17,100 unqualified teachers, which accounted for almost 3.7 per cent of the total teaching force.

In 2015, the DfE launched a TV advertising campaign to recruit 35,000 new teachers a year (www.bbc.com/news/education-34647833 - 28 Oct. 2015).

Retention of teachers

During the nineteenth century, excessive demands and rigidity of the school curriculum, the irregularity of pupil attendance, the insufficiency of staff, long hours, excessive paperwork and school inspections were cited as reasons for the failure to recruit and retain teachers. In 1890, teachers complained about the amount of additional paperwork associated with recording pupil attendance and producing Labour Certificates. Head teachers were expected to train pupil-teachers before and after school and undertake voluntary work in the village outside school hours.

In the twenty-first century, constant changes to the school curriculum, excessive paperwork, long hours and school inspections were all factors given as reasons why teachers chose to leave the profession.

In 2014, the Teaching and Learning International Survey found that the average number of hours worked by all teachers in England was 52 hours per week, compared with 32 hours per week in Finland and 29 hours per week in Italy.

In 2000, research carried out by the Health and Safety Executive (HSE) found that teaching was the most stressful profession in the UK, with 41.5 per cent of teachers reporting themselves as 'highly stressed' (The Scale of Occupational Stress HSE, 2000). The seriousness of stress cannot be underestimated, since it is recognised as a cause of cardiovascular issues, diabetes, cancer and many other life-threatening and life-changing conditions.

School inspections have always been one cause of stress. In 1886, when John Dorling, the head teacher of Great Barton School, took his own life, the report of his inquest mentioned his concern about a forthcoming inspection as a contributory factor.

Since 1998, coroners' inquests into the suicides of teachers revealed that eight of them took their lives shortly before or after Ofsted inspections. Between 2003 and 2013, 35 to 63 teachers killed themselves each year and, in 2013, the suicide rate of teachers was one-third higher than the national average.

Between 2014 and 2015, 17,000 new graduates were trained in England, but 18,000 teachers left the UK in order to teach overseas. In 2016, 100,000 teachers who had trained in the UK were employed in British International Schools. To alleviate the shortage within the UK, supply agencies recruited qualified teachers from Canada, Australia, New Zealand, South Africa, Jamaica and the Irish Republic.

In 2015, nearly 40 per cent of newly qualified teachers left teaching after one year, and there were 2,000 unfilled places in teacher training colleges in September 2015.

According to an analysis of statistics produced by the DfE, the number of teachers who completed their training but did not enter the teaching profession rose from 3,600 in 2006 to 10,800 in 2011 (The Independent, 31 March 2015).

School discipline

During the 1890s, some MPs suggested that there should be national guidelines on the management of pupil behaviour. These were never drawn up but schools were required to record details of corporal punishment from the early twentieth century. The use of corporal punishment was permitted by law until 1986, but its use was controversial and as its use declined, schools devised alternative systems of rewards and punishments.

Following the Elton Report (1989), entitled *Discipline in Schools*, which enquired into the state of school discipline in England and Wales, schools were required to produce a behaviour policy.

In January 2014, Sir Michael Wilshaw, the Ofsted chief inspector, stated that many new recruits were quitting the classroom because they were inadequately prepared for dealing with unruly pupils (*The Guardian*, 15 Jan. 2014). In 2015, poor pupil behaviour cost an average of 38 days of learning time so the government appointed a discipline tsar to head a task force to improve teacher training on classroom behaviour in England.

The purpose of education

There has always been a wide diversity of opinions about the purpose of education.

During the nineteenth century, the teaching of literacy and religion were the main objectives for the education of the poor. In contrast, John Sleath (1767-1847), High Master of St Paul's School, London, from 1814 to 1837, told the parents of his pupils that, 'If you want your boy to learn anything else [apart from grammar and the classics] you must have him taught at home and. for that purpose, we give him three half-holidays a week' (BBC History Magazine June 2015. *Schools of Hard Knocks*. David Turner).

A more modern view was expressed by Dr Elizabeth Garrett Anderson in 1880, when she stated in a speech to the Social Science Association that the use of education is as 'much to fit a child for acquiring future knowledge as to furnish him with facts, which he may soon cease to remember' (*BFP*, 15 May 1880).

By the end of the nineteenth century, preparation for future employment was also seen as a purpose of education and the school curriculum included vocational subjects such as gardening and domestic subjects as well as reading, writing, arithmetic, geography, history, science, PE, art, craft, music and RE.

During the next 70 years, some teachers in elementary schools based their teaching on a belief that primary education should be aimed at the training of pupils to pass the scholarship examination at the age of 11.

In 2016, primary schools in England were measured by their performance data based on their pupils' results in the tests at the end of year 6. Consequently, one of the objectives of primary teaching in 2016 was to ensure that pupils performed well in these tests.

The debate about the purpose of education is an ongoing issue and there will inevitably be a wide diversity of opinion on the subject.

For several decades, schools have been required to agree the aims and objectives of their school and to publish them.

The curriculum

The education codes of the nineteenth century regulated what subjects were to be taught. However, as a consequence of the system of payment by results, introduced in 1862, which linked school finances to test results, schools often taught religion and the three Rs to the exclusion of other subjects, in order to secure the highest school grant. Even within literacy and numeracy lessons, the curriculum was further narrowed whenever teachers taught to the test.

During the twentieth century, primary schools were increasingly able to determine the details of their own curriculum within certain parameters, but this risked a lack of continuity and created problems for pupils who changed from one primary school to another.

National Curriculum 5-16 laid down exactly what was to be taught and Melissa Benn commented in *School Wars, The Battle for Britain's Education* that, 'some noted an uncanny similarity between the 1988 curriculum and that of the syllabus of 1904'. The contents of the National Curriculum have continued to be debated, and have been subject to several revisions since 1988.

From 2012, there were increasing demands by the government for the collection of data and evidence, which again risked squeezing out those parts of the curriculum that did not produce measurable units of progress.

During the nineteenth century, the government aimed to regulate how lessons were taught.

Consequently, in 1888, the National Union of Teachers submitted a petition to parliament, which requested that the government should allow teachers to use 'the most intelligent methods of teaching'.

Since then, pedagogy, the method and practice of teaching, has been in a continuous state of experimentation, and many alternative curricula, teaching methods and testing regimes have been introduced, sometimes without adequate trials or evidence of their effectiveness.

The Primary School (1931) recommended a child-centred approach to learning, collaborative learning, the adoption of the 'project' approach to teaching, and learning by activity and experience. It advocated the appropriate use of 'look and say', phonics, and sentence methods for teaching children to read, and urged that children should be encouraged to express themselves freely in writing.

Many of these ideas were reiterated in the Plowden Report (1967), entitled *Children and their Primary Schools*, which influenced much of the teaching for the next 30 years.

The National Literacy and Numeracy Strategies, introduced during the 1990s, reduced the opportunity for innovation and flexibility, but the Education Act 2002 gave certain schools greater autonomy to implement innovative teaching methods.

New technology has had a significant impact on teaching methods during the twenty-first century, but its efficacy has yet to be proven.

Infant education

Infant education was first included in the Education Code 1871. Since that time, educationalists have debated whether infant education should be an academic or a practical, play-based one.

In 1893, the Education Department issued a circular to HMIs on the *Training and Teaching of Infants (1893),* which recommended the wider use of kindergarten methods. In 1905, five of the recently appointed women HMIs conducted an inquiry into infant education. Their report concluded that children aged between three and five did not benefit from school, and that mechanical teaching dulled their imagination and weakened their powers of independent observation.

Infant and Nursery Schools (1933) supported the idea that children learn from their surroundings. It favoured an 'open air environment' with semi-open-air buildings and garden playgrounds.

The level and quality of pre-school provision improved after the Second World War and young children who attended a nursery school or playgroup had the opportunity to learn through play and develop at their own pace under the supervision of trained staff.

The Plowden Report (1967) expounded the importance of play activities and of early year's education.

The Childcare Act 2006 introduced the Early Years Foundation Stage for nought to five-year-olds.

From 2008, five-year-olds were assessed against the Early Years Foundation Stage Profile (EYFSP) to ascertain what level they had achieved in certain areas and the results were published. This profile put pressure on staff in pre-schools and nurseries to increase the amount of academic teaching at the expense of play activities.

In 2013, only 49 per cent of five-year-olds in Suffolk reached the required levels in the EYFSP, and Suffolk's schools were amongst the lowest achieving schools in the country.

In response, Suffolk County Council introduced Raising the Bar, a school improvement strategy to raise achievements by supporting schools and publicly rewarding success. By 2015, the percentage of five-year-olds in Suffolk who reached the required levels in the EYFSP was 67.6 per cent, which was above the national average of 66.3 per cent.

The gender gap

Pupils

HMI reports during the nineteenth century stated that, in spite of the fact that girls spent most afternoons studying needlework, more girls than boys were proficient readers.

In 1876, girls in the Bury St Edmunds area out-performed boys in the Prize Scheme Examinations organised by the National Society.

During the 1990s, the results of the reading tests at Great Barton School indicated the underperformance of boys, so the school, in common with many others, implemented strategies to improve the reading standards of boys.

In 2012, national research revealed that 'boys were almost twice as likely as girls to fail basic reading tests.' (*The Telegraph*, 20 Sep. 2012).

Between 2013 and 2015, the EYFSP results for five-year-olds revealed that girls in English schools outperformed boys in all of the early learning goals, but especially in writing. The gender gap continued throughout each key stage and was evident in the GCSE results for 2013 to 2015.

In 2016, the results of the new key stage 2 assessments, introduced in 2014, showed that 57% of girls achieved the expected standard in reading, writing and mathematics compared to 50% of boys.

Teachers

In 1938, only 29 per cent of all teachers were male, in spite of the fact that married women were forbidden to teach in most areas.

In 1967, the Plowden Report identified the need to employ more male members of staff and the problem was still apparent nearly 50 years later, when the Training and Development Agency emphasised not only the difference that teachers can make to the lives of students, but also the rewards of a good salary and career path, as those incentives were a higher priority for men.

In 2010, 25 per cent of all teachers were male, and the shortage was especially noticeable in the primary sector, where men comprised only 12 per cent of the workforce. 25 per cent of all primary schools had no male teachers (http://data.worldbank.org/indicator/SE.PRM.TCHR.FE.ZS).

The percentage of female head teachers fell from 57 per cent in 1927 to 38 per cent in 1976, but gradually increased to 63 per cent in 2010 (*TES*, 30 March 2011).

By 2013, in spite of this increase and the fact that equal rates of pay for men and women had been in place since 1955, the average pay for all qualified teaching staff was £39,900 for men and £36,600 for women (http://www.sec-ed.co.uk/news/school-workforce-suffers-gender-inequality-lower-wages-and-fewer-teachers - 9 May 2013).

Pupil attendance

Teachers have always been concerned about pupils with irregular school attendance.

In Suffolk during the 1890s, teachers blamed non-attendance on a lack of support from parents who allowed their children to work in paid employment, and on the ineffectiveness of school boards.

Great Barton School presented awards from 1874 onwards and Suffolk County Council awarded good attendance certificates from the 1900s.

In 1958, the school managers of Great Barton School identified an added complication when they expressed their concern about the fact that parents were taking their children on holiday during term-time to take advantage of cheaper travel and holiday costs.

Until 2013, head teachers were empowered to grant up to 10 days' leave in exceptional circumstances, which included illness, bereavement or bad weather. Although it did not include family holidays, these were often authorised, and almost 5 million school days were missed because of family holidays during the academic year 2011 to 2012.

The *Education (Pupil Registration) (England) Regulations* (2006), which came into force in September 2013, tightened up the guidelines and obliged local authorities to impose a fine on parents whose child was absent from school without the school's authorisation.

Small schools and federation

In 1888, members of the NUT submitted a parliamentary petition, requesting additional pecuniary help for small schools to enable them to provide an efficient staff and suitable school appliances (*BNP*, 21 Aug. 1888).

In 1893, a questionnaire was sent to the teachers and managers in the Great Barton area seeking their views on a proposal to federate small schools. The idea was overwhelmingly supported but never implemented, although the Bury St Edmunds branch of the NUT set up a branch of the Confederation of Rural Teachers in 1893 to address the concerns of small rural schools (*BNP*, 6 June 1894).

In 1896, an Education Bill included a proposal to federate voluntary schools into associations, each of which would be eligible to receive a lump sum from a Special Aid Grant Fund, but the bill was rejected.

The Education Act 2002 allowed schools to federate and suggested a range of models, which would enable schools to share teachers, governance, resources and expertise.

To improve the viability of small schools, Suffolk Education Authority encouraged federation of small schools, some of which found it difficult to attract or afford head teachers.

The Academies Act 2010 stated that schools, which chose to federate, were eligible to receive a start-up government grant to help with the costs of converting, on condition that they chose to become an academy or multi-academy trust.

More than 120 years after the original proposal to federate, Great Barton Primary School was still concerned about the school's viability. In order to safeguard its future, it joined with the primary schools at Woolpit, Rattlesden and Thurston to form Thedwastre Education Trust, a multi academy trust.

Afterword

Despite all the educational legislation, regulations and reports, and the countless hours of discussions and debates, it would appear that there is no single solution to the issue of how to educate children in Britain; just a wide range of alternatives and adaptations in an ever-changing world.

Until education policy is based on well-researched evidence, rather than political ideology, the education system will be subjected to new policies each time a new government is elected. Consequently, many of these recurring issues may never be resolved.

Great Barton School has progressed a long way from its humble beginnings as a Victorian, one-roomed, elementary school. It will continue to evolve and, as with all histories, there is no ending but only the place where this story ends.

HEADTEACHERS OF GREAT BARTON SCHOOL SINCE 1846

NAME (birth-death)	DATE OF EMPLOYMENT
GREAT BARTON GIRLS' SCHOOL	
Susan Kerry (1825-1894)	1846-1891
Emma Daine (1864-1947)	1892-1916
Florence Pickworth (1884-1953)	1917- 1918
GREAT BARTON BOYS' SCHOOL	
William George Plummer (1812-1886)	c.1857- c.1871
James Handley (1850-?)	c.1871- 1874
John Dorling (1837-1886)	1874-1886
James Daine (1864-1910)	1886-1893
James Killick (1860-1922)	1893-1897
Robert Evans (1857-1932)	1897-1918
GREAT BARTON MIXED SCHOOL	
Robert Evans (1857-1932)	1918-1922
Cecil Frank Channell (1894-1951)	1923-1933
Ernest Edmund Reed (1889-1949)	1933-1949
Elsie Evelyn Carter (1897-1997)	1950-1960
Rene (Ron) Ceurstemont (1918-2000)	1960-1978
John Dawkins	1978-1990
Sue Spiller (1946-)	1990-2004
Sarah Rees	2004-

SUSANNA (SUSAN) KERRY (1825-1894)

Susan Kerry [364] taught at Great Barton School from 1846 until 1891 and was the longest serving head teacher in its history.

She was born in Bury St Edmunds on 2 May 1825 to Elizabeth and Thomas Kerry, and christened 'Susanna Kerry' at St Mary's Church, Bury St Edmunds. She had at least three brothers. Charles became a carpenter and William and Frederick became bricklayers, like their father. Her sister, Elizabeth Louisa, worked as a servant when she left school, married Henry Parish a gamekeeper, and moved to Halstead, Essex, where she brought up seven children.

According to the government report of 1833 and *Pigot's Directory* of 1830, Bury St Edmunds was well served with schools. These included a Lancasterian School for boys in College Street, several charity or free schools, at least 20 privately run day and boarding schools, an infants' school, and two Central Schools run by the National Society. The nearest school to Susan Kerry's home at 68 Field Court was the Central School for Girls in Elephant Court, near the Theatre Royal, which was a 'normal' school, authorised to train teachers.

In 1841, Susan was employed as one of three servants of Hester and Elizabeth Bloomfield, who lived on Angel Hill, Bury St Edmunds.

From the age of 21, she worked at Great Barton School as an unqualified teacher (Article 50) but in 1875, applied to the Education Department for a teaching certificate under Article 59.

She taught at Holy Innocents' Sunday School, Great Barton, and helped to set up the local branch of the Diocesan Sunday School Society in 1883.

At first, she lodged in Barton Hall, whilst Sir Henry, his wife and niece stayed at Alverbank House at Gosport in Hampshire. By 1861, she had moved to Carpenters House in School Lane, and by 1871 into the Girls' Schoolhouse, a five-roomed cottage in School Lane, where she lived for the remainder of her life. At Easter 1881, she was staying at Wokingham, Berkshire, with Cecilia Bunbury, the widow of Henry William St Pierre Bunbury.

Susan never married and had a greater degree of independence as a single woman than as a married one, who had no separate legal identity until the passing of the Married Women's Property Act 1870, which allowed women to retain their own wages and inherit property.

Susan retired in December 1891 at the age of 67, but superannuation legislation, campaigned for by the National Union of Teachers, was not passed until 1892 so she would not have received any pension.

She died in November 1894 from abdominal dropsy, and was buried in the churchyard at Holy Innocents' Church, Great Barton. Her death certificate was witnessed by Susanna Rolfe [755] her neighbour, who lived in Great Barton until her death in 1933 at the age of 95.

WILLIAM GEORGE PLUMMER (1812-1886)

William Plummer [246] was the first headmaster of Great Barton Boys' School. According to the population census, he was born in Central Africa and was a British subject.

His father, who was a soldier, died when William was very young and his mother, Mary (1782-1874), who came from Great Livermere, married James Sturgeon (1771-1836) in 1821. They lived in Great Barton and had three more sons, but James died in 1836 leaving Mary as a widow for a second time.

In 1840, William lived in Bury St Edmunds at 1 Field Lane, Turkey Court, in the parish of St Mary and worked as a tailor. On 20 June 1840, he married Ann Gibson Long (1818-1890), the daughter of a Great Barton farm labourer, who was a servant at the time of her marriage, living at 4 Eastgate Street in the adjacent parish of St James. Ann and William were not married in either St James' Church or St Mary's Church, but in the Superintendent's Office in Bury St Edmunds, where the ceremony was conducted by Frederick Wing, the Superintendent Registrar, and witnessed by Marianne Feakes and William White, both of whom were from Great Barton.

Under the Marriage Act 1753, the only legally recognised marriages in England and Wales were those performed by the Church of England, the Quakers or under Jewish law. However, the Marriage Act 1836 legalised civil marriages in England and Wales and allowed Nonconformist and Roman Catholic ministers to act as registrars and conduct civil marriage ceremonies in local registry offices after 1 July 1837. The first couple to be married at the Superintendent's Office in Bury St Edmunds went to the Baptist Chapel after the ceremony for their union to be blessed by the Revd Elven, a Baptist minister, and it is possible that William and Ann had done something similar.

In 1841, William worked as an agricultural labourer and he and Ann lived in a cottage at Cattishall, Great Barton, with two of his stepbrothers and his mother, who was described in the 1841 population census as 'independent'. In 1851, William and Ann had four children and lived in a cottage at Conyers Green with William's mother and one of the stepbrothers. The 1851 population census described both William and his mother as paupers. William's fortune changed during the 1850s when he was appointed as headmaster of Great Barton Boys' School. He and his family moved into the Boys' Schoolhouse and his mother moved into one of the widows' homes and worked as a charwoman until her death at the age of 84.

William taught at Great Barton Boys' School for about ten years and was described by Sir Charles Bunbury as 'an excellent man' (*BNP* 28

Jan.1862). The Revd Harry Jones, Vicar of Great Barton from 1882 to 1886, interviewed William after retirement and wrote about him in *Dead Leaves and Living Seed*. William Plummer was apparently bed-ridden, and the Revd Harry Jones wrote of 'our old pensioned schoolmaster, a cripple' who 'had beaten most Barton men in their youth'. He went on to write that, 'when provided with a paper block and pencil, so he could write his recollections in bed, it was apparent that William Plummer had never learned to write properly' and 'was as slow at writing as he was at running' (*BNP*, 11 June 1895).

William was described as a 'pensioned schoolmaster', so he may have subscribed to Barton Friendly Society, which provided financial and social services to individuals, or have been eligible for a small income from the West Suffolk Benevolent Institution.

William died on 18 February 1886 from renal disease and exhaustion, and Ann [297] died four years later. They were both buried in the churchyard at Holy Innocents' Church, Great Barton.

The children of William and Ann Plummer
William George Jnr, (1842-?) worked as an agricultural labourer at the age of eight. He was caught poaching at the age of 19 and found guilty of using snares for taking game. As it was his first offence and Sir Charles Bunbury interceded on his behalf, he was fined 1s. with 8s. costs and given a caution (*BNP*, 28 Jun. 1862).

Frederick George (1845-1917) worked as a gardener for most of his life. In 1864, he married Elizabeth Ollington, from Brettenham, Suffolk, and their first daughter, Catherine, was born in Great Barton. They subsequently lived at Whelnetham and Bacton in Suffolk, and then Romford in Essex, where they spent the remainder of their lives and brought up nine children.

Eliza Ann (1847-1920) worked as a housemaid at Fornham All Saints in the household of John Jackson, a retired solicitor. She married Frederick Sturgeon, a farm labourer, and they lived in Ingham for 20 years and then in a three-roomed cottage at East Barton. George (1881-1951), the eldest of their eight children, was blind from childhood and worked as a basket maker at the age of 20 and as a tea agent at the age of 30.

Walter George (1854-?) gave evidence in a court case in 1869, in which he claimed that he had seen Robert Soames, a carpenter, stealing wood from Charles Rolfe, another carpenter, for use as firewood (*BNP*, 13 Apr. 1869). Walter joined the army for a short time, but was unemployed and living at home by 1881.

Sarah Ann Caroline (1858-1940) worked for the Revd Thomas Godfrey Law Lushington (1851-1928), who had stayed at Great Barton Vicarage in 1881. She worked as a parlour maid at the Vicarage at Swavesey, Cambridgeshire, in 1891, at Sittingbourne, Kent, in 1901, and as a lady's maid to his sister at Maidstone, Kent, in 1911. She died in Romford, Essex.

JOHN DORLING (1837-1886)

John Dorling, the headmaster of Great Barton Boys' School from 1874 to 1886, was born and brought up in Bury St Edmunds, where generations of his family had lived for 200 years.

He lived in Raingate Street, Bury St Edmunds, and attended a local school until the age of 14. His father, Bilby Dorling (1795-1879), was a journeyman tailor, who was descended from generations of tanners and dyers. Bilby Dorling married Sarah Chapman (1808-1885) from Wickhambrook, Suffolk, on 10 October 1826 at St James's Church, Bury St Edmunds, and they had eight children, four of whom became schoolteachers, as did some of their grandchildren.

John became a teacher in 1856, at the age of 19, and four years later married Charlotte King (1832-1912). She was a young widow, living in Cambridge, who was born in Melton Mowbray, Leicestershire, and was the daughter of Catherine and Richard Whitchurch, a grazier. Charlotte and John were married in the church of St Peter and Paul, Bardwell, the village where John was the schoolmaster of the local school. Charlotte was appointed as the schoolmistress of Bardwell School and they lived in Bardwell Schoolhouse.

John was one of the founder members of the local branch of the Church Teachers' Association (CTA), set up in 1871 at Fornham St Martin, Suffolk, and was an active member. In 1873 and 1874, Bardwell School received a good inspection report, and many of its pupils were successful in the Prize Scheme Examination organised by the National Society to encourage pupils to study the Bible. He was clearly a religious man and keen to improve his own education. In 1873, whilst at Bardwell School, he took an examination in divinity and received a second-class award with 175 marks out of 300. He took a further examination in divinity in 1875, but was not judged 'sufficiently advanced in preparation' until 1876 when he received his certificate with honours, signed by the Bishop of Ely.

At Bardwell, John and Charlotte appear to have been popular and well-respected teachers, but were obliged to leave Bardwell School in 1874 when Charlotte, who was losing her hearing, was described as being 'quite incapable of performing her share of school duties'. Their leaving presents from the managers and parents included an 'electro-plated tea and coffee pot, a sugar basin, a cream jug, a handsome walnut table and two gold pencil cases' (*BNP* Oct. 1874).

After John's appointment as the headmaster of Great Barton Boys' School, he and Charlotte moved into the Boys' Schoolhouse. John took an active role in village life and played the church organ. He continued to be active in the CTA and acted the role of Bernardo in a CTA performance of *Hamlet*, held at Badwell Ash School (*BNP*, 10 Feb. 1885).

In 1884, the local branch of the CTA sent a questionnaire to all of its members, the results of which showed that many of them were suffering from stress (*BNP*, 20 Jun. 1885). Pressure arising from school inspections by Her Majesty's Inspectorate) was cited as one of the causes.

Tragically, on 30 April 1886, John Dorling committed suicide, whilst in a state of temporary insanity, by cutting his throat with a razor' (*BNP*, 4 May 1886).

DISTRESSING SUICIDE AT GREAT BARTON
(Bury and Norwich Post, 4 May 1886)

On Friday last, Mr. John Dorling, schoolmaster, Great Barton, committed suicide by cutting his throat in the private grounds at Great Barton, under somewhat distressing circumstances. It appears that the deceased, who is between 40 and 50 years of age, had been suffering from sleeplessness, caused, it is supposed, from over-anxiety as to the government examination of his school, which will shortly take place. He had been attended by Dr Henry, of Bury St. Edmund's, but it was never suspected that he was at all likely to commit such a rash act as that which terminated his life. On Friday morning, Dorling went to the stables at the Hall, and told Thomas Strait he should like to go for a drive with him if he were going out. As Strait was not going out then he promised to give him a drive in the afternoon. The parties then walked to the home farm, where they parted, the deceased proceeding towards home by the Navarrino Road. He was not seen again until six o'clock, when he was discovered in the plantation, dead, with his throat cut. By his side was a razor, and he had a razor case in his pocket. An inquest was held at the Crown beer house, Great Barton, on Saturday afternoon, before Mr. R. H. Wilson, coroner for the liberty of Bury St. Edmunds, and a jury of which Mr. J. S. Phillips was chosen foreman.

Thomas Strait, coachman, deposed: I last saw the deceased alive yesterday morning about half-past nine, when I was with him near the home farm. About a quarter-past nine, he came into the stables, and asked me if I was going for a drive, and would I take him. I told him I was not going. He then walked from the stables to the farm with me. I thought he was not looking quite so well as usual, and told him so, but I cannot remember what he said in reply. I promised to give him a drive later in the day, and afterwards sent round to his house, but the deceased's wife thought he had gone to Bury. When I saw the deceased I thought he seemed more "flighty" than usual, but there was nothing which led me to suppose that there was anything wrong with him; the place where I left him was about five minutes' walk from where he was found. On the way to the farm, we passed a well where a man was drowned, and the deceased turned and looked at it. I did not think anything about that at the time. I have known the deceased for many years; I don't think he suffered from depression of spirits, but I think he was rather excitable. —

The Coroner: You never thought he would have committed suicide.

Witness: Not at all; that was the last thing I would have thought.

Mr Scott: He did not say he would wait for you until you came out of my house?

Witness: No, he said he would walk home the other way, as it would be a change. That would be the Navarrino Road, where he was found. He went in that direction.

Albert Clutterham, a boy 14 years of age, deposed: About six o'clock last evening, I was returning from the post by the Navarrino Road, and went into the plantation. I there saw the deceased lying face downwards: about 10 or 12 yards from the road. I thought he was "shamming "to be dead and I came out of the plantation. I went to my master's house and told Harry Hunt. We both went back and saw the body, but did not go near it. We did not know who it was. We then went and told P.C. Peake. We returned with him to the place. I did not see that the man had his throat cut.

P.C. Peace deposed: About a quarter to seven last night, the last witness came to my house, and I went with him to the plantation. I there found the deceased lying face downwards, his face being embedded in leaves and moulds. His hat was on the back of his head, his left arm was under him across his breast, and his right arm was by his side. On his right hand was some blood, and close to his hand was an open razor. I turned him over, and found his throat badly cut. He was dead, but his breast was still warm, and his arms and legs were limpid. I have been told there has been insanity in the deceased's family.

Dr G. F. Henry, Bury St. Edmund's, deposed: I have lately been treating the deceased, and he last came to my surgery on Tuesday. He has been suffering from sleeplessness; I had previously attended him for the same thing. I think it arose from anxiety with regard to the coming school examination. He spoke to me about the examination, and his anxieties that it should it pass off satisfactorily. I made an external examination of the body, and found a wound six inches long in the neck, extending as far as the ear upon the right side. I found no other marks of violence, and I think the wound might have been self-inflicted. The wound was not sufficient to cause death. I have seen a much larger wound, which did not cause death for two hours. There was a wound of the common carotid artery, and death was caused by loss of blood. The deceased was a very nervous man, and rather disposed to magnify his ailments. I have heard from his sister that there was insanity in the family - a sister having been insane; but the deceased never mentioned the subject. He used to complain of his head and muscular twitching of the eyebrows.

The Coroner having summed up, the jury returned a verdict that the deceased committed suicide whilst suffering from temporary insanity.

His obituary in the *Bury Free Press* stated that,

'The deceased possessed an amiable deposition, and was very greatly esteemed by those who knew him. He had been a schoolmaster for the long period of 30 years, and was very much respected and beloved by his pupils, in who took quite a fatherly interest, and his good influence over them will not soon pass away, and many of them will keep his memory green. It may truly be said of him, "his works will follow him." He was kind, loving, and affectionate husband, and his home was very happy one. He is gone to his reward, and will greatly be missed' (BFP, 8 May 1886).

John Dorling left a personal estate of £98. 2s. 9d. to his wife, Charlotte, who moved into a cottage next door to Great Barton Post Office. Ten years after the death of her husband, Charlotte visited a neighbour's house to inquire after the health of 81-year-old Hannah Wright and discovered the dying body of Hannah's daughter, Eliza, who had committed suicide in the kitchen (*BFP*, 16 May 1896).

During the 1900s, Charlotte moved into a three-roomed house at 79, Southgate Street, Bury St Edmunds, near her sister-in-law, Emma. In 1912, she died childless and bequeathed her estate, valued at £43, to Lita Jarratt (1856-1918), an American professional musician and vocalist who lived in Lambeth, South London, and was married to Arthur Frank Jarratt (1848-?), the composer of the music for *Action Songs for Infant Schools*, published in 1885.

The sisters of John Dorling, who became teachers

Emma (1833-1918) taught at Hepworth School, Suffolk, but gave up work after her marriage in December 1861 to Wilson Rainbird (1841-1911) from Hepworth, who worked as a domestic gardener, thatcher and rough carpenter. They moved to Southgate Street, Bury St Edmunds, and had nine children, the youngest of whom became a schoolteacher.

Jemima (1842-1919) taught at Hessett National School, Suffolk, from 1874. Two years later, she married Frederick Cornish from Rougham, who was a coal-merchant, had three children and continued to teach at Hessett until the 1880s when she and Frederick moved to Combs Hall near Stowmarket, Suffolk, where Frederick was employed as a farm steward. They later moved into a six-roomed house in Lime Tree Place, Stowmarket, where Frederick worked in the cordite factory as a night watchman and then as a labourer. Their eldest daughter, Evelyn, became a schoolteacher.

Eleanor (1845-1919) trained as a schoolteacher at the Central School for Girls in Bury St Edmunds. In 1870, she married Frederick Brooke, who was also a schoolteacher, and she and Frederick taught at Bocking School, Essex, and had four children, and then at Hemsby School, Norfolk, where they had four more children. Eleanor continued to teach until the 1890s. Her husband suffered from cerebral paralysis and died in 1901 leaving her to bring up the three youngest children who were still living at home.

JAMES DAINE (1864-1910) AND EMMA DAINE (1863-1947)

James Daine [530] was the headmaster of Great Barton Boys' School from 1886 until 1894. His wife, Emma (née Harris), was the headmistress of Great Barton Girls' School from 1891 until 1916.

James was born at Barton-upon-Irwell, near Manchester. His mother, Emma Daine (née Hesketh), was a dressmaker. His father, Strethill Daine, was employed at various times as a labourer in a timber yard, a cowman, a farm labourer and a gardener. James, the oldest of ten children, was a pupil-teacher before qualifying as a certificated teacher.

Emma Harris was born on 15 January 1863 at Ordnance Place, Chatham, Kent. Her father, George Henry Harris, joined the Royal Marines in 1849 and rose to the rank of sergeant. In 1851, her mother, Ann Ward, was working as a servant at the Royal Marine barracks. In 1861, George, Ann and their three children lived at New Street, Chatham, together with a 48-year-old Greenwich Pensioner who lodged with them. George left the Royal Marines soon after the birth of Emma, their fourth child, and worked on the railways as a ticket collector. In 1871, George and Ann lived in Otway Terrace, Chatham, with 15-year-old Agnes and five-year-old Rose. Eight-year-old Emma lived in Frimley, Surrey, with her 20-year-old sister, Cordelia, who was a certificated teacher in a national school, and Emma was a pupil-monitor. Following the death of their father during the 1870s, Rose lived at home with her mother and worked as a dressmaker. After Rose left home, Cordelia who was teaching at a school in Kingston, Surrey, moved back home with her mother. They took in a lodger, Nellie Jackson, another schoolteacher.

In 1881, Emma studied at Bishop Stortford, Hertfordshire, at the Hockerill Training School for Mistresses, founded in 1852 by the Rochester Diocesan Institute for the Training of Schoolmistresses. The college was attended by 60 students, aged 18 to 22, all of whom had been recommended by their local clergyman and had passed a written examination conducted by a clergyman. Students undertook a probationary period of six weeks before embarking on a two-year training course, and were taught by governesses, who had themselves trained at Hockerill Training School. Pupils were instructed in arithmetic, grammar, history, geography and basic needlework, and were expected to improve their knowledge of reading and writing by themselves. In 1885, science was added to the school curriculum. Teaching practice took place on the same site as the college in one of two 'practising schools' and criticism lessons were held in the training room.

Sir James Kay-Shuttleworth, the Assistant Secretary of the Committee of the Privy Council on Education from 1839 to 1849, advocated that England's teachers should not suffer from 'intellectual pride, assumption of superiority, and selfish ambition'. Consequently, the Hockerill students, along with their contemporaries in other colleges, set and cleared away their own meals, washed dishes, did the laundry, dusted, polished, and swept the floors.

James Daine taught at St James Elementary School, Bury St Edmunds, until his appointment as head master of Great Barton Boys' School in 1886. On 22 August 1887, his marriage to Emma at St Paul's Church, Chatham, was witnessed by her sister Rose and brother George. Emma moved into the Boys' Schoolhouse with James and, in 1888, gave birth to their only child, George Harris Strethill Daine. When Susan Kerry retired in December 1891, Emma was appointed as headmistress of Great Barton Girls' School and remained living in the Boys' Schoolhouse.

James Daine played cricket for the village team and was secretary of Great Barton Quoits Club. Whilst at Great Barton School, he served on the local committee of the National Union of Teachers, and addressed the local association on the subject of 'What our Association is; why is it as it is; what it should be and the best way of making it what it should be' (*BFP*, 11 June 1892).

James contracted Addison's disease and resigned in 1893 on grounds of ill health. Addison's disease, a rare disorder of the adrenal glands that can be exacerbated by stress, is characterised by weight loss, muscle weakness, fatigue, low blood pressure and sometimes darkening of the skin. President John F. Kennedy also suffered from this condition and was one of the first Addisonians to survive major surgery.

James was replaced as headmaster of the Boys' School by James Killick, but remained living in the Boys' Schoolhouse until the death of Susan Kerry, at which point he and Emma moved into the Girls' Schoolhouse.

In 1901, he presented the leaving present to Frances Firman, the infant teacher, and gave an address in old English. James recovered well enough to return to work for a short time as an assistant teacher at Great Barton Boys' School in 1903, and then for a longer time at St James Elementary School, Bury St Edmunds.

He died on 18 February 1910 at the age of 46, and was buried in the churchyard at Holy Innocents' Church, Great Barton. Amongst the floral tributes, were those from the pupils and master of the schools at Great Barton and St James, the Vicar of Great Barton, and Frank and Mary Riley Smith, of Barton Hall (*BFP*, 26 Feb. 1910).

Emma Daine served on the committee of the National Union of Teachers, taught at Great Barton Sunday School and was the treasurer of the Doctors Club, the Clothing Club and the Children's Boot Club. She also helped with Missionary Society activities and regularly assisted with charitable and other village events, including the organisation of 'long night' dances (*BFP*, 25 Jan. 1913).

In 1916, Emma resigned from Great Barton Girls' School after 25 years, and was appointed as head teacher of the mixed elementary school at Tuddenham St Mary, near Bury St Edmunds. She moved to Tuddenham and lived with her sister, Cordelia, who died in October 1917, leaving £161. 16s. 11d. to Emma and their sister, Rose. Emma taught at Tuddenham School until her retirement.

During the following 20 years, she moved to Station House, Feltham, West London, to live near her son. She died in a nursing home at Twickenham, Surrey, on 6 January 1947 from 'myocardial degeneration and senile decay'.

Their son, *George* (1888-1954), attended Great Barton Boys' School and King Edward VI Grammar School, Bury St Edmunds, where the school uniform consisted of a red gown and cap for all the boys and coat tails for the sixth form boys at dinner. The Bury Guide of 1906 described the school as having two dormitories, a headmaster's house, four classrooms, a fine dining room, science laboratory, museum, gymnasium, sanatorium and workshops, with playing fields, five courts and a pavilion. As a 'foreigner' because he lived outside the town, he had to pay fees, but was awarded the Sutton Exhibition of £4 in 1905 (*BFP*, 22 Jul. 1905). Set up in 1696 by John Sutton after the death of his two sisters, this fund provided £30 a year towards the maintenance and education of six poor boys at King Edward VI Grammar School. In 1905, George won the Headmaster's Prize for the design of a memorial, which was unveiled by General Anderson and placed in the schoolroom.

He started to train as a schoolteacher at St Mary's School, Bury St Edmunds, but on 6 November 1906, he enlisted as a gunner in the Royal Regiment of Artillery, formed in 1899 to operate the guns of the British Empire's forts and fortresses. His service record of November 1906 described him as being over 6 foot 5 inches, weighing 171 lbs, with brown hair and eyes and a fresh complexion. After six months 'service and gymnastic course', his record stated that he was just over 6 foot 6 inches and weighed 193 lbs. On 3 February 1908, he was put on trial by the army, found guilty, imprisoned with hard labour for 28 days (reduced to 14) and dishonourably discharged on 20 February 1908. He later fought in the First World War and was a sergeant major and instructor at Seaford Army Camp, Sussex, in 1918.

In 1918, George married Rose Elizabeth Honey, the daughter of a domestic gardener, who was an assistant to a druggist at the time of their marriage. The couple moved to Twickenham, Surrey, (Rose's birthplace) and lived at 65 Prospect Crescent, Twickenham, from 1927 until 1930, when they moved to 105 Staines Road, Feltham, Surrey. Rose died in 1945 and George died two years later, at which time he was working as a wages clerk. He left £185. 3s. 5d. to his son, Peter Michael, who was a professional librarian.

JAMES KILLICK (1864-1922)

James Killick was the headmaster of Great Barton Boys' School from September 1893 until 1897.

He was born in 1860 in Rotherfield, Sussex, and brought up in West Sussex where his father ran Bucksteep Mill, Warbleton, and then Cowfold Mill. After his father died in 1890 his mother, Mary, and his youngest brother, John, ran the mill at Lower Bleeding where John was a corn manager and his mother a corn dealer. William, the middle son, worked as a corn store manager and foreman, then as a miller's traveller. In 1911, William lived in a seven-roomed house at Crowborough, Berkshire, with his wife and three children, one of whom was employed as a watch and clock improver and another as a steam tractor engine driver.

James trained as a teacher and, at the age of 21, taught in a school at St Woolos, Monmouthshire, and lodged in a boarding house with two other young teachers.

Whilst at Great Barton Boys' School, he took part in village activities and attended meetings of the CTA. When he resigned, he was given a silver mounted pipe and case inscribed, 'To J. Killick from the boys at Barton School - 1897' and a tobacco pouch and silver matchbox from Charles and George Clinton. In thanking everyone, James said that 'he had had three and a half, happy years at Barton School' (*BFP*, 27 Feb. 1897).

He subsequently taught in elementary schools at Boyton in Cornwall, Nantgaredig in Cardiganshire and Liphook in Hampshire.

His mother died in 1919 at the age of 84, and left £2,124. 6s. 1d. to her three sons. James never married and died in 1922 from nephritis, accelerated by fatty degeneration of the heart. He bequeathed his money to his two brothers - £2,315. 11s. 2d. to William and £698. 5s. 1d. to John. William died four months later, leaving £2,582. 14s. 7d. When John died in 1937, he left £4,537. 16s. 6d.

ROBERT EVANS (1857-1932)

From 1897 until 1922, Robert Evans [743] was the head teacher of Great Barton Boys' School, which became Great Barton Voluntary Mixed School in 1918.

He was born in West Bromwich, Staffordshire, where he spent his childhood. His father, Joseph, also born in West Bromwich, was a tinsmith for one of the five spring-making companies in West Bromwich, Staffordshire. His mother, Mary Clamp, was born in Nuneaton,

Warwickshire, and brought up 10 children of whom Robert was the fourth oldest and the only one to become a teacher. His brothers, Joseph and John, became blacksmiths; Thomas became a pattern maker and James a spring-balance maker, possibly for Salters who produced a wide range of weighing scales, including the United Kingdom's first bathroom scale. His oldest sister, Sarah, worked as a balance adjuster, and his other sisters as dressmakers.

In 1886, Robert married Edith Emma Cripps (1860-1946) from Shrewsbury, Shropshire, who was one of 13 children. Her brothers became clerks and she and her sisters became teachers or governesses. Her father, Gordon Henry Cripps (1821-1902) was a commercial traveller in the wine business, who had been accused and acquitted of fraud in 1846. He died in 1902, in the billiard room of the Bull and Star, a public house in Putney High Street, South London, [demolished in 1971]. He left £817. 4s. 6d. to his unmarried daughter, Gertrude, who was also left £428. 18s. 6d, by her mother when she died in 1917.

In 1881, Edith worked as a governess for the family of a grocer in Leominster, Hereford, who had six children under the age of 12. Robert, who was a pupil-monitor at the age of 13, trained as a teacher and then taught in a national school in Uxbridge. In 1891, he and Edith lived at Armthorpe, in Yorkshire, where Robert was a schoolmaster and organist, and Edith a sewing mistress. They had two daughters, Dorothy and Winifred, and employed a living-in servant.

After Robert Evans was appointed as the headmaster of Great Barton Boys' School, he and Edith moved into the Boys' Schoolhouse where Robert Gordon was born.

Robert played a very active part in village activities. He was a part-time journalist, a parish councillor, and clerk of the Poor's Farm Firing Charity from 1908 until April 1925 when he was replaced by T.E. Fryer, who served as clerk until 1948. He supported church activities and was clerk of the Parochial Church Council from 1896 until 1922 and of the Church Institute Committee. He was a lay reader from 1917, and the church organist and choirmaster from 1897 until 1924 when he was replaced by Mr Cheveaux, a former pupil of Mr R A Onien of the Royal Choral Society and the Royal Albert Hall, London. He was a rate collector from 1912, assistant overseer from 1916 and in charge of Barton Volunteer Training Corps. In recognition of his additional workload, which included the preparation of the Assessment Books, the school managers increased his salary in 1916 (*BFP*, 29 Apr.1916).

He enjoyed gardening and was highly commended in an article in *The Gardener* magazine, for an effective flower stand arrangement (*BNP*, 16 May 1899). His garden at Garden House was used by Great Barton Bowls' Club, and for the village garden parties.

After his retirement in December 1922 at the age of 65, he continued to be active in the village. He returned to the school on special occasions to give talks or show slides.

Robert died in Great Barton in 1932 and was the last head teacher of Great Barton School to be buried in the churchyard of Holy Innocents' Church, Great Barton. In his will, he bequeathed his estate of £997. 10s. 3d. to his son, Robert. A few years later, Edith Evans [64] sold Garden House to Marmaduke Lawther.

The children of Robert and Edith Evans

Dorothy (1890-1983) played the piano and the organ from a young age and often performed at events in the village. In December 1899, the local paper reported that 'Young Dorothy Evans played her piano with great confidence for one so young' (*BFP*, 23 Dec. 1899). She never married and retired to Montana House, Great Barton, where she died at the age of 93.

Winifred (1893-1953) also played the piano from a young age. After she left school, she worked as a governess for the Vicar of Roxwell in Chelmsford, Essex, but returned to Great Barton, where she was employed as the village librarian in 1911. She taught at Great Barton School from 1912 until her marriage in 1930 to Archie Ainsworth Hunt, who was an architect, churchwarden and school manager. They lived at The White House, Great Barton and Winifred played an active role in the Women's Institute (WI). In 1933, she helped to found a group in Great Barton and served as it secretary and president. She was one of the founders of West Suffolk Federation of WIs, helped to found many WI groups, served on the county executive, was a voluntary county organiser, gave demonstrations on organisation, drama, music and speech making and was the prime mover in the inauguration of the annual WI carol service.

Archie died on 4 December 1949 leaving £14,713. 13s. 1d. to Winifred, and she died on 3 March 1953 leaving £7,052. 19s. 4d.

Robert Gordon (Robert Evans Jnr) (1899-1981) attended Great Barton School. He was awarded a medal for school attendance by Suffolk County Council in 1908 and a prize for gardening in 1909. He was a member of Barton Cricket Club. From the age of 11, he attended King Edward VI Grammar School, Bury St Edmunds. In 1918, he enlisted in 4th Battalion of the Suffolk Regiment as a second lieutenant and, after the war, studied at Peterhouse College, Cambridge. In 1921, the *Bury Free Press* reported that 'R.G. Evans, son of the headmaster of the village school, was awarded a cricket blue at Cambridge. His forte is in bowling, but he scored a number of runs for the Bury and West Suffolk Club, which he hopes to play for again this year' (*BFP*, 25 June 1921). He trained as a teacher and was teaching at Studley Church of England School when he applied, unsuccessfully, for the post of head teacher of Great Barton School in 1933. He died in Chichester, West Sussex, in September 1981.

FLORENCE ELIZABETH PICKWORTH (1884-1953)

Florence Pickworth who was born in Garston, Lancashire, was the acting headmistress of Great Barton Girls' School from January 1917 until 1918.

Her father, Alfred Joseph Pickworth (1858-1943) from Market Rasen, Lincolnshire, was a doctor. He was educated at Kingswood School, Bath, an independent day and boarding school, and was trained as a physician and surgeon at Liverpool Medical School.

Florence's mother, Sarah Hannah Hart (1861-1890), who was born in Glanford Brigg, Lincolnshire, was the daughter of William Hart, an engineer millwright.

In 1885, Florence and her parents moved to Lakenheath, Suffolk, where her brothers William and Frederick were born. After the death of Florence's mother in 1890, two of Alfred's sisters, Caroline and Jesssie, moved to Lakenheath to look after Florence and her two brothers. In 1893, Florence's father married Mary Elizabeth Household (1866-1944), with whom he had two more children, Thomas and Eric, and the family lived in a nine-roomed house at Lakenheath.

Florence attended the elementary school at Lakenheath and at the age of 17 was living at home and described in the 1901 population census as a 'Board School Teacher'. In the 1911 census, she was living in Wisbech and described as a 'Certified School Mistress'. By 1916, she was employed by West Suffolk Education Committee as a supply head teacher, working in schools with a temporary vacancy.

In 1926, she married George Simpson (1869-1959), a widower and mechanical engineer, at the Wesleyan Chapel at Lakenheath.

Florence's family were Methodists and her father's obituary was published in The Methodist's *Who's Who*. He was a circuit steward in the Methodist ministry, chairman of Sedge Fen Free Church and of Lakenheath Consolidated Charities, a school manager, vice-chairman of the Parish Council, a local magistrate, the medical officer of Lakenheath District Mildenhall Union and Surgeon of Foresters, Oddfellows and Shepherds. He died on 23 December 1943 and bequeathed property, valued at nearly £6,000, to two of Florence's brothers; William a garage proprietor, and Thomas a bank clerk.

Florence died in Doncaster leaving an estate of £4,308. Her husband, who was by then a retired locomotive erector, died six years later.

CECIL FRANK CHANNELL (1894-1951)

Cecil Channell was born in Ingham near Great Barton and was the head teacher of Great Barton Voluntary Mixed School from 1923 until 1933.

His paternal grandmother, Maria Feakes (1839-1896), was born and brought up in Great Barton, but was living in Guildhall Street, Bury St Edmunds, in 1861, working as a general servant for William Cooper a licensed physician and surgeon. She later moved to Shoreditch, London, and worked as a servant for Henry Plumb, a gutta-percha dealer who sold rubber for waterproofing. In 1871, she married Charles Channell an agricultural labourer from Drinkstone, Suffolk, and moved to a four-roomed cottage called Botany Bay House, at Seven Hills, near the Culford Arms at Ingham.

Their eldest daughter, Annie Maria (1873-1932), was Cecil Channell's mother. In 1891, she was working as a domestic housemaid for Henry Waspe who farmed at Gusford Hall near Ipswich, but she returned home in 1894 to give birth to Cecil. Her mother died two years' later and Annie remained living at the family home to look after her father, older brother and son.

Cecil attended Ingham School, founded in 1846 by the Revd Benyon, MA. He was awarded the Ampton Calthorpe Scholarship, was a pupil at West Suffolk County School, a pupil-teacher at Ixworth Voluntary School and an unqualified teacher at St Michael's Boys' School, Bishop Stortford. During the First World War, he joined the Hertfordshire Yeomanry with whom he served in France, Egypt and Syria. In November 1923, he gave a lantern lecture with 60 slides in Great Barton Church Institute, during which he described his personal experiences in Egypt and the Holy Land.

In 1920, he attended St Mark's College, Chelsea, set up by the National Society in 1841, which included a teacher training college, and a 'practising school' attended by local children.

By 1922, the Schoolmaster's House at Great Barton had been sold so Cecil lived with his mother at Ingham. From there, he and cycled to school each day until he bought a motor bike in 1925. He became secretary of Ingham Parish Council and Ingham Men's Club.

In 1933, he was appointed as a teacher at Kentford School, near Newmarket, Suffolk, but I can find no evidence of his career until his death in 1951, at which time he was living at 10 Grove Estate, Brampton, Hertfordshire, and working as a clerical officer for the Royal Air Force.

He never married and died intestate on 7 November 1951 from 'pneumonia, hemiplegia and cerebral thrombosis'. On the *Andrews Newspaper Index Cards, 1790-1976*', which includes people with unclaimed wills, he is described as a 'bachelor and bastard without natural mother'. The Crown acquired his estate valued at £542. 14s. 2d.

ERNEST EDWARD REED (1889-1949)

Ernest Reed was the head teacher of Great Barton Voluntary Mixed School from 1933 until his death in 1949, except for four years of the Second World War, during which he was granted leave of absence to serve in the Royal Navy.

Ernest was born on 28 May 1889 in Almondsbury, Gloucestershire, and christened on 14 June 1889 in the parish church of St Mary the Virgin, Almondsbury, Gloucestershire, the village where his family had lived for at least three generations.

His grandfather, Giles (1835-1915), worked as an agricultural labourer and then in a brickyard, married Anna Maria Hunt in 1857 and had five children, including Ernest's father, Stanley Herbert (1866-1940). Stanley worked as a labourer in a brickyard and as an engineer, married Elizabeth Riddeforde and had four children, of whom Ernest was the second oldest.

Ernest spent two years as a pupil-teacher in Gloucestershire before the First World War.

In June 1914, Archduke Ferdinand was assassinated and Ernest, who was on holiday in Austria at the time, was forced to take refuge inside his hotel after he experienced hostility from Germans. He travelled back to England via Ostend, Belgium, where he was subject to a vigorous search by soldiers carrying drawn swords.

In August 1914, he enlisted in the Warwickshire Horse Artillery, Leamington, and trained at Barton Mere, Norwich and Newbury. He served in France and was with the army of occupation, which proceeded into Germany in 1918.

Ernest's younger brother, Augustus Ewart Reed (1900-1918), was a private in the 1/5th Duke of Cornwall Light Infantry. He was posted as missing in France on 11 April 1918 and was commemorated on the Loos Memorial, France, and the war memorial at Almondsbury, Gloucestershire.

On 19 October 1917, Ernest married Emily May Kate Brunning (1886-1969), who lived in the Lodge House, Barton Mere, where her father was the estate gardener. Emily's sister, Alice Maud, who later married Edmund Pawsey an ex-pupil of Great Barton Boys' School, witnessed their wedding.

Emily taught at Guildhall Feoffment School, Bury St Edmunds, and then Great Barton School from 1917 until 1926.

After Ernest was demobilised in 1919, he worked as an uncertificated teacher at Guildhall Feoffment Boys' School, Bury St Edmunds, for five years. In 1924, he decided to train as a qualified teacher and attended the teacher training college of St Mark and St John, Chelsea, the same college that Cecil Channell had attended, which changed its name in 1923 when St Mark's College, Chelsea, amalgamated with St John's College, Battersea.

He qualified in 1927 (registration number 27/10545) and taught at St James School, Bury St Edmunds, where he sometimes had an additional responsibility for St Mary's Boys' School nearby. He taught sports and athletics and, according the *Bury Free Press*, had a 'wonderful eye for picking out athletes'. Two of his boys gained places in the all-England Sports at Stanford Bridge and many of his pupils won prizes at the county sports where he was the chief marshal.

He was a keen gardener and his work in the school gardens was especially appreciated. His leaving gift from St James School was a motoring picnic set for four people.

Ernest was appointed as head teacher in 1933 and he and Emily lived at Highfield, Thurston. Ernest took an active part in sports activities in Great Barton and Thurston. He was the master of ceremonies at a whist drive and

Edward Ernest Reed

dance at the Church Institute, which raised £4 for Barton Football Club (*CM*, Nov 1935. pp 110, 126). He was a member of Thurston Parish Council and secretary of the Thurston branch of the British Legion.

In 1939, he joined the National Defence Corporation Territorial Army Reserve. From September 1939 to July 1943, he served in the Royal Navy, operating guns on a convoy escort ship. In July 1940, he was granted an emergency commission as second lieutenant.

He died in 1949, a few months before he was eligible to retire. After undergoing lumbar sympathectomy surgery at West Suffolk Hospital, he died on 4 July at the age of 59 from 'post-operative shock and haemorrhage, complicating hypertension and arteriosclerotic gangrene of his right foot'.

Amongst the mourners at his funeral at Peter's Church, Thurston, on 9 July 1949 were some of his pupils. He left £986. 17s.4d to his widow, Emily, who died 20 years afterwards, at Samford, Suffolk.

ELSIE EVELYN CARTER (1897-1997)

Elsie Carter was the head teacher of Great Barton Church of England Voluntary Controlled Primary School from April 1950 until July 1960.

Her father, John, was born in Chelmarsh, Shropshire. He worked as a farm labourer when he left school and then as a coachman at Bridgnorth, Shropshire, for Harriet Maynard the widow of a commander in the Royal Navy. In 1884, John married Amelia, who was from Fakenham, Norfolk, and they lived in Wallasey, Cheshire, where Amelia, Lucy and John were born, and then at Pakenham, where Bertram and Elsie were born.

Elsie spent her childhood in the Gardener's Cottage at Nether Hall Estate, Pakenham, where her father was head gardener. At one time, Nether Hall Estate included parts of Great Barton as well as Pakenham, Thurston, Stowlangtoft and Tostock. In 1897, it included a grand house, stables, pack of hounds and herd of deer. It was owned by Sir Edward Walter Greene, 1st Bt (1842-1920), who was the Conservative Member of Parliament for Bury St Edmunds from 1900 until 1906 and was a member of the Greene King family who owned the brewery in Bury St Edmunds. In Pakenham, villagers were expected to raise their caps or curtsey when Sir Walter Greene or his wife passed by in their carriage or on horseback.

Whilst John Carter was in charge of excavating a lake at Nether Hall, Sir Walter Greene had a serious quarrel with his neighbour Sir Compton-Thornhill who owned the Lodge adjacent to Nether Hall. Walter Greene ordered that the soil from the lake be used to build a high embankment, which became known as Spiteful Bank, between the two properties.

Elsie attended the village school at Pakenham, where John Carter, who had been awarded a certificate in horticulture, taught at the Evening Continuation School. Three of his children became teachers. Lucy taught in an elementary school in Shropshire and John in an elementary school in Sheffield.

Elsie's father died at Nether Hall in November 1934 leaving effects valued at £621. 15s. 6d. to his son, John. Elsie and her mother, Amelia, moved to The Lowe, Pakenham, where Amelia died in March 1939 leaving effects valued at £439. 7s. 1d. to John. Elsie continued to live at The Lowe.

Elsie taught at Pakenham Primary School until 1950 and then at Great Barton for the remainder of her career. She travelled to school in her Austin 7, an economy car produced in the United Kingdom between 1922 and 1939.

She was well respected by parents and pupils at Great Barton School. Ex-pupils commented that she was very strict but that she used to lick the chalk whilst writing on the board, and would constantly tug at her skirt, whenever her petticoat threatened to peep out below it.

She was particularly fond of the natural world. One former pupil said that 'she grounded nature study in our world in a way that no subsequent teacher ever managed.' Another said that she was 'a petite lady, country-like, old fashioned and very strict' and a third one described her as 'strict and scary, rather blunt' and added that she 'rarely smiled, but when she did so her pupils were a bit suspicious'.

When she retired in July 1960 at the age of 63, the oldest pupil at the school presented her with a cheque and the youngest one gave her a bouquet of roses.

After retirement, Elsie continued to live in Pakenham where she played the piano and the organ in Pakenham Church and at village functions, and became secretary of the Over 60 Club. She sold her Austin 7 and bought a Morris 1000, which she found much easier to drive.

Her nephew, Michael, recalled going on holiday with her and his mother to Scotland. Eventually she moved into Hillside Retirement Home at Great Cornard and died in Walnut Tree Hospital, Sudbury, Suffolk, from congestive cardiac failure a few months before her 100th birthday.

RENÉ (RON) FREDERICK FRANCOIS CEURSTEMONT (1918-2000)

René (Ron) Ceurstemont was the head teacher of Great Barton Church of England Voluntary Controlled Primary School from September 1960 until 1978.

He was born in Edmonton, London, on 13 February 1918 and was the only child of Adele Maria Ceurstemont (1890-1995) a refugee from the Flemish area of Belgium, who moved to London during the First World War. René's mother worked in a hotel, but was unable to support her son, so René was brought up by Frederick Robearts and his wife, who lived in Tottenham, and Ron saw his mother only when she could get time away from her job.

In December 1925, René was dangerously ill in the North Middlesex Hospital, where he received the last rites but made a full recovery. He attended St Ignatius College, Tottenham, run by Jesuits, but left school without any formal qualifications. He was largely autodidactic and studied and read widely in his spare time.

After he left school he worked as a wages clerk for McNamara's, a transport company, which carried goods for the Post Office. He studied in his spare time and matriculated in English, maths, French, geography and economics in June 1939. He made enquiries about becoming a teacher, but the Second World War intervened.

In 1935, he joined Crouch Hill Cycling Club and rode 200 miles in a 12-hour race, completed 100 miles in five and a quarter hours, and became 'point's runner up' for that year. He met Mary Davis during a cycle trip to Cornwall and married her at St Peter's Church, Old Woking, Surrey, in 1940.

In 1940, he was unsuccessful in his application to join the Royal Air Force, so he joined the Royal Army Ordinance Corps. He anglicised his name to Ron and his army record stated that he was just over 6 foot tall and had brown eyes. He served as a corporal, and was posted to Egypt and Palestine for the rest of the war. He worked as a clerk and prepared technical reports, which were distributed throughout the world. He used his love of English literature to write and perform in plays, which included 'Cinderella in Three Acts' in December 1943.

During the war, Mary moved to Ashford, Kent, and worked in the army stores in White City, Shepherds Bush, London, and Ron and Mary wrote many letters to each other, some of which included poems.

Following his discharge from the army in May 1946, Ron transferred to the Army Reserve in White City and trained as a teacher at Camden Training College, run by London County Council, where he specialised in English literature and handicrafts.

In January 1948, he was appointed as a teacher at Longford County Secondary Modern Boys School in Feltham, Middlesex, where he taught arts and crafts and was in charge of the special class. He was an active member of the Teacher Parent Association and helped to organise school plays and produce the school magazine. After completing a three-year extra-mural course at City Literary Institute, London, he was awarded a diploma in English literature.

He and Mary continued to enjoy poetry and often recited verses of their favourite poems. In 1949 Ron and Mary, accompanied by Mary's sister, Helen, went on a cycling holiday to the Ardennes in Belgium with their three-year old son Peter in a sidecar.

Ron attended evening classes where he widened his craft skills to include fabric printing, paper sculpture, basketry, bookbinding, pottery, woodwork and copper work. He enjoyed making and renovating things and built bikes for his sons and a two-man kayak for his family, which they used on the River Wye and Loch Ness.

In September 1953, he was appointed as a teacher at Guildhall Feoffment Junior Mixed School, Bury St Edmunds. At first, he travelled to and from London in a car, which he built himself from a 1926 Austin 7 chassis. He lodged temporarily with the Revd Jones, a Methodist minister, in Well Street, Bury St Edmunds, whilst his own family home was being built at Fornham Road, Bury St Edmunds.

In 1954, he and his family moved into this house, together with Ron's mother, who lived with them until her death in September 1985 at the age of 95. In order to pay the mortgage, they took in lodgers and French students and Ron worked for a short time for W.H. Smith, delivering newspapers to local shops each morning before school in his 1932 Ford Model Y.

Mary took a Pitman's Shorthand Course and worked as a secretary at Silver Jubilee School, Bury St Edmunds.

Ron was the secretary of the West Suffolk Primary Schools Athletic Association and played an active role in the Annual Inter Schools Sports Day. In 1959, he studied rural education, for which he was awarded an associateship of the Cambridge Institute of Education. During the same year, he completed a study of the growth and development of Bury St Edmunds, a copy of which is held in Suffolk Record Office.

**Ron Ceurstemont
teaching in
United States of America**

In 1959, he was promoted to deputy head teacher, which stood him in good stead when he successfully applied for a post as head teacher of Great Barton School, where he soon earned the nickname of 'Custard' because pupils found it difficult to pronounce his surname. He taught the older pupils and embraced the job with energy and enthusiasm. He particularly enjoyed teaching poetry, drama, arts and crafts and he produced several school plays. One year he produced illustrated individual Christmas cards for each pupil in his class.

He was a keen member of the National Union of Teachers and attended several national conferences on behalf of the Bury St Edmunds branch. In 1967, he was elected as one of the teacher representatives on Suffolk Education Committee, and was the secretary of the Benevolent and Orphans' Fund for many years.

In 1969, he answered an advertisement for the Educational Exchange Programme of the Government of United States of America (USA), administered by the Department of State under the direction of the Office of Education.

As a result, he and Mary swapped their house and car with that of Harry Harris, his American exchange partner, for a year. Harry lived in their home and taught at Tollgate Primary School, Bury St Edmunds. On arrival in the USA, Ron and Mary spent three days in Washington DC, where they attended briefing sessions and receptions, and then nine days on the journey to California on a Greyhound Bus. Ron taught at Malaga Elementary School, Fresno, California, where most of the 350 students were of Mexican or Hispanic-American origin and the school's grant was dependent on the annual number of student attendances. His experiences at the school gave him a fascinating insight into the social and educational life in California and he spoke at the State Capitol in Sacramento in support of a bill to provide additional financial support for foreign exchange teachers.

In April 1971, Mary Ceurstemont was appointed as an ancillary classroom helper and school nurse at Great Barton School for 20 hours a week.

During the early 1970s, Ron enrolled with the Open University, and studied 'Decision making in the British Education System', for which he was awarded a BA degree in 1976.

Ron and Mary both retired in 1978. Ron joined Probus Club, an organisation of retired and semi-retired professionals, and became a Town Guide in Bury St Edmunds. He worked as a driver for the Royal Voluntary Service and delivered Meals on Wheels to the homes of individuals, who were unable to prepare their own meals. He and Mary became Samaritans, a charity that provides 24-hour-a-day confidential support for people who are experiencing suicidal feelings. They played bridge with the University of the Third Age and bowls with the Probus Club. They enjoyed caravanning in the UK and France, walking, studying ornithology and using the binoculars, which Ron had received as a leaving present.

In 1990, at the age of 72, Ron had triple bypass heart surgery at Papworth Hospital, Cambridgeshire, and continued to enjoy active retirement for another decade.

In July 2000, Ron and Mary received a telegram from the Queen to celebrate their diamond-wedding anniversary. Such telegrams have been arranged since 1917 by the Anniversaries Office at Buckingham Palace to celebrate significant birthdays and anniversaries.

Ron died a few months later, in November 2000, at the age of 82. Amongst the words in his memorial book were some lines from *Invictus* by William Ernest Henley, which summed up Ron's positive and determined approach to life: 'I thank whatever gods may be / For my unconquerable soul'.

SUSAN (SUE) MARGARET DIXON SPILLER (1946 -)

Sue Spiller (née Payne) was the head teacher of Great Barton Church of England Voluntary Controlled School from 1990 until 2004.

She was born in Grimsby, Lincolnshire, but brought up in Surrey. Her maternal great grandfather, the son of a Lincolnshire shepherd, joined the police force and rose to the position of Detective Chief Inspector of Grimsby Police Force. Sue's mother graduated from an agricultural college and worked as a bacteriologist until she gave up work to bring up her two children.

Sue's paternal great grandfather was a shipwright in Poplar, London, and seven of his nine children and at least two of his grandchildren, including Sue's father and aunt, became teachers. Her father was educated at Stratford Grammar School, London, and then at Peterhouse College, Cambridge, where he gained a double first degree in classics and history. From 1947 until his death in 1977, he taught at Wandsworth Grammar School, which became a comprehensive school in 1957.

At the age of five, Sue attended an infant school in Grays, Essex, where her grandmother worked as a supply teacher. After one term, her family moved to Woking, Surrey, where she lived until the age of 18. She attended Maybury County Primary School in Woking, where her mother was an active member of the Parent Teachers Association. Sue passed the Eleven Plus examination and was awarded a scholarship to Guildford High School for Girls, an independent day school, which was founded in 1888 by the Church Schools Company as a progressive school. The teachers were all single women who were passionate about their subjects and had high expectations of the standards of work and behaviour of their students.

Between school and university, Sue worked as a nursing auxiliary in a maternity hospital and then as an unqualified teacher in a challenging secondary modern school where she taught French, English, religious and moral education to pupils aged 11 to 15; an experience which left her with serious misgivings about the choice of teaching as a career.

She studied geography and history at Leicester University with the intention of becoming a social worker after gaining life experience outside academia. However, during her university vacations, she worked for Woking Town Planning Department and decided to become a town planning officer instead. After graduating with a BA (Hons), she studied for a year at Birmingham University, where she was awarded a Postgraduate Diploma in Urban and Regional Studies. In 1969, she joined a team of town planners and engineers from Leicester and Leicestershire Town Planning and Engineering Departments, who were given the task of preparing plans for the city of Leicester in the year 2000. Her involvement with this team gave her a good insight into the workings of local government and experience of forward planning and decision-making.

After one year, she decided that, in spite of her earlier reservations, she would like to become a teacher and take advantage of the opportunity offered to 'good' graduates of qualifying as a teacher by working as a probationary teacher for two years, instead of attending a post-graduate teacher training course for one year.

Her first appointment, in 1970, was at Lutterworth Upper School, Leicestershire, a co-educational comprehensive school where she taught history, geography and environmental studies to pupils of all abilities, aged 12 to 16. After two terms, she married Roger Spiller whom she had met at Leicester University, and they moved to Oulton Broad, Suffolk.

Sue taught at secondary, middle and primary schools in Suffolk for the remainder of her career. Her first post was in the geography department of Denes Grammar School, Lowestoft, which was renamed Denes High School in 1971. At that time, Lowestoft was in the process of converting from a two-tier bilateral system into a three-tier comprehensive one and, as a first step, selected pupils from the two secondary modern schools in Lowestoft were offered a place at the grammar school in 1971.

In 1972, Sue was appointed as the co-ordinator for environmental studies at Elm Tree Middle School, Lowestoft, a newly built middle school that catered for pupils aged 9 to 13. Whilst there, she also gave one-to-one tuition in literacy to underachieving pupils during her spare time.

In 1974, she moved to a village near Diss, Norfolk, and decided to teach children with special educational needs. She was appointed as teacher-in-charge of the younger Special Class at Stowmarket Middle School, where she taught nine and ten-year-old pupils with learning difficulties.

In 1975, West Suffolk adopted the three-tier system and opened Blackbourne Church of England Voluntary Controlled Middle School, Stanton, which was nearer her home. Sue was appointed as the co-ordinator for special needs and taught there for 11 years during which time she brought up two children and a teenage foster son, represented the teaching staff on the board of governors, was an active member of the NUT and served as a member of the Industrial Tribunal in East Anglia.

In 1984, Blackbourne Middle School was given a stand-alone RM Nimbus PC-186 16-bit microcomputer as part of a government initiative, and Sue was asked to use it with pupils with special educational needs. In spite of the severe limitations of the software, speed and reliability of computers at that time, she endeavoured to teach pupils a computer language programme called BASIC and to make use of some of the available educational software.

She really enjoyed teaching computer studies (information technology) and when the school acquired more computers, she produced resources for and taught information technology throughout the whole school.

In 1985, she attended a term's course at Cambridge Institute of Education on 'Special Needs in Ordinary Schools' and wrote a paper on 'Good Practice in Special Needs Provision'. The course gave her the opportunity to visit primary, middle, secondary and special schools in West Suffolk and she decided that she would like to teach primary-aged children.

She was appointed as humanities co-ordinator and class teacher at Eye Church of England Voluntary Aided (CEVA) Primary School, north Suffolk, which had 260 pupils, aged four to 11. Whilst there, she gained valuable teaching experience with primary aged children and co-ordinated information technology and religious education, as well as humanities. She also had responsibility for curriculum development, multicultural education, equal opportunities and audio-visual materials. Within the Hartismere pyramid of schools, she set up and managed a resources centre at Eye CEVA Primary School for use by other rural primary schools, and took a leading role in the Primary Maths Year Project, the Primary Science Group and the Humanities Support Team. At county level, she contributed to in-service training courses on mathematics, language development, information technology, gender equality and special educational needs.

In 1990, she was seconded by Suffolk County Council to work as an advisory teacher for information technology. She ran training courses and worked alongside primary school teachers in the classroom, teaching them how to use *Logo*, an educational programming language designed in 1967 and popularised in 1980 by Seymour Papert in *Mindstorms*. She set up a County Logo Users Group and co-authored a book with Mike Page entitled *See More Logo*, published by Suffolk County Council, which described ways of using *Logo* in the classroom and was distributed to every primary school in Suffolk.

In 1990, she was appointed as head teacher of Great Barton CEVC Primary School where she was able to put her previous experience to good use.

In 2004, she took early retirement and moved to South West France to continue to renovate the two hundred year old house, which she and her husband had bought seven years earlier, and to write this book.

Appendix II

A DAY IN THE LIFE OF A PRIMARY SCHOOL HEAD TEACHER by SUE SPILLER

One day in the early 1990s, I wrote an account of a particular school day in my diary. I came across it again whilst writing this book and realised that it illustrated the wide variety of tasks carried out daily by many primary school head teachers, in particular those in small schools with full-time class responsibilities.

The date was April the First. I arrived at school at 8.00 a.m. and planned to do some administrative tasks before going to my classroom. I was about to start making some phone calls when the cook told me that I had left my car lights on. I went outside to switch them off and saw two of the older pupils who were standing by the gate and wanted to show me a dead mammal they had found on their way to school. They thought it was a mole but, when I saw that that was not the case, I suggested that they came into school and carried out some investigative research in the school library.

The phone was ringing in my office so I dealt with the caller and then phoned the school vicar to arrange a meeting later in the week. I made two further phone calls, sorted the paperwork I had taken home the previous night, located my lesson plans for the day and rewound the video I needed for one of my afternoon lessons.

On the way to my classroom, I checked on the progress of the boys in the library and offered further guidance. I prepared for my first lesson and wrote a daily welcome message on my roller board, together with instructions for what pupils should do in the classroom before the start of school, which that day involved finding as many words with three or more letters, using only the letters in the word CATERPILLAR.

The boys with the mammal came into my classroom to tell me that they now thought the animal was a shrew, so I praised them and sent them to their classroom to show their class teacher.

I returned to my office, where I found an irate mother who wished to complain about the state of her son's clothes after a painting lesson the previous day. I apologised and assured her that I would investigate why the child had not been wearing a painting overall.

Then a group of girls from my class came to my office and told me that there was a spider under my desk. When I bent down to look, they called out, 'April Fool'. I walked back to the classroom with them and was joined on the way by a child who handed me an envelope which contained a hand-drawn card with 'I love you Mrs Spiller' written in it.

I called the register of my class of six to eight-year-olds, talked to them about the activities for that day, shared the list of the words that they had found before school and took them into the hall where a teacher was waiting to take hymn practice and school assembly.

In my office, the mother of a boy in the top class was waiting to see me. She accused a lunchtime assistant of victimising her son by insisting that he should sit with younger children to eat his lunch. I listened, promised to investigate and arranged to see her at the end of the day.

I then spent time with the school secretary demonstrating how to do something new on the computer, dictating two letters and discussing some financial matters. I also spoke to a teaching assistant about the painting lesson, and a lunchtime assistant about the lunchtime issue. After assembly, I taught mathematics to my class for an hour.

During the morning break, I dealt with a child who had behaved badly during assembly and helped a child to edit a story she had written at home. I showed two children how to measure the weather for that day and how to enter the results on the computer. Then I went to my office to speak to the electrician about the relocation of the school cooker and an increase in the number of electric sockets throughout the school.

I hastily drank a cup of coffee and raced back to my class to teach English and handwriting. Whilst the children were writing, I carried out some reading conferences with less able readers until interrupted by a teaching assistant accompanied by a four-year-old child (let's call him Ernest) who was in school that week for pre-school morning visits. On the previous day, Ernest had been in trouble at play time for urinating on a classmate, and on this day had deliberately attacked another child (let us call her Mildred) with scissors. Leaving my class with a teaching assistant, I made my way to the classroom of the youngest pupils, where I found Mildred being comforted by her mother, who was helping in the classroom that day. The class teacher explained what had happened and I asked her to record the incident. Outside the classroom, I severely reprimanded Ernest and he agreed to apologise to Mildred and to try to do something kind for her. I returned to my classroom to finish teaching my lesson.

During the lunch break, I set up my classroom for a technology lesson and spoke to the parent of a child in the top class about the provision of additional support for her child who was struggling with schoolwork.

I spoke to Ernest's mother when she collected him after lunch, explained what had happened in the classroom that morning and discussed the school discipline policy.

I had a discussion with a teaching assistant about amendments to her job description and a proposal to increase her hours during the following term so that she could assist me with the Key Stage One Standard Assessment Tests.

I gave the secretary, who only worked part-time, further help with the computer before she went home, read the correspondence for that day, tackled some paperwork and ate yoghurt, which constituted my lunch.

During the afternoon, I taught technology to my class with the help of two mother-helpers. I was interrupted several times by phone calls which I answered on the phone in my classroom, and by a weeping child from the top class who was clutching his stomach and complaining of tummy pains. I phoned his mother and arranged for her to collect her son from my classroom.

During the afternoon break, I briefly talked to my mother-helpers about the technology curriculum for the following term and went outside to do playground duty with another member of staff. I taught my class for the remainder of the afternoon without further incident.

After school, I had a meeting with other head teachers at a school five miles away and needed to leave promptly. I searched out the mother of the child who had complained that morning about the dinner woman and made her aware of all the facts so that she could appreciate that she had not been told the whole story and that her son had not been victimised.

The Educational Welfare Officer was waiting for me in my office and whilst I was talking to her, I received phone calls from a prospective parent who wanted to look round the school, and from a local shop about some curtains that had been ordered for the school hall.

On my way out, I found a girl who had still not been collected from school. I phoned her home, but the call was answered by her sister, who did not know the whereabouts of her mother and had no means of contacting her [this was in the days before mobile phones]. By then I was late for my meeting, so I asked a teacher to look after the child until she was collected.

After a two hour meeting, I returned to school to check that the child had been collected and to talk to Brown Owl about her Brownies having the use of a school cupboard, in which to store their equipment, and of the hall for discos and holiday activities.

I tidied my classroom, sorted my paperwork into urgent and less urgent matters, picked up a pile of papers to work on during the evening and arrived home at 7.45 p.m.

The school logbook for that day recorded only the following:
George Cater, electrician, came to discuss the proposed cookery area with Mrs Spiller. After school, Mrs Baxter, the EWO called to see Mrs Spiller.

Appendix III

TEACHING STAFF AT GREAT BARTON SCHOOL (1846-2004)

Year (number of classes)	Teaching staff (dates of employment)
1846 to 1857 (1)	Susan Kerry (1846-1891) Mary Last (?-1851)
1857 to 1871 (2)	Susan Kerry (1846-1891) William George Plummer (c.1857-c.18
1871 to 1881 (3)	Susan Kerry (1845-1891) James Handley (1871-1874) John Dorling (1874-1886) Jane Prike or Miss Frost (1871) #William George Stockley (1874)
1881 to 1891 (3)	*Susan Kerry (1845-1891) John Dorling (1874-1886) *James Daine (1886-1893) Kate Louisa Kerry (c.1871-1894) #Frank Last (1881-bef. 1891)
1891 to 1901 (3)	*Susan Kerry (1845-1891) *Emma Daine (1891-1916) *James Daine (1886-1893) James Killick (1893-1897) *Robert Evans (1897-1922) #Annie Corley (1891) #Agnes Mary Trudgett (1891) Frances Firman (1894-1901) Walter Foulger (c.1897)

1901 to 1912 (3)	*Emma Daine (1891-1916) *Robert Evans (1897-1922) Jessie Fraser (Article 68) (c.1902-c.1903) ^ Rachel Elizabeth Edwards (1903-1904) #Herbert Rudling (1903-1907) Lilian Agnes Clinton (1905-1907) #A.M.Wright (1907-1910) Jennie Clinton (1907-1920) Mary Cordelia Frost (1908-1910) Stanley Thompson (1910) Miss Pinpoint (?-1912) Clara Amy Weller (1910-1912)
1912 to 1916 (4)	*Emma Daine (1891-1916) *Robert Evans (1897-1922) Jennie Clinton (1907-1920) Archibald Barnett (1914) Winifred Evans (1912-1930) Catherine Hogg (1912)
1917 to 1922 (4)	Robert Evans (1897-1922) Florence Pickworth (1917- 1918) Jennie Clinton (1907-1920) Winifred Evans (1912-1930) Miss Addison (1921-?) # Doris Robinson (1921 -1925) # Cicely Clara Bloomfield (1921-1925) Emily May Kate Brunning / Reed (1917 -1926)
1923 to 1933 (4)	Cecil Frank Channell (1923-33) Winifred Evans (1912-1930) Emily May Kate Brunning / Reed (1917 -1926) E.J. Ransom (1923-1932) # Winifred Mothersole (1924) % R.J.Farrants (1925) # Constance Brown (1926) # Rose Mayhew (1926) Hilda Lincoln (1926-1933) Kathleen Thoburn (1930-1935)

1933 to 1939 (4)	*Ernest Edward Reed (1933-1949)
	Hilda Lincoln (1926-1933)
	Kathleen Thoburn (1930-1935)
	Vera A. Gorham (1933-1952)
	Winifred Mothersole (1933-1944)
	*Monica Legge (1935-1941)
	% Ellen Crawley (1933-1935)
	% Malcolm Cutter (1935)
	Phylis Reeve (1935)
1939 to 1948 (4)	*Ernest Edward Reed (1933-1949)
	Vera A. Gorham / Reeve (1933-1952)
	Winfred Mothersole / Bridge (1933-1944
	*Monica Legge (1935-1941)
	Mrs Ozanne (1939-1943)
	Mrs Winsall (1941-1942)
	*Zoe Ward (1942-1943)
	% Mrs M. Mayes (1943-1944)
	Irene Edith Grace Forsdike (1944)
	Rose Mayhew (1944-1969)
	Mrs H. E. Lovett (1945)
	Mrs A.N. Rolfe (1946)
	Mrs Pickering (1946)
1948 to 1950 (3)	*Ernest Reed (1933-1949)
	*Rose Mayhew (1944-1969)
	*Vera Reeve (1933-1952)
	*Mr Bartholomew (1949)
1950-1960 (3)	*Elsie Evelyn Carter (1950-60)
	*Rose Mayhew (1944-1969)
	*Vera Reeve (1933-1952)

*Certificated teacher
^Article 68 teacher
Pupil teacher
% Student teacher

Date (number of classes)	Full-time teaching staff (dates of employment)	Part-time teaching staff (dates of employment)
1960 to 1967 (3)	Ron Ceurstemont (1960-1978) Rose Mayhew (1944-1969) Margaret Huggins (1961-1986) Mrs Jones (1952-1960)	
October 1967 to August 1969 (4)	Ron Ceurstemont (1960-1978) Rose Mayhew (1944-1969) Margaret Huggins (1961-1986) Mrs M.S. Trodden (1967-1969) C. Hammond (1968) J.P. Richards (1969)	Mrs Jones (1967-1968) C. Hammond (1968-1969) Mrs Richards (1969)
September 1969 to August 1970 (5)	Mr J.E. Nock (1969-1970) Margaret Huggins (1961-1986) Mrs J.V. Gladwell (1969-1970) Mrs E.S. Davis (1969-1970) Mrs C. Edwards (1969-1970)	
September 1970 to March 1971 (5)	Ron Ceurstemont (1960-1978) Margaret Huggins (1961-1986) Mrs Aldous (1970-1971) Mrs Haytack (1970-1974) Mrs D. Hill (1970-1973) Pat Barratt (1971-1984)	
April 1971 to August 1975 (6)	Ron Ceurstemont (1960-1978) Margaret Huggins (1961-1986) Mrs Hill (1970-1973) Mrs J. Gladwell (1971-1973) Mrs Haytack (1970-1974) Pat Barratt (1971-1984) Jennifer Barber (1971-1978) Wenda Pennells (1973-1982) Julia Briggs (1974-1982) Miss S. Gray (1974-1975)	Sally Bulbrook (1972-1976)

September 1975 to March 1978 (5)	Ron Ceurstemont (1960-1978) Margaret Huggins (1961-1986) Pat Barratt 1971-1984) Jennifer Barber (1971-1978) Wenda Pennells (1973-11982) Julia Briggs (1974-1982) Reinhild Raistrick (1978-1987)	Sally Bulbrook (1972-1976)
April 1978 to 1982 (5)	John Dawkins (1978-1990) Margaret Huggins (1961-1986) Pat Barratt (1971-1984) Wenda Pennells (1973-1982) Reinhild Raistrick (1978-1987)	Julia Briggs (1976-1982)
1982 to1988 (4)	John Dawkins (1978-1990) Margaret Huggins (1961-1986) Pat Barratt (1971-1984) Reinhild Raistrick (1978-1987) Sandra Williams (1985-1988) Rosemary Roe (1987-1990) Sylvia Taylor (1986-1993)	Wenda Pennells (1982-198◄ Mrs Thomas (1984-1986) Mrs Copping (1986-1987) Liz Chapman (1987-1990)
1988 to August 1990(3)	John Dawkins (1978-1990) Rosemary Roe (1987-1990) Sylvia Taylor (1986-1993)	Liz Chapman (1987-1990)
September 1990 to December 1990 (3)	Sue Spiller (1990-2004) Rosemary Roe (1987-1990) Sylvia Taylor (1986-1993)	
January 1991 to December 1992 (3)	Sue Spiller (1990-2004) Sylvia Taylor (1986-1993) Susan Smith (1991-2007)	Rosemary Scales (1991) Diane Grimes (1991-1993
January 1993 to August 1993 (3.8)	Sue Spiller (1990-2004) Sylvia Taylor (1986-1993) Susan Smith (1991-2007) Christine Holden (1993-1998)	Diane Grimes (1991-1993

September 1993 to August 1994 (4)	Sue Spiller (1990-2004) Liz Babbedge (1993-1999) Susan Smith (1991-2007) Christine Holden (1993-1998)	Diane Grimes (1991-1993) Chris Overy (1993-1994)
September 1994 to August 1995 (4)	Sue Spiller (1990-2004) Liz Donnelly (1994) Liz Babbedge (1993-1999) Susan Smith (1991-2007) Christine Holden (1993-1998)	Trudy Lindsay (1994-1995)
September 1995 to August 1998 (5)	Sue Spiller (1990-2004) Hilary Bilonick (1995-2009) Liz Babbedge (1993-1999) Susan Smith (1991-2007) Christine Holden (1993-1998) Trudy Lindsay (1995-2001)	
September 1998 to August 1999 (5)	Sue Spiller (1990-2004) Hilary Bilonick (1995-2009) Liz Babbedge (1993-1999) Susan Smith (1991-2007) Freya Smith (1998-2005) Trudy Lindsay (1995-2001)	
September 1999 to August 2001 (5)	Sue Spiller (1990-2004) Hilary Bilonick (1995-2009) Karen Rees (1999-2003) Susan Smith (1991-2007) Freya Smith (1998-2005) Trudy Lindsay (1995-2001)	
September 2001 to August 2003 (5)	Sue Spiller (1990-2004) Hilary Bilonick (1995-2009) Karen Rees (1999-2003) Susan Smith (1991-2007) Freya Smith (1998-2005) Carolyn Cooper (2001-2003)	

September 2003 to December 2003 (5)	Sue Spiller (1990-2004) Hilary Bilonick (1995-2009) Rachel Bailey (2003-) Susan Smith (1991-2007) Freya Smith (1998-2005) Carolyn Cooper (2001-2003)
January 2004 to March 2004 (5)	Sue Spiller (1990-2004) Hilary Bilonick (1995-2009) Rachel Bailey (2003-) Susan Smith (1991-2007) Freya Smith (1998-2005) Angela Jones (2004)
April 2004 (5)	Sarah Rees (2004 -) Hilary Bilonick (1995-2009) Rachel Bailey (2003-) Susan Smith (1991-2007) Freya Smith (1998-2005) Angela Jones (2004)

Sources:
Census of Great Britain, 1851, 1861, 1871, 1881, 1891, 1901, 1911;
The Return of Voluntary Schools (County of West Suffolk, 1902);
Minutes of Managers' Meetings (1903-1923);
Great Barton School staff record book (1934 -1983;
Great Barton School logbooks (1925-2000).

Appendix IV

VICARS OF HOLY INNOCENTS' CHURCH, GREAT BARTON
SINCE 1781

VICAR	Date of appointment
Henry Soame	1781
Thomas Cowper	1781
Thomas Scotman (curate)	1813
Nathan Orman, M.A.	1823
William Robert Blake, M.A.	1826
Harry Percy Smith, M.A.	1868
Harry Jones, M.A.	1882
Henry Stewart Gladstone	1886
James Arthur Hervey	1897
John Elwin Eddis, M.A.	1902
Henry Taylor, M.A.	1908
William Hatt Lipscomb, DCL	1915
David Duval, M.A.	1949
Harold Grayson, B.A.	1960
B. Vaughan Parry, Dip Th. Hon. CF	1969
Derek S. Hill, AKC	1978
Alan Beardsmore	1987
David W. Herrick	1996
Stephen John Abbott, LLB BJH	2000
Alan Gates, Dip Hed	2005
Manette Crossman	2015

Appendix V

UNITED KINGDOM EDUCATION DEPARTMENTS
(1839 – 2016)

Committee of the Privy Council on Education (CPCE)	1839-1899
Education Department (CPCE combined with Science and Art Dept.)	1856-1899
Board of Education	1899-1944
Ministry of Education	1944-1964
Department of Education and Science (DES)	1964-1992
Department for Education (DfE)	1992-1995
Department of Education and Employment (DfEE)	1995-2001
Department for Education and Skills (DfES)	2001-2007
Department for Children, Schools and Families (DCSF)	2007-2010
Department for Education (DfE)	2010

Appendix VI

POPULATION OF GREAT BARTON PARISH AND SCHOOL

YEAR	POPULATION OF GREAT BARTON PARISH	NUMBER OF PUPILS AT GREAT BARTON SCHOOL
1801	523	0
1831	778	0
1841	774	0
1851	855	95
1861	848	94
1871	878	126
1881	819	147
1891	766	119
1901	645	102
1911	718	
1921	666	80 (in 1918)
1931	728	150
1941	c780	88
1951	813	66 (in 1955)
1961	979	100 (in 1960)
1971	1495*	184 (217 in 1972)
1981	1810 * 1991 **	110 (in 1978)
1991	1967**	41
2001	1512***	143
2011	1600***	202 (in 2015)

Sources:
1801-1961   http://www.visionofbritain.org.uk/unit/10250171/cube/
TOT_POP
1971-1981   *https://heritage.suffolk.gov.uk/Data/Sites/1/media/parish-histories/great_barton.pdf
1981-1991   **1991 Census statistics from the Ward and Civil Parish Monitors
2001-2011   ***http://www.citypopulation.de/php/
uk-england-eastofengland .php?cityid=E34002527

Appendix VII

RANKS OF THE BRITISH ARMY AND ROYAL NAVY
(in descending order of seniority)

BRITISH ARMY	ROYAL NAVY
Commissioned Officers	**Commissioned Officers**
Marshall or Field marshal	Admiral of the fleet
General	Admiral
Lieutenant general	Vice admiral
Major general	Rear admiral
Brigadier general or Brigadier	Commodore
Colonel	Captain
Lieutenant colonel	Commander
Major or Commandant	Lieutenant commander
Captain	
Lieutenant or First lieutenant	Lieutenant
Second lieutenant or Ensign	Sub lieutenant
	Ensign
	Midshipman

Enlisted grades and Other Ranks (NCOs)	**Enlisted grades and Other Ranks (NCOs)**
Warrant officer Class I (or Regimental sergeant major)	Warrant officer or Chief petty officer
Warrant officer Class II (or Company sergeant major)	
Staff Corporal or Staff Sergeant	Petty officer
Sergeant	Leading rate or seaman
Corporal or Bombardier	Able rate or seaman
Private (Trooper, Gunner, Sapper, Signalman, Guardsman, Rifleman, Ranger, Air trooper, Driver, Craftsman)	Ordinary rate or seaman

BIBLIOGRAPHY

PRIMARY SOURCES

Original documents
Barton Estate sale plan (1915).
Educational Guidance Tests (October 1976).
Future of Very Small Schools in Suffolk (1980).
Head teachers' Report to Managers (Jan 1979).
Head teacher Report on Religious Instruction to Managers (23 Jan 1978).
Head teacher's Reports to Governors: 1997 to 2004.
Letter from Messrs. Bankes, Ashton & Co. to Mr Hooper about the ownership of Great Barton School (20 February 1969).
Letter to Mr Creese about a boundary fence (24 May 1962).
Letter to the Revd Duval about lease and Trust Deed (14 December 1949).
Logbooks: 1925 to 2000.
Memorandum by Suffolk County Council (18 April 1978).
Memorandum of Agreement between Sir Henry Charles John Bunbury and Managers of Great Barton School (1918).
Minute books of Managers' meetings: 1903 to 1968.
Minute books of Parent Teacher Association: 1964 to 1978.
Minute book of Trustees of the Poor's Firing Farm Charity (1913-1925).
Punishment book for boys at Great Barton School: 1907 to 1960.
Punishment book for girls at Great Barton School: 1907 to 1960.
Register of Title, Title number SK1835 (Land Registry 2008).
School Admissions Register: 1926 to 1972.
School Reorganisation in the Beyton and Ixworth Areas (West Suffolk Education Office, 1971).
School Staff Record Book: 1933 to 1983.
Suffolk Voluntary Controlled Schools (Articles of Government) Order 1989 (Suffolk County Council Local Education Authority, 1986).
Suffolk Voluntary Controlled Primary Instrument of Government (Schools under 100 pupils) Order 1989 (Suffolk County Council Local Education Authority, 1986).
Village Study (part of) by Senior Class (1963).

Great Barton School inspection reports

Reports by Diocesan Inspector: 1900, 1902, 1903, 1925, 1927, 1933-38, 1942, 1943, 1955.
Report by HMI: 1904, 1905, 1906, 1925, 1926, 1929,1935, 1953.
Report by Office for Standards in Education (Ofsted): 1996, 2000, 2006, 2009.
Inspection Report under Section 13 of the 1992 Education Act: 1996, 2000.
Report by Office for Standards in Education (Ofsted): 2006, 2009.
Report of Statutory Inspection of Anglican Schools (SIAS): 2006, 2009.
Report of Statutory Inspection of Anglican Schools and Methodist Schools (SIAMS): 2014.

Records kept by the National Archives about Great Barton Church of England School

Inspection of Returns: 1872.
Minutes from the Education Department: 1873 to 1875.
Correspondence with the Education Department: 1891 to 1900.
Board of Education Accommodation: 1909 to 1910.
Board of Education Inspector's Report: 1914.
Correspondence with the Board of Education : 1917 to 1918.

Newspapers

www.britishnewspaperarchive.co.uk (on subscription).
Bury and Norwich Post (BNP).
Bury Free Press (BFP).
East Anglian Daily Times (EADT).
The Church Magazine (CM).
The Guardian
The Independent
The Telegraph
Times Educational Supplement (TES).
Westminster Gazette

Other documents

Census of England and Wales, 1841-1911.
Poll Books for two members to serve in Parliament for the Western Division of Suffolk (5 May 1859, 21 November 1868).
Church of England Council for Education Schools Council – *Agreed Syllabuses of Religious Instruction* (69 Great Peter Street, London SW1, 1949).

SECONDARY SOURCES

Websites
www.greatbartonprimaryschool.co.uk
www.greatbarton.onesuffolk.net
www.bertunaschildren.wordpress.com
www.ancestry.co.uk (on subscription).
www.findmypast.co.uk (on subscription).
www.freebmd.org.uk
www.1914-1918.net
www.bbc.co.uk/history/domesday/dblock/GB-588000-267000
www.bbc.com/news
www.cwgc.org
www.educationengland.org.uk/history
(Gillard, Derek (2011), Education in England: a brief history)
www.english-heritage.org.uk
www.fitzroyhistorysociety.org.au/images/file/6-
BSL%26F_TheBunburyLettersFromNewTown.pdf
www.gov.uk/government/organisations/department-for-education
www.gro.gov.uk/ (General Register Office)
www.history.ac.uk
www.historyhome.co.uk
www.historyofparliamentonline.org
www.nationalarchives.gov.uk
www.stedmundsburychronicle.com/index.htm
www.visionofbritain.org.uk
en.wikipedia.org/wiki
hansard.millbanksystems.com
oa.anu.edu.au

Books
Ames, Mrs Ernest, *ABC for Baby Patriots 1899* (Old House Books, 2010).
(© Mrs Ernest Ames, 'An ABC for Baby Patriots', first published 1899, this edition 2010, Old House Books, used by kind permission of Bloomsbury Publishing Plc.)
Barr, William, *Arctic Hell-Ship: The Voyage of HMS Enterprise 1850-1855* (University of Alberta Press, 2003).
Benn, Caroline and Chitty, Clyde, *Thirty Years On* (David Fulton Publishers, 1988).
Benn, Melissa, *School Wars; The Battle for Britain's Education* (Verso, 2011).

Birchencough, C., *History of Elementary Education in England and Wales from 1800 to the Present Day* (University Tutorial Press Ltd, 1914).

Brown, A.F.J., *Chartism in Essex and Suffolk* (Essex Record Office, 1982).

Bunbury, Edward Herbert, *A History of Ancient Geography Among the Greeks and Romans* (J. Murray, 1879).

Burt, Cyril L. *Mental and Scholastic Tests* (London, 1921).

Burt, Cyril, *The Measurement of Mental Capacities* (London 1928).

Crawford, Elizabeth, *The Women's Suffrage Movement in Britain and Ireland: A Regional Survey* (Routledge, 2008).

Davies, Alan and Denyse Ritchie, *Teaching Handwriting, Reading And Spelling* (THRASS (UK) LIMITED, 1 Mar 2003).

Dennis, Norman, *The Uncertain Trumpet* (Civitas, 2001).

Dymond, David and Martin, Edward (ed), *An Historical Atlas of East Anglia* (Planning Dept. Suffolk County Council, 1989).

Dymond, David and Northeast, Peter, *A History of Suffolk* (Phillimore, 1995).

Edwards, B., *The Burston School Strike* (The Gresham Press, 1974).

Elliot, R.W., *The Story of King Edward 6th Free Grammar School* (Foundation Governors of School, 1963).

Fowler, Simon, *Workhouse* (The National Archives, 2009).

Frith, Francis, *East Anglia* (Frith Book Co, 1999).

Glyde, John, *Suffolk in the Nineteenth Century: physical, social, moral, religious, and industrial* (London, Simpkin and Marshall and Co., 1856).

Halliday, Robert, *Around Bury St Edmunds* (Sutton Publishing, 2004).

Horn, Pamela, *My Ancestor was in Service* (Society of Genealogists Enterprises Ltd, 2009).

Jones, Harry, *Dead Leaves and Living Seeds* (New York, Macmillan and Co., 1895).

Jones, Harry, *Prince Boohoo and Little Smuts* (Gardner Darton 1896).

Joyce, Rev. Jeremiah, *The Scientific Dialogues: Intended for the Instruction and entertainment of Young People: in which the First Principles of Natural and Experimental Philosophy are Fully Explained Vol. 1 – Mechanics* (M.Carey) (Philadelphia, USA, 1815).

Knight, Roger, *Britain against Napoleon, The Organisation of Victory 1793-1815* (Penguin, 2013).

Lawson J. and Silver H., *A Social History of Education in England* (Methuen and Co Ltd London, 1978).

Leverett, Richard, *Great Barton Free Church* (unpublished, 2010).

MacDonald, Nina, *Wartime Nursery Rhymes* (British Library, 2014).

Richardson, Marion Elaine, *Writing & Writing Patterns* (London, 1935).

Roberts, W. M., *Lost Country Houses of Suffolk* (Boydell Press, 2010).

Rubenstein, David, and Simon, Brian, T*he Evolution of the Comprehensive School, 1926-1966* (Galton, Simon and Croll, 1980).

Sellman, Roger R, *Devon Village Schools in the Nineteenth Century* (Newton Abbot 1967), pp 77-78.

Stephen, W.B., *Education, Literacy and Society, 1830-70: The Geography of Diversity in Provincial England* (Manchester University Press, 1989).

Steer, Mary, *Opals From Sand: A Story Of Early Days At The Bridge Of Hope (*1912*) p.41).*

Suffolk Past - The Country Our Parents Knew (East Anglia Film Archives, 2007).

Summers, Julie, *Jambusters* (Simon and Schuster UK Ltd, 2013).

The Missionary Service Book, 1936.

Thompson, Paul, *The Edwardians* (Weidenfeld and Nicholson, 1975).

Towns, Elmer L., *History of Sunday School* (Sunday School Encyclopedia, 1993).

Tropp, Asher, *The School Teachers* (William Heinemann Ltd, 1957).

Trowler. P., *Education Policy: a policy sociology approach* (Gildredge Press, Eastbourne, 1988).

Waller, Ian, *My Ancestor was an Agricultural Labourer* (Society of Genealogists Enterprises Ltd, 2007).

Wardle, David, *English Popular Education 1780–1970* (CUP, 1970).

Webb, Sidney, *The Education Muddle and the Way Out* (London: the Fabian Society 1901).

West, H. Mills, *Suffolk Country Schooldays* (Countryside Books, 1995).

Google Books

Reports of Special Assistant Poor Law Commissioners on the Employment of Women and Children in Agriculture (HMSO 1843).

Report of the Commissioners Appointed to Inquire Into the State of Popular Education in England (HMSO, 1861).

Page, Augustine *Supplement to the Suffolk Traveller* (Joshua Page 1844).

Articles in magazines

Jones, Harry, 'Religious Education: Ways and Means' (Education Review, 1893)

Neuberg ,V.E., 'Literacy in Eighteenth Century England: A Caveat' (Local Population Studies Magazine and Newsletter, no. 2 (Spring 1969) pp. 44-6).

Newbould, Ian D.C., The Whigs, the Church, and Education, 1839 (Journal of British Studies Vol. 26, No. 3 (Jul., 1987), pp. 332-346) Cambridge University Press).

Northeast, Peter, The Charity School Movement in Suffolk: Evidence from Records of the S.P.C.K.(Suffolk Local History Council, 2003).

Northeast, Peter, The Provision of Elementary Education in Nineteenth Century Rural Suffolk (Suffolk Local History Council, 2003).

The Architectural Review – Vol CXLVII No. 875 (January 1970), p.25.

'Village Schools in Suffolk, Building Appraisal No.5' (date unknown).

'Village Schools in West Suffolk' (*Era: Journal of the Eastern Region of the Royal Institute of British Architects, vol.1, No.3. p.24*).

Biographies of Bunbury family

Henry William Bunbury (Dictionary of National Biography volume 07.djvu/272)

Memorandum of Bunbury's meeting with Napoleon 31 Jul 1815 (Suffolk Record Office, E18/740/7/14C).

Bunbury, W. St Pierre and Morrell, W. P. (eds), *Early Days in Western Australia, Being the Letters and Journal of Lieut H. W. Bunbury* (London 1930).

Bunbury, Henry. *Memoir and Literary Remains of Lt. General Sir Henry Bunbury, Bart.* Bunbury, Charles James Fox (ed*.),* (Spottiswoode and Co., New Street Square, London, 1868).

Bunbury, Charles James Fox, *Life, letters and Journals* of Sir Charles F. Bunbury Bt. Frances Joanna Bunbury (ed.) (privately printed 1894).

Fraser, Trudie E., *The Bunbury Letters from New Town* (Fitzroyhistorysociety.org.au).

Gregory, Desmond, *No Ordinary General: Lt. General Sir Henry Bunbury (1778-1860) the Best Soldier Historian* (Fairleigh Dickinson University Press, 1999).

Lyell, Mrs. Henry (ed.), *The Life of Sir Charles J. F. Bunbury, Bart.: With an Introductory Note by Sir Joseph Hooker* (Vol. 1) (John Murray, London, 1906).

Local publications

Holmes, Frank, *Stern Days in Suffolk* (unpublished).

Holmes, Frank, *Barton Bygones* (Great Barton Newsletter 1998 – 2004).

Holmes, Frank, *History of the Bunbury Family* (unpublished).

Holmes, Frank, *History of Holy Innocents' Church, Great Barton* (unpublished).

Holmes, Frank, *A Life of Riley* (Diomed Production, 1997).

List of Gravestones from Women's Institute Survey 1979. List1. Pre 1900. Record Office Ref:-H.D.1179.
Burials Holy Innocents Church, Great Barton. June 1868 to 11 April 1939. Suffolk Record Office Ref:-FL 526/4/11.
Burials Holy Innocents Church, Great Barton. 27 May1939 to 30 October 1992 (Book 13).
Curtis, Roger, *A Brief History of Great Barton* (http://greatbartonvh.onesuffolk.net).
Leveritt, Richard, *History of Great Barton Free Church* (unpublished).
Scott Fulcher Merritt, Eliza, Granny's Life Story (privately printed).

Directories and lists
Biographical List of Boys Educated at King Edward 6th Free Grammar School, 1550-1900 (Bury St Edmunds, Suffolk).
Ekwall, Eilart, *Concise Oxford Dictionary of English Place Names* (OUP, 1974).
Kelly's Directory of Suffolk: 1879, 1883, 1892, 1896, 1900, 1912, 1916, 1925.
Pigot's Directory of Suffolk: 1830, 1839.
Post Office Directory of Suffolk: 1869, 1875.
W. White's History, Gazetteer and Directory of Suffolk: 1844, 1855, 1874, 1892 .

Government publications
Great Britain. Parliament. House of Commons. Select Committee on Education of the Poor, A digest of parochial returns made to the select committee appointed to inquire into the education of the poor: Session 1818 ([London] : House of Commons, 1819-1821).
Board of Education, *Handbook of Suggestions for Teachers in Elementary Schools:1905* (HMSO,1905).
Board of Education, *Handbook of Suggestions for the Consideration of Teachers and Others Concerned in the Work of Public Elementary Schools: 1934* (HMSO, 1934).
Board of Education, *Handbook of Suggestions for the Consideration of Teachers and Others Concerned in the Work of Public Elementary Schools* (HMSO, 1937).

Speeches
Alexander, Robin, The Curriculum in Successful Primary Schools: A Response (University of Cambridge Text of keynote address given to the HMI Invitation Conference on the 2002 Ofsted report *The Curriculum in Successful Primary Schools*).

Other

Shorter Oxford English Dictionary (OUP, 2007)

Waite, Maurice, *New Oxford Spelling Dictionary: The writers' and editors' guide to spelling and word division* (Oxford, 2005).

Ritter, R.M., *New Oxford Dictionary for Writers and Editors: The essential A-Z guide to the written word* (Oxford, 2005) adapted from Ritter, R.M. *The Oxford Guide for Writers and Editors*.

Ritter, R.M., *New Hart's Rules: The handbook of styles for writers and editors* (Oxford, 2005) adapted from Ritter, R.M. *The Oxford Guide to Style*.

Dymond, David, *Researching and Writing History* (Carnegie Publishing Ltd, 2009).

INDEX

INDEX OF FORMER PUPILS OF GREAT BARTON BOYS' SCHOOL AND OTHERS, WHO WERE FROM OR ASSOCIATED WITH GREAT BARTON, WHO FOUGHT IN WORLD WAR ONE

Lightning Source UK Ltd.
Milton Keynes UK
UKOW05f1122230117
292661UK00001B/16/P